LATE MEDIEVAL POPULAR
PREACHING IN BRITAIN AND IRELAND

SERMO: STUDIES ON PATRISTIC, MEDIEVAL, AND REFORMATION SERMONS AND PREACHING

Editors

Dr Roger Andersson *Riksarkivet (National Archives), Stockholm*
Prof. Dr Hans-Jochen Schiewer *Albert-Ludwigs-Universität, Freiburg*

Editorial Board

Dr Jussi Hanska *Tamperen Yliopisto (University of Tampere)*
Prof. Dr Thom Mertens *Universiteit Antwerpen*
Dr Veronica O'Mara *University of Hull*
Dr Riccardo Quinto *Università degli Studi di Padova*

Previously published volumes in this series are listed at the back of this book.

VOLUME 5

LATE MEDIEVAL POPULAR PREACHING IN BRITAIN AND IRELAND

Texts, Studies, and Interpretations

by

Alan John Fletcher

BREPOLS

British Library Cataloguing in Publication Data

Fletcher, Alan J. (Alan John)
Late medieval popular preaching in Britain and Ireland :
texts, studies, and interpretations. -- (Sermo ; v. 5)
1. Preaching--Great Britain--History--Middle Ages,
600-1500. 2. Preaching--Ireland--History--Middle Ages,
600-1500. 3. Sermons, Medieval--Great Britain--History
and criticism. 4. Sermons, Medieval--Ireland--History and
criticism.
I. Title II. Series
251'.00941'0902-dc22

ISBN-13: 9782503523910

D/2009/0095/146
ISBN: 978-2-503-52391-0

Printed in the U.S.A. on acid-free paper

For Helen

CONTENTS

ILLUSTRATIONS

PREFACE

Many individuals and institutions have helped me with my work on medieval preaching over the years. If I mention a few names here, it is not to the exclusion of others, but only to indicate those who spring soonest to mind as direct contributors to the present volume. Rodney Thompson made a congenial fellow reader when I was working in the library of Worcester Cathedral. Not to mention his making freely available to me his unrivalled grasp of the content and make-up of the medieval manuscripts there, he cheered my stay and the work I was doing to no end. To the librarian of Salisbury Cathedral, Suzanne M. Eward, I owe my thanks for her various good offices and for having answered several queries in connection with the subject of Chapter 6. I must say the same of Rosalind Caird and the library staff of Hereford Cathedral, who assisted me in my work for Chapter 5 with the greatest friendliness and efficiency. When Patrick Horner presented me with a copy of his edition of the sermons of Oxford, Bodleian Library, MS Bodley 649 over a memorable dinner in Manhattan four years ago, he could hardly have foreseen its consequences for Chapter 4 of this book. I would like to record here that I rate his scholarly diligence as highly as I do his choice in convivial places in which to eat; indeed, without his expertise in both those regards, Chapter 4 may not have been written. About the dedicatee of this volume I will say little, since the self-effacing modesty that I have come to associate with her would doubtless not welcome too ostentatious a blazon of the credit that she deserves for the contributions to our field that she has made and continues to make. But she knows who she is.

Those chapters of this book that have appeared in earlier publications have all been revised and are reissued here with the kind permission of the original publishers. Chapter 2: *The Cambridge History of the Book in Britain*, II: *1100–1400*, ed. by Nigel Morgan and Rodney M. Thomson (Cambridge: Cambridge

University Press, 2008), pp. 317–39; Chapter 3: *Mediaeval Studies*, 56 (1994), 217–45 (© 1994, The Pontifical Institute of Mediaeval Studies, Toronto); Chapter 7: *Mediaeval Studies*, 66 (2004), 27–98 (© 2004 The Pontifical Institute of Mediaeval Studies, Toronto); Chapter 8: *Irish Preaching 700–1700*, ed. by Alan J. Fletcher and Raymond Gillespie (Dublin: Four Courts, 2001), pp. 56–81; Chapter 9: *A Companion to the Middle English Lyric*, ed. by Thomas G. Duncan (Cambridge: Brewer, 2005), pp. 189–209. Finally, my thanks are due to the staff of Brepols Publishers, and especially to Roger Andersson, head of the Editorial Board of the Sermo series, whose care and eagle-eyed vigilance have been such a boon. They have efficiently seen to press a manuscript that must from time to time have tried their patience.

NOTE TO READER

In editing the texts that appear in Chapters 3 to 7 of this book, modern punctuation, capitalization, and word division have been introduced and all abbreviations silently expanded. Where appropriate, Arabic numerals have been expanded to their full medieval Latin form (for example, *3m* as *tercium* or *4º* as *quarto*). The Greek letters chi and rho which are sometimes used in the *nomen sacrum* are rendered by the letters Chr-. The use of *ff* for capital *F* has been retained. Pen flourishes added to certain letters but appearing to have no significance as abbreviations are treated as otiose and disregarded. For the sake of clarity, the letters *Y* and *y* in certain Middle English texts have been changed to *Þ* and *þ* as appropriate. (This *Y* and *y* orthographical habit is regionally significant, however, and one of the indicators of northern Middle English; see Michael Benskin, 'The Letters <þ> and <y> in Later Middle English and Some Related Matters', *Journal of the Society of Archivists*, 7 (1982), 13–30.)

Scribal copying errors have been silently cleared from the main body of the text but noted in the apparatus. In most other respects, however, editorial emendation is conservative and has been kept to a minimum. No provision has been made for routinely recording marginalia, although if considered of interest, these may be referred to in the notes. Text marked for insertion is given in the place intended between two slanting strokes, ` ´, and angle brackets, < >, enclose text that is either illegible or irrecoverable for some other reason (but that may sometimes be conjecturable), or parts of words that the scribe omitted either to copy or to indicate by an abbreviation mark.

Latin quotations remain as they appear in context in cited works. All other Bible quotations in Latin are taken from *Biblia sacra iuxta vulgatam versionem*, ed. by Robertus Weber and others, 4th edn (Stuttgart: Deutsche Bibelgesellschaft, 1994).

ABBREVIATIONS

AFH	*Archivum Franciscanum Historicum*
AH	*Analecta hymnica medii aevi*, ed. by Guido Maria Dreves, Clemens Blume, and Henry Marriot Bannister, 55 vols (Leipzig: Fues, 1886–1922)
CCCM	Corpus Christianorum Continuatio Mediaevalis (Turnhout: Brepols, 1966–)
CCSL	Corpus Christianorum Series Latina (Turnhout: Brepols, 1953–)
ChauR	*Chaucer Review*
CompD	*Comparative Drama*
EETS	Early English Text Society
EPLMA	H. Leith Spencer, *English Preaching in the Late Middle Ages* (Oxford: Clarendon Press, 1993)
JEGP	*Journal of English and Germanic Philology*
JEH	*Journal of Ecclesiastical History*
JTheoS	*Journal of Theological Studies*
LALME	Angus McIntosh, Michael L. Samuels, and Michael Benskin, *A Linguistic Atlas of Late Mediæval English*, 4 vols (Aberdeen: Aberdeen University Press, 1986)

LCL	Loeb Classical Library
LeedsSE	*Leeds Studies in English*
LSCLME	Siegfried Wenzel, *Latin Sermon Collections from Later Medieval England: Orthodox Preaching in the Age of Wyclif* (Cambridge: Cambridge University Press, 2005)
MÆ	*Medium Ævum*
MED	*Middle English Dictionary*, ed. by Hans Kurath, Sherman M. Kuhn, and Robert E. Lewis, 14 vols (Ann Arbor: University of Michigan Press, 1956–99)
MLN	*Modern Language Notes*
MLQ	*Modern Language Quarterly*
MP	*Modern Philology*
MS	*Mediaeval Studies*
NM	*Neuphilologische Mitteilungen*
NIMEV	Julia Boffey and A. S. G. Edwards, *A New Index of Middle English Verse* (London: The British Library, 2005)
N&Q	*Notes & Queries*
OED	*Oxford English Dictionary*, ed. by John A. Simpson and Edmund Weiner, 2nd edn, 20 vols (Oxford: Clarendon Press, 1989)
PBA	*Proceedings of the British Academy*
PG	*Patrologiae cursus completus [...] Series Graeca*, ed. by Jacques-Paul Migne, 161 vols (Paris: Migne, 1857–66)
PL	*Patrologiae cursus completus [...] Series Latina*, ed. by Jacques-Paul Migne, 221 vols (Paris: Migne, 1844–64)

PPPLME	Alan J. Fletcher, *Preaching, Politics and Poetry in Late-Medieval England* (Dublin: Four Courts, 1998)
PRIA	*Proceedings of the Royal Irish Academy*
RES	*Review of English Studies*
RS	Rolls Series (Rerum Britannicarum medii aevi scriptores; or, Chronicles and Memorials of Great Britain and Ireland during the Middle Ages)
YLS	*Yearbook of Langland Studies*

INTRODUCTION

The Project in Outline

In the last analysis, anthologizing almost always proves to be an invidious task, and, from a purist's perspective, an indefensible one. 'Why this text and not that?', the critic may well ask. Yet the alternative, unprejudiced publication of an entire textual corpus, may often simply not be practicable, or at least not be one that is currently feasible, as is certainly the case in respect of the vast corpus that has been selectively sampled to produce this book. The late medieval sermons of Britain and Ireland constitute a huge body of material, one that we are still many years away from coming to terms with. Yet some great strides forward have been taken in the last decade or so. With respect especially to the material written in English, Helen Leith Spencer's landmark study *English Preaching in the Late Middle Ages* (1993) continues to be the most authoritative introduction to the field; and more recently, an invaluable reduction to order of the daunting corpus of sermons in Latin has been provided in Siegfried Wenzel's *Latin Sermon Collections from Later Medieval England* (2005).[1] These two works between them are indispensable guides for students intending to enter this field in any serious and substantial way, and the contributions made in these two books continue to be enhanced by the publications appearing in the journal *Medieval Sermon Studies*, as well as by the Sermo series of which the present book forms a part.[2]

---

[1] H. Leith Spencer, *English Preaching in the Late Middle Ages* (Oxford: Clarendon Press, 1993); Siegfried Wenzel, *Latin Sermon Collections from Later Medieval England* (Cambridge: Cambridge University Press, 2005). Henceforth referred to respectively as *EPMLA* and *LSCLME*.

[2] The first publication of the Sermo series, an essential tool for research into the corpus of Middle English sermon manuscripts and their contents, is *A Repertorium of Middle English*

As Spencer and Wenzel would be the first to acknowledge, however, and as all members of the larger community of students of the medieval sermon would doubtless agree, much more remains to be done. At our current technological juncture, a further significant step towards doing such proper justice might be the digital scanning and storing of the entire known medieval sermon archive. Once that archive becomes electronically accessible and searchable, the obligatory second step, the critical edition of its sermons, will be greatly facilitated, for while an electronic archive may be a prerequisite database, it is only through the processes of edition and an engagement with the demands that editing makes that a text may truly be brought up close and the student provoked to ask of it systematic questions of the sort that will not only illuminate the text under review, but also shed light on the intriguing networks of relations that it was capable of entering into; these networks in themselves have much to reveal about the vagaries of the textual history of sermons and about the ways in which they came to serve the communities in which they were originally conceived, or by which they were subsequently inherited.

In the interim, before such counsels of perfection can be achieved, what to do? Rather than abjectly despair and do nothing, the alternative course that I have chosen to pursue here, by way of a small contribution towards the larger desired project and also, it is hoped, as a stimulus to it, is to present an anthology of sermons that are little known, some of which, indeed, appear printed in these pages for the first time, and to attach to them a series of studies that the sermons anthologized have prompted. Some of these studies move beyond the sermons to which they are attached and accumulate into what could be considered a parallel anthology of sermon studies, engagements with selected current issues in the field.

However, even as some of these studies may lead us in a variety of directions away from the immediate sermons that have prompted them, the anthology of sermon texts themselves is not arbitrarily chosen. While confessing the necessary limitations of selectivity that all anthologies impose, that selectivity is at least consistently driven and its principles of selection explicable. In this collection I have sought, first, to illustrate something of the range of late medieval preaching across all of the principal departments of the late medieval orthodox Church. By 'orthodox', I intend the exclusion of sermons emanating from that reformist wing of the Church that the late fourteenth-century ecclesiastical establishment increasingly sought to ban, namely, sermons produced by John Wyclif or by his

Prose Sermons, ed. by Veronica O'Mara and Suzanne Paul, Sermo, 1, 4 vols (Turnhout: Brepols, 2007).

confessional fellow travellers and heirs. Wycliffite sermons have attracted considerable critical attention in recent years, even though, of course, some important examples still remain unpublished.[3] This is not to say that the repercussions of Lollard preaching and dogma will not be heard echoing in various places in this anthology: many orthodox sermons were galvanized by, perhaps indeed actually owe their very existence to, a rereguard action fought against Lollardy by the orthodox establishment. The orthodox counterattack will therefore not surprisingly be heard in the pages ahead. Self-evidently, however, the bulk of our surviving medieval preaching is not Wycliffite. Students with niche interests in reformist preaching will thus be better served elsewhere.[4] Excepting any direct products of Wycliffite pens, then, samples of sermons will be offered here that were produced under the aegis of the friars, the regulars, the canons regular, the secular canons, and the seculars, allowing this anthology in some measure to be considered a representative cross-section of preaching as conducted throughout the various chief branches of the late medieval orthodox Church.[5] Most of the sermons in it are by anonymous authors; one or two are by authors whose identity can be inferred.

In addition to having this general representative aim, the anthology's principles of selection admit a second common purpose. I have preferred to choose only such sermons as seem, whether more or less evidently, to have been designed for delivery *ad populum*, to the laity, rather than ones composed for intramural clerical consumption by elite groups of churchmen, like sermons preached in synod or at visitations. The reason for the anthology's 'popular' emphasis stems from the fact that not only did preaching to the laity occupy the lion's share of

---

[3] For example, the collection studied by Christina Von Nolcken, 'An Unremarked Group of Wycliffite Sermons in Latin', *MP*, 83 (1986), 233–49.

[4] They can turn up the Latin sermons of the heresiarch himself, for example, or, thanks to more recent editorial industry, the English sermons of his co-religionists; see, respectively, *Iohannis Wyclif Sermones*, ed. by Iohann Loserth, 4 vols (London: Trübner, 1887–90; repr. New York: Johnson Reprint, 1966), or *English Wycliffite Sermons*, ed. by Pamela Gradon and Anne Hudson, 5 vols (Oxford: Clarendon Press, 1983–96), *Lollard Sermons*, ed. by Gloria Cigman, EETS, o.s., 294 (Oxford: Oxford University Press, 1989), *Two Wycliffite Texts*, ed. by Anne Hudson, EETS, o.s., 301 (Oxford: Oxford University Press, 1993), and *The Works of a Lollard Preacher*, ed. by Anne Hudson, EETS, o.s., 317 (Oxford: Oxford University Press, 2001).

[5] Of course, it must be admitted that each of these branches itself comprises various sub-departments or orders (the friars, for example, comprise Franciscans, Dominicans, etc., the regulars comprise Cistercians, Benedictines, etc., and so forth). Part of the selectivity imposed by the present anthology necessarily requires that choices between these orders be made.

clerical endeavour and professional commitment — hence its special centrality to the Church's mission to the world and its reciprocal worthiness as a subject for our critical attention — but also that, from the point of view of students whose interests in medieval sermons may only be incidental, sermons to the laity are more likely to have something to offer. Thus *ad populum* preaching would seem to cater to the widest range of potential tastes (unless, that is, the student's concern is confined exclusively to intraclerical aspects of Church history).[6]

Literature and Pulpit

When in the 1920s and 1930s Gerald R. Owst pioneered extensive study of the sermon in late medieval England, one of his chief ancillary preoccupations was with the liaison that he had noticed between sermons and the vernacular literature of the period. This preoccupation, which registered in his first book, *Preaching in Medieval England: An Introduction to the Sermon Manuscripts of the Period c. 1350–1450* (1926), became ever more conspicuous in his second, *Literature and Pulpit in Medieval England* (1933), whose very title placed literature centre stage alongside the sermons themselves. His works and their thrust in this respect succeeded in setting an agenda whose influence continues to be felt even some eight decades later. At the time he was writing, Owst was a little apologetic about his subject, and the note of defensiveness struck as he sought to justify it, laundering what he anticipated many of his contemporaries would consider a dusty topic, is easy to hear. Today, all that defensiveness has gone, and medieval sermon studies have emerged as a confident, international topic of enquiry in their own right. Nevertheless, the interest that Owst stimulated in the literary application of sermon study, even if to some extent he did so as an apologia for sermon study proper, has persisted — indeed, has flourished in some quarters. In an anthology such as this, which has declared *ad populum* preaching to be one of its key concerns, aspects of the commerce between preaching and vernacular literature similarly continue to find a natural place. A chapter has therefore been permitted to round off the substantive part of book, the title of which offers implicit homage to Owst's first forays into this field. The chapter explores a particular aspect of this commerce that has benefited in recent years from considerable literary critical momentum. It illustrates the ways in which vernacular verses were drafted into preaching, some of them having no originally

[6] For an excellent summary of the nature of *ad populum* preaching, see *LSCLME*, pp. 245–46.

independent life outside the sermon in which they appear but being invented solely to meet the preacher's needs.[7] In some senses, the topic of this chapter is only one of the more obvious among those set many years ago by Owst's 'Literature and Pulpit' agenda. Avenues into the territory of 'Literature and Pulpit' that are as equally fundamental, yet which are also at once far less obvious and more sophisticated, await exploration.[8] In pursuing only one of their more obvious instances here, this anthology has again simply confessed to the imperative of any anthology in operating selectively.

The Project in Detail

Owst's cultural patriotism and Anglocentrism, flagged also partly as another of his means of justifying his topic to an audience whom he evidently judged temperamentally susceptible to such displays, is as clear as is his defensiveness about the worthiness of his chosen subject. Such a strategy would similarly no longer be countenanced today in scholarly discussions within a field that has assumed a pan-European scope (although, to be sure, the field comprises national regional units which may usefully be studied either comparatively or individually and within their own terms). The regional unit in which the evolution of England's tradition of medieval preaching makes fullest sense includes the islands both of Britain and Ireland, and it is this unit that the present book proposes to consider. Yet, certain obstacles to coverage emerge that are of a different, non-Owstian order: there arises, fundamentally, the issue of survival. Medieval preaching in Scotland has left no unequivocal primary textual traces, as it similarly seems not to have done in Wales either, even though Wales produced the most substantial indigenous vernacular literature of any of the Celtic territories in Britain.[9] Something similar

[7] Siegfried Wenzel has made this field characteristically his own in a number of important studies; most notably, his *Verses in Sermons: Fasciculus Morum and its Middle English Poems* (Cambridge, MA: Medieval Academy of America Press, 1978), and his *Preachers, Poets, and the Early English Lyric* (Princeton: Princeton University Press, 1986).

[8] For example, for a recent illustration of how the 'culture of preaching', thus more loosely defined, may be thought to respire in one of the masterpieces of late fourteenth-century English literature, the poem known as *Pearl*, see Alan J. Fletcher, '*Pearl* and the Limits of History', in *Studies in Late Medieval and Early Renaissance Texts in Honour of John Scattergood*, ed. by Anne Marie D'Arcy and Alan J. Fletcher (Dublin: Four Courts, 2005), pp. 148–70.

[9] Some medieval Welsh texts, while they seem to be in touch with the culture of preaching, are nevertheless not actually sermons; G. E. Ruddock, 'Siôn Cent', in *A Guide to Welsh Literature*

may be said in the case of Cornwall, in Britain next after Wales for its legacy of medieval texts in a Celtic language, yet none of these is a sermon, even though we know for a fact from external historical evidence that medieval sermons were sometimes preached in Cornish.[10] However, notwithstanding these issues of survival, we are not quite left entirely shiftless and thrown back, *faute de mieux*, upon Owst's Anglocentrism: Ireland is the exception, and from here survives a quantity of sermon texts, in English, Irish, and Latin, that become candidates for our attention. As well as yielding actual sermons, late medieval Ireland also provides many indirect evidences of how preaching was conducted there: the production of preaching aids of different sorts, or surviving historical accounts of sermons delivered, or of sermon tours undertaken, all contribute to the picture. Consequently, a chapter of this book has been devoted to Irish preaching activity to help offset an Anglocentrism that, although not imposed for Owst's reasons, unavoidably impinges nevertheless as a function of the sheer scale of the evidence surviving from England.

This Irish chapter concludes the series of previous chapters (Chapters 3 to 7) whose chief task will be the presentation of sermons produced within each of the principal branches of the late medieval Church, and where selected issues to which some of those sermons give rise will also be explored. Though all of the sermons in these earlier chapters of the anthology hale from England, they have at least been chosen in such a way as not to cluster in any one English corner, county, or shire. Thus they may be thought at least to aspire to some measure of

---

1282–c. 1550, ed. by A. O. H. Jarman and Gwilym Rees Hughes, rev. by Dafydd Johnston (Swansea: Davies, 1976), pp. 150–69 (see pp. 153–54). Also, see J. E. Caerwyn Williams, 'Medieval Welsh Religious Prose', in *Proceedings of the Second International Congress of Celtic Studies* (Cardiff: University of Wales Press, 1966), pp. 65–97. I am grateful to Jenny Rowland for helpful discussion on this point. And while a Welsh translation of an early printed edition of what was probably late medieval England's most popular vernacular sermon collection, the *Festial* of the Augustinian canon John Mirk, was undertaken in the sixteenth century, it lies too late for our present consideration; see Martyn F. Wakelin, 'The Manuscripts of John Mirk's *Festial*', *LeedsSE*, n.s., 1 (1967), 93–118 (pp. 112–13).

[10] For example, John Grandisson, Bishop of Exeter (1327–69), had occasion to preach a sermon of reconciliation at St Buryan, Cornwall. He spoke both in French and in English, but his words were also translated into Cornish by Henry Marseley, rector of St Just, for the benefit of the humbler sort present who spoke only Cornish; see *The Register of John de Grandisson, Bishop of Exeter (AD 1327–1369)*, ed. by F. C. Hingeston-Randolph, 3 vols (London: Bell, 1894–99), II, 820. The earliest sermons extant in Cornish are works translated from English originals during the reign of Queen Mary (1553–58); see Brian Murdoch, *Cornish Literature* (Cambridge: Brewer, 1993), pp. 129–30.

English representativeness in their geographical spread. For example, the scribe of the sermon edited in Chapter 3, when writing in English, produced a late thirteenth-century linguistic variety that seems locatable in the region of either north Lancashire or west Yorkshire, while the scribe of the sermons in Chapter 4, conversely, active perhaps in the first third of the fifteenth century (although probably after 1409), whenever he wrote in English reflected orthographies characteristic of Norfolk. Other forms of historical evidence than the linguistic may allow the location of certain sermons to be determined exactly and with confidence, since a regionally distinctive scribal English dialect, while it may indicate where a scribe was writing, need not necessarily do so.[11] The sermon in Chapter 6, for example, was an autograph composition, one amongst a series that survive from a diligent preacher whose final years were spent in Salisbury where he was a canon of the cathedral.[12] Thus the sermons of Chapters 3, 4, and 6 triangulate between them the north, east, and south of England; and the west can be added if one of the sermons edited in Chapter 7 is also taken into account (Text D of that chapter).

But before these individual chapters take up their individual (and in some cases collateral) threads and concerns, the book will begin with a general introductory survey in Chapter 2 of the codicology of late medieval sermon manuscripts from Britain and Ireland, and again track sermon manuscript production in each of those same principal departments of the Church whose preaching will be exemplified in subsequent chapters. In one notable case, Chapter 2 will also introduce a relative novelty: a sermon manuscript produced not by any professional Church department member but by a layman (and a sermon from it will be edited as Text C of Chapter 7). From all these sermon manuscripts that Chapter 2 surveys, and which stand by proxy for a host of others of which nothing has been said in this book, a general calibrated rule may be observed to emerge: rarely are sermon manuscripts opulent; some are handsome; and many are workmanlike. As we move down this pyramidal scale of codicological finesse, away

[11] Strictly, a scribe's written dialect will indicate only one of three things: either a) the region in which he was trained to write (when he reproduces his own orthography, unconstrained by any alternative orthography in his exemplar); or b) the region in which the person who copied his exemplar was trained to write (when he reproduces the orthography of his exemplar faithfully); or c) some mixture of these two things. In whichever case, the regional location of a written scribal dialect may, but need not necessarily, indicate where a manuscript was copied.

[12] Although no Middle English appears in the sermon edited in Chapter 6, the linguistic complexion of this man's written Middle English elsewhere is entirely consistent with a Salisbury location, however; I am grateful to Michael Benskin for information on this matter.

from quality at the apex and towards the broad base of pure pragmatism and serviceability at the bottom, so we might also imagine ourselves to be exchanging elegance and the relative pastoral distance that elegance may imply for a nearer contact with pastoral actualities and with real-life situations in which these lower-end manuscripts were immediately implicated and in which, indeed, many that now no longer exist must once have been read and consulted over and over until they finally fell apart and were discarded. Perhaps we see the near cousins of this lost manuscript class amongst some of the lowliest products surveyed in Chapter 2, manuscripts whose modest production values, as well as their content, suggest that they may have answered with particular immediacy to perceived pastoral needs. In that immediacy they perhaps convey one of the best impressions that we are ever likely to gain of clerical life lived at the coal face of the *cura animarum*.

Future Projects

Sermons of the *ad populum* sort, as earlier observed, are informative on a number of fronts, some of which will be broached in this anthology and permitted to lead certain chapters off on specialized tangents of their own. Others are left to the reader to discover and explore, and it is one of the potential strengths of an anthology that it should facilitate multiplicity in this respect, offering more for subsequent thought than it chooses to ruminate on directly. But this introduction might conclude by pointing out at least one track not explicitly signposted in the pages ahead that others may wish to consider following. While it may be hard to know now what the exact impact of preaching on the mentalities of late medieval men and women may have been, that impact, for better or worse, was a profound one. Granted, many sermons may have been met with apathy, one of the preacher's most insidious opponents, a topic that Chapter 9 will reflect on further. Yet, there may have been as many others capable of provoking strong reactions of one kind or another in those who heard them: for example, a member of a congregation might strenuously object to what was said or to the preacher's manner of saying it; might be moved to laughter, either accidentally or by the preacher's conscious design; or conversely be moved to tears; or even to transports of religious devotion and enthusiasm. In all of these reactions congregations showed not indifference but a wide range of different sorts of affective response to what they heard. Thus *ad populum* preaching was potentially powerfully constitutive of one corner of late medieval popular consciousness. For many, this preaching would have furnished the mental plans whereby they organized their lives (or at least, by which they were encouraged to organize them); it would have provided compass points by which to take their bearings amongst the contours of their experience, perceiving and interpreting the facts of their existence in Church-sanctioned ways. Part of the interest of the sermons of this anthology resides in their demonstration of some of the strategies adopted by the Church in its attempts to explain and negotiate the experiences of lay lives. By identifying and attempting to medicate sin and its consequences, these *ad populum* sermons aimed to orientate the disposition and outlook of their congregations aright. They provided the moral and spiritual route maps that the Church urged on medieval men and women if they were to chart their way safely through the 'valley of restless mind'. The structural ideologies of these sermons, and their chosen devices for inculcating them, cannot fail to fascinate historians of all persuasions, and may provide anyone interested in this earlier phase of our culture with insights into an important forum in which that culture rendered itself intelligible unto itself, a site where it projected its lineaments, here through the lens of preaching, into the minds and hearts of its members.

Sermon Manuscripts from Late Medieval Britain and Ireland: A Codicological Typology

Introduction

When Christ commissioned his twelve apostles and exhorted them to preach the gospel to all nations, he also told them that, when the time came for them to give witness, they should not carry what they would say premeditated in their heads; instead, the Holy Spirit would speak for them spontaneously *in illa hora* (in that hour).[1] It is curious to reflect, then, that the formidable array of sermon manuscripts and anthologies of material compiled to support preachers in their task that survives from Britain and Ireland in the later Middle Ages betrays how little confidence medieval preachers reposed in the original dominical advice. Miracles now were in shorter supply than in gospel times, it was said, and so preachers were driven to the expediency of mere human assistance. The modern historian of medieval preaching, needless to say, has every reason to be grateful for this medieval failure of nerve.

Copious though the legacy of compilations for preaching may be, this is not to imply, of course, that there was never any such thing as the medieval preacher who acted according to strict evangelical precept and who preached as he felt the Holy Spirit had moved him. Necessarily, the efforts of such a man would, of their nature, have left no palpable traces to posterity, unless someone other than him troubled to make notes of his words before they evaporated in the

[1] Mark 13. 11.

air.[2] Yet even at the best of times the Holy Spirit needed something to work with: the extensive scribal industry that developed in response to the need to stock the preacher's mind with preachable matter, leave alone to confer an enduring parchment or paper existence upon evanescent sermon words, would ensure that in future, the aspiring preacher, provided that he was sufficiently well tutored in such premeditated materials, could at least give the semblance of spontaneous, evangelical simplicity, seeming to invent his sermon on the spot. Indeed, whatever the historical actuality, contemporary illustrations of medieval preachers in action rarely depict them preaching from a book, and such instances as might suggest the contrary are not unambiguous.[3] In some cases, the mise-en-page and convenient size of certain sermon manuscripts suggests that they were laid out so as to facilitate easy reading, appropriate, therefore, for carrying into a pulpit where they could serve, if not as a direct crib, then as a handy prompt;[4] but while their layout and dimensions may suggest such possible use, we have no clear evidence that they actually so functioned. At the other end of the scale, the sheer readerly inconvenience attending the tiny, crabbed hands that often crowd the small-format manuscripts so typical of those late medieval preachers par excellence, the friars, entails a clearer conclusion: while these small codices would have conduced to portability, thus suiting them perfectly to their peripatetic mendicant users who might wish to travel as lightly as possible on their preaching tours, in terms of actual pulpit use they would have been less helpful. Ideal as vade mecums, they are nevertheless most unlikely to have also accompanied friars into the pulpit.[5] *In illa hora*, in the very moment of preaching, minute and highly contracted handwriting is self-evidently inconvenient.[6]

---

[2] Such note-takings, or *reportationes*, are relatively rare. See Helen L. Spencer, 'Middle English Sermons', in *The Sermon*, ed. by Beverly Maine Kienzle, Typologie des sources du moyen âge occidental, fasc. 81–83 (Turnhout: Brepols, 2000), pp. 597–660 (pp. 609–10). However, it should be observed that several summaries, taken down in *reportatio* form, survive of sermons delivered at openings of Parliament; these specimens of *reportatio* have received little critical attention.

[3] Compare the comments on the early sixteenth-century sculpture in the parish church at Tong, Shropshire, depicting Arthur Vernon 'preaching' from a book, in *EPLMA*, p. 77.

[4] For example, the group of professionally produced late fifteenth-century sermon manuscripts discussed in *PPPLME*, pp. 154–59.

[5] See especially David L. d'Avray, *The Preaching of the Friars: Sermons Diffused from Paris before 1300* (Oxford: Clarendon Press, 1985), pp. 57–62.

[6] Equally, our *heftiest* extant sermon manuscripts are unlikely to have been carried up into the pulpit by preachers either.

Plentiful though they are, it would thus seem that the bulk of our surviving medieval sermon manuscripts and preaching anthologies tracked the actual preaching event at one or other kind of remove: either they followed in the wake of it (as, for example, when sermons were preached and subsequently written up into sermon diaries); or they anticipated it, by providing the staple material from which the sermon eventually preached would be tailored. Therefore, in the majority of cases, the books of sermons that have come down to us are de facto of a literary and a consultative kind. A very few, to be sure, claim to contain a faithful, *in illa hora* record of sermons delivered at historical times and places by named preachers;[7] more usually, however, sermon manuscripts preserve texts by named, or by anonymous, authors, either *in extenso* or in abbreviated form and, save in the case of sermons belonging to the Temporale or Sanctorale, whose normal use coincided with their corresponding liturgical occasion, without any indication of when they had originally been preached or might be preached again in the future. There are signs that the tolerance of medieval congregations for longwinded 'predicacioun' may have been no more robust than that of modern ones,[8] but even supposing that early sermongoers were a more indulgent lot, it nevertheless remains clear that some sermons, as recorded in manuscript, are so unpreachably vast that they cannot have been delivered quite as they stand.[9] And in some cases, the provision of sermon manuscripts with indices, or with other forms of textual *accessus*, further supports the case that they were initially conceived as quarries for preachers — important, but essentially ancillary, resources for their own proper efforts in the pulpit and thus bearing only more, or less, directly upon the words actually preached.[10] So although by the late Middle Ages preaching was a familiar and culturally central phenomenon, the codices which contain its chiefest traces witness to it only obliquely: in the moment of their codification, sermons were

---

[7] For example, the *reportationes* mentioned in note 2, above. But even *reportationes*, like a student's lecture notes, abbreviated what was actually said.

[8] *EPLMA*, pp. 91–108; the topic is further touched on below in Chapter 9.

[9] For example, the *Sermones dominicales* of Philip Repyngdon, Bishop of Lincoln († 1419). For some recent account of Repyngdon's sermons, see Simon Forde, 'New Sermon Evidence for the Spread of Wycliffism', in *De ore Domini: Preacher and Word in the Middle Ages*, ed. by Thomas L. Amos, Eugene A. Green, and Beverly Maine Kienzle, Studies in Medieval Culture, 27 (Kalamazoo: Medieval Institute Publications, 1989), pp. 169–83.

[10] However, collections like *Dormi secure* (see below, p. 23 and n. 39) suggest a heavier (and indolent) degree of reliance upon pre-prepared words.

inevitably entering the domain of the literary and the consultative, and becoming estranged from their pulpit actuality.[11]

Of course, the literary and the consultative aspects of the manuscripts, as these preliminary comments have begun to suggest, were themselves shaped by diverse market requirements, and thus liable to be manifested in a range of formal ways. Hence it follows that a codicological typology of medieval compilations for preaching is only likely to be broadly conceivable. As a sampler of this codicological variety, and as a codicological preface to some of the sermons that will be published in the chapters that lie ahead, the rest of this chapter will introduce and briefly describe a (generally representative) selection of sermon manuscripts from Britain and Ireland designed for different late medieval orthodox interest groups: first, inside the professional Church, for the friars, the regulars (including the regular canons), and the seculars (including the secular canons); and second, outside it, for the laity, a group whose readership of books of sermons might on the face of it come as a surprise. Certain of the manuscripts discussed here, their content, and the issues for medieval preaching that they raise, will form the subject for more extended discussion in subsequent chapters.

Preaching Compilations for the Friars

Our first manuscript, a more detailed account of which will follow in Chapter 3, is Oxford, Bodleian Library, MS Bodley 26, most of whose texts are in Latin. Its 206 leaves measure approximately 151 × 116 mm, and as such is the smallest of the manuscripts to be considered here. Stints by at least sixteen different scribes can be distinguished in it, and these range in date from the first half of the thirteenth century to the early years of the fourteenth.[12] Traces in it of four medieval foliation systems, combined with its scribal arrangement, reveal how it was put together. Its first seven quires (fols 1–103, roughly half its entire length) were originally conceived as a unit in their own right, and were copied by three scribes, two of whom certainly worked in collaboration. The work of the scribe of the ninth and earliest quire, done in the first half of the thirteenth century, was originally part of an independent compilation that was later broken up and eventually accommodated within the present manuscript. The remainder

---

[11] Reasons for the distance between the actual sermon event and its literary traces are also usefully surveyed in *LSCLME*, pp. 16–20.

[12] For a detailed examination of its scribal stints, see Chapter 3, below.

of Bodley 26 includes leaves which, like those of quires 1–7 and quire 9, also originally belonged to another, independent compilation. Thus Bodley 26 was pieced together by some unknown compiler who had at his disposal at least three other, originally discrete, books, booklets, or *quaterni*. Since various of his sources were Franciscan in origin, it is likely that he had access to the resources of an English conventual scriptorium or centre. He was active probably in the first half of the fourteenth century. With its cluster of scribes, its small format, and its evidence of having been assembled from other books or booklets, Bodley 26 also seems paradigmatic of a characteristic mode of mendicant book production everywhere in Britain and Ireland (for comparable late medieval Irish cases, for example, see the further discussion in Chapter 8 below).[13] The balance of the evidence — a number of different sources of Franciscan origin, coupled with the characteristic portable format of the manuscript — suggests that Bodley 26 was a mendicant compilation.

We may compare with Bodley 26 a slightly later case in London, British Library, Additional MS 46919: this is the product of a Franciscan who, in the early years of the fourteenth century, brought together into one codex of 213 leaves various, originally separate, booklets or *quaterni*.[14] The leaf size is approximately 230 × 170 mm (though many leaves are irregular). Their contents include sermons, plus other assorted materials mainly of theological import. These texts are mostly in Anglo-Norman, with a few in English, Continental French, or Latin. Again as with Bodley 26, several scribal stints (about thirteen in all) are discernible, but a notable difference is that the identity of one of the scribes is known, and he, moreover, was none other than the manuscript's actual compiler, the Franciscan preacher, poet and theologian, William Herebert (†1333).[15] If Bodley 26 originated as a personal mendicant anthology, even more surely did Additional 46919. Precisely why Herebert found the eclectic mix of matter that he compiled appealing is hard to gauge, though the principal interests evinced are in preaching and preachable material.[16] Some of the material is Herebert's own — certain of the sermons, for example, recorded in Latin, plus a set of Middle

---

[13] This codicological habit amongst the mendicants was, of course, a pan-European one; see d'Avray, *The Preaching of the Friars*, pp. 57–62.

[14] Originally there would have been some additional leaves, since the manuscript's index includes the *Proverbs of Hendyng* and the *Epistola Valerii ad Rufinum*, both now missing.

[15] For his biography, see *The Works of William Herebert, OFM*, ed. by Stephen R. Reimer, Studies and Texts, 81 (Toronto: Pontifical Institute of Mediaeval Studies, 1987), pp. 1–6.

[16] See the summary of contents in *The Works of William Herebert*, pp. 8–9.

English lyrics — and this personal work consorts with matter by others in a codex that witnesses to Herebert's habituation to a cultural milieu where writings in Latin, French, and English could associate freely. Such linguistic amphibiousness in the compiler was also glimpsed, to a lesser extent, in Bodley 26, where words in English and French are occasionally to be found amongst the (preponderant) Latin. Such codices challenge conventional wisdom about the status of these three languages in Britain and Ireland in the late thirteenth and early fourteenth centuries,[17] but more particularly for present (and future) purposes, the trilingual mélange may entail codicological corollaries worthy of further research. In Additional 46919 we also see Herebert returning to his sermons and poems in order to revise them, thus giving them the air of works fluidly in progress; this ongoing editorial activity may perhaps be regarded as a local, textual analogue to the general flexibility apparent in the way mendicant preaching compilations freely combined and recombined their materials, the sort of process to which the multiple stages in the manufacture of Bodley 26 have already testified.

Given the centrality to the mendicant orders of preaching, it is unremarkable that friars perennially had a taste for compilations in which sermons featured prominently. The small format so characteristic of their books might not always be paramount, however, for cherished portability was also to be achieved by copying sermons into slim, unbound booklets. (Of course, Bodley 26 enjoyed the additional advantage of having a leaf size that was itself small-scale.) Thus while the leaf size of our final example is a little larger (though at 204 × 150 mm, still smaller than Additional 46919),[18] it is worth stressing that the manuscript first existed as individual booklets and that their current assembly was only the afterthought, albeit an important one, on the part of their mendicant scribe and compiler. In Oxford, Bodleian Library, MS Lat. th. d. 1, we see another Franciscan, Nicholas Philip, copying booklets of sermons for his personal use — indeed, he also tells us when and where he preached some of them — before eventually marshalling his booklets into one codex. They are mainly recorded in Latin, although some admit words and verses in English. Between 1430 and 1436, this

---

[17] Also, the mendicant miscellany in Dublin, Trinity College, MS 667 (discussed further below in Chapter 8) contains matter side-by-side in English, Irish, and Latin.

[18] This measurement is taken from Oxford, Bodleian Library, MS Lat. th. d. 1, fol. 74ʳ, which probably gives the clearest impression of the original leaf size (in this portion of the manuscript at least); extensive modern repairs throughout have obscured original leaf sizes. I am grateful to Helen L. Spencer for taking measurements for me. The folio size of MS Lat. th. d. 1 is almost that of recently mentioned Dublin, Trinity College, MS 667: its folios measure 214 × 143 mm.

high-ranking Franciscan travelled the length and breadth of England, preaching at places as far apart as King's Lynn, Oxford, Newcastle upon Tyne, and Lichfield. His mobility as a friar is thus well attested.[19] MS Lat. th. d. 1 exhibits nothing of the scribal multiplicity of the earlier mendicant codices reviewed above. All the booklets appear to be in Philip's hand, and for whatever reason, he did not incorporate work by other scribes. When late in the fifteenth century his booklet collection was provided with an index — and in the early years of the sixteenth, the collection continued to circulate as a resource within the order — this late medieval change continued a codicological evolution that Philip initiated when he first drew his booklets together. The format of his collection was steadily becoming more literary, more consultative, as time went by.

Preaching Compilations for the Regulars (Including the Regular Canons)

Although the mendicant preaching compilations just considered were Franciscan, our typology risks no distortion on that account, for no material differences in book production seem to distinguish one mendicant order from the next. If only by virtue of the fact that in the later Middle Ages the regulars are less famously known to have invested in preaching than are the mendicants and the seculars — the case of the Canons Regular of St Augustine, to be discussed later in this section, is something of an exception — production of sermon books by regulars might be anticipated to be somewhat different. And this, for the most part, is what we find. It therefore seems appropriate that our first example of one of their preaching compilations (though it can only loosely be thus classified since the abiding impression it leaves is of eclecticism) should be an exception to prove this rule. It comes, moreover, from an order virtually invisible in modern scholarship on late medieval preaching in Britain and Ireland, the Cistercian.[20] Before the

---

[19] For further details see *PPPLME*, pp. 41–57; also, *LSCLME*, pp. 95–99 (advocating a slightly less determined opinion on the identity of the scribe), and pp. 572–78.

[20] And this despite an attribution in recent times of a substantial number of Latin sermons to Aelred, Abbot of Rievaulx (1109–1167); see Aelredus Rievallensis, *Opera omnia II: Sermones I–XLVI (Collectio Claraevallensis prima et secvnda)*, ed. by Gaetano Raciti, CCCM, 2A (Turnhout: Brepols, 1989) and Aelredus Rievallensis, *Opera omnia III: Sermones XLVII–LXXXIV (Collectio Dunelmensis sermo a Mattheo Rievallensi Servatus sermones Lincolnienses)*, ed. by Gaetano Raciti, CCCM, 2B (Turnhout: Brepols, 2001). Even more invisible has been the association of sermon manuscripts with houses of Carthusians, yet we have a notable case in Aberdeen, University Library, MS 154; for a summary description, see Montague Rhodes James, *A Catalogue of the*

sixteenth century, when they were parted, the two manuscripts now preserved as Dublin, Trinity College, MS 114 and London, British Library, MS Cotton Faustina A.v, comprised a single codex.[21] This book, of some 185 leaves (the Dublin portion measuring 240 × 166 mm and the London 240 × 172 mm), was formerly in the possession of the library of the great Cistercian abbey of Fountains in Yorkshire.[22] The compilation, chiefly of items in Latin, contains the stints of nine principal scribes, whose work ranges widely in date between the first half of the twelfth century and the second half of the fifteenth. The twelfth-century material, executed in the Benedictine scriptorium at Durham, had arrived at Fountains by *c.* 1200. Here its quires were supplemented with newer ones until finally, out of various later accretions, there emerged the codex as it stands (though now divided between two libraries).

It is difficult to know exactly when the later additions to the twelfth-century core were made. Perhaps some abbey librarian decided that, rather than keep unbound quires in his custody at random and separately, it would be tidier to sweep them together into one compilation. Alternatively, like a growing pearl, perhaps the later layers coagulated around the twelfth-century seed in an orderly, incremental series corresponding to the chronology of the various subsequent scribal stints (if so, this growth would again seem to have occurred within the walls of the abbey). Whatever the manuscript's precise evolution, its sermon component was the work of four scribes who were all probably active in the second quarter of the fourteenth century. Thus while the impressive tally of scribes at

---

Medieval Manuscripts in the University Library of Aberdeen (Cambridge: Cambridge University Press, 1932), pp. 50–51. This manuscript contains a collection of sermons owned in the fourteenth century by the Carthusians of Hinton, Somerset. Their priory was begun in 1227 and completed in 1232; see David Knowles and R. Neville Hadcock, *Medieval Religious Houses: England and Wales*, 2nd edn (London: Longman, 1971), pp. 133–34. The sermons were not, however, Carthusian in origin, but Dominican: they seem either to have been the work of Thomas de Lisle or Thomas Brito († 1361), as was thought by Johannes Baptist Schneyer, *Repertorium der lateinischen Sermones des Mittelalters, für die Zeit von 1150–1350*, Beiträge zur Geschichte der Philosophie und Theologie des Mittelalters, 43, 11 vols (Munster: Aschendorff, 1969–90), V, 631 and 663–70, or, as more recently argued by Louis-Jacques Bataillon, 'Les Sermons attribués à saint Thomas: Questions d'authenticité', in Bataillon, *La Prédication au XIIIᵉ siècle en France et Italie: Études et documents*, Variorum Collected Studies Series, 402 (Aldershot: Ashgate, 1993), item XV (first publ. in *Miscellanea Mediaevalia*, 19 (1988), 325–41), to be by one Thomas Lebreton, a contemporary of Aquinas (p. 333).

[21] See further *PPPLME*, pp. 21–40.

[22] I am grateful to Julia Boffey for taking measurements of London, British Library, MS Cotton Faustina A.v for me.

work in the Fountains codex might seem to invite comparison with certain mendicant preaching compilations, especially those of the late thirteenth and early fourteenth centuries, the resemblance is skin deep. And one feature of the codex that tends to set it apart from the general run of mendicant preaching compilations is its inclusion of material inherited from the scriptorium of one of the more ancient, pre-mendicant orders within the Church.

However, more conspicuous in the late medieval preaching field than the Cistercian, another regular order whose preaching activity has become increasingly clear of late is that which provided the twelfth-century seed around which Dublin, Trinity College, MS 114 and London, British Library, MS Cotton Faustina A.v grew, the Order of St Benedict. In the early years after the Conquest, the works of that giant among Anglo-Saxon preachers, Ælfric, abbot of the Benedictine monastery at Eynsham, were still commanding attention and in demand. His work was being recycled in such collections as London, British Library, MS Cotton Vespasian D.xiv (datable to the mid-twelfth century),[23] or Lambeth Palace Library, MS 487 (datable to c. 1200),[24] both codices possibly the products of Benedictine scriptoria.[25] Nevertheless, an appreciable number of late medieval sermon books whose provenance is demonstrably Benedictine has survived.[26] As in the mendicant fashion, Benedictines too were capable of compiling sermon codices out of smaller booklets or *quaterni*, though this time in most cases these booklets were of an ampler format, both in terms of their script and leaf size. One such larger example is to be found in Worcester, Cathedral Library, MS F.126, the product of several scribes working between the last quarter of the fourteenth and the beginning of the fifteenth centuries.[27] It comprises 294 leaves that measure

---

[23] See Neil Ripley Ker, *Catalogue of Manuscripts Containing Anglo-Saxon* (Oxford: Clarendon Press, 1957), pp. 271–77.

[24] Montague Rhodes James, *A Descriptive Catalogue of the Manuscripts in the Library of Lambeth Palace: The Mediaeval Manuscripts* (Cambridge: Cambridge University Press, 1932), pp. 673–76.

[25] London, British Library, MS Cotton Vespasian D.xiv can be assigned either to Christ Church, Canterbury, or, less likely, to Rochester. The possible role of this manuscript within its community is considered by Elaine Treharne, 'The Form and Function of the Twelfth-Century Old English *Dicts of Cato*', *JEGP*, 102 (2003), 465–85 (pp. 477–81).

[26] For an overview, see Siegfried Wenzel, *Monastic Preaching in the Age of Chaucer*, Morton W. Bloomfield Lectures on Medieval English Literature, 3 (Kalamazoo: Medieval Institute Publications, 1993).

[27] For a description of this manuscript, see Rodney M. Thomson, with Michael Gullick, *A Descriptive Catalogue of the Medieval Manuscripts in Worcester Cathedral Library* (Cambridge:

365 × 250 mm and is, as such, the largest of the codices reviewed in this chapter. A fifteenth-century inscription at the top of fol. 66ʳ declares the late medieval ownership of the manuscript by Worcester's Benedictine priory, and its provision with indices suggests that it may be a more carefully finished and presented specimen of the sort of sermon compilation witnessed, for example, in another Benedictine compilation most likely of Worcester provenance, Worcester, Cathedral Library, MS F.10, a manuscript with which F.126 also shares some sermons in common.[28] Many of the F.126 sermons were evidently produced within the Benedictine order (though it also includes much material from without),[29] and their particular form of codification confers upon them an existence suited rather to the cloister than to the pulpit.[30]

Our final sermon book in this section on preaching compilations for the regulars, produced in the first third of the fifteenth century (but probably after 1409) and very likely under the aegis of the Canons Regular of St Augustine, will make an appropriate bridge to those sermon books produced by and for the last group for consideration within the professional Church, the seculars. This is because the Canons Regular, unusual amongst regulars in that they were frequently entrusted with the cure of souls, resembled the seculars in that respect.[31]

Brewer, 2001), pp. 87–91; also, *LSCLME*, pp. 146–50. The texts in this manuscript are either entirely or chiefly in Latin.

[28] For an analysis of the sermon contents of Worcester, Cathedral Library, MS F.126, see *LSCLME*, pp. 630–57. Worcester, Cathedral Library, MS F.10 is described by Thomson, *A Descriptive Catalogue*, pp. 182–83. Its texts are either entirely or chiefly in Latin.

[29] For example, the fifty-five *Collationes dominicales* of Archbishop John Pecham, identified by Siegfried Wenzel, *Macaronic Sermons: Bilingualism and Preaching in Late-Medieval England*, Recentiores: Later Latin Texts and Contexts (Ann Arbor: University of Michigan Press, 1994), p. 59, or the *confessio* of the Franciscan friar John Tyssyngtone, see *Fasciculi Zizaniorum Magistri Johannis Wyclif cum Tritico*, ed. by W. W. Shirley, RS, 5 (London: Longman, 1858), pp. 133–80.

[30] This is what the codicology would seem to suggest. Nevertheless, the Benedictines of Worcester had practical experience as preachers, and it is to be suspected that anthologies like MSS F.126 and F.10 served in some ultimate way their own practical ends. On the preaching of the Worcester Benedictines in the later Middle Ages, and their exercise of the *cura animarum*, see Joan Greatrex, 'Benedictine Monk Scholars as Teachers and Preachers in the Later Middle Ages: Evidence from Worcester Cathedral Priory', in *Monastic Studies*, II: *The Continuity of Tradition*, ed. by J. Loades (Bangor: Headstart History, 1991), pp. 213–25, and her 'Benedictine Sermons: Preparation and Practice in the English Monastic Cathedral Cloister', in *Medieval Monastic Preaching*, ed. by Carolyn Muessig, Brill's Studies in Intellectual History, 90 (Leiden: Brill, 1998), pp. 257–78.

[31] This they normally did, episcopal licence having been obtained, at churches impropriate to their priories.

If their notable record of service to the literature of preaching is enough to judge by, the various congregations of Augustinian canons took their pastoral responsibilities seriously; indeed, one of their number, John Mirk, eventually prior of Lilleshall Abbey in Shropshire, amongst various other pastoralia compiled, probably between *c.* 1382 and 1390, what arguably became the most influential late medieval sermon collection written in English.[32] And while in a different part of the country his much earlier confrère, Orrm, who composed in the last quarter of the twelfth century at Bourne in Lincolnshire a collection of versified vernacular sermons, seems to have had no discernible impact on later tradition — his sermons are solely extant in a unique and orthographically idiosyncratic holograph manuscript, Oxford, Bodleian Library, MS Junius 1 — he nevertheless remains an early witness to a general application to preaching evidenced elsewhere by members of this order, an application that has left several traces for study in manuscript form.[33]

A handsome specimen of what may have been an Augustinian canons' preaching anthology, two of whose sermons are edited below in Chapter 5, is to be found in Hereford, Cathedral Library, MS O.iii.5, a book of 145 leaves that measure 290 × 198 mm. This manuscript contains two main items, each by a different scribe: first, a collection of sermons, either exclusively or chiefly in Latin, some *de tempore*, some *de sanctis*, and some for special occasions like visitations; and second, a Latin version of the *Gesta Romanorum*.[34] Cross-references within certain sermons suggest that the collection (though not necessarily every item in it) was assembled by a single compiler. Whether this compiler was one and the same with the scribe of the first part of the manuscript, a man evidently trained to write

---

[32] A new edition of this sermon cycle (the *Festial*) is currently being prepared for EETS by Susan Powell. For discussion of the possible date bands of its composition, see Alan J. Fletcher, 'John Mirk and the Lollards', *MÆ*, 55 (1987), 59–66. A general cultural study of the *Festial* is now available in Judy Ann Ford, *John Mirk's 'Festial': Orthodoxy, Lollardy and the Common People in Fourteenth-Century England* (Cambridge: Brewer, 2006). Augustinian canons feature amongst the earliest vernacular preachers on record in English in the post-Conquest period.

[33] And amongst these should probably be included the manuscripts of another sermon collection, the *Northern Homily Cycle* (whose earliest version dates to *c.* 1300). Its provenance amongst the Canons Regular of St Augustine has been convincingly argued by Thomas J. Heffernan, 'The Authorship of the "Northern Homily Cycle": The Liturgical Affiliations of the Sunday Gospel Pericopes as a Test', *Traditio*, 41 (1985), 289–309.

[34] See Roger A. B. Mynors and Rodney M. Thomson, *Catalogue of the Manuscripts of Hereford Cathedral Library* (Cambridge: Brewer, 1993), pp. 19–20. For some further discussion and list of sermon contents, see *LSCLME*, pp. 159–65 and 461–65 respectively.

somewhere in Norfolk, is not known.[35] In any event, the compiler was probably working not long after 1409 because one sermon appears to refer to the Oxford Constitutions promulgated in that year under Archbishop Thomas Arundel.[36] Familial references to St Augustine in some sermons suggest that the compiler was also a member of one of the congregations of Canons Regular.[37] The relatively careful finish of O.iii.5 has resulted in the effacement of any evidence of its sermons having formerly existed in booklet form, save perhaps in one respect: occasional duplication of certain items suggests that O.iii.5 is to be compared with codices like Worcester, Cathedral Library, MS F.10, referred to briefly above and whose booklet composition is more self-evident, or indeed with the manifest booklet composition of Friar Nicholas Philip also referred to above in Oxford, Bodleian Library, MS Lat. th. d. 1. In both these manuscripts certain items, as in O.iii.5, have been copied twice. It is easy to imagine this happening if the exemplar of the item duplicated existed as a small, mobile unit (most individual sermons, after all, were short enough to fit onto a single quire) which, unless the compilation was produced in stringently supervised circumstances, might find itself inadvertently recopied.

Preaching Compilations for the Seculars (Including the Secular Canons)

All the compilations discussed so far, both mendicant and regular, have something of the haphazard about them, and this applies even to those finished with relative care, like Worcester F.126 and Hereford O.iii.5. All seem to have been unique, once-off productions. True, individual sermons in them occasionally reappear in yet other compilations,[38] but this only serves to emphasize the same basic point:

---

[35] An alternative, though perhaps less likely, explanation is that the scribe was not from Norfolk, but was copying *literatim* the Norfolk forms of his exemplar.

[36] MS O.iii.5, fol. 62ᵛ, col. b; the Constitutions are printed in *Concilia Magnae Britanniae et Hiberniae*, ed. by David Wilkins, 4 vols (London: Gosling and others, 1737; repr. Brussels: Culture et civilisation, 1964), III, 314–19.

[37] The visitation sermon in MS O.iii.5, fols 38ʳ, col. b–40ᵛ, col. b, for example, refers to a monastery, to brothers and canons, and to the Rule of 'beatissimus pater noster Augustinus' (fol. 40ʳ, col. a).

[38] For example, the Latin funeral sermon in MS O.iii.5, fols 104ᵛ, col. a–106ʳ, col. b is known in a Middle English version in three other manuscripts (see *EPLMA*, pp. 300–02, and *PPPLME*, pp. 126–27). One of these, Cambridge, University Library, MS Gg.6.16, is considered briefly below. Further cases of sermons that this manuscript shares with others are noted in *LSCLME*,

the circulation of many late medieval sermon texts was piecemeal; texts often travelled either individually or in small clusters, and thus lent themselves to a potentially endless series of recombinations with other materials when anthologizers were casting about for preachable matter. Yet alongside this piecemeal transmission, whose consequences are most clearly seen in the sheer variety of content that preaching compilations tend to exhibit, there also circulated larger, frequently more stable, groups of sermons, like the 'standard' sermon cycles of the Fathers, or those by such newer arrivals as the Dominican Jacobus de Voragine or the Franciscan Nicholas de Aquevilla. While the sermon cycles of these authors could be, and sometimes were, broken up for circulation as smaller units, a need for sermon collections offering systematic coverage of the Church year, apart from collections of a piecemeal sort, caused the larger cycles to cohere centripetally and helped ensure their transmission en bloc. Certainly, piecemeal sermon compilations were often not so utterly eclectic that they neglected the prime preaching seasons of Advent and Lent — many such compilations compare in catering for these times — but they might not go so very much further. Some preachers, conversely, were under an obligation to preach on a more regular basis outside the periods of peak demand, and they too needed to be equipped. Thus systematic sermon cycles had a prospective market, an extreme example being the notorious *Dormi secure* collection which, by providing a year's worth of off-the-peg sermons, let preachers sleep tight knowing that they would not be embarrassed for something to say on the Sunday — hence the collection's arch title.[39] The chances are, then, that when a preaching compilation is found to be thoroughly eclectic in its sermons and other contents, it will also prove to be a personal product, while the manuscript that contains the longer and systematic sermon cycle, by contrast, will prove to be institutionally sanctioned or a product of professional scribes who had a practical eye to the clerical book market. Exceptions to this rule can always be found, of course, but it is fundamentally serviceable.

pp. 161–66, and see pp. 147–49 for Wenzel's detection of similar kinds of overlap between the sermons of Worcester, Cathedral Library, MS F.126 with other manuscripts.

[39] Gerald R. Owst, *Preaching in Medieval England: An Introduction to Sermon Manuscripts of the Period c. 1350–1450* (Cambridge: Cambridge University Press, 1926; repr. New York: Russell and Russell, 1965), pp. 237–38. On *Dormi secure*, see also John W. Dahmus, '*Dormi secure*: The Lazy Preacher's Model of Holiness for His Flock', in *Models of Holiness in Medieval Sermons*, ed. by Beverly Mayne Kienzle and others, Textes et études du moyen âge, 5 (Louvain-la-Neuve: Fédération internationale des Instituts d'études médiévales, 1996), pp. 301–16.

Sermon books are rarely ornate and de luxe; on the contrary, they incline towards the workaday, as certain of the manuscripts considered above and others to be considered later testify. Nevertheless, some may be handsome, especially those made professionally, such as were many of the manuscripts containing the systematic sermon cycles already alluded to. One prominent and systematic late medieval Latin cycle whose popularity doubtless owed something to its being well placed to catch the attention of an established network of professional copyists is the *Sermones dominicales* collection of the Oxford preacher, John Felton.[40] In turning to Felton, we also arrive at the third group within the professional Church who routinely undertook preaching, the seculars. Felton died in Oxford as vicar of St Mary Magdalen's in 1434.[41] Not merely a preacher to his Oxford congregations in the minimum terms his office would have required, but by all reports a devotee of regular Sunday preaching, he achieved some celebrity, even a local reputation for sanctity, on account of his pulpit skills. What seems to have happened is that his *Sermones dominicales*, completed probably in 1431, were taken up and promoted by Oxford's copying houses, since of the thirty odd manuscripts in which they are currently known to survive, in whole or in part, about half may have been Oxford products.[42] One of this Oxford batch, Oriel College MS 10, stands very conspicuously at the 'handsome' end of the book production range. Written by one principal scribe in a university book hand of the mid-fifteenth century, this substantial manuscript of 446 leaves, measuring 348×228–30 mm, and which also includes two other works eminently useful to preachers (the vast *Summa predicantium* of the Dominican John Bromyard, plus the substantial *Manipulus florum* of Thomas of Ireland),[43] could not, in terms of

---

[40] A convenient list of the content of the *Sermones dominicales* is printed in *LSCLME*, pp. 479–84.

[41] On John Felton, see *PPPLME*, pp. 58–118.

[42] To the twenty-nine manuscripts listed in *PPPLME*, pp. 62–63, should now be added Cambridge, University Library, MS Ii.3.22, fols 43ʳ–144ʳ; also, Cambridge, Jesus College, MS 13, fols 126ᵛ–128ᵛ, contains a copy of Felton's Easter Sunday sermon on the *thema, Qui manducat hunc panem vivet in eternum* (John 6. 59), and Oxford, Bodleian Library, MS Bodley 687, fols 74ᵛ–76ʳ, contains a copy of his sermon on the *thema, Acceperunt corpus Iesu* (John 19. 40).

[43] The *Summa predicantium* awaits a modern edition; for the most up-to-date details concerning its author, see Peter Binkley, 'John Bromyard and the Hereford Dominicans', in *Centres of Learning: Learning and Location in Pre-Modern Europe and the Near East*, ed. by Jan Willem Drijvers and Alasdair A. MacDonald (Leiden: Brill, 1995), pp. 255–64. The *Manipulus florum*, also awaiting a modern edition, has nevertheless been extensively researched by Richard H. Rouse and Mary A. Rouse, *Preachers, Florilegia, and Sermons: Studies on the*

its bulk and quality format, be more remote from certain other compilations for preaching that seculars are known to have used. Admittedly, not all the *Sermones dominicales* manuscripts are as handsome as Oriel College 10, but most show signs of having been manufactured with more than average care.

By contrast, at the bottom end of the market, but perhaps here bringing us closer to the commoner realities of everyday pastoral use, stand many far humbler compilations owned by seculars. Often they are of paper, or predominantly so: for example, Oxford, Bodleian Library, MS Hatton 96, a rag-bag of cursive hands and quires which an intercalated paper slip containing a memorandum of some wedding banns suggests may have provided a mid-fifteenth-century secular cleric, active possibly in or near Bewdley, Worcestershire, with a fund of sermons and preachable matter (one of its texts is edited below as Text D of Chapter 7);[44] or Cambridge, University Library, MS Gg.6.16, the work this time of a single scribe writing in the third quarter of the fifteenth century and assembling what seems to have been intended as a personal anthology, mainly of sermons, presumably to help supply his own pastoral requirements.[45] This lone sermon compiler seems either to have been a Suffolk man or to have copied faithfully Suffolk orthographies from his exemplar. No doubt numerous preaching compilations of this more friable sort formerly existed that in time were simply read to bits.

That this was indeed most probable, and that even seculars of higher intellectual capacity than the compilers of either MS Hatton 96 or MS Gg.6.16 are

---

'*Manipulus Florum*' *of Thomas of Ireland*, Studies and Texts, 47 (Toronto: Pontifical Institute of Mediaeval Studies, 1979). An electronic edition of the *Manipulus* is being prepared by Chris L. Nighman at Wilfrid Laurier University, Canada; see Chris L. Nighman, 'The Electronic *Manipulus florum* Project (www.manipulusflorum.com)', *Medieval Sermon Studies*, 46 (2002), 97–99, and also his 'Commonplaces on Preaching among Commonplaces for Preaching? The Topic *Predicacio* in Thomas of Ireland's *Manipulus florum*', *Medieval Sermon Studies*, 49 (2005), 37–57.

[44] Most folios measure 201 × 138–40 mm; one cluster, however, fols 213ʳ–217ᵛ, measures 201 × 147–50 mm. For an analysis of the written dialects of this manuscript and its constituent parts, see Angus McIntosh and Martyn F. Wakelin, 'John Mirk's *Festial* and Bodleian MS Hatton 96', *NM*, 84 (1983), 443–50.

[45] The folios of MS Gg.6.16 measure 217 × 146 mm. Its written dialect has been placed in Suffolk by *LALME*, III, 487–88 (Linguistic Profile 8430). MSS Hatton 96 and Gg.6.16 are but two instances; several others could be added: for example, Oxford, Bodleian Library, MS Bodley 95, still in its original blind-stamped binding of leather on wooden boards, has been shown by Helen L. Spencer, 'The Fortunes of a Lollard Sermon Cycle in the Later Fourteenth Century', *MS*, 48 (1986), 352–96 (p. 359), to have been owned by the secular cleric John Jeffys, who between 1485 and 1491 was vicar of Sandford St Martin, Oxfordshire.

likely to have been might similarly resort to such humbler, paper *quaterni* for recording sermons, is quickly demonstrated. The career of Thomas Cyrcetur († 19 February 1453), fellow of Merton College, Oxford, parish priest, canon of Wells and then also of Salisbury, furnishes a case in point.[46] He evidently attended diligently to the office of preaching — one of his compositions is edited below in Chapter 6 — and a short consideration of how this diligence was expressed codicologically shall be allowed to conclude this chapter's section on preaching compilations for the seculars.

A particularly interesting feature of Cyrcetur's sermons and sermon notes, either exclusively or predominantly written in Latin, is that they are all authorial holographs; with the exception of only two manuscripts earlier noted in this chapter,[47] most, if not all, of the other manuscripts surveyed here can lay no claim to comparable status.[48] The fact that Cyrcetur's compositions are also holograph is necessarily likely to bring us closer, if not to the actual preaching event, then at least to the actual preacher's notions concerning that event, and as such they acquire a special interest. Further, Cyrcetur seems to have preserved his sermons in two formats, either as unbound paper *quaterni*, of which he owned a large quantity (as many as forty-five or more) but which have failed to survive,[49] or as personal additions in spare spaces in more durable manuscript books of other

---

[46] The basic study of his intellectual formation, preaching interests, and career is by R. M. Ball, 'Thomas Cyrcetur, a Fifteenth-Century Theologian and Preacher', *JEH*, 37 (1986), 205–39.

[47] That is, those portions of London, British Library, MS Additional 49619 that were copied and authored by William Herebert, and the versified sermon collection of Orrm in Oxford, Bodleian Library, MS Junius 1.

[48] It seems impossible to determine whether any of the sermons compiled by Nicholas Philip in Oxford, Bodleian Library, MS Lat. th. d. 1 were actually by him; some at least were palpably not.

[49] A *quaternus 45* is referred to in a note that Cyrcetur made in Salisbury, Cathedral Library, MS 166, fol. 140ᵛ. On Salisbury, Cathedral Library, MS 174, fol. vᶦ, he added the following interesting note, significant for indicating his two major ways of preserving sermons: 'Pro thematibus quaternorum de papiro non ligatorum, respice quaternum ligatum de papiro cuius secundo folio 'illa recoleret' folio 152 et sequentibus, et in eodem quaterno folio 119 et sequentibus, et folio 305 et sequentibus' (for the *themata* of the unbound, paper *quaterni*, look at the bound paper *quaternus* whose second folio is 'illa recoleret', folio 152 and following, and folio 119 in the same *quaternus*, and folio 305 and following). It should be mentioned that not all the sermons in these unbound *quaterni* were Cyrcetur's own compositions; some were patently not, for he makes reference elsewhere to a 'grossus quaternus in quo continentur quaterni M. R. Stabul' (a large *quaternus* in which are contained the *quaterni* of M. R. Stabul) (cited in Ball, 'Thomas Cyrcetur', p. 220); 'M. R. Stabul' was Master Richard Stabul († 1410 or 1411), a colleague of Cyrcetur while at Merton College. Evidently, Cyrcetur had come into possession of some of Stabul's sermon *quaterni*.

works in his possession. Of these latter, three are extant: Salisbury, Cathedral Library, MSS 126, 170, and 174.[50] There is an informal, cursive rapidity, too, in Cyrcetur's hand that carries its own palaeographical story: these are unselfconscious memoranda that evince a scribe addressing his own needs before anyone else's. It is even conceivable that Cyrcetur's additions to MSS 126, 170, and 174, had we his unbound *quaterni* available for comparison, would have appeared the least premeditated in respect of their appearance and presentation, for even *quaterni*, as has been seen, might circulate freely among preachers, and hence, however informal in preparation they were, they may always have been produced with some sense of a wider useability that the codicological genre of the *quaternus* came associated with in preaching circles. Therefore an author copying his sermons into a *quaternus*, even if in the first instance for his own use, might be more conscious of their possible afterlife for others than an author who tucked his sermons or sermon notes into spare spaces in bound manuscript books that he owned.[51] Thus the very inconsequentiality of Cyrcetur's sermon memoranda, from a codicological perspective, paradoxically confers significance upon them, at least from the point of view of the historian of medieval preaching.

Preaching Compilations for the Laity

As noted earlier, once codified, sermons, especially those set down in English, became available for any potential reader, not only for professional clerics, even if the largest sermon readership throughout the Middle Ages doubtless remained clerical. The preface to the Middle English *Myrrour*, for example, a translation of a thirteenth-century Anglo-Norman sermon cycle by Robert de Gretham that was undertaken probably in the late fourteenth century, envisaged its use not specifically by preachers but by *readers* and *hearers*, people wont, moreover, to consume such profitless romances as *Guy of Warwick* or *Sir Tristram*; the *Myrrour's* sermons were offered to the likes of these as a healthily pious antidote to their unregenerate taste.[52] It is to be suspected that this target readership/audience was

[50] The cathedral library still preserves some eleven other manuscripts that were formerly Cyrcetur's (see further on these in Chapter 6, below).

[51] This point is not belied by the fact that the manuscript books themselves were ultimately intended to be passed on to other institutions and users; what was being passed on was the book and its primary contents, not its accretions at the hands of its previous owner.

[52] See Oxford, Bodleian Library, MS Holkham misc. 40, fol. 1ʳ.

either non-clerical or at least included non-clerical elements.[53] Also, the quality format and mise-en-page of certain *Myrrour* manuscripts — the outstanding instance being Oxford, Bodleian Library, MS Holkham misc. 40 — recall those of certain books produced under Wycliffite auspices and that may have been the products of London workshops.[54] Indeed, the translation of the *Myrrour* itself was conceivably undertaken in the wider context of a great vernacularizing enterprise so characteristic of late fourteenth-century England and with which the aims of English Church radicalism at that date in part overlapped. The endeavour of the radicals to put theological matter, especially the naked text of Scripture,

---

[53] MS Holkham misc. 40, fol. 1ᵛ: 'þat han god wylle to here þys boke oþer to reden hit' (who have a good will to hear this book or to read it); fol. 3ᵛ: 'þerfore Ich haue mad þys bok þat iche man may haue delyt forto here and rede openlyche what appendeþ to God and to hym' (therefore I have made this book so that every man may have delight in hearing or reading openly what pertains to God and to himself); fol. 5ʳ: 'Y beseche hem alle comynlyche þat hit reden or heren þat ȝyf þer beo ony defawt in þat hii amende hit' (I beseech them all generally who read it or hear it that if there is any lack in it that they repair it).

[54] Thomas G. Duncan, 'The Middle English *Mirror* and its Manuscripts', in *Middle English Studies Presented to Norman Davis in Honour of his 70th Birthday*, ed. by Douglas Gray and Eric Gerald Stanley (Oxford: Clarendon Press, 1983), pp. 115–26. The leaves of MS Holkham misc. 40 measure 285 × 190 mm. I am grateful to Helen L. Spencer for taking this measurement for me. London has been suggested as a possible place of origin for copies of the English Wycliffite Bible, particularly in its Later Version, by A. I. Doyle, 'English Books in and out of Court from Edward III to Henry VII', in *English Court Culture in the Later Middle Ages*, ed. by V. J. Scattergood and J. W. Sherbourne (London: Duckworth, 1983), pp. 163–81 (p. 169); see also now Maureen Jurkowski, 'Lollard Book Producers in London in 1414', in *Text and Controversy from Wyclif to Bale: Essays in Honour of Anne Hudson*, ed. by Helen Barr and Ann M. Hutchison, Medieval Church Studies, 4 (Turnhout: Brepols, 2005), pp. 201–26. For a general study of London literary culture, see also Ralph Hanna, *London Literature, 1300–1380* (Cambridge: Cambridge University Press, 2005). Given the demonstrable scribal overlap between copyists of certain manuscripts of the English Wycliffite Sermon Cycle and the copy of the Wycliffite New Testament contained in Dublin, Trinity College, MS 75 (see *PPPLME*, pp. 119–42, and Chapter 7, pp. 236–39, below), it may be that at least some manuscripts of the English Wycliffite Sermon Cycle itself will similarly become candidates for investigation as possible products of London copyists. A systematic palaeographical comparison of the scribal hands of a range of Lollard manuscripts produced *c.* 1400 (a range which should include not only manuscripts of the English Wycliffite Sermons and the Wycliffite Bible, but also of the various other tracts and treatises associated with the sect) with the hands of known London scribes is a desideratum; only once this comparison is done will it be possible to set our understanding of the question of provenance on a surer footing. See further in respect of this issue Alan J. Fletcher, 'The Criteria for Scribal Attribution: Dublin, Trinity College, MS 244, Some Early Copies of the Works of Geoffrey Chaucer, and the Canon of Adam Pynkhurst Manuscripts', *RES*, 58 (2007), 1–36.

into lay hands was an endeavour that encouraged, as it was itself a response to, a growing lay appetite for spiritual writings in English. This radical endeavour was not exclusively Wycliffite (although no doubt its vociferous Lollard advocacy would have helped to bring it into disrepute): another vernacular sermon collection which may be near in date to the *Myrrour*, the postils on the Sunday Gospels preserved uniquely in another manuscript of handsome aspect and presentation, Longleat House, MS 4, was apparently written for some eminent lay patron; its author, furthermore, was a friar, thus hardly a fellow traveller with John Wyclif. Yet the Longleat collection implicitly shared an objective characteristically Lollard in that it too sought to make the Scriptures available in English.[55]

As time went by, there may have been some lessening of the anxieties that initially prompted Archbishop Arundel's Constitutions of 1409 — Constitutions which thereafter prohibited all unlicensed Bible translation into English and which would thus have stalled works like the *Myrrour* or the Longleat 4 postils[56] — for signs reappear later in the fifteenth century of some resumption of the lay attempt to appropriate clerical texts. Our final case is perhaps the most striking of all in that it raises not just the issue of sermons diverted to lay readership, but also illustrates how the very manuscripts containing them, contrary to all expectation, might be copied, not by a cleric or by a professional scribe, but by a layman for his personal use (a sermon from this manuscript is edited as Text C of Chapter 7, below). For on the face of it, Lincoln Cathedral Library, MS 133, a manuscript cursively and casually, though clearly, written, might reasonably be guessed to be precisely the sort of personal pastoral anthology that a secular cleric would choose to compile: leave alone the patent clerical interest of its contents, in measuring 220 × 145 mm it is practically identical in size to the secular clerical sermon compilation reviewed earlier in Cambridge, University Library, MS Gg.6.16; also like that manuscript, MS 133 is written on paper in the unpretentious, though clear, hand of its compiler, in this case Giles Wright of Flixton, Lancashire. Wright, however, was no cleric but a draper.[57] In 1480 when he copied some (if not all) of his manuscript, he was married, had at least one child,

---

[55] See Anne Hudson and Helen L. Spencer, 'Old Author, New Work: The Sermons of MS Longleat 4', *MÆ*, 53 (1984), 220–38.

[56] On the Constitutions and their repercussions, see Nicholas Watson, 'Censorship and Cultural Change in Late-Medieval England: Vernacular Theology, the Oxford Translation Debate, and Arundel's Constitutions of 1409', *Speculum*, 70 (1995), 822–64.

[57] In an earlier article, 'Unnoticed Sermons from John Mirk's Festial', *Speculum*, 55 (1980), 514–22, I was mistaken in supposing that MS 133 may have been copied by a secular cleric.

and had property interests in Oxford.[58] Perhaps his Oxford connection suggests how he chanced by a greater degree of education than is usually associated with members of the lay estate: evidently he could both read Latin and compose it.[59] Amongst the principal items that he copied were an abridged and edited version of the *Provinciale* of the early fifteenth-century canonist, William Lyndwood, a tract on the drafting of wills and testaments (Wright included himself as testator amongst some of his specimens), a portion of a Latin version of the *Speculum Christiani*, a tract on the Mass, and finally a selection of ten Middle English sermons, nine of which derive from the *Festial* of John Mirk.[60] The contents of Wright's manuscript reveal what formidable clerical resources the laity by this date might aspire to assimilate, exceptional among laymen though Wright doubtless was. Had Archbishop Arundel been alive to see Wright's compilation, while he would have had to confess its content theologically blameless, he may nevertheless have cavilled at the general principle of a layman having such intimate access to preserves traditionally clerical.

Conclusion

In sum, this codicological typology of medieval compilations for preaching uncovers certain recurrent patterns of features, and these characterized the manuscript media in which the sermons to be studied in the chapters ahead have been delivered to us. These features are often explicable as reflexes of the peculiar circumstances of each manuscript's point of origin and, all things being equal, that point of origin is reasonably to be inferred on the basis of these reflexes, whether that origin was professionally commercial and targeting a clerical book market, or in-house, when clerics copied for private use matter which, in some cases, subsequently reverted to confrères. Yet any recurrent features notwithstanding, individual sermon codices are also ever liable to contain a margin of surprise that individuality, of its nature, entails.

As might be expected, the professionally commercial products tend to be well finished. They are, however, seldom ornate: characteristically de luxe features (historiated initials, floriate borders and writing frames, polychrome decoration, and

---

[58] Rodney M. Thomson, *Catalogue of the Manuscripts of Lincoln Cathedral Chapter Library* (Cambridge: Brewer, 1989), pp. 102–04.

[59] Conceivably, Wright had formerly undergone vocational training for a Church ministry.

[60] They are listed in Fletcher, 'Unnoticed Sermons', p. 522.

so forth), while not impossible to find, are nevertheless very rare.[61] Like the professionally commercial products, in-house products too may be handsome; they are more likely, though, to reflect the workaday pastoral circumstances for which they were devised, both in terms of a comparative eclecticism of content, and of a presentation that is unadorned and pragmatic. They may also contain indications, more or less evident, that the sermons compiled in them had a prior written existence in one of the humblest of codicological forms, the unbound *quaternus* or booklet. Some in-house products may also reflect the values and ethos of the order producing them (as when, for example, the friars, for whom itinerant preaching tours were routine, preferred codices of portable format, or when the regulars indulged in a format more leisurely and consultative, qualities germane to cloistral life).

More conspicuous than in the case of some of the other books produced for the Church's use whose format was more rigid and content more standard, the greater margin of idiosyncrasy in the codicology of books of sermons may constitute an informative counterbalance to those aspects of ecclesiastical book production that might be deemed conventional. On such preciously idiosyncratic occasions, compilations for preaching afford (less routine) insights into how the late medieval Church locally and nationally went about conducting this particular, fundamental aspect of its worldly mission.

[61] Compare, for example, the historiated initial depicting a tonsured preacher in a hexagonal pulpit that appears in the copy of John Mirk's *Festial* preserved in Durham, University Library, MS Cosin V.III.5, fol. 1ʳ; such depiction is unique among the extant *Festial* manuscripts. Or again, floreate illuminated initials, and two pages having full illuminated borders, may be found in the unique manuscript containing the Latin sermons of Robert Rypon, London, British Library, MS Harley 4894. Both codices are exceptions to the rule, however, and indeed, none of the manuscripts from which the sermons of this anthology have been gathered falls into this top-end category.

THE FRIARS: AN ANONYMOUS SERMON
FOR THE FIRST SUNDAY IN ADVENT

Introduction

Oxford, Bodleian Library, MS Bodley 26, a manuscript briefly introduced in the previous chapter, has not been widely noticed, and none of the texts in it, apart from a Middle English carol copied near the end, has been edited *in extenso*.[1] Its comparative neglect, symptomatic of a malaise that has long afflicted the study of manuscripts of its kind, has consequently obscured its general interest as a compilation probably of Franciscan provenance, as well as

---

[1] Printed notices of MS Bodley 26 are not numerous. Among the more noteworthy are the following: *Religious Lyrics of the XIVth Century*, ed. by Carleton Brown, 2nd edn, rev. by G. V. Smithers (Oxford: Clarendon Press, 1957), pp. 110–11, no. 88 (where the carol 'Honnd by honnd' is printed) and p. 272 (where the manuscript is described); Johannes Baptist Schneyer, 'Eine Sermonesliste des Nicolaus de Byard, O.F.M.', *AFH*, 60 (1967), 3–41 (where on p. 9 the Advent sermon beginning on fol. 173ʳ is identified as the work of Nicholas de Byard); Lynn Thorndike, *A History of Magic and Experimental Science during the First Thirteen Centuries of our Era*, History of Science Society Publications, n.s., 4, 8 vols (New York: Columbia University Press, 1923–58), I, 694 (where fols 207ʳ and 216ᵛ are observed to contain the *Sphere of Pythagoras* or Apuleius); *The Early English Carols*, ed. by Richard Leighton Greene, 2nd edn (Oxford: Clarendon Press, 1977), p. 6, item 12a (where 'Honnd by honnd' is printed and dated as *c*. 1350) and p. 316 (where the manuscript is described); Rossell Hope Robbins, 'The Earliest Carols and the Franciscans', *MLN*, 53 (1938), 239–45 (on p. 243 he incorrectly states that the sermon on the *thema Audi, filia, et vide*, fols 192ʳ–201ʳ, has a carol embedded in it; rather, the suspected carol proves to be rhymed English lines used to mark the sermon's structural parts); and Homer G. Pfander, 'The Popular Sermon of the Medieval Friar in England' (unpublished doctoral dissertation, New York University, 1937), p. 46 (where he takes the manuscript to be Franciscan, and notes the use of verse in *Benedictus qui venit in nomine Domini*, as well as in the sermon *Audi, filia, et vide*).

its particular interest for students of the medieval sermon. I have no intention of making exaggeratedly large claims for its importance in some attempt to re-dress the balance, but it deserves to be brought to wider notice as a manuscript containing an early example — one of the earliest of which I am aware — of a phenomenon that is more frequently associated in the field of medieval sermon studies with manuscripts of the fourteenth and fifteenth centuries, and one that has caused no little debate: this is the phenomenon of macaronic prose and its status in the culture of preaching.[2]

It may be useful first, however, to describe this manuscript more thoroughly than was done in the previous chapter, before turning to the item in it with which this chapter is chiefly concerned, and from which the issues that it subsequently explores stem.

The Manuscript

Given its complexity and the interest that that complexity stimulates, MS Bodley 26 and its construction repay detailed consideration. It is a small parchment compilation of iii + 206 + iv leaves (flyleaves i–ii are of paper, as are endleaves iii–iv). The leaves are approximately 151 × 116 mm. A medieval foliation was added, with consecutive numbers in the top right-hand corner of each leaf in ink, and runs between folios 1 and 218. It is complete, except where folios have gone missing, and where it skips one folio after folio 76 and another, on which a modern foliator has written '201a', after folio 201. In addition, three other medieval foliation systems which must be slightly earlier, as will become clear, make a brief appearance in the manuscript: one in quire 9, which is added in ink at the top centre of each leaf, runs from '184' to '194'; another in quire 10, also in ink and in the same place though in a different hand, runs from '56' to '67'; and a third in quire 12, in ink and in a different hand again but this time in the top right-hand corner, runs from '45' to '54'. The original folio numbers on the first six leaves of quire 12 (that is, '45' to '50') are cancelled, probably in the ink of the hand that added the final consecutive foliation. The collation of the manuscript is straightforward, though occasionally leaves have been lost, and a quire of twelve, it appears, has gone missing between quires 8 and 9. The collation is as follows (folio references are those of the first foliation system described above): iii + 1[24],

---

[2] The question of the language of actual sermon delivery which this phenomenon broaches has been particularly insistent; it will be given further attention below.

$2-3^{12}$, 4^{16}, 5^{14}, 6^{13} (fols 80–92; wants one after 9), 7^{10}, || singleton completing quire 7 ||, 8^8 (fols 104–11; wants two after 8), 9^{11} (fols 124–34; wants one after 8), 10^{12}, 11^8, 12^{10}, 13^8, 14^{19} (fols 173–91; wants one before 1), $15–16^{12}$, 17^2 + iv. The manuscript has a postmedieval binding, but traces of wood grain and thong impressions on the recto of flyleaf iii and on the verso of endleaf ii (both raised parchment pastedowns) suggest it had an earlier, medieval binding of wooden boards. The dimensions of the written text on a leaf vary according to the scribes at work, and of these there are at least sixteen. Their stints are described in the following table, and an approximate palaeographical date is given for each:[3]

Scribe	Folios Covered
A (s. xiii ex.)	1^r–64^v (quires 1–4)
B (s. xiii ex.)	65^r–83^v (quire 5 and the first four leaves of quire 6)
C (s. xiii ex.)	84^r–103^r (the rest of quire 6 plus quire 7 and the singleton added to it before quire 8)
D (s. xiii ex.)	104^r–111^v (quire 8)
E (s. xiii^1)	124^r–134^r (quire 9)
F (s. xiv in.)	135^r–146^r (quire 10)
G (s. xiv in.)	147^r–154^r (quire 11)
H (s. xiv in.)	155^r–164^r (quire 12)
I (s. xiv in.)	165^r–172^r (quire 13)
J (s. xiii ex.)	173^r–191^r (quire 14)
K (s. xiv in.)	192^r–202^r (quire 15)
L (s. xiv in.)	203^r–206^r (the beginning of quire 16, to the recto of the fourth leaf)
M (s. xiv in.)	206^{r-v} (beginning halfway down the recto of the fourth leaf of quire 6 and ending three lines down its verso)

[3] Dating formulas used here and elsewhere in this book follow Neil Ripley Ker, *Medieval Manuscripts in British Libraries*, I: *London* (Oxford: Clarendon Press, 1969), p. vii.

N (s. xiv in.)	206^v–207^r (beginning where M leaves off, and continuing to the recto of the quire's fifth leaf)
L	207^v–209^r (the verso of the fifth leaf, the sixth leaf, and three quarters of the recto of the seventh)
O (s. xiv in.)	209^r–214^v (beginning where L leaves off, and continuing to the end of quire 16)
N (s. xiv in.)	215^r–216^r (beginning of quire 17, and continuing onto the recto of the second leaf)
P (s. xiv in.)	216^v (the verso of the last leaf of quire 17)

The scribal arrangement and the evidence of the four foliation systems suggest various conclusions about how MS Bodley 26 was put together. Its first seven quires, roughly half its entire length, were originally intended to form a unit in their own right. The scribes active in them, A, B, and C, were all contemporary with each other, and wrote late thirteenth-century varieties of script. They may all have worked in collaboration; A and B certainly did. This collaborative pattern ceases after the gap, apparently of twelve leaves, that follows quire 8. When the manuscript resumes with quire 9, the scribe, E, writes with a much earlier hand, the earliest in fact in the manuscript. It probably dates to the first half of the thirteenth century.[4] Also, his stint is accompanied by the first of the alternative foliation systems, located at the top centre of each page. Scribe E's quire, then, would seem originally to have belonged to an earlier, independent compilation that was later broken up and eventually reallocated here. Something similar also appears to have occurred in the case of the next quire. Quire 10, which like quire 9 shares the general top-right foliation of the manuscript, introduces the second of the alternative foliation systems, again located at the top centre of each page. Since its top-centre foliation was not written by the same person who wrote the top-centre foliation in quire 9, however, it appears that quire 10 was derived not from the compilation which yielded quire 9 but from yet another one which shared a similar fate. This seems also to have been the case with quire 12. Quires 11, 13, 14, and 15 were written respectively by scribes G, I, J, and K, who were

---

[4] Compare Andrew G. Watson, *Catalogue of Dated and Datable Manuscripts c. 700–1600 in the Department of Manuscripts, The British Library*, 2 vols (London: The British Library, 1979), II, pl. 135.

more or less contemporary (J is a little earlier in style, dating to the late thirteenth century), but it is impossible to tell whether or not they were collaborating (scribe H could not have collaborated with these four, since quire 12 may have derived from an independent compilation). However, the last two quires, 16 and 17, must have been either the product of collaboration once more or the product of a group of scribes who variously had access to the same two quires.

MS Bodley 26, therefore, an evident compilation, is most efficiently explained as being the product of some final, unknown compiler[5] to whom different manuscripts or *quaterni* were available, including material from at least three other originally discrete compilations.[6] Since certain of his sources were of Franciscan origin, it seems likely that he had his hand on the resources of a conventual scriptorium or centre.[7] Where this may have been is not known: though scribe D produces a variety of written Middle English locatable in the north Lancashire or west Yorkshire region, and scribe K produces one locatable in the region of

[5] Perhaps he shows his hand in the top right-hand corner foliation that runs throughout the manuscript. This seems evidence of an early (fourteenth-century?) attempt to coordinate the manuscript. There are other signs of such attempts. On fol. 2^v, in a hand intruded into what was originally a spare space, is written 'Themata subscripta continentur in quaternis sequentibus et que non sunt hic scribuntur post' (The *themata* written below are contained in the following *quaterni*, and those which are not are written afterwards). At the foot of fol. 36^v, in a hand similarly intruded, is written 'hic deficiunt collaciones nisi possint inuenire [read *inueniri*]' (here collations are wanting, unless they can be found). Also, on fol. 84^r at the bottom of the list of *themata* is written 'Iste collaciones continentur in quatuor quaternis sequentibus' (these collations are contained in the four *quaterni* following), and on fol. 84^v at the top, 'Iste themata sunt de collacionibus precedentibus super Lucam' (these *themata* are from the preceding collations on Luke).

[6] On the *quaternus*, see Pamela R. Robinson, 'The "Booklet": A Self-Contained Unit in Composite Manuscripts', *Codicologica*, 3 (1980), 46–69. Occasionally, MS Bodley 26 refers to *quaterni*: the list of *themata* on fol. 84^r (see n. 9, below) refers to collations 'in quatuor quaternis sequentibus' (in the four following *quaterni*) and these begin on fol. 85^r and extend as far as fol. 103^r. These folios must have constituted the first part of the original four *quaterni*, though the remainder are lost (probably two, since a quire of eight, fols 85^r–92^v, and a quire of ten, fols 93^r–102^v, plus a singleton, fol. 103^{r-v}, are extant).

[7] There are various indications of Franciscan provenance throughout the manuscript. For example, on fol. 147^r, before copying the sermons that ensue, scribe G wrote at the top of the page *Ihesus Maria Franciscus*. A similar formula in another hand, but of comparable date, appears at the top of fol. 192^r, though here it is partially cut away by the binder's knife. In other respects, too, the manuscript seems a typical mendicant product: see Kenneth Williams Humphreys, *The Book Provisions of the Medieval Friars 1215–1400*, Studies in the History of Libraries and Librarianship, 1 (Amsterdam: Erasmus, 1964), pp. 46–66 and 99–118.

Gloucestershire or Worcestershire, this is of no real help in determining the provenance of the compilation as a whole, especially not when the various component *quaterni* of that compilation, if indeed of mendicant origin, would formerly have been liable to roam with their owners.[8] The centre in which the components were finally assembled may nevertheless have been one of some importance, to judge by the extent of the resources to which the compiler had access. He was probably active some time in the first half of the fourteenth century, and his principal interest, to judge by the contents of his compilation, was in preaching.[9] The most reasonable assumption would seem to be that he was a Franciscan himself. Certainly his practice of compiling a manuscript of small format is characteristic of the mendicant movement generally, where practical portability would have been one of the first considerations of the itinerant preacher.[10]

The Sermon

Amongst the material he selected was a macaronic sermon for the first Sunday in Advent on the *thema, Benedictus qui venit in nomine Domini* (Matthew 21. 9). This sermon is the second in a group of five that constitute the whole of quire 8. The group is somewhat heterogeneous: the first sermon, based on an Old Testament *thema*, is for no specified occasion (*Egressus es in salutem populi tui*; Habakkuk 3. 13); the third is for Trinity (on the *thema, Testimonia tua, Domine, credibilia facta sunt nimis*; Psalm 92. 5); the fourth is for Pentecost (on the *thema,*

---

[8] These are approximate locations which I have broadly deduced from resources published in *LALME*. Linguistic analysis of the earlier corpus of Middle English is still in progress.

[9] A summary of contents, following the latest medieval foliation, is as follows: fols 1ʳ–2ᵛ, preaching notes; fol. 2ᵛ, *themata* for collations on Luke (that is, for the collations that follow on fols 3ʳ–39ᵛ); fols 3ʳ–83ᵛ, collations on Luke; fol. 84ʳ, *themata* for the preceding collations on Luke (that is, for those that came on fols 39ᵛ–83ᵛ); fols 85ʳ–103ʳ, collations; fols 104ʳ–111ᵛ, sermons (including the Advent sermon edited here); fols 124ʳ–134ʳ, sermons; fols 135ʳ–145ᵛ, sermons; fols 147ʳ–172ʳ, notes (including a sermon by Nicholas de Byard); fols 192ʳ–201ʳ, sermon (on the *thema Audi, filia, et vide*, with English verses); fol. 202ᵛ, carol 'Honnd by honnd we schulle ous take'; fols 203ʳ–216ᵛ, works on arithmetic and physiognomy and grammatical sophismata (including two diagrams of the *Sphere of Pythagoras* or Apuleius). (A briefer list of contents may be found in Falconer Madan and H. H. E. Craster, *A Summary Catalogue of Western Manuscripts in the Bodleian Library at Oxford*, 7 vols (Oxford: Clarendon Press, 1895–1953), II, pt 1, pp. 91–92, *SC* 1871.

[10] See above in Chapter 2, p. 15 and n. 13.

Accipietis virtutem supervenientis spiritus sancti in vos; Acts 1. 8); and the fifth is
for the feast of St John the Baptist (on the *thema, Iohannes est nomen eius*; Luke
1. 63). All are written in scribe D's tiny hand, one rendered even more condensed
by his liberal use of abbreviations. His advanced tachygraphy shows him capable
of writing at speed, though there is no indication that the five sermons of this
group were copied as *reportationes*; he seems to have simply been economical
with his parchment.[11] Similarly, his manner of copying would suggest that he
was writing his text for consultative purposes rather than for any immediately
practical purpose of providing the preacher with a manuscript from which he
might preach directly.[12] *Benedictus qui venit in nomine Domini* is not the only
sermon in the group to contain English, but it contains it the most extensively.
The fourth sermon, for example, draws attention in the left-hand margin of fol.
110 to a vernacular proverb, 'Nota prouerbium "Wen þe bale", et cetera', which
is probably that which appears in the better known context of *The Owl and the
Nightingale* (a literary text whose composition, incidentally, may lie close in date
to this group of sermons).[13] As Wenzel observes, proverbs in the vernacular were
amongst the earliest specimens of rhymed English to find their way into Latin
sermon collections.[14] Use of 'Wen þe bale' would thus run true to form and, with
the two brief snippets of English which occur in the fifth sermon,[15] its appearance here at this date is neither remarkable nor surprising. But the English of
Benedictus qui venit in nomine Domini is in quite another class. In order to
illustrate it and its function in context adequately, the complete sermon is edited
here.

---

[11] See Malcolm B. Parkes, 'Tachygraphy in the Middle Ages: Writing Techniques Employed
for "Reportationes" of Lectures and Sermons', *Medioevo e Rinascimento*, 3 (1989), 159–69.

[12] In fact, the weight of evidence suggests that he was copying guides for prospective sermons.
Note, for example, the advice to the preacher of *Benedictus qui venit in nomine Domini*: 'pone
exemplum de beato Francisco' (present an exemplum about blessed Francis; see below, p. 42, lines
97–98), which sounds more like a memorandum to someone reading over notes in advance than
an instruction to a preacher in full flow to start improvising.

[13] 'Wone þe bale is alre hecst, | Þonne is þe bote alre necst' (*The Owl and the Nightingale*, ed.
by Neil Cartlidge (Exeter: Exeter University Press, 2001), p. 17, lines 687–88); the poem
attributes the proverb, which also appears at lines 699–700 of the poem, to King Alfred. The
earliest appearance that Bartlett Jere and Helen Wescott Whiting, *Proverbs, Sentences and
Proverbial Phrases from English Writings Mainly Before 1500* (Cambridge, MA: Belknap, for
Harvard University Press, 1968), p. 20, B22, cite is in the *Wohunge of Ure Laverd, c.* 1225.

[14] Wenzel, *Verses in Sermons*, pp. 95–97.

[15] MS Bodley 26, fol. 111[r], 'he es a man', and fol. 111[r–v], 'gret clergie'.

A Sermon for the First Sunday in Advent from Oxford, Bodleian Library, MS Bodley 26

|fol. 107ʳ|

DE ADUENTU

'Benedictus qui uenit in nomine Domini.' Matthei.

> 'Blisced be his holi com
> Þat cums in ur Lord nom.'

5   Thre thinges do þe messenger be ondrefongen wyt menskkful chere. If he com fram gret lording, if he bring þe god tyþng, if þat gode be ner comminge. Et ista tria fuerunt in nuncio nostro Christo. Nam if you see þe gret lordinge, he coms in our Lordes nom. If you ask þis gode tiþng, he brings Goddis bliscyng ʽon to monʼ. If you thinke of þis comynge he coms, lo, fort onon.

10 Primum ibi, 'in nomine Domini.' Iste enim non quiuis est dominus, sed 'rex regum et dominus dominancium.' Dominus, inquam, quo maior cogitari non potest. Quia 'Scitote,' inquit, 'quod Dominus ipse est Deus.' Secundum ibi, 'benedictus,' nam word bringging of gode tiding es i-called blisced tiþnge. Non ne com neuer onto mon so gode tiʽdʼyng als thoruh þis com. 'Est enim

15 super omnia benedictus in secula,' Romanos. Tercium ibi, 'qui uenit.' Nota languorem antiquorum dominancium. Num putas ueniet? Scio quod ueniet. Tarde uenit. Et tandem, 'prope est ut ueniat tempus eius,' et cetera. In Anglice sic: 'Ne think þe noht his day to longe, for his tym es her and hond.' Sin he coms tan fram swilk lording, and bringes til us so gode tiþng, and þis gret

20 gode es so ner comyng, wyt alkyn scil þis messengere syould be welcomd wit lofly chere.

  Sed in quibus, putas, stat Christi cultus? In riche cloþnge? In mangeries? In fair dihtinge? In drueries? Þis riche cloþng es noht skarlet na ueluet, bot a serk of chastite and a kirtil of humilite, a sourcot of charite and mantil trouht

25 of þe Trinite. Primum, quia iocale pulcrum non ponitur in fimario sed in forceario. Secundum, quia humilis non habitat cum superbis. Tercium, quia 'ubi caritas et amor, ibi Deus est.' Quartum, quia magister non admittit discipulum qui eius non uult suscipere documentum.

  Þis mangeries nes nouþer flesly daynte ne fysly plente, sed deuocioun and

30 orisoun, huselyng at Godʽdʼes borde and herkening of Goddes worde. Hec enim sunt quatuor fercula conuiuii spiritualis, quibus libenter Ihesus

· Christus et omnis reficitur christianus. Primum, quia sancta tempora sunt
in sanctis operibus occupanda. Secundum, quia in sanctis temporibus magis
propicius est Deus hominibus, modo mangnorum qui in diebus suis festis et
35 peticiones exaudiunt et donaciones distribuunt. Tercium, propter exemplum
antiquorum, qui primo cotidie, demum omni die dominica, post ter adminus
in anno communicauerunt. Quartum, quia 'qui ex Deo est uerba Dei audit.'
Nota: casus appetitus est signum infirmitatis.

Þis proud tiffynge nes na crokettes na shauinge quantum ad homines, na
40 lokettes na smeringe quantum ad mulieres, sed sunt hertly compunccioun,
clenli confessioun, þe warme tere in þe yhe and a sobbyng bot nohȝt on heye.
Quia it ne es so foul macula in facie anime, quin ista non alluant, nec ita
paruus capillus in capite, quin ista ad suum locum non dirigant.

Þis drueries ner na ringge in þe finger, na cuifhefftis of siluer, na gret bedes
45 of coral, na gildin gaudes þer wital, bot swet speche and holi werkes, for þes
of Goddes worshep er þe merkes. Que ut digne mereamur habere, in primis
debemus orare, et cetera. |fol. 107ᵛ|

Iste mangnus dominus est Pater et Filius et Spiritus Sanctus. Pater enim
mittit appropriate loquendo wit a selli miht, Filius wit a semli riht, Spiritus
50 Sanctus wyt a seli lyht. Et correspondenter his uenit Filius primo onto mans
kynd, secundo onto mans mind, tercio onto þe demyng. Primum de preterito,
secundum de presenti, tercium de futuro. Et ex hiis tribus aduentibus et
cetera appropriate loquendo, correspondenter et cetera tria nobis commoda
seu benediciones uenerunt. Et quia opposita iuxta se posita magis apparent,
55 ideo primo memorandum est que et quot dampna incurrimus ex peccato
primi parentis, et sunt tria, scilicet Goddes wrehtfol werraynge, mans ruful
utlauhyng, and þe deu`e´ls myhtful masteryng. Et contra hec tria dampna
conferuntur nobis per hos aduentus lof and pes twihs Godd and man, and
reles of þis thraldam, and leue fort com til oure kyngdam.

60 Primo ergo dico quod Pater misit wyt a selli miht. Quod enim mirabilius siue
potencius quam facere Deum hominem, et matrem uirginem? Similiter Filius
wiht a semly ryht. Racio`na´bilius enim etiam ut Filius Dei fieret Filius
hominis quam alia persona, ne duos haberemus filios in diuinis.

Similiter Spiritus Sanctus wyht a sely lyht. Lyht, dico, non ab illuminando,
65 sed a condescendendo. Quia 'Spiritus Sanctus superueniet in te, et uirtus

Altissimi obumbrabit tibi.' De quorum mittencium indiuiso diuino, patet in
figura Abrahe demonstrata. Recepit enim tres in mensa et tamen loquebatur
indiuisa reuerenter: 'loquitur ad Dominum meum,' et cetera. Unde in simbolo
Atthanasi, 'Ita Dominus Pater, Dominus Filius,' et cetera. Iste ergo Dominus
70 Pater appropriate misit Filium onto mans kynd propter raciones predictas.
Unde ad Romanos, 'cum autem uenit plenitudo temporis,' et cetera. Nota
quare tunc erat plenitudo temporis magis quam prius uel post, ex quarto
Sentenciarum. Et per istum aduentum facta est lof and pes twyhs God and
man. Ista enim persona Christi incarnata est signum federis quod posuit
75 Dominus cum Noe quando benedixit ei. Cuius tres colores sunt tres nature,
quod et bis curuatur ad terram et in medio eleuatur ad celum, quia in
ingressu est humiliatus ad carnem, in egressu autem in mortem, cuius cum
tota conuersacio est in celis per iugem Dei contemplacionem. Unde de
hoc pacis federe in Psalmo, 'Benedixisti, Domine, terram tuam,' 'ubi'
80 dicitur, 'misericordia et ueritas,' et cetera. Unde et Ysaac benedicens filio, qui
significat Christum et populum Christianum, in primis ait, 'Accede et da
michi osculum, fili mi.' Ergo, karissimi, illam huius temporis inuocacionem
frequencius replicemus, 'Ueni, Domine, uisitare nos in pace, ut letemur
coram te corde perfecto.' Et prosequere de tercia pace, et de natura perfecti,
85 quia perfectum est cui nichil deest, et cetera.

Secundo, dico quod Dominus Spiritus Sanctus appropriate mittit Filium
onto mans mind, et hoc wiht a seli lyht. Nisi enim Sancti Spiritus gracia corda
nostra uisitando preueniat et ad nos condescendendo perueniat, nequaquam
corda nostra Dei Filius inhabitat. Et hoc est quod angelus ad Mariam
90 querentem quomodo Dei Filium nedum carne sed et corde conciperet,
respondit 'Spiritus Sanctus superueniet in te,' et sic 'quod nasceretur ex te
Sanctum uocabitur Filius Dei.' Quamdiu enim hec gracia Spiritus Sancti
nobiscum fuerit, totum sanctum, totum in nomine Filii Dei factum erit,
quia si ingrediens fueris per contemplacionem uel egrediens per accionem,
95 benedictus eris. Deuteronomium, 'Benedictus eris ingrediens et benedictus
egrediens.' Nota signum aduentus Spiritus Sancti, scilicet per graciam.

Et dic per quantam recipi debeat reuerenciam. Et pone exemplum de beato
Francisco, qui ad motus Spiritus Sancti pedem fixit. Per istum aduentum
facta est reles of þis thraldam, quia 'Benedixisti, Domine, terram tuam;
100 auertisti captiuitatem Iacob.' Unde et Ysaac benedicens Iacob dixit, 'Esto
dominus ffratrum tuorum.' Isti ffratres sunt mali spiritus per creacionem et

racionis participacionem, quibus homo ante huius benediccionis aduentum subiectus, nec eis per Dominum est prelatus. Ergo, karissimi, et illam huius temporis et cetera inuocacionem frequencius replicemus, 'Ueni, Domine, et
105 noli tardere, relaxa facinora plebi tue Israel.'

Tercio et ultimo dico quod Dominus Filius appropriate mittet seipsum at te werld end, et hoc wiht a semly riht. Quod autem mittet seipsum patet, quia indiuisa sunt opera trium ad extra. Quod autem appropriate, quia racionabile est ut iudicet qui redemit. Quod autem wiht a semly scyl,
110 quia 'Ecce,' inquit, 'uenio cito, et merces mea mecum est dare unicuique secundum opera sua.' |fol. 108ʳ|

Secundum hunc aduentum fiet finalis introduccio onto mans kyngdam. Unde in figura huius, Axa filia Caleb accepit in benediccionem irriguum superius et inferius: hoc est, graciam in presenti et gloriam in futuro. Unde
115 et Ysaac benedicens filio 'frumento, uino et oleo `eum perpetuo stabiliuit´,' et uictus `ei´ plenitudinem que in contemplacione stat Patris et Filii et Spiritus Sancti repromisit. Quam nobis concedat, et cetera.

Critical Notes and Glosses

14 so gode] so co gode MS.
19 and¹] *sic* MS for 'an' or 'on'.
22 mangeries: 'feasts' (the earliest example of this word given in the MED is late fourteenth-century).
23 dihtinge] 'adorning', 'arraying' (the earliest example of this word in this sense given in the MED is fourteenth-century); drueries: 'love-tokens'.
29 daynte] 'choice food', 'dainty' (the earliest example of this word given in MED is fourteenth-century); fysly: a hapax legomenon, evidently an adjective meaning 'of fish', 'fishy'.
30 huselyng] 'receiving Holy Communion' (the earliest example of this word given in MED is fourteenth-century).
34 mangnorum] *sic* MS (nasal suspension over the a) for 'magnorum' (and see comparably below, line 48).
39 proud] proud de MS; crokettes: 'ornamental curls', 'rolls of hair' (the earliest example of this word given in MED is fourteenth-century).
44 cuifhefftis] a hapax legomenon, evidently a plural noun, and possibly meaning 'fashionable caps' (perhaps from COIF + HEADS).
45 gaudes] 'gewgaws', 'trinkets' (the earliest example of this word given in MED is fifteenth-century).
48 mangnus] *sic* MS (nasal suspension over the a) for 'magnus'.

Apparatus fontium and **Commentary**

2 Matthew 21. 9. Here, as elsewhere, the scribe's tendency is to underline biblical lemmata.

11 Deuteronomy 10. 17.

11–12 quo ... potest: possibly deriving from Anselm's ontological argument (see *St. Anselm's Proslogion*, trans. and ed. by Maxwell John Charlesworth (Oxford: Clarendon Press, 1965), p. 116), where God is *aliquid quo maius nihil cogitari potest*.

12 Psalm 99. 3.

15 Romans 9. 5.

17–18 Isaiah 14. 1.

27 Though possibly inspired by 1 John 4. 8 or 4. 16, perhaps more directly a reminiscence of the Maundy hymn *Ubi caritas et amor, Deus ibi est* (see *AH*, 12 (1892), pp. 24–26; and compare André Wilmart, 'L'hymne de la charité pour le Jeudi-Saint', in *Auteurs spirituels et textes dévots du moyen âge latin* (Paris: Études augustiniennes, 1932), pp. 26–36).

37 John 8. 47.

44–45 Censure of excessive finery is a theological commonplace, inspired here perhaps by I Timothy 2. 9–10 or I Peter 3. 3.

48–49 Pater ... mittit: the understood object of this sentence appears to be *Christum*. The Father, the Son, and the Holy Spirit send Christ respectively 'wit a selli miht', 'wit a semli ribt', and 'wyt a seli lyht' (and compare again line 60, below).

50–51 The three comings of Christ became a sermon commonplace; compare, for example, their appearance in Cambridge, Jesus College, MS 13, part vi, fol. 91^v (in a sermon for the third Sunday in Advent on the *thema Tu es qui venturus est*).

54 opposita ... apparent: possibly an Aristotelian epitome. See *Les Auctoritates Aristotelis*, ed. by Jacqueline Hamesse (Louvain: Université catholique de Louvain, Publications de CETEDOC, 1974), p. 267 (57): *Contraria juxta se posita magis apparent, sive elucescunt*; this derives from the *Rhetorica*, III.3 (1405a12–13). The proposition appears to have had some currency in contemporary mendicant collections. Compare its use in Cambridge, Trinity College, MS 43, fol. 28^r, in a Palm Sunday sermon on the *thema Ecce rex tuus venit tibi mansuetus*, fols 27^v–28^v. (This manuscript is better known for its 'Atte wrastlinge' sermon, fols 41^v–42^r.)

63 ne ... diuinis: possibly a reminiscence of Peter Lombard, III *Sent.*, 1.1; see *Magistri Petri Lombardi Sententiae in IV libris distinctae*, ed. by Collegium S. Bonaventurae, 3rd edn, Spicilegium Bonaventurianum 4–5, 2 vols in 3 (Grottaferrata: Editiones Collegii S. Bonaventurae ad Claras Aquas, 1971–81), II, 24–26.

65–66 Luke 1. 35.

68 Genesis 18. 27 and 31.

68–69 in simbolo Atthanasi: the full clause in the Athanasian Creed is *Ita dominus Pater, dominus Filius, dominus Spiritus Sanctus; et tamen non tres domini, sed unus est dominus* (see J. N. D. Kelly, *The Athanasian Creed* (London: A. and C. Black, 1964), p. 18, lines 17–18).

71 Galatians 4. 4.

72–73 ex quarto *Sentenciarum*: the reference is problematic in that IV *Sent.* does not discuss the three comings; I *Sent.*, 15.8, however, cites the lemma (*Sed cum venit plenitudo temporis ...*) in the context of a discussion of the two comings — the Incarnation and the coming to the *animae piae* who recognize Christ (*Magistri Petri Lombardi Sententiae*, I, 136).

74 signum federis: an allusion to Genesis 9. 1–17.

78 tota ... celis: an allusion to Philippians 3. 20.

79–80 Psalm 84. 2 and 11.

82 Genesis 27. 26.

83–84 Ueni ... perfecto: an Advent antiphon (after Sarum Use, for Compline on the first Sunday of Advent; see *Breviarium ad usum insignis ecclesiae Sarum*, ed. by Francis Procter and Christopher Wordsworth, 3 vols (Cambridge: Cambridge University Press, 1879–86), I, p. xii).

91–92 Luke 1. 35.

95–96 Deuteronomy 28. 6.

100–01 Psalm 84. 2.

102 Genesis 27. 29.

105–06 Ueni ... Israel: an Advent antiphon (after Sarum Use, for use either during None on the ferias of Advent or for Lauds on the sixth feria of the third week of Advent; see *Breviarium*, II, 68 and I, p. cxxv respectively).

111–12 Revelation 22. 12.

113–14 Axa ... inferius: an allusion either to Joshua 15. 19 or Judges 1. 15.

116 Genesis 27. 37. However, published Vulgate variants do not feature *perpetuo* (pp° MS) as part of this lemma, and the reading should be regarded as problematic.

The Sermon's Use of English and the Macaronic Problem

The sermon, an interesting specimen of mendicant (probably Franciscan) preaching, is intricately organized and displays allegiance to the highly structured 'modern' form of sermon composition. 'Modern' sermons opened with the announcement of a *thema*, normally taken from Scripture, which was then systematically divided into a set of *principalia* or *membra*, each of which might in turn be further sub-divided, the resultant branching structure providing the pegs from which the bulk of the sermon was made to hang.[16] The extensive use of English to mark major

---

[16] 'Modern' sermon form has been discussed in several places; see notably Rouse and Rouse, *Preachers, Florilegia and Sermons*, pp. 65–90. The Rouses base their account on actual sermon practice. A survey of the form as advocated by the *artes predicandi* is given in James J. Murphy, *Rhetoric in the Middle Ages: A History of Rhetorical Theory from Saint Augustine to the Renaissance* (Berkeley and Los Angeles: University of California Press, 1974), pp. 269–32. See also *EPLMA*, pp. 228–68. For texts of some of the *artes*, see T. M. Charland, *Artes praedicandi: Contribution à l'histoire de la rhétorique au moyen âge*, Publications de l'Institut d'études médiévales d'Ottawa, 7 (Paris: Wetteren, 1936). Wenzel, *Preachers, Poets, and the Early English Lyric*, pp. 61–62, and again in *LSCLME*, pp. 11–14, prefers to use the term *scholastic* to describe sermons of this form. Whatever its limitations, however, the word *modern*, unlike *scholastic*, was a contemporary medieval term used of such sermons; moreover, *scholastic* risks

structural parts (the translation of the opening *thema* into a four-stress couplet, the threefold rhymed *distinctio* on what the *Christi cultus* comprises, to mention only the structural markers that occur in the first part of the sermon before the bidding prayer at lines 46–47) is earlier than anything in the examples collected by other scholars in their study of the function of English verse in Latin sermons.[17] Moreover, since its use of English at this early date is already particularly elaborate, any idea, based presumably upon an evolutionary model of thinking, that the use of English verses in Latin sermons became steadily more flexible and diverse from about the mid-fourteenth century, would seem to be discountenanced: this sermon is already more advanced in this respect than many that follow it, even if it remains true that there are proportionally far more examples of the extended use of English verses in Latin sermons extant from the later period.[18] If an evolutionary model has any validity, we must suppose from *Benedictus qui venit in nomine Domini* that an extensive introduction of English verses into preaching was taking place earlier still in the thirteenth century. Perhaps this did take place, with the mendicants in the vanguard of it, but substantial evidence has not survived.

There is another use of English in the sermon, of a different kind, whose function has also contributed to the speculation and debate noted at the start of this chapter. English, as we have seen, is used extensively to articulate the structural nodes of *Benedictus qui venit in nomine Domini*, and twice it is used to paraphrase a preceding piece of Latin text.[19] Invariably on these occasions, the English is versified. But in two cases English appears within sentences of Latin *prose* (at lines 42–43 and 106–07).[20] This sort of linguistic switching within the boundary of a single prose sentence unit (that is, intrasentential code-switching)

---

conveying a false impression of the milieu in which a substantial number of sermons composed in this *modern* form were preached.

[17] See for example Wenzel, *Verses in Sermons*, pp. 74–81.

[18] Wenzel, *Verses in Sermons*, p. 94, suggests manuscript loss may partly explain this impression, and notes too the upsurge in confidence in the vernacular generally after the mid-fourteenth century. For further reflections on the increase of English usage at around this time, see Tim William Machan, *English in the Middle Ages* (Oxford: Oxford University Press, 2003), pp. 71–110.

[19] See lines 3–4 and 17–18.

[20] It should, however, be noted that the syntactic balance and repetition evident in lines 42–43 suggest the lines are close to being verse. (Do they reflect an underlying English verse original, incompletely digested into Latin?)

is in England more familiarly associated with certain manuscripts of the fourteenth and fifteenth centuries, all again later than the date of the hand that wrote the sermons in quire 8 of MS Bodley 26.[21] Some of the later specimens of this curious macaronic style are particularly arresting, because the alternation between English and Latin may happen within the same sentence rapidly and repeatedly, as in this reflection on the upwardly mobile on Ezechiel's wheel:

> Gape vpward ful fast. Quidam ar qwirlid vp subito super illam rotam et fiunt de pore gentilmen grete astates and gret lordis.[22]

> (Gaze intently upwards. Quidam are whirled up subito super illam rotam et fiunt de poor gentlemen men of great estate and great lords.)

Admittedly, the two cases in *Benedictus qui venit in nomine Domini* are more modest than this, and two cases in the entire sermon, even if we were to increase this number by also including cases where lines initially given in rhymed English are then dislocated for incorporation into Latin prose,[23] are far fewer proportionally than those in the rest of the early fifteenth-century sermon from which the sentence above was excerpted. But what is interesting is that they seem to be of exactly the same order.

An obvious question provoked by macaronic usage, whether of English verse in Latin sermons or of English and Latin words alternating within sentences in prose, concerns the language in which the sermons displaying this usage were delivered, where preaching intention is evident or can be inferred. Were congregations treated to the curious linguistic confections that some manuscripts, if taken at face value, suggest? Siegfried Wenzel believes that they were.[24] Not until well into the second half of the fourteenth century do sermon collections largely

---

[21] Wenzel, *Macaronic Sermons*, has proposed a classification of such sermons of the randomly macaronic sort. They belong to his type C category, which is distinguished by its intrasentential code-switching back and forth between Latin and English.

[22] *A Macaronic Sermon Collection from Late Medieval England*, ed. by Patrick J. Horner, Studies and Texts, 153 (Toronto: Pontifical Institute of Mediaeval Studies, 2006), p. 525, lines 136–38.

[23] There are nine examples of this sort (at lines 60, 61–62, 64, 64–65, 70, 73–74, 86–87, 106–07, and 109).

[24] Wenzel, *Macaronic Sermons*, pp. 105–29. Before him, a similar view had been expressed of the sermons in Oxford, Bodleian Library, MS Bodley 649 by Roy Martin Haines, *Ecclesia Anglicana: Studies in the English Church of the Later Middle Ages* (Toronto: University of Toronto Press, 1989), p. 204: 'A marked feature of the Bodley [649] sermons is their macaronic form — a mixture of Latin and English. It is possible that they were actually delivered in this manner.'

in English begin appearing in any significant quantity.[25] Of these, collections either demonstrably or probably intended for preaching were doubtless intended for preaching in English.[26] It would be perverse to imagine anything else. Before the second half of the fourteenth century, what exceptions there are, though some are major works, are comparatively few: Latin is normally the language in which sermons are recorded.[27] There survive from this earlier period, however, several sermons that are known to have been delivered in English but written down in Latin after the event.[28] Others — cast like *Benedictus qui venit in nomine Domini* in the 'modern' form, admitting English verse renderings of their structural parts — may similarly have belonged to this category, either set down substantially in Latin after the event or perhaps composed in the study before it. It is easy to see why vernacular rhyme should be preserved in such sermons: in the case of a sermon originally delivered mainly in English, English verses are more likely to have resisted the sermon's subsequent translation into its Latin literary form, since

[25] For example, most of the manuscripts cited in the conspectus of shelfmarks compiled by Thomas J. Heffernan and Patrick J. Horner, 'Sermons and Homilies', in *A Manual of the Writings in Middle English 1050–1500*, ed. by Peter G. Beidler (New Haven: Connecticut Academy of Arts and Sciences, 2005), XI, pp. 3969–4167, date from this period. Thomas J. Heffernan, 'Sermon Literature', in *Middle English Prose: A Critical Guide to Major Authors and Genres*, ed. by A. S. G. Edwards (New Brunswick, NJ: Rutgers University Press, 1984), pp. 177–207, speculates (p. 186) on the reasons for the dearth of Middle English sermon manuscripts from just after the Black Death in 1349.

[26] That is, where a preaching intention, above mere private consultation, seems demonstrable, as it does, for example, in the case of John Mirk's *Festial* (see *Mirk's Festial: A Collection of Homilies*, ed. by Theodor Erbe, EETS, e.s., 96 (London: Paul, Trench, Trübner; repr. Millwood, NY: Kraus, 1973)).

[27] Among the major earlier sermon collections are the *Ormulum* (ed. by R. M. White, rev. by R. Holt, 2 vols (Oxford: Clarendon Press, 1878)), the Lambeth Homilies (*Old English Homilies and Homiletic Treatises*, ed. by Richard Morris, EETS, o.s., 29 (London: Trübner, 1868)), and the so-called Kentish sermons (*An Old English Miscellany*, ed. by Richard Morris, EETS, o.s., 49 (London: Trübner, 1872; repr. New York: Greenwood, 1969)); also the *Northern Homily Cycle: The Expanded Version in MSS Harley 4196 and Cotton Tiberius E vii*, ed. by Saara Nevanlinna, Mémoires de la Société néophilologique de Helsinki, 3 vols (Helsinki: Société néophilologique, 1972–84).

[28] Some of the sermons of Richard FitzRalph are a prime example. See Aubrey Gwynn, 'The Sermon-Diary of Richard FitzRalph, Archbishop of Armagh,' *PRIA*, 44 (1937–38), 1–57. Also, G. Mifsud, 'John Sheppey, Bishop of Rochester, as Preacher and Collector of Sermons' (unpublished B.Litt. thesis, University of Oxford, 1953), pp. 39–41, convincingly argues for Sheppey having composed at least one, and probably more, of his sermons in Latin for delivery in English.

they would demand a modicum of extra effort to render them into Latin verse equivalents; and certainly in the case of a sermon set down beforehand in Latin by someone intending eventually to preach it in English, such things as rhymed themes and divisions might not be left to be improvised on the spot, whereas the portions in straightforward Latin prose could be more easily translated or paraphrased at the time of delivery.[29] This much at least would be prepared in advance should the Spirit not move the preacher on the day quite as far as *ex tempore* verse. Verse like this of itself might give grounds for suspecting that *Benedictus qui venit in nomine Domini* too was delivered or intended for delivery *ad populum* and mainly in the vernacular.[30] (If it was, for some reason English was not found to be the appropriate medium for committing it, no less the later sermons with which it compares, to posterity.)[31] This interpretation might explain the presence of English verse in the sermon, but what is the status of the more curious macaronic style in prose, here incipient but found fully-fledged in sermons only a generation or two later, which alternates English and Latin within a single sentence? This calls for some further consideration, given recent arguments that sermons thus recorded may really have been thus preached.[32] Necessarily they either were or were not, and even were it possible to determine that they were not, how might we then explain the strange macaronic mixture given to them on parchment?

While these questions may return no decisive answers, it is nevertheless worth expanding the scope of enquiry further than has been customary if any answers are to be ventured at all, and this means in effect by going beyond medieval sermon texts. Thus it may be possible to locate their macaronic style in the context of

[29] Wenzel, *Preachers, Poets and the Early English Lyric*, p. 86. There is always a possibility, of course, that English verses became items of *curiositas* through self-conscious introduction into sermons otherwise preached predominantly in Latin.

[30] Compare Wenzel, *Verses in Sermons*, p. 87. The sermon's subject matter also suggests such a conclusion; see further below.

[31] It has commonly been thought that not until the second half of the fourteenth century, when theological matter in Middle English prose starts appearing in any quantity, did Middle English start to slough the stigma of being a second-class literary language. But the reasons for the preference of Latin to English before this time may be a little more complex: Latin may simply have been found quicker to write, more economical on space on account of its richer repertory of abbreviations, and generally a more familiar written language than English currently was, even to scribes who natively spoke English.

[32] Henceforth my references to macaronic texts will intend specifically cases of macaronic prose, not merely cases of English verse in an otherwise Latin prose text.

a much wider contemporary phenomenon, to suggest how this sermon style may have come about, to come as near as possible to settling the question of the original language of preaching, and to try to offer some explanation of its raison d'être.

The Macaronic Style in England

We are fortunate to have surviving the work of another Franciscan, not this time his sermons, though he was evidently an active preacher, but a collection of his letters written between 1456 and 1461. Friar John Brackley, confidant to the Paston family of Norfolk in the mid-fifteenth century, was a man in touch with clerical culture and someone whose prose style, characterized by Norman Davis as exhibiting 'a strange mixture of Latin and English',[33] was capable of the more extreme sort of random macaronic usage which is of especial concern here. Thirteen of his fourteen extant letters were addressed to John Paston I, and the remaining one was addressed to John's brother, William Paston II.[34] Both Pastons, Cambridge educated, may be assumed to have had some familiarity with Latin, and thus Brackley's use of it in letters to them probably needed no interpretation. Five were written entirely in Latin, and are therefore not of present interest.[35] Of the remaining nine, three are also in Latin so substantially that they too may be set aside.[36] This leaves six letters from which to deduce what may have been the reasons behind Brackley's macaronic usage. Whenever he quoted Bible lemmata, he invariably did so in Latin. This use of Latin to report sacred text, so utterly without exception that it looks to have been with him a point of principle, is akin to his tendency to shift from English into Latin wherever his drift took a spiritual turn away from more secular matters. For example, approximately the first half of his letter of 24 October 1460 to John Paston I, in English, is concerned with political consequences arising from the Coventry parliament of 1459, but its second half, containing several Bible lemmata with

---

[33] *The Paston Letters: A Selection in Modern Spelling*, ed. by Norman Davis (Oxford: Oxford University Press, 1963), p. 33 n. 2.

[34] See *Paston Letters and Papers of the Fifteenth Century*, ed. by Norman Davis, Richard Beadle, and Colin Richmond, EETS, s.s., 20–22, 3 vols (Oxford: Oxford University Press, 2004–05), II, nos 557, 581–83, 605–06, 608–12, 617, 655, and 705.

[35] *Paston Letters and Papers of the Fifteenth Century*, nos 581, 605, 608, 611, and 612.

[36] *Paston Letters and Papers of the Fifteenth Century*, nos 606, 610, and 655.

theological commentary, is entirely in Latin.[37] Most of this second half is taken up with Brackley's discussion of the matter of a sermon he preached on the *thema*, *Non credas inimico tuo in eternum* (Ecclesiasticus 12. 10), and of how a bishop — 'vtinam non indignus' (would that he were not unworthy) adds Brackley in a sideswipe — had claimed that these words were not to be found in Scripture; which goes to show, he thinks, that sometimes even a bishop nowadays may be ignorant of what Scripture actually says.[38] After this, the remainder of the letter is a conclusion, comprising a dark hint of things still to be said but which 'iam non expedit calamo commendare' (it's not now expedient to entrust to writing), a little family news, and pious good wishes, mixed with biblical lemmata.[39] Brackley concludes each of his macaronic letters in Latin, a habit he perhaps learned by analogy with Latin epistolary valedictions elsewhere whose terms are likely to have been formulaically familiar.[40] Equally, the secular material and news intercalated into Brackley's conclusions and the pieties that they routinely contain are drawn into Latin.[41]

Brackley was sometimes inclined to use Latin to point the direction that a conversation was taking, using markers like *Cui ego* or *Et ille* before reporting what *ego* or *ille* actually said.[42] This usage produces a macaronic style a little like that under discussion, but only in terms of the rapidity of its English/Latin alternation, for unlike the style under discussion it seems more systematic than haphazard. Sometimes, though, Brackley was indeed capable of much less predictable macaronic shifts, where within a sentence prose alternates between languages for no very obvious reason:

> And now he seyth he wil labowr and ryde and do hise part, &c. And he wold haf me to help hym, &c., quod non fiet, &c., or ell a man of credens of my maysterys, &c., quod dubito fieri, &c. God bryng ʒow sone hidyr, &c., for I am weri tyl ʒe come.[43]

---

[37] *Paston Letters and Papers of the Fifteenth Century*, no. 617, pp. 221–22.

[38] *Paston Letters and Papers of the Fifteenth Century*, no. 617, p. 222, lines 29–49.

[39] *Paston Letters and Papers of the Fifteenth Century*, lines 54–65; the ending of letter no. 582, p. 185, lines 38–53, is somewhat comparable.

[40] See Murphy, *Rhetoric in the Middle Ages*, pp. 194–268.

[41] For example, *Paston Letters and Papers of the Fifteenth Century*, II, no. 582, p. 185, lines 38–53.

[42] *Paston Letters and Papers of the Fifteenth Century*, no. 583, p. 186, lines 21–22.

[43] *Paston Letters and Papers of the Fifteenth Century*, lines 13–16 (in this quotation and in the subsequent quotations I have retained Davis's expansions but without notice). Both shifts into Latin are precipitated by *quod*-clauses (another instance is in the text cited below, as n. 51). Why this should be, however, is not clear.

(And now he says he will labour and ride and do his part, et cetera. And he would have me help him, et cetera, quod non fiet, et cetera, or else a credible man of my master's, et cetera, quod dubito fieri, et cetera. God bring you quickly to this place, et cetera, for I am weary until you come.)

At times, then, the alternation looks motivated, as again when words registering various kinds of status (*germanus vester, judex*) were introduced into the English sentence,[44] while at others, the alternation is less readily explicable. These latter cases are the moments when Brackley's macaronic style is at its most comparable to the apparently random macaronic prose alternation under review here.

The most interesting of Brackley's letters in respect of macaronic versatility is that sent to William Paston II sometime before Easter 1460. It displays almost all of the varieties of macaronic usage noted above, but an additional feature is the way in which Latin is introduced into the direct speech that Brackley attributes to himself when reporting an exchange that took place in public between him and Justice William Yelverton. The exchange concerns the circumstances surrounding a dispute that had broken out between Yelverton and John Paston I, the latter part of which Brackley had overheard, and Yelverton is moved to remind Brackley that if he is to report the matter, he has a responsibility for getting the facts right:

'For sothe,' seyd I, 'whan I came in-to the chambre there the fyrst word I hard was this, that ʒe seyd to my Maystyr J. P., "Who that evyr seyth so, I sey he lyeth falsly in hise hede,"' &c. 'Ya,' quod the justise, 'ʒe schuld haf told what mevyd me to sey so to hym'; and I seyd I cowde not tellyn that I not herd, &c. Et judex, 'ʒe schuld haf examyned the matyr,' &c. And I seyd, 'Sire, it longyd not to me to examyne the matyr, for I knew wele I schuld not be jvge in the matyr, and alonly to a juge it longyth to seue and stodyen illam Sacre Scripture clausulam whiche holy Job seyd, "Causam quam nesciebam diligentissime investigabam."'[45]

('Indeed', I said, when I came into the room, the first word I heard was this, that you said to my master J.P., "Whoever says so, I say he lies through his teeth", et cetera. 'Yes,' said the Justice, 'you should have declared what prompted me to say so to him.' And I said I could not say what I had not heard, et cetera. Et Judex, 'You should have examined the matter, for I knew well that I shouldn't be the judge of the matter, and it's only up to judges to follow and study illam Sacre Scripture clausulam which holy Job said, "Causam quam nesciebam diligentissime investigabam."')

Eventually a prior, unnamed but also evidently privy to the conversation, intervenes with a reproof both to Yelverton and to the absent John Paston I about the

---

[44] *Paston Letters and Papers of the Fifteenth Century*, no. 705, p. 333, lines 30 and 52 respectively.

[45] *Paston Letters and Papers of the Fifteenth Century*, lines 45–56 (punctuation modified).

propriety of haggling over a dead man's goods, the disposal of which has given rise to their quarrel:

> Et ille [Yelverton], 'I knowe ʒe haf a gret hert,' &c., 'but I ensure ʒow the lordys a-bove at London am infoormyd of ʒow, and they schal delyn wyth ʒow wele anow.' Cui ego, 'He or they that hafe infoormyd the lordys wele of me, I am behold to hem. And yf they be oþyrwyse infoormyd I schal do as wele as I may; but be myn trowthe I schal not be aferd to sey as I knowe for none lord of this lond, yf I may go saf and come, quod non credo, per deum, propter euidencias multas,' &c. Tunc Prior, 'Domine, non expedit nec racioni seu vere consciencie congruit quod vos contendatis cum Magistro Paston, vel ipse vobiscum, pro bonis defuncti, que solum sua et non vestra sunt; miror valde,' inquit, 'cum prioribus temporibus tam magni fuistis amici, et non sic modo, quare valde doleo.' Cui judex, 'There is no man besy to bryng vs to-gydere,' &c.[46]

> (Et ille [Yelverton], 'I know you are big hearted, et cetera, but I assure you, the lords in London are informed about you, and they shall deal with you well enough.' Cui ego, 'He or they who have spoken well of me to the lords, I am obliged to them. And if they are otherwise informed, I shall do as best I may; but upon my word, I shan't be afraid to say what I know, for any lord of this land, if I may come and go safely, quod non credo, per deum, propter euidencias multas,' &c. Tunc Prior, 'Domine, non expedit nec racioni seu vere consciencie congruit quod vos contendatis cum Magistro Paston, vel ipse vobiscum, pro bonis defuncti, que solum sua et non vestra sunt; miror valde,' inquit, 'cum prioribus temporibus tam magni fuistis amici, et non sic modo, quare valde doleo.' Cui judex, 'There isn't anyone actively seeking to bring us together', et cetera.)

What is of interest in these passages is the way Brackley apparently shifts between English and Latin in two different sentences when addressing Yelverton. Moreover, when the prior joins the conversation, which despite the linguistic oscillation of Brackley has hitherto been conducted mainly in English, he speaks entirely in Latin. Are we then to understand, as Brackley's report would seem to imply, that this conversation actually took place with one speaker (Yelverton) speaking in English, another (Brackley) alternating between English and Latin, and a third (the prior) speaking in Latin exclusively? Either this was what really happened or, alternatively, so curious a mélange may reflect to some unquantifiable degree other considerations that came into play once Brackley took up the pen and whose nature I will address later.

Whatever the spoken actuality behind this, it is at least clear that interchange between English and Latin on the written page was for Brackley a relatively easy matter. In many instances, a rationale for his macaronic usage seems deducible (broadly, Latin supersedes English for spiritual topics, epistolary formulas, status

---

[46] *Paston Letters and Papers of the Fifteenth Century*, p. 334, lines 68–79 (punctuation modified).

words, conversation markers, and conclusions, and it is used when Brackley is writing at speed), but there is a small residuum of English/Latin usage whose explanation is less readily forthcoming, where alternation seems more a matter of whim. These cases are interesting, for wherever language choice seems not determined by any evident literary or practical considerations, it would suggest that English and Latin for Brackley shared moments of linguistic coequivalence: he was sufficiently bilingual for his two languages to slip in and out of each other without much forethought. What Brackley's usage presents us with is perhaps an example of what modern linguists would identify as code-switching.[47]

The writing habits of this Franciscan, a man in touch with clerical culture and a preacher by profession, are also those of someone who kept company with lawyers and their legal dealings, as the passages quoted above indicate. No doubt during his career he would have made his acquaintance too with the prose of the courts. If we turn to the writing that certain legal notaries of his day were producing, an interesting point of comparison emerges: some of it is cast in precisely the random macaronic mould of chief concern here. To draw attention to the comparison is not to suggest lines of influence and to imply that macaronic legal prose provided Brackley's model; rather, it is to introduce alongside the sermons and the letters another province of texts in which macaronic writing was manifesting itself, and hence to widen further the contexts in which writing of this kind had also established itself as acceptable written practice.

Although in the case of macaronic legal prose the mixing of Latin and English is much less frequent than the mixing of Latin and French, macaronic mixtures can be quite as comparable in terms of randomness. No attempt was made to establish English officially as the language of the courts until after the passing of the Act of 1362, which required the substitution of 'la lange du paiis' (the country's language) for 'la lange francais, qest trope desconue' (the French language which is too unfamiliar), but even after 1362 the act seems to have had little widespread effect.[48] Consequently, the Latin, French, and English usage of the notary who recorded the case of Alblaster v. Bendisch in Trinity Term, 1470, is

---

[47] See Carol Myers-Scotton, *Contact Linguistics: Bilingual Encounters and Grammatical Outcomes* (Oxford: Oxford University Press, 2002), pp. 153–57. She makes the point from analysis of modern examples that borrowed linguistic items and code-switching differ in regard to predictability. Borrowing is predictable, in that the item in question will reoccur, whereas the code-switching item may or may not reoccur.

[48] *Year Books of Edward II*, I: *1 and 2 Edward II, A.D. 1307–1309*, ed. by Frederic William Maitland, Publications of the Selden Society, 17 (London: Quaritch, 1907; repr. London: Professional Books, 1974), pp. xxxiv–xxxv.

very much a late medieval phenomenon; such trilingual alternation as his would
be far less likely in the thirteenth or early fourteenth century, when any extensive
macaronic usage was normally limited to Latin and French.[49] By the fifteenth
century, this Latin and French tradition of macaronic legal prose had grown
sturdy, as this excerpt — a discussion of some niceties of marriage law taken from
a Year Book of 7 Henry VI—demonstrates:

> June: 'La cause del fesance del lestatute fuit en auantage des heires maries deins age, et pur
> ii causes: vn que le roy auera le garde de corps, pour ceo que il serra adonques en le election
> le heire, sil voet ipsum vel ipsam habere, cui, et cetera, ou celuy que le roy offera: et mesque
> le roy granta cel election a luy, il ne poet estre entend*u*, que par cel benefice done al heire,
> le roy serra exclude de son duite, scilicet, le forfeiture del mariage, que nen pas peyne, eins
> vn veray duite.' Ad alium diem Huls baccalaureus vtriusque iuris argua moulte en latin et
> dit quod 'consensus matrimonii tribus modis cognoscitur, scilicet, inspectatione corporis,
> vt per pubertatem, id est pilositatem, per cursum etatis, scilicet, xiiii an*norum* in viro, in
> sexu femineo xii, et per carnis copulationem. Et modis presuppositis est consensus in
> heredibus notabiliter approbatur. Et a ceo que mon maister June dit, que le seignior fuit
> cause del fesance del estatute, [...] a ceo moy semble que par cel parole *eligat* tout est
> extient, quia electio est sine compulsione, vna res ab alia libera seperatio. Et sil paiera le
> value, cel election nest pas sine compulsione, nec est libera.'[50]

> (June: 'The reason for the making of the statute was for the advantage of heirs married
> within age, and for two reasons: one, that the king will have guard of the body, because
> he will then be the heir in the election, if he wishes ipsum vel ipsam habere, cui, et cetera,
> or the one who the king will offer: and unless the king granted this election to him, he
> cannot be heard, apart from by this benefit given to the heir, the king will be excluded
> from his obligation, scilicet, the forfeiture of the marriage, without penalty, thus a true
> obligation.' Ad alium diem Huls baccalaureus vtriusque iuris argued many things in Latin

---

[49] *Year Books of Edward IV: 10 Edward IV and 49 Henry VI, A.D. 1470*, ed. by Nellie Neilson,
Publications of the Selden Society, 47 (London: Quaritch, 1931; repr. London: Spottiswoode,
Ballantyne, 1965), p. 96: 'En dette sur obligacion porte par Jamez Alblaster enuers T. Bendisch
le defendaunt dit qe lobligacion est enclose sur tiel condicion et in hec verba, setassauer: That iff
the said Thomas B. sufficiently proue that itt was the wille off John Bendisch that the said James
Alblaster suld mak an estat to the said T. B. and J. C. off certein lands and tenementez en D. etc.
and that a bille concernyng the said wille be signyd with hys aune hande and sent to the said Jamez
A. etc. and that thies condicion be performyd within xii moneth nex after the makyng off the
obligacion qe adunqe lobligacion soit voide, et dit qe le dit J. B. a D. auaunt dit fist sa volunte
setassauer qe lez ditz Jamez enfeoffe lez ditz T. B. et J. C.'.

[50] Year Book, Michaelmas Term, 7 Henry VI, fol. xi^v (London: Wyllyam Myddylton, [n.d.]).
Here it might be noted that some of the macaronic alternation occurs where there is little
question of some underlying original act of speech. Hence it appears essentially literary (as at lines
7–8, for example). (I have silently emended the printed text at line 10, which reads *notabilter* for
notabiliter, and at line 14, where sense demands *sine* before *compulsione*.)

and said quod 'consensus matrimonii tribus modis cognoscitur, scilicet, inspectatione corporis, vt per pubertatem, id est pilositatem, per cursum etatis, scilicet, xiiii an*norum* in viro, in sexu femineo xii, et per carnis copulationem. Et modis presuppositis est consensus in heredibus notabiliter approbatur. And to what my master June said, that the lord was the reason for making the statute, [...] in this respect it seems to me that by the word *eligat* everything is overridden, quia electio est sine compulsione, vna res ab alia libera seperatio. And if he will pay the value, this election is not sine compulsione, nec est libera.')

Although passages like this would have been rare in the earlier period, where French predominates, even there a certain macaronic tendency that is more fortuitous than predictable may be discerned.[51] Evidently, Latin came as quickly to mind as French for certain legal scribes.[52] All this supports the case that by the fifteenth century, macaronic prose was well entrenched within the field of certain sorts of legal text too. Consequently, the frequent and random macaronic variation that some of the later sermon manuscripts display should again appear less curious than it has; it was certainly not an isolated textual phenomenon.

Indeed, for reasons we may now consider, it would be the more surprising if it were confined exclusively to some single prose genre rather than featuring more widely, as has been seen to be the case, in contiguous fields of text. The bilingual competence which macaronic usage of the random kind may imply, whether manifested in sermons, letters, or legal records,[53] is perhaps to be traced to a common origin, and as such, its appearance in a wide variety of texts is only what might be expected.

---

[51] As sentences like 'Et secundum quosdam la femme avera heide del heir' (in the case of Hemegrave v. Bernake, Trinity Term, I Edward II (1308)) or 'Et bota avaunt la chartre quod dictum donum testatur' (in the case of London v. Tynten, 2 Edward II (1308–1309)) might suggest (see *Year Books*, ed. by Maitland, p. 38 and p. 148 respectively).

[52] Of course, it is conceivable that some scribes' knowledge of French and Latin may not have been absolutely coextensive, so that lapses from the former into the latter, or sometimes vice-versa, might naturally occur in consequence.

[53] And these are not the only textual genres in which random macaronic usage may appear. There are instances of it, too, in literary works, where intrasentential code-switching may be found. I would like to thank Judith Tschann for helpful discussion on this point, especially in the context of examples found in the late thirteenth-century poetic anthology in Oxford, Bodleian Library, MS Digby 86. Examples in scientific and medical prose have been usefully studied by Linda Ehrsam Voigts, 'What's the Word? Bilingualism in Late-Medieval England', *Speculum*, 71 (1996), 813–26, and examples in business and accountancy prose by Laura Wright, 'Bills, Accounts, Inventories: Everyday Trilingual Activities in the Business World of Later Medieval England', in *Multilingualism in Later Medieval Britain*, ed. by David A. Trotter (Cambridge: Brewer, 2000), pp. 149–56.

The formation of any English-speaking child in Latin grammar would necessarily have required the child being taught through an English medium, at
least in the earliest stages of instruction. It was not until 1346, when the Oxford
grammarian John of Cornwall issued his *Speculum gramaticale*, that English
was officially recognized for the first time after the Conquest as an appropriate
means for instructing in Latin.[54] Yet as early as 1311, in the *Memoriale iuniorum*
of Thomas of Hanney, there are signs that the vernacular was not being neglected
for the purposes of teaching Latin, though here the vernacular used was French.[55]
It is, in fact, unimaginable that English was never used at any time before 1300
in schools as an access to Latin, even if some fifty years would elapse before John
of Cornwall's overt acknowledgement that English was a convenient teaching
medium: after all, since medieval children were not normally born, as far as we
are aware, into Latin-speaking households, or even into ones fluently bilingual in
English and Latin, we must suppose that their access to Latin came subsequently
and via English.[56] By the fifteenth century, some Latin grammars in the Oxford
tradition make it abundantly clear where the use of English in teaching circumstances might potentially end, for they reproduce the macaronic style under
review here so markedly that it may be a matter of doubt about what language
classroom instruction actually took place in. The following excerpt is from a
unique treatise on English grammar, contained in Cambridge, Trinity College,
MS 1285, fols 4^r–7^v. Its text is composite, incorporating an English adaptation of
Donatus's *Ars minor*:

> In how many maners schal the nominatyf case be gouernyd of a verbe? In on, by strengthe
> of person, as Ego sum homo: ego is gouernyd of sum ex vi persone. Quare? 'Quia'
> verbum personale est et regit nominatiuum casum ei supponentem personam. Homo
> regitur in the same manere of sum for that is a certeyne reule of P.H., in 'Absoluta'.[57]

---

[54] For a short recent history, see Cynthia Renée Bland, *The Teaching of Grammar in Late
Medieval England: An Edition, with Commentary, of Oxford, Lincoln College MS Lat. 130*, Medieval Texts and Studies, 6 (East Lansing, MI: Colleagues; Woodbridge: Boydell and Brewer, 1991).

[55] David Thomson, *A Descriptive Catalogue of Middle English Grammatical Texts* (New
York: Garland, 1979), p. 37.

[56] See now the evidence assembled by Tony Hunt, *Teaching and Learning Latin in Thirteenth-
Century England*, 3 vols (Cambridge: Brewer, 1991). He concludes, 'In the medieval schoolroom,
as in medieval England throughout the thirteenth century, Latin, French and English were
complementary' (I, 434). See also James J. Murphy, 'The Teaching of Latin as a Second Language
in the 12th Century', *Historiographia Linguistica*, 7 (1980), 159–75.

[57] The text is printed in Sanford Brown Meech, 'An Early Treatise in English Concerning
Latin Grammar', in *Essays and Studies in English and Comparative Literature*, University of

(In how many ways must the nominative case be governed by a verb? In one, by strength of the subject, as Ego sum homo: ego is governed by sum ex vi persone. Quare? Quia verbum personale est et regit nominatiuum casum ei supponentem personam. Homo regitur in the same way by sum for that is a definite rule of P.H., in 'Absoluta' .)

It is worth pausing to consider what is going on in this excerpt. Is the densely macaronic style a faithful transcription, in fact, of a classroom patois? Here there would seem more grounds for suspecting that indeed it might be, because the intermittent replacement in speech of English words and phrases by ones in the language that the English was aiming to inculcate might have usefully reinforced the pupils' Latinity.[58] Yet the possibility here of a faithful transcription of an actual macaronic way of speaking need not be denied as we also acknowledge the necessarily *literary* status of this transcription, just as we did with the legal passages cited earlier: by the fifteenth century there is nothing amiss, to put it simply, in *writing* sentences in prose that switch internally between Latin and English, even if this tends only to occur in certain specialized contexts.[59] Within the methods adopted for teaching Latin grammar to children may lie an important clue, then, to understanding how the prompt commerce between English and Latin could have arisen, whether in the spoken or the written language. Moreover, this explanation would seem endorsed by the findings of modern linguistics: as Uriel Weinreich observed several years ago, abnormal proneness to bilingual switching 'has been attributed to persons who, in early childhood, were addressed by the same familiar interlocutors indiscriminately in both languages'.[60] The grammar text quoted above might be a reflex of just such a situation. But whatever its reality in speech within the classroom, its existence nevertheless as a written fact demonstrates that macaronic bilingualism, if such it was, was equally comfortable in manifesting itself as a written prose *Misch-sprache*. The process, therefore, is circular: though there may have been forms of

Michigan Publications, Language and Literature, 13 (Ann Arbor: University of Michigan Press, 1935), pp. 81–125 (see p. 121 for the excerpt quoted here, from fol. 7ʳ of the manuscript). For a careful description of the text and manuscript, see Thomson, *A Descriptive Catalogue*, pp. 158–68.

[58] Thomson, *A Descriptive Catalogue*, p. 72, reminds us that 'classroom routine, despite these English texts, would still often have been conducted in basic Latin'.

[59] As well as from the sermons, so far I have illustrated cases of random macaronic prose from epistolary, legal, and grammatical texts. All these constitute categories that are formally definable, and which, however indirectly, may be thought to posit some spoken referent (see further below).

[60] Uriel Weinreich, *Languages in Contact: Findings and Problems*, Publications of the Linguistic Circle of New York, 1 (New York: Linguistic Circle of New York, 1953; repr. The Hague: Mouton, 1963), p. 74.

speech in which English and Latin alternated, we now identify them perforce through written texts, and this in turn means that such texts, whether or not we are right in identifying behind them actual spoken usage, were themselves acceptable phenomena in a wide variety of textual genres.

Some support for this conclusion is found in texts that neither belong to any very obviously identifiable genre nor function as texts to which any very obvious spoken referent can be imputed. So far, cases of random macaronic prose, in addition to the sermons, have been illustrated from epistolary, legal, and grammatical texts, all of which belong to genres that are formally definable and which, however indirectly, may be thought to be predicated upon some spoken referent (pulpit delivery, reading aloud by a letter bearer or messenger, forensic pleading, or instruction in the classroom).[61] In cases less evidently definable and whose relation to some speech event is also at best obscure, there is harder evidence for the acceptability of macaronic prose purely as a written phenomenon in its own right. The marginal scribbles and jottings that feature in Shrewsbury, Shrewsbury School, MS 13, for example, seem to be a case in point. This manuscript, a fifteenth-century collection of short Latin homilies on the Gospels, contains notes on its earlier folios which include the following: 'mulier mersa cum nauis and hokis ser(c)he downe þe water sponsus dixit non [ita] sed vp þe strem quia semper contrarius fuit' (fol. iv͏ʳ); 'schort mas and longg dener displicit deo' (fol. vi͏ᵛ). The random macaronic prose alternation shown here is precisely of the sort under review, though this time it surfaces in jottings having the character of unsystematic, personal memoranda.[62]

But, to rein this excursus back now towards the earlier specific question, what may have been the language of delivery of sermons written down in macaronic form? An answer has already been emerging, but it must be prefaced by a few further considerations. If macaronic speech of the kind that has been posited

---

[61] This may apply, too, in the case of literary examples, which have not been directly discussed here (and see n. 53, above).

[62] Other cases of this kind may come to light as the *Index of Middle English Prose* is completed. In two of its more recent volumes, compare the macaronic *Modus tenendi curiam baronum cum visu francplegii* in Oxford, Trinity College, MS 30, and the macaronic version of George Ripley's *Accurtationes et practica raymundinae* in Oxford, Bodleian Library, MS Ashmole 759 (respectively in *The Index of Middle English Prose Handlist VIII: A Handlist of Manuscripts Containing Middle English Prose in Oxford College Libraries*, ed. by Sarah J. Ogilvie-Thomson (Cambridge: Brewer, 1991), p. 132, and *The Index of Middle English Prose Handlist IX: A Handlist of Manuscripts Containing Middle English Prose in the Ashmole Collection, Bodleian Library, Oxford*, ed. by L. M. Eldredge (Cambridge: Brewer, 1992), p. 111).

may have existed in reality, it was certainly a speech variety that specialized, and therefore limited, sociolinguistic contexts had engendered; to that extent it may have sounded unusual, perhaps even distinctly reminiscent of those contexts, whenever heard outside them. In fact, there are good grounds for believing that sometimes macaronic speech of this kind *was* actually heard. Some of the macaronic usage of *Piers Plowman*, for example, compares with that under investigation inasmuch as certain Latin locutions, the reason for whose selection is not always readily explicable, are tailored with morphological precision into sentences whose lexical and syntactical fabric is otherwise English. On any occasion when *Piers Plowman* may have been delivered aloud, such usage would have been heard and, as I have suggested, it may have sounded reminiscent of an actual spoken register, in this case that of clerkly authority:[63] interestingly, those whose speech in *Piers Plowman* is macaronic — and most of its examples occur in direct speech that the narrator is reporting — are either authority figures or figures who, arguably, are laying claim to authority.[64] A century later, the preacher Mercy in the moral play *Mankind* not only is capable of the fulsome aureations that provoke one of the vices to dismiss him as a body stuffed 'full of Englysch Laten',[65] but he also speaks macaronically. For example, 'My predylecte son, where be ye? Mankynde, vbi es?' is a snatch of Mercy's dialogue that another vice mockingly echoes:[66] and in the case of a play, of course, there can be no doubt that all such discourse is intended eventually to be spoken aloud for an audience to hear.[67] Nor

---

[63] Even mental reading posits a spoken voice.

[64] The following tabulation of characters in *Piers Plowman* who speak macaronically is based solely on investigation of the B text (William Langland, *Piers Plowman: A Parallel-Text Edition of the A, B, C, and Z Versions*, ed. by A. V. C. Schmidt, I: *Text* (London: Longman, 1995); II: *Introduction, Textual Notes, Commentary, Bibliography, and Indexical Glossary* (Kalamazoo: Medieval Institute Publications, 2009),I). The number of instances for each character is indicated in parentheses. It includes only macaronic usage in direct speech. Latin not worked into the syntax of sentences otherwise in English has been excluded (this mostly covers self-contained and explicit quotations, many of which are from the Vulgate). Also excluded are the more familiar Latin tags (e.g., *ergo, contra,* and *in extremis*): Holy Church (4); Theology (1); Civil Law (1); Reason (1); Hunger (3); Wit (2); Dame Study (1); Scripture (1); Covetousness of Eyes (1); Lewtee (1); Scripture (2); Trajan (3); Imaginatif (1); Patience (8); Conscience (4); Anima (10); Samaritan (3); Faith (2); Peace (2); Book (1); Christ (1); Curate (2); Narrator (16).

[65] *The Macro Plays*, ed. by Mark Eccles, EETS, o.s., 262 (London: Oxford University Press, 1969), p. 158, line 124.

[66] *The Macro Plays*, p. 179, line 771 (and line 774).

[67] See also Hans Jurgen Diller, 'Code-Switching in Medieval English Drama', *CompD*, 31 (1997–98), 506–37.

does the phenomenon stop on the eve of the Reformation. When a century later the pedants who populate several of the scenes of *Love's Labour's Lost* parade in macaronic rhetorical colours, their author was parodying a register whose parentage the evidence suggests may be sought in a substantially earlier age. Shakespeare may not merely have been glancing at nonce habits of speech that had followed in the wake of newer Renaissance enthusiasms, for his pedants, it will be recalled, were schoolmaster and priest,[68] the descendants of the John of Cornwalls and the Friar Brackleys of the later Middle Ages.

Yet it must be understood that these examples of macaronic speech, if indeed reminiscent of particular provinces of social usage, define a *strategic spoken register*, for there remains a vast difference between the quantity of macaronic usage in texts like these and that of some of the macaronic sermons that start appearing a generation or two after *Benedictus qui venit in nomine Domini*. The much greater macaronic frequency and randomness of these sermons constitute a qualitative difference: frequency, conversely, diminishes what more sparing usage bestows, effacing the very thing from which a stategic spoken register would derive its effectiveness. Ultimately in these cases, any spoken rhetorical cachet is lost. (Chaucer's Pardoner, it will be recalled, was careful to use only a sprinkling of Latin with which to 'saffron' his preaching.)[69] Just as significantly, we should understand that a speech variety which is randomly and frequently macaronic would confound itself as meaningless if spoken to monolinguals; hence sermons intended for monolingual audiences but written in a style like this return us primarily to considerations of the sociolinguistics of *writing*. Perhaps what is telling in such sermons, then, is not so much a matter of what is recorded in Latin and what in English, since that — as we have seen — is partly arbitrary anyway, but the fact that code-switching, to put it in linguistic terms, has occurred at all.

As is well known, Latin was pre-eminently the language of written clerical discourse in this period. The man who wrote down his sermon to an English-speaking lay audience, however, was recording something either actually preached or intended for preaching largely in English, and thus the vernacular was never far from his mind as he wrote. In the act of writing, his English sermon was now also being conceived as a text for reading, either for him or for other *litterati* to consult. Therefore, once his words entered the domain of writing, a second

---

[68] *Love's Labour's Lost*, ed. by Richard David, 5th edn (London: Methuen, 1956).

[69] Even if the imputation may also be that he knew little Latin in the first place. See *The Riverside Chaucer*, gen. ed. Larry D. Benson, 3rd edn (Boston: Houghton Mifflin, 1987), p. 194, lines 344–46.

audience came within view.[70] This envisaging of two different types of audiences simultaneously, a situation which required the sermon author to be linguistically bifocal, as it were, might well encourage his disposition towards macaronic prose, a disposition fostered in his earliest years of Latin schooling and later endorsed and fortified by his encounter with the macaronic practice of other varieties of written text.[71] But there is an additional possibility. The very fact of bilingual competence displayed by the sermon author's code-switching could impress clerical readers of his text — the only people likely to read it, after all — as a gesture of cultural solidarity, and this is precisely the sort of function that some modern studies have found code-switching to carry.[72] And lest the importance of signalling cultural solidarity linguistically be overlooked, the following conversation between two scholars, taken from an early Tudor *vulgaria*, should help to recall it:

> 'Gode spede, praty childe!' 'And youe also.' 'I know that ye have lurnede youre grammer, but wher, I pray youe?' 'By my faith, sum at wynchester, sum in other places.' 'And I am an Oxforde man. Woll youe we shall assay how we cann talke in latyn?' 'Yee, for gode, ryght fayne!'[73]

> ('God speed you, fair child!' 'And you too.' 'I know that you have learnt your grammar, but where, I pray you?' 'By my faith, some in Winchester, some in other places.' 'And I am an Oxford man. Will you have a go at seeing how we can talk in Latin?' 'Yes, by God, very willingly!')

Winchester and Oxford, centres well known for the teaching of Latin grammar, are the common coin that both exchange in the preliminaries to establishing their mutual social identity. Once it is established, the invitation to celebrate this identity by switching the conversation into Latin, an invitation enthusiastically welcomed, could not be plainer.

---

[70] He was himself part of that second audience, even if he originally wrote his manuscript solely for his private consultation.

[71] Compare Peter C. Erb, 'Vernacular Material for Preaching in MS Cambridge University Library Ii. III. 8', *MS*, 33 (1971), 63–84; he appropriately suggests (p. 66) that as the preacher composed his sermon in Latin, 'intending his words for an English audience, [he] continually had it [English] in mind and entered vernacular phrases as they came to him'.

[72] Ronald Wardhaugh, *An Introduction to Sociolinguistics* (New York: McGraw-Hill, 1986), p. 104. The code-switching discussed here is found in speech, to be sure, but both languages being spoken are mutually intelligible to addresser and addressee.

[73] *A Fifteenth Century School Book from a Manuscript in the British Museum (MS. Arundel 249)*, ed. by William Nelson (Oxford: Clarendon Press, 1956), p. 23.

In view of all this, the nature of the actual or projected audience of the macaronic sermon (just as much as that of a sermon preserved entirely in Latin), wherever it can be determined, should help to resolve the question one way or another: either the sermon had been — or would be — delivered predominantly in English or, if preached to clerics, perhaps predominantly in Latin. In the light of the analysis made in this chapter, the common-sense approach advocated by Lecoy de la Marche over a hundred years ago to the question of which language was used, and subscribed to by several subsequent commentators, remains largely intact, and survives, in my view, the challenges made to it by Siegfried Wenzel.[74]

Wenzel, as earlier noted, believes that many of the sermons whose sentences may manifest random macaronic variation could actually have been preached virtually in the form in which they appear on the written page. His evidence, however, seems insecure. First, he sets some store by a ruling in the statutes of the Carthusian order about preaching. This declares, 'In dispositione facientis sermonem sit loqui latine vel vulgariter vel mixtim' (Let it be up to whoever gives the sermon to speak in Latin or in the vernacular or in a mixture). Wenzel interprets this as licensing preaching which is of the random macaronic sort.[75] But the ruling need not necessarily be understood in this way at all. It may simply be allowing the preacher scope to deliver parts of his sermon in Latin and other parts in the vernacular (*mixtim* simply in that sense). And second, in order further to justify his thesis that random macaronic sermon prose mirrored a spoken event, he finds it convenient, understandably, to hypothesize the existence of a bilingual audience capable of understanding such prose. Thus he conjectures a university or monastic audience for these sermons — at Oxford, for example, or at some monastic centre.[76] Certainly, a place like Oxford may have been a special case, offering unusual opportunities for clerical and lay contact and congregational mixing, and where such bilingual competence may not have been in short supply, even amongst the laity.[77] Yet, are we also to believe that comparable cultural situations also obtained in medieval Lichfield, for example, or in medieval Newcastle upon Tyne (where some of the randomly macaronic sermons in the early

---

[74] Wenzel, *Macaronic Sermons*, pp. 114–19 (with an account of the view held by Albert Lecoy de la Marche).

[75] Wenzel, *Macaronic Sermons*, p. 123.

[76] Wenzel, *Macaronic Sermons*, p. 124.

[77] It is interesting to note that Lincoln, Cathedral Library, MS 133, which is discussed in Chapter 7, below, seems to have been compiled by a layman who possibly had an Oxford connection.

fifteenth-century anthology of Friar Nicholas Philip were preached)?[78] Of course, short of an unlikely discovery, some medieval policy statement on macaronic usage in sermons (having discounted Wenzel's Carthusian example on account of its ambiguity), probability is as far as we can come to deciding the matter for certain. In the case of *Benedictus qui venit in nomine Domini*, the audience intended seems to have been secular, and therefore probably not fluently conversant with Latin.[79] Again for this reason, *Benedictus qui venit in nomine Domini* would seem likely to have been preached, or intended for preaching, mainly in English.

When random macaronic prose alternation is infrequent, as here, we may in some measure be facing a use of English still underconfident before the overpowering prestige of Latin, and also perhaps underconfident in the most basic sense that a scribe, happily *litteratus* in Latin, may have been less happily literate in English; even though a fluent native speaker, he may have been more accustomed to writing in Latin than in his mother tongue.[80] When random macaronic prose alternation is frequent, as in the later sermons, then, conversely, that confidence may have increased, and also any inhibiting sense of Latin's absolute appropriateness may have decreased correspondingly. But whether frequent or infrequent, arbitrary macaronic usage in sermons should be suspected of testifying both to a *written* version of the phenomenon of code-switching (which, if for anyone's benefit, was for that of a clerical coterie) and to the linguistic versatility of the sermon author (or of some later copyist of his work), rather than to any actual mode of sermon delivery. Each text must be judged individually on its merits, of course, but macaronic sermon prose of this kind seems *prima facie* a reflex of a written — before a spoken — practice (especially whenever there is reason to suspect that the sermon's audience, unlike the sermon's readership, was monolingual).

Arbitrary macaronic usage in the thirteenth-century *Benedictus qui venit in nomine Domini* sermon is tentative; there is no disputing that. By the late Middle Ages and among certain sermon writers, such usage was endemic. This was the

---

[78] *PPPLME*, pp. 41–57.

[79] At the very least, for the author of this sermon to have sought, in front of an audience of clerics, to encourage the exchange of high fashion, tonsorial extravagance, make-up, and the trinkets of love-making for such chaster fare as 'huselyng at Goddes borde and herkening of Goddes worde' (line 30) would have seemed, were the audience strictly clerical, strangely inappropriate and an unnecessary preaching to the converted.

[80] And see the reasons given in n. 31, above. Wenzel, *Verses in Sermons*, p. 94, identifies a possible 'scribal uneasiness' about the writing of English in the earlier period.

case not only in sermons written in England but in some Continental ones as well,[81] and here too it has sometimes been maintained that congregations simply took everything in as written, that extant texts may be more or less accurate transcripts of original spoken events. For medieval England, at least, the present study finds that assumption unwarrantable. The usage shown in *Benedictus qui venit in nomine Domini* should not be regarded as an early moment in a particular sort of sermon genre, for comparable usage, as we have seen, was certainly not unique to sermons. Even less should it be regarded as what a congregation actually heard.

But I also suggest that it need not merely be viewed as an early example of how — especially in the peculiar circumstance of sermons — the force of the distinction between the learned language of written record and the probable language of delivery was occasionally liable to break down. Those occasional 'breakdowns' might equally be construed as significant markers of clericalism, as evidence of status destined for the eyes of the *litterati*, rather than as lapses in the hegemony of Latin.[82] Viewed more broadly than this, perhaps macaronic

[81] For example, Bruno Migliorini, *The Italian Language*, abridged, recast and rev. by T. Gwynfor Griffith (London: Faber, 1984), p. 164, points out that the most curious examples of macaronic mixture are to be found in sermons, and gives an example (pp. 164–65) from a fifteenth-century Lenten sermon of Valeriano da Soncio: 'Scis quod facit vulpes quando abstulit galinam illi pauperculae feminae? La se ne va in lo boscheto e se mette in la herba fresca e volta le gambe al celo e sta a solazar cum le mosche. Sic faciunt isti prophete, questi gabadei, questi hypocritoni, sangioni dal collo torto, quando habent plenum corpus de galini, caponi, fasani, pernise, qualie e de boni lonzi de vitello e qualche fidegeti per aguzar lo apetito, e lo capo de malvasia, vernaza, vino greco, tribiani e moscatelli cum qualche prosuto, salziza, cerveladi, mortadelli, beroldi o vero cagasangui a la bresana per bevere melio. Non vedesti mai, madre mia, li meliori propheti.' (Scis quod facit vulpes quando abstulit galinam illi pauperculae feminae? He goes away into the copse and sits down in the cool grass and turns the legs to the sky and besports himself with the flies. Sic faciunt isti prophete, these tricksters, these old hypocrites and holy Joes when habent plenum corpus of hens, capons, pheasants, partridges, quails and good cheeks of veal and some 'fidegeti' to fill their bellies and turn their heads with wines from Malvasia, Vernaza wine, Greek wine, Trebbiano and Muscatel wines, along with hams, sausages, saveloys, mortadellas, pigs' trotters or real black pudding from Brescia to work up a thirst. Never have you seen, madre mia, better prophets.) I am grateful to Dr George Talbot for help with this passage. For the reasons given in this chapter, Migliorini's statement that 'the frequency of texts of this kind must lead us to the conclusion that the sermons were actually delivered in this mixture of two languages' (p. 165) may not be secure.

[82] Compare Herbert Schendl, 'Linguistic Aspects of Code-Switching in Medieval English Texts', in *Multilingualism in Later Medieval Britain*, ed. by Trotter, pp. 77–92 (p. 79). I am also grateful to Professor Schendl for allowing me to see an advance copy of his paper, 'Code-switching in Late Medieval "Macaronic" Sermons', due to appear in a forthcoming volume of proceedings

sermon texts may have something to reveal about the history of the diglossic rivalry between Latin and English, and about the substantial emancipation and emergence of the latter in writing which philologists normally associate with the second half of the fourteenth century. In the macaronic sermons, English is being allowed to contest Latin by invading the space that Latin was usually privileged to occupy. A cultural legitimacy is thereby being displaced into English. Yet equally, English is not allowed a complete usurpation, for it in turn continues to be contested by Latin. By the fifteenth century, we find texts alternating extensively between the two languages and with an unpredictability that seems founded on a linguistic self-confidence in both; both approach a sort of symbiosis in which cultural legitimacy may be all the more evenly distributed. It was doubtless the prestige of English which had most to gain from this relationship, but in the macaronic distribution of legitimacy, both languages were finally protected and affirmed. It may be that the ready macaronic interplay attested in the fifteenth century, something seen only in fledgling form in *Benedictus qui venit in nomine Domini*, is a barometer of a culture in which the anxiety implicit in the vernacular's earlier challenges to the relative exclusiveness of Latin had now been substantially overcome.

But whichever way we choose to look at the macaronic sermons, texts like these can offer no real accommodation to anyone who, persuaded by the jeremiads of medieval Church reformers, may be tempted to regard them as signs of clerical Latinity in decay. An effective case for that would be better served by other evidence. On the contrary, the author of *Benedictus qui venit in nomine Domini*, and even more conspicuously the authors of the later sermons in the randomly macaronic vein,[83] may have been demonstrating how well able they were to take both languages in their stride.[84]

---

of the conference on Multilingualism in Medieval Britain, 1100–1400, held at the University of Bristol in July 2008.

[83] For a conspectus of sermon manuscripts in which sermons of a macaronic order may be found, see Wenzel, *Macaronic Sermons*, pp. 133–211.

[84] Indeed, it is now generally thought that modern manifestations of code-switching imply high levels of competence in both languages used. In addition to the Myers-Scotton study cited above, n. 47, see Shana Poplack, 'Sometimes I'll Start a Sentence in Spanish y termino in espanol: Toward a Typology of Code-Switching', *Linguistics*, 18 (1980), 581–618; also, David Sankoff and Shana Poplack, 'A Formal Grammar for Code-Switching', *Papers in Linguistics: International Journal of Human Communication*, 14 (1981), 3–45.

THE REGULARS: A SERMON OF HUGH
LEGAT FOR THE THIRD SUNDAY IN LENT

Introduction

While the sermon at the centre of this chapter brings us forward by the best part of a century and more, and introduces an example of late medieval *ad populum* preaching this time as the regulars practised it,[1] it remains in touch with one of the issues explored at length in the previous chapter in the way it too moves between Latin and English throughout its course. Yet it does so almost in a mirror image of the linguistic oscillation found in the earlier MS Bodley 26 sermon. There, Latin predominated, with sorties into English that were occasional; here, it is the turn of English to predominate, with occasional sorties into Latin, even if the opening nine lines of the sermon are in Latin entirely.

The (atelous) sermon under review, one for the third Sunday in Lent on the *thema, Estote sicut filii* (Ephesians 5. 1), is known to exist uniquely in Oxford, Bodleian Library, MS Laud misc. 706, a manuscript in which the hands of a number of scribes writing in the first third of the fifteenth century (but after 1412) are at work, and which contracts a close connection with another near contemporary Bodleian manuscript, MS Bodley 649, the first set of sermons in which depends similarly on sources assembled under the aegis of the regulars; here,

---

[1] There seems little doubt but that the sermon edited below was destined for a lay audience. Translations into English of key Latin terms, as happens, for example, at lines 168–71, would be a redundant procedure were the sermon intended for delivery before a clerical audience presumably already competent in such elementary Latin.

four sermons found in MS Laud misc. 706 reappear.[2] Like the earlier mendicant anthology of MS Bodley 26, so too the anthology in MS Laud misc. 706 seems to have been assembled from several booklets, though they are ones of a larger format. Unquestionably, however, MS Laud misc. 706 is a Benedictine compilation. It was bound at St Peter's Abbey, Gloucester, either in the late fifteenth or early sixteenth century, and prior to that was owned by one of the monks of that house, John Paunteley, when he was a professor of the sacred page at Oxford around the year 1410.[3]

It contains thirty-three sermons in total, of which the liturgical occasions of four are indeterminate.[4] Of the remaining twenty-nine, a large proportion, eight, are for Sundays in Lent (the third Sunday faring particularly well with possibly as many as six sermons out of those eight),[5] and five are for Passiontide. This concentration of some thirteen sermons within the prime penitential season of the ecclesiastical year is hardly fortuitous, and reflects the fact that, as for the other orders of the Church, so too for late medieval English Benedictines, Lent and the period immediately preceding Easter evidently constituted a time of heightened preaching activity, when consciences could be pricked and compunction stimulated for confessions in advance of Easter Day when all confirmed Christians would be making their mandatory annual communion.[6] Of the manu-

---

[2] For details of the overlap, see *A Macaronic Sermon Collection*, p. 5; *LSCLME*, p. 90, notes the appearance of one further sermon from MS Laud misc. 706 also in another Benedictine compilation (Worcester, Cathedral Library, MS F.10, a manuscript introduced in Chapter 2, above; see note 9, below, for further details of this sermon). On *Estote sicut filii* see also *A Repertorium of Middle English Prose Sermons*, III, 2187–91.

[3] One of Paunteley's own sermons, a funeral sermon preached 3 May 1412 for Walter Froucetur, Abbot of St Peter's, may be found in it; see Patrick J. Horner, 'A Funeral Sermon for Abbot Walter Froucester of Gloucester (1412)', *American Benedictine Review*, 28 (1977), 147–66. Both Horner, in his edition of *A Macaronic Sermon Collection*, p. 6, and *LSCLME*, p. 85, speculate that Paunteley may have composed the first set of sermons in the MS Bodley 649 anthology, but this seems to me most unlikely; see further below on this question of authorship.

[4] There are two scientific works at the end; Patrick J. Horner, 'Benedictines and Preaching in Fifteenth-Century England: The Evidence of Two Bodleian Library Manuscripts', *Revue Bénédictine*, 99 (1989), 313–32 (p. 317). For a list of its sermons, see *LSCLME*, pp. 578–82.

[5] Five are securely for the third Sunday in Lent but the sixth, which comprises the seventeenth sermon in the collection, may either be for that day or for a synod. *LSCLME*, p. 582, assesses the occasion of *Estote sicut filii* as 'T21?'.

[6] This was the 'Easter duty' legislated for in Canon 21 of the Fourth Lateran Council, *Omnis utriusque sexus*, which also found its way into the Decretals of Gregory IX; see *Corpus iuris*

script's remaining sixteen sermons, four are for other occasions of the Temporale, six are for the proper of the saints, three are for synods, one for a funeral, one for a memorial, and one for a visitation. As might be predicted of a piecemeal booklet conglomeration such as this, and as was similarly seen in the previous chapter in the case of the mendicant collection in MS Bodley 26, the sermons do not seem to have been arranged in any intelligible sequence, even if Lent and Passiontide lend the collection a certain centre of gravity.

As earlier noted, the former owner of the anthology, and the author of at least one of the sermons in it, Dom Paunteley, spent part of his career in Oxford, and it is probable that at least two sermons in MS Laud misc. 706 reflect Benedictine preaching undertaken there.[7] However, the sermon *Estote sicut filii* edited below may well have had a connection with St Albans, Hertfordshire.[8] Thus the manuscript may be thought to witness within its pages to something of a confluence of late medieval English Benedictine preaching activity and tradition: its booklets, later bound at St Peter's Abbey, Gloucester, were formerly owned by Dom Paunteley, monk of that place and a preacher himself, who had spent time in Oxford where he evidently had access to at least two sermons (including the one under present review) which were probably either preached at, or intended for preaching at, the Benedictine abbey at St Albans, an abbey that maintained a presence in Oxford at this date at Gloucester College, as well as to another sermon on the *thema Ascendit aurora, ascendit aurora* (Genesis 32. 26), a second version of which may also be found in the great Worcester Benedictine collection briefly referred to in Chapter 2, above, and now preserved in Worcester, Cathedral Library, MS F.10.[9] There is evidence here for some kind of network for the circulation and exchange of sermons, however informal, amongst the

canonici, ed. by Emil Friedberg and Emil Ludwig Richter, 2nd edn, 2 vols (Leipzig: Tauchnitz, 1879–81; repr. Graz: Academische Druck- u.Verlagsanstalt, 1959), II, 887–88. The Lenten emphasis of MS Laud misc. 706 is matched in the other manuscript to which it is most nearly related, MS Bodley 649, in the first set of sermons there (in *A Macaronic Sermon Collection*, ed. by Horner; two sets of sermons are found in this manuscript).

[7] Sermon items 15 and 24 in this manuscript; see *LSCLME*, p. 90 n. 13.

[8] There is another sermon in the manuscript, on fols 153ʳ–156ʳ and immediately following *Estote sicut filii*, composed for the feast of St Alban on the *thema, Coronavit eum in die laetitiae* (Song of Solomon 3. 11), whose internal evidence suggests that it may similarly have been delivered, or intended for delivery, at St Albans. Sources used in this patronal sermon are of especial importance in helping to determine the author of this sermon as Hugh Legat; see further on this below.

[9] See *LSCLME*, p. 579 and p. 608.

English Benedictines in the late Middle Ages, just as there had also been, though somewhat more conspicuously, amongst the friars from the earliest years of the mendicant movement.

The Sermon's Audience and its Author

Wenzel's account of the sermons of MS Laud misc. 706 perhaps conveys an impression that *ad populum* preaching was not represented in its pages or was represented only in some qualified sense and to the extent that a few of its sermons seem cognizant of a mixed audience of clerics and laity of the kind that might have existed at the university or in certain monastic contexts. Yet, this impression should not be allowed to overwhelm due respect for the *ad populum* thrust that certain sermons in this manuscript seem to share. While some were without question intended for elite clerical audiences, the orientation of others, including that of the present *Estote sicut filii*, is resolutely popular — for example, *Estote sicut filii*'s chosen terms of audience address, 'Gode men', are unvaryingly consistent (at lines 73–74, 87, 96, 124–25, 160, 502, and 524), and are of a piece with certain internal references and comments that seem to imply a congregation that may (at least predominantly) have been lay.[10] This is not to say that no clerics other than the preacher himself would have been present at the sermon; quite possibly they were (and compare, for example, lines 328–32). Rather, it is to say that its general pitch is primarily towards a lay audience.[11] The particular investment that it makes in attempting to mould lay expectations and outlook will be revisited in more detail later.

As so often happens with medieval sermon texts, the name of the sermon author, who was more often than not also likely to be its original preacher, is withheld. Here in the case of *Estote sicut filii*, by contrast, good grounds exist for identifying who that author/preacher was. Appropriately, these grounds are consistent with what has so far been inferred about the sermon, namely, that its author was probably a Benedictine with a St Albans connection. Attribution of its paternity to Dom Paunteley, the one known name attaching to a single sermon

---

[10] See n. 1, above. A variety of terms of sermon address is considered in *EPLMA*, p. 112.

[11] *Three Middle English Sermons from the Worcester Chapter Manuscript F.10*, ed. by Dora M. Grisdale, Leeds School of English Language Texts and Monographs, 5 (Leeds: Wilson, 1939), p. xxv, strikes an astute balance in her estimation of the composition of the audience of the Hugh Legat sermon; and see the further argument below for why her view may be especially judicious.

in MS Laud misc. 706, would not, however, seem very compelling, for, in addition
to encountering the inconvenience of Paunteley's connection with Gloucester,
rather than St Albans, little in the organization, style, or content of his one
known sermon, that for Abbot Walter Froucetur's funeral, coincides with *Estote
sicut filii* in any especially remarkable way.[12] Conversely, comparison of *Estote
sicut filii* with the work of Hugh Legat, an eminent Benedictine preacher active
at St Albans and elsewhere in the early fifteenth century, yields similarities so
striking that there seems little doubt but that this sermon too is another of his
compositions.[13]

Hugh Legat's name is currently known to appear explicitly in connection with
a sermon in only one place, on fol. 8 of Worcester, Cathedral Library, MS F.10,
where it prefaces a vernacular Passion Sunday sermon on the *thema Accipiant
repromissionem vocati* (Hebrews 9. 15).[14] The nature of the organization of this
Passiontide sermon closely resembles that of *Estote sicut filii* (notwithstanding
the fact that the final part of the latter is missing and therefore unavailable for
comparison), and both sermons share a number of characteristic themes (for
example, observations on the reluctance of people to accept due correction, on
misguided preaching and preachers, on the importance of making a confession

---

[12] Horner, 'A Funeral Sermon for Abbot Walter Froucester'. While the Paunteley sermon
may share a few *auctoritates* with *Estote sicut filii* (Isidore, Augustine, Jacobus de Voragine, Lincolniensis), these sources were common homiletic fare, hence little can be made to depend upon
the coincidence of their appearance.

[13] In the following argument for Legat's authorship, it should be stressed that the appearance
singly of any of the criteria outlined in greater detail below (see n. 23) cannot be regarded as
constituting sufficient evidence; the criteria only become compelling if a substantial number of
them, and ones found across a range of the four different categories of criteria, can be identified
congregating in one sermon.

[14] *Three Middle English Sermons*, pp. 1–21. Grisdale dated this sermon 'in all probability' (p.
xxiii) to around the same time as two other vernacular sermons in the manuscript whose date can
be established between 1389 and 1404 on the basis of internal references. However, Hugh Legat's
sermon *Accipiant repromissionem vocati* possibly reflects awareness of the terms of the first of
Archbishop Thomas Arundel's Oxford Constitutions of 1409; this restricted the content of
preaching by simple clergy and vicars to the rudiments of catechesis promulgated by his pre-
decessor, Archbishop John Pecham, at the Lambeth Council of 1281; see *Three Middle English
Sermons*, p. 8, lines 39–42, and compare *Concilia Magnae Britanniae et Hiberniae*, III, 315. If
Legat was indeed aware of the Constitutions, the composition date of *Accipiant repromissionem
vocati* to some time after 1409 would more nearly coincide with the composition dates of those
of the first set of sermons in MS Bodley 649 which yield internal dating evidence: these sermons
belong to the reign of Henry V (1413–22).

that is exact in its particulars)[15] that between them suggest the possibility of their origin in a common author. But especially suggestive is the coincidence between both of a number of favourite locutions and forms of expression that cumulatively, and in company with the other evidence, build a strong presumptive case for common authorship.[16] On a similar evidentiary basis, certain other sermons in MS Laud misc. 706, and indeed, all of the first set of sermons in its 'companion' manuscript, MS Bodley 649, deserve serious consideration as being by him.[17]

Two more examples in support and illustration of this thesis, that Legat authored far more sermons than he is currently credited with, may be permitted to suffice, although additional candidates from MS Laud misc. 706 could conceivably present themselves once further analysis has been undertaken:[18] first, another sermon in MS Laud misc. 706, like *Estote sicut filii* also atelous and chiefly

---

[15] *Three Middle English Sermons*, p. 7, lines 21–30, pp. 7–8, lines 31–42, and p. 19, lines 33–39 (compare respectively below, lines 108–21 and 471–79; 42–59; and 479–91). The first two of these themes may also be found in the first sermon of the first set of sermons in MS Bodley 649 (*A Macaronic Sermon Collection*, p. 7, lines 21–30, and pp. 7–9, lines 31–42), and constitute further reason for believing that this first set may also be Legat's work; see further below on this.

[16] *Three Middle English Sermons*, p. 2, line 34: 'Ich vndurstonde at tis time' (compare below, line 12, 'I vndurstond at this tyme'); p. 4, lines 1–2: '*Accipiant* [...] as I seide before' (compare below, lines 203–04, '"Estote" [...] as Y seyde before'); p. 5, line 29: 'For þe processe of this sermon' (compare below, line 204, 'Ffor the prosces of thes schort sermone'); p. 5, line 29: 'I seyde firste and principalich' (compare below, line 213, 'Ffyrst than Y sey and prinspaliche'); p. 13, line 118: 'I seide þe secunde time principaliche' (compare below, line 448, 'I seyde the secunde tyme prin<s>palyche'); p. 16, line 209: 'I seide firþurmore' (compare below, line 333, 'I seyde also fyrthermore').

[17] James G. Clark, *A Monastic Renaissance at St Albans: Thomas Walsingham and his Circle c. 1350–1440* (Oxford: Clarendon Press, 2006), p. 233, has convincingly proposed that the MS Laud misc. 706 sermon for the feast of St Alban on folios 153ʳ–156ʳ, on the *thema*, *Coronavit eum in die laetitiae* (Song of Solomon 3. 11), which immediately follows *Estote sicut filii*, is by Legat on the basis of its combined use of the *De consolatione philosophiae* of Boethius and, more tellingly, of the much rarer *Architrenius* of Johannes de Alta Villa. Legat wrote commentaries on both of these works; see further on this below.

[18] Certain aspects of the first vernacular sermon in MS Laud misc. 706, again for the third Sunday in Lent though this time on the *thema*, *Venit ira Dei* (Ephesians 5. 6), suggest that this sermon, too, may have been Legat's work (for a fuller outline of what may be considered the salient criteria for authorial identification, see n. 23, below). For example, Origen on Leviticus — not the commonest of sources — is used in *Venit ira Dei*, as it also is in *Estote sicut filii*, and the sermon attacks the Lollards, a signature theme of the Legat corpus (in the undisputable Legat sermon *Accipiant repromissionem vocati* in Worcester, Cathedral Library, MS F.10, heresy is mentioned without being specifically attributed).

in English, again for the third Sunday in Lent but this time on the *thema*, *Fructus lucis est in bonitate* (Ephesians 5. 9), may be his;[19] as may, second, a macaronic sermon in Latin and English in MS Bodley 649 for the first Sunday of Lent on the *thema Nunc dies salutis* (II Corinthians 6. 2), and which is the opening sermon of the first of two sermon sets that this manuscript contains.[20] The *Fructus lucis est in bonitate* sermon exhibits several of the characteristic Legat traits, both in terms of its organization, its favoured topics, and its shared locutions.[21] Something similar may be said in respect of the *Nunc dies salutis* sermon of MS Bodley 649 and since, as Wenzel has convincingly argued,[22] all of the sermons belonging to the first sermon set in this manuscript are by one and the same author, it necessarily follows that there is reason to believe that all these particular Bodley 649 sermons are unattributed Legat compositions as well.[23] Haines, Wenzel, and most recently

---

[19] MS Laud misc. 706, fols 156ʳ–163ᵛ, available in Patrick J. Horner, 'An Edition of Five Medieval Sermons from MS Laud misc. 706' (unpublished doctoral dissertation, State University of New York, Albany, 1975), pp. 147–79. See also *A Repertorium of Middle English Prose Sermons*, III, 2191–94.

[20] MS Bodley 649, fols 1ʳ–8ʳ; see *A Macaronic Sermon Collection*, pp. 26–53. There are twenty-five sermons in this first set, of which two are entirely in Latin, and the remaining twenty-three in a macaronic mixture, to greater or lesser extents, of Latin and English. Since the sermons of this first set are probably the work of the same author (see n. 22, below), it follows from my argument that they are all attributable to Hugh Legat.

[21] Signs of possible Legat composition of *Fructus lucis est in bonitate* consist in the appearance of: characteristic themes, like the lay reluctance to accept due correction and lay transgression into provinces of clerical responsibility (fol. 160ᵛ); characteristic locutions, like 'Ffurst þan I say and principalyche' (fol. 159ᵛ); and a close organizational similarity of the sermon to other Legat preaching. (For a fuller outline of what the salient criteria for authorial identification may be considered to be, see n. 23, below.)

[22] Wenzel, *Macaronic Sermons*, p. 50 and n. 57.

[23] A selection of evidence for Legat's composition of the first sermon of the first set of sermons in MS Bodley 649 (and hence of the whole of the first set) might be cited under four categories as follows: the thematic; the organizational; shared locutions; and shared sources of the less common kind. Amongst characteristic Legat themes, note: the even-handed apportioning of blame for the cause of the world's various ills (*A Macaronic Sermon Collection*, p. 31, lines 84–97; compare below, lines 260–64); observation of lay disrespect for the Church (*A Macaronic Sermon Collection*, p. 31, lines 93–97; compare below, lines 229–37); extended use of a comparison between spiritual ills and human medical conditions (*A Macaronic Sermon Collection*, p. 35, lines 163–67; compare below, lines 527–33). Compare the general organizational procedure announced in the *processus* of this sermon (*A Macaronic Sermon Collection*, p. 33, lines 140–50; compare below, lines 203–12). Amongst shared locutions, note such correspondences as: 'Lego in scriptura sacra' (*A Macaronic Sermon Collection*, p. 27, line 4; compare below, line 450); 'In ista

Horner, have suggested Dom John Paunteley as their author, but this suggestion is hindered by the fact that very little in the organization, style, or content of the one undisputed Paunteley sermon, that for Abbot Walter Froucetur's funeral, resembles aspects of the organization, style, or content of all the rest, whereas the situation in the case of these putative Legat sermons is entirely different.[24] Here, correspondences between the sermons are extensive in all these three departments.

Hugh Legat's Career

Little is known of Hugh Legat's origins, but it is conceivable that he was eponymously named after a place called Leggats in the parish of St Paul's Walden, Hertfordshire, where St Albans possessed a manor.[25] A reasonable estimate for his date of birth would be *c.* 1380. He first appears on record in 1401, at the election of Abbot William Heyworth (1401–20), by which time he had entered the St Albans monastery.[26] He eventually went to Oxford, probably no later than

---

oracione recommendatis singulis, etc.' (*A Macaronic Sermon Collection*, p. 33, line 122; compare below, lines 201–02); 'Dico primo et principaliter' (*A Macaronic Sermon Collection*, p. 33, line 151; compare below, line 213); 'sicut dicitur in premissis' (*A Macaronic Sermon Collection*, p. 33, line 123; compare below, lines 90, 143, and 203–04); 'Go to your curate for counsel' (*A Macaronic Sermon Collection*, p. 37, lines 203–05; compare Worcester, Cathedral Library, MS F.10, in *Three Middle English Sermons*, p. 19, line 36). Amongst shared sources of the less common sort, note the use of the *Stratagemata* of Sextus Julius Frontinus (*A Macaronic Sermon Collection*, p. 39, lines 251–55; compare below, lines 1–9).

[24] Roy Martin Haines, 'Reginald Pecock: A Tolerant Man in an Age of Intolerance', in *Persecution and Toleration*, ed. by William J. Sheils, Studies in Church History, 21 (Oxford: Blackwell, 1984), pp. 125–37; see p. 129 n. 29, and p. 135; Wenzel, *Macaronic Sermons*, p. 50 n. 58, and p. 53; and *A Macaronic Sermon Collection*, p. 6. Five years after his 1984 article, however, Haines, *Ecclesia Anglicana*, p. 203, qualified his former view: 'On maturer reflection, having re-examined the sole sermon in the Laud manuscript specifically attributed to Paunteley, I would have to admit that the case for his authorship is not substantiated, and hence that the Bodley sermons could almost equally well have been composed by some contemporary of his, a fellow Benedictine'.

[25] *Annales Monasterii S. Albani a Johanne Amundesham, Monacho, ut videtur, conscripti, A.D. 1421–1440. Quibus praefigitur Chronicon rerum gestarum in Monasterio S. Albani, A.D. 1422–1431, a quodam auctore ignoto compilatum*, ed. by Henry T. Riley, RS, 28, 2 vols (London: Longman, 1870–71), I, 428: 'manerium de Legattys in Walden'. The following biographical information is much indebted to *Three Middle English Sermons*, pp. xi–xii; see also the entry on Legat in *Oxford Dictionary of National Biography*, ed. by H. C. G. Matthew and Brian Harrison, 60 vols (Oxford: Clarendon Press, 2004), XXXIII, 178.

[26] Clark, *A Monastic Renaissance*, p. 227 n. 72.

1405, since he had completed his bachelor in theology degree by 1412.[27] Thereafter, he remained in Oxford for several years studying the classics. By the time of the election of Abbot William Heyworth's successor, John Wethamstede, in 1420, Legat is referred to as being prior of Redbourne, a cell of St Albans,[28] and his last recorded appearance is in the St Albans Chronicle under the year 1427, where it is noted that he was removed from the priorate of Redbourne in that year and sent to live at Tynemouth, another St Albans' cell.[29] His death date, sometime after 1427, is not on record.

Legat was a man of wide intellectual interests and rich classical acquaintance; an impression can be formed of their scope and depth both from the books with which he is known to have been associated, as well as from his own original compositions. Two former St Albans books are known to have been connected with him: one, Oxford, Bodleian Library, MS Rawlinson G. 99, is a thirteenth-century collection of grammatical tracts that he formerly owned; and the other, London, British Library, MS Harley 2624, is an early twelfth-century copy of Cicero's *De inventione* and the popular pseudo-Ciceronian *Rhetorica ad Herennium* that he evidently arranged to have bound.[30] As for his own original compositions, Bale records that Legat wrote a commentary on the *De consolatione philosophiae* of Boethius. This has not survived, though another commentary, dedicated to Abbot Heyworth, on the *Architrenius* of Johannes de Alta Villa, has, if imperfectly.[31] A letter, written in the persona of *Discretio*, is also attributed to Legat in a fifteenth-century formulary of model letters.[32] Other than these particular works, the remainder of his extant literary corpus consists entirely

[27] A. B. Emden, *A Biographical Register of the University of Oxford to A.D. 1500*, 3 vols (Oxford: Clarendon Press, 1957–59), II, 1125–26.

[28] *Three Middle English Sermons*, p. xii.

[29] *Annales Monasterii S. Albani*, I, 13. Clark, *A Monastic Renaissance*, pp. 233–34, has misunderstood the chronicler's observation that Legat was sent to the Tynemouth cell 'ibi moraturus' (there to dwell), as meaning that he was sent there to die (having apparently confused the verb *moror* with the verb *morior*).

[30] *Three Middle English Sermons*, p. xiii.

[31] John Bale's statement is cited in *Three Middle English Sermons*, p. xi. For the manuscripts of Legat's works known to date, see *A Handlist of the Writers of Great Britain and Ireland before 1540*, ed. by Richard Sharpe, Publications of the Journal of Medieval Latin, 1 (Turnhout: Brepols, 1997), pp. 187–88. Another work no longer known to be extant but which Bale noted having seen a copy of at Norwich was a set of *Epistolae ad diversos*.

[32] See Clark, *A Monastic Renaissance*, pp. 227–30, for a good account of this letter and its companion pieces.

of sermons. The attribution to him of the vernacular sermon in Worcester, Cathedral Library, MS F.10, noted above, seems straightforward enough; and if my attribution to him of all the remaining ones earlier described be also accepted, his sermons would come to loom largest in his extant output, far outweighing the rest of it. Furthermore, acceptance of his authorship of this expanded sermon corpus would extend what we know of his career and ground the outspoken political views for which the first sermon set in MS Bodley 649 has long been famous in an identifiable individual whose cultural context and formation it is possible in large part to reconstruct. The rest of the present discussion will proceed on the presumption that all of these sermons are indeed his work.

Legat's stay for many years at Oxford would be consonant with the fact that one of the sermons in MS Bodley 649 refers to Oxford as its author's place of study and also specifies a university audience there.[33] Legat was evidently a preacher of some standing within his order, being one of the monks entrusted with responsibility *pro sermone in vulgari* at the General Chapter of the English Benedictines held in Northampton on 8 July 1420. Moreover, it seems reasonable to suppose that the distribution of his preaching across at least three extant manuscripts (MS Laud misc. 706, MS Bodley 649, and Worcester, Cathedral Library, MS F.10) further endorses the view of his stature as a preacher well known among the Benedictines.[34] The range of sources drawn on in his sermons, and the thematic preoccupations displayed there, enlarge our appreciation of the width of his cultural repertoire and of the way this was enlisted in the service of a particular project that he intended his preaching to achieve.[35] Moreover, this project was one which he seems to have pursued singlemindedly.

The Sermon and its Sisters

In this latter regard, their sheer determination of focus, Legat's sermons are especially interesting. A distinct social politics breathes throughout the *Estote sicut filii* sermon edited below, one that closely corresponds to a reciprocal agenda by

---

[33] The eighth sermon of the first sermon set; see *A Macaronic Sermon Collection*, pp. 210–33.

[34] *Documents Illustrating the Activities of the General and Provincial Chapters of the English Black Monks, 1215–1540*, ed. by William A. Pantin, Camden Third Series, 45, 47, and 54, 3 vols (London: Royal Historical Society, 1931–37); see II, 97.

[35] For a useful outline of his preaching aims, see *A Macaronic Sermon Collection*, pp. 15–19.

which many of its sister sermons are driven.[36] The bulk of our extant medieval preaching concerned itself with timeless topics. The Scriptures and pastoralia, things that never aged, were the essential business of sermons, and provided the kernel from which most messages from the pulpit were grown. Indeed, the Advent sermon edited in the previous chapter was a case in point for, although it occasionally seems to respond to and address the local condition of its (lay) audience by alluding to sins that such an audience might typically have found congenial, it is otherwise taken up with an artful discant on the three advents of Christ to mankind, requisitioning in passing some exemplum about St Francis, enjoined on the preacher to introduce but never actually committed to parchment, that may have been aired as much in honour of the preacher's patron and by way of advertisement of his mendicant affiliation as it may have come apropos to his theme. By contrast, *Estote sicut filii*, like its sister sermons, conveys a far more urgent sense of an orthodox preacher's sociopolitical situation via the intensity of his response to it. This response had formed in a deep orthodox reaction to a historically contingent and evolving social actuality, one which the preacher abhorred, that he sought to reverse, and that might almost be credited with having stirred him to preach in the first place, so frequently does consciousness of it stir his discourses.

Certainly, Legat touched upon various social and spiritual ills in the course of his sermons, as many a medieval preacher was routinely wont to do, but his comments are often articulated with a degree of particularity that suggests that, if not the product of an exclusively personal view, they nevertheless expressed the view of a tightly knit, like-minded clerical coterie whose preaching agenda may have been notable for a certain characteristic intellectual pressure and committed intensity of emphasis. Chiefly what Legat lamented were the changes that he perceived taking place in society that were damaging the institution of the Church that he had come to recognize and cherish. As he watched and regretted respect for the orthodox ecclesiastical establishment leaking away amongst the

---

[36] A number of further studies by Roy Martin Haines are germane to establishing the wider profile of Legat's social politics (always on the strength of my presumption, of course, that all these sermons are his): '"Wilde Wittes and Wilfulness": John Swetstock's Attack on those "Poyswunmongeres", the Lollards', in *Popular Belief and Practice*, ed. by G. J. Cuming and Derek Baker, Studies in Church History, 8 (Cambridge: Cambridge University Press, 1972), pp. 143–53; 'Church, Society and Politics in the Early Fifteenth Century as Viewed from an English Pulpit', in *Church, Society and Politics*, ed. by Derek Baker, Studies in Church History, 12 (Oxford: Blackwell, 1975), pp. 143–57; and '"Our Master Mariner, Our Sovereign Lord": A Contemporary Preacher's View of King Henry V', *MS*, 38 (1976), 85–96.

laity, so ultimately his regrets stemmed from awareness of a concomitant ebb in institutionally established clerical power. *Estote sicut filii* focuses this state of affairs in a vignette from Bede (lines 377–82), where Legat notes that in the good old days, a layman happening across a cleric would go down on one knee to him and treat him with deference. Not so anymore. Moreover, the prime cause of contemporary disrespect and anticlericalism Legat saw as located in an infection of the lay mentality by the contagion of Lollardy. So for him, the realm's chiefest woes were theologicopolitical, and one of the ways he sought their cure was through preaching powered by a formidably resourced moral imagination.

For there is no doubt but that Hugh Legat was a literary artist of great imaginative skill, even without our ever being able to ascertain whether or to what extent that skill was matched by the quality and effectiveness of his performance art in the pulpit.[37] It would be no exaggeration to claim that in some of the processes through which the pressure of his moral imagination released itself we see analogies to some of William Langland's characteristic methods of imagining and projecting his own concerns some two generations earlier. Necessarily for us today, all that remains of Legat's preaching is the still life of his words frozen on the page, not their life in flesh-and-blood when actually heard in delivery. Yet these written evidences nevertheless witness to a care in the craft of composition, something that his concern with rhetoric, glimpsed elsewhere in his diligence that London, MS Harley 2624 should be newly bound, was also likely to vouch for.[38] Not only well in control of the verbal texture and arrangement of his discourses, Legat, a practised writer too in other provinces, chose words apt for dressing a content that was rich and varied, one calculated to appeal to a wide number of interests, and many of these sometimes all within the scope of one and the same sermon. He was capable of shifting between, amongst other things, allusions to classical history, canon and civil law, mythology, astrology, astronomy, medicine, music, the Scriptures, the Fathers, contemporary experience and anecdote, politics, the natural and physical sciences, philosophy, scholastic writing, and the

[37] Although self-evidently, he would not have been named amongst those responsible for vernacular preaching at the General Chapter of the Benedictines in 1420 had he been seriously deficient in matters of sermon delivery (*Documents Illustrating the General and Provincial Chapters of the English Black Monks*, II, 97). Legat's work is perhaps the most sophisticated and 'literary' of all the preaching samples included in this present anthology.

[38] London, British Library, MS Harley 2624, dated to *c.* 1125–50; see Rodney M. Thomson, *Manuscripts from St Albans Abbey, 1066–1235*, 2 vols (Woodbridge: Boydell and Brewer, 1982), I, 93. There is some discussion of Legat's compilation of the grammatical booklets in MS Rawlinson G.99 in Clark, *A Monastic Renaissance*, p. 93.

encyclopedists, so changing the stimulus of his content and yet always doing so in the service of a few unchanging key concerns.[39] As very much a preacher of the Lenten and Passiontide period, to judge by the surviving evidence, Legat's principal emphasis would necessarily be on the focusing of his audience's need, indeed of the nation's need, for repentance and renewal.[40] First, their sin must be identified and acknowledged by holding up before them a mirror in which they could see their condition reflected. Next, the prerequisite for effective confession, their contrition, must be stirred up, and then they must be urged to go to their curate so that the sacrament of penance might be administered to them in due orthodox form. Legat took some pains to defend orthodox Church teaching concerning those sacraments whose traditional theology Wycliffism had been assailing, sometimes entering into a degree of detail unusual for a preacher when discussing such matter.[41] Above all, for Legat, no one should trespas beyond the appropriate bounds of their class or capacity by meddling in matters in which they had neither right of access nor understanding. All the evident energy that he devoted to preaching essentially conduced to this one end: people should know their appointed place and shun the newfangled alternative vision of what that place might be that heresy was encouraging and holding out before them. His voice, profoundly conservative, was also compellingly articulate.

It was earlier observed that, while these sermon preoccupations may sound like Legat's own idiosyncrasies, they may in fact have already been those of a close coterie of which he was an eloquent member. There is some evidence to suggest that this may indeed have been the case and that his emphasis reflected and voiced that of a group. Legat's preaching should probably therefore be regarded as a component in a wider Benedictine preaching programme having a notable head-quarters at St Albans, but that was also supported in other leading Benedictine

---

[39] See *A Macaronic Sermon Collection*, pp. 14–15, for a summary of the sources used in the MS Bodley 649 collection, and ibid., pp. 541–44, for a more systematic account of the same.

[40] It is clear from one of the MS Bodley 649 sermons that Legat envisaged a course of seven sermons being preached *ad populum* during this penitential season (one on each of the six Sundays in Lent and the seventh on Good Friday; see *A Macaronic Sermon Collection*, p. 69, lines 265–67).

[41] For example, in MS Bodley 649 on the Eucharist in certain places, although he does not go into comparable detail in the sermon edited below here. See *A Macaronic Sermon Collection*, pp. 437–39, lines 31–44, where there is significant orthodox discussion of the essentials of Eucharistic consecration, and also of pilgrimages and of the veneration of images. Legat also insisted upon the inviolability of other traditional Church devotional practices that had similarly come under Wycliffite fire, as, for example, indulgence. His respect for papal power was pronounced, also in contrast to the scepticism of the Wycliffites.

centres.[42] Thomas Walsingham († *c.* 1422), another St Albans inmate and famed chronicler of the period, seems to have recognized the role that preaching had as an effective weapon against heresy when he approvingly recalled the endeavours of one of his and Legat's confrères, Simon Southerey. This man who, like Legat, had also spent time in Oxford, 'multos per suas praedicationes ab errore predicti Johannis revocavit' (by his preaching recalled many from the error of the aforesaid John [Wyclif]).[43] By implication, preaching for Walsingham had great value in helping to reclaim ground lost by traditional Church authority. The fact that St Albans monks preached regularly in the local parish churches also suggests something of the extent to which they were collectively moved at this historical juncture to take part of their *opus Dei* out of the cloister and into the world, especially a world that in some influential quarters was ill disposed to the cloister's privilege and that might benefit from a salutary reminder of what the sanctioned social order had been in the past and must continue to be in the future.[44] Legat was part of a second generation of Benedictines who were carrying forward the anti-Wycliffite campaign in which Benedictines had played a prominent part as early as the 1370s when Wyclif was at the beginning of his controversial career and first starting to attract adverse notice and then finally official censure.[45] The Abbot of St Albans during that period, Thomas de la Mare († 1396), had claimed that his monks had been amongst the first to warn against Wyclif's opinions, almost as if the vocal anti-Wycliffite stance of the Benedictines generally, not to mention that of the St Albans Benedictines in particular, had become a point of pride within the order.[46] At the time when Hugh Legat was active — his sermons

---

[42] For example, at the Benedictine foundation at Worcester Cathedral, as sermons in MS F.10 would seem to imply, and also at Durham Priory, where the monks were wont to preach *ad populum* after dinner on holy days; see *Rites of Durham*, ed. by J. T. Fowler, Surtees Society, 107 (Durham: Andrews, 1903; facsimile repr. 1998), p. 46.

[43] *Annales Monasterii S. Albani*, II, 305–06.

[44] In 1426, John Wethamstede, abbot of St Albans, preached a Latin synodal sermon in St Peter's Church, St Albans, in which he denounced Lollardy; see *Annales Monasterii S. Albani*, I, 229–31. (The latter half of the sermon was in verse; Wethamstede seems habitually to have concluded synodal proceedings with verse.)

[45] The Benedictine Uthred of Boldon was one of Wyclif's earliest opponents; see M. D. Knowles, 'The Censured Opinions of Uthred of Boldon', *PBA*, 37 (1951), 305–42.

[46] De la Mare seems himself to have been a capable preacher in English, French, and Latin; see *Gesta abbatum monasterii Sancti Albani, a Thoma Walsingham [...] compilata*, ed. by Henry T. Riley, RS, 28, 3 vols (London: Longmans, Green, Reader, and Dyer, 1867–69), II, 419–66 (pp. 419–31).

in MS Bodley 649 seem contemporaneous with the reign of Henry V (1413–22) — he might look back to antecedents in a line of two generations of reactionary Benedictine preachers, one of the most egregious amongst whom had been Thomas Brinton, Bishop of Rochester († 1389). Brinton, like Legat subsequently, spoke against Wycliffism from the pulpit on a number of occasions, and, even if he did so without such a degree of detail as Legat could be capable of, he had the advantage over his later confrère of having crossed with the heresiarch in person and thus of having had a personal stimulus for his preaching.[47] The mutual dislike between Brinton and Wyclif was strong; indeed, it may have been Brinton whom Wyclif had it in mind to denigrate when speaking in a sermon of his own of a certain 'black dog' (a *canis niger*) who, with his whelps, had reported him to the pope, thus helping to earn him the papal condemnation visited on him in 1377.[48]

Apart from composing sermons whose edge was whetted in reaction to Lollardy, Brinton had certain other sermon preoccupations that echo again and characteristically in Legat's preaching. Brinton's lament about the encroachment on the rights and privileges of the Church, for example, and about the contempt being meted out to the clergy resurface in Legat, as we have already seen, as also does a strong sense of the preacher's patriotism and loyalty to the Crown.[49] In view of all this, and without going quite as far as to deprive Legat of his own particular voice, we should balance what appear the personal preoccupations of his preaching with an awareness that some of them also witness to a certain

[47] Brinton is on record as having preached in 1382 and 1383 against four characteristic Lollard positions: a) that sacraments ministered by a bishop or a priest in a state of mortal sin were invalid, and that he neither consecrated nor baptized; b) that contrition, without external oral confession to a priest, was sufficient; c) that the substance of bread and wine remained in the Sacrament of the Altar after the prayer of consecration; and d) that no veneration should be afforded to the cross of Christ nor to religious images. See especially Brinton's sermon 101, delivered in 1382, for positions a), b), and c), and his sermon 107, delivered in 1383, for all four positions; see *The Sermons of Thomas Brinton, Bishop of Rochester (1373–1389)*, ed. by Mary Aquinas Devlin, Camden Third Series, 85–86 (London: Royal Historical Society, 1954), II, 466 and 495 respectively. While Brinton attacked Lollardy in various places, Legat's zeal, by comparison, seems to have been the greater, for of the MS Bodley 649 sermons, all, with one sole exception (sermon 4), mention Lollardy.

[48] *Iohannis Wyclif Sermones*, III, 70.

[49] Devlin, *The Sermons of Thomas Brinton*, I, 68 (for disrespect of the Church) and II, 354–57 (for loyalty to king and country). The latter loyal theme might well be anticipated in Legat, since his monastery, a royal foundation, was especially set fair to benefit from royal patronage; see Clark, *A Monastic Renaissance*, p. 35.

thematic consistency amongst the preachers of his order more widely, and that may include a consistency shared not only with his immediate contemporaries, but also with his confrères of the recent past. This larger consistency through time would also have had the advantage of publicizing the order's solidarity and giving Benedictine preachers in the troubled decades of the late fourteenth and early fifteenth century a certain fellow-feeling and sense of their unity in a common cause. *Estote sicut filii*, then, is eloquent both in itself, and in terms of its testimony to a broader scheme, to ways in which Benedictines were now serrying ranks, increasingly seeing the perennial waywardness of the human condition dimensioned in historically contingent terms. Their preaching, in short, was becoming more overtly politically aware and engaged.[50]

Legat's Structural Eloquence

If before presenting the text of *Estote sicut filii* we may briefly and finally return to a specific aspect of its eloquence, the aspect attributable to Legat's command of procedures of sermon structure that relate to those characteristic of 'modern' sermon form,[51] we find that his particular achievement in this department consists in the way in which those procedures have been deployed: there is little sense that *Estote sicut filii* is mechanically cranking out its matter, even though the sheer systematism inherent in 'modern' form may in the hands of other practitioners be conducive to sermons of such a sort. The reason for this seems to lie in the nature of Legat's treatment of the characteristic procedures, for while it is respectful, it is not slavish. In sum, he controls them rather than they him, and does so to the extent that his customizing of them constitutes another of the stylistic fingerprints leading us to suspect that his hand has been at work.

The sermon starts by announcing its *thema*, *Estote sicut filii*, and follows this with a classical exemplum. The *thema* is repeated, translated now into rhymed English but also having its original scriptural sense blended with a motif derived from the classical exemplum (lines 9–10). The moral interpretation of the exemplum is then explained. This explanation consists of a threefold *distinctio* on the qualities and conduct of the good preacher, and contrasts, first, illegitimate

---

[50] They were, of course, also becoming involved in polemic and the writing of defences of their order; their preaching should also be seen in such a context. See Clark, *A Monastic Renaissance*, pp. 254–57.

[51] See on 'modern' form above in Chapter 3, pp. 45–46 and n. 16.

preachers who for one reason or another are delinquent in their office. The congregation is warned against these in another repetition of the *thema*. The sermon proceeds to discuss, second, preachers who preach well but live badly, and again repeats the *thema*. St Paul's declaration about subduing his body is introduced, and the *thema* repeated yet again. Then, third, God's preachers are discussed, whose reproof of sin earns them enemies. These enemies are unlike the obedient sons envisaged in the *thema*. A second group who react badly to preaching are those who declare the preacher's discourse too profound to follow. An exemplum is adduced against such objectors and the *thema* repeated. A third group whose reaction to preaching is also inappropriate comprises people who during sermons may be pierced with devotion and stirred to sob and sigh, but whose feelings prove skin deep and ephemeral. The congregation is then advised to receive deeply the sharp arrow of preaching. The three parts of an arrow (head, shaft, and nock) are then specified, each part having two Latin words inscribed upon it. Each pair of words is explained, and how they relate to three different aspects or stages of the preacher's project. The preacher encourages his congregation to pray, and adduces another classical exemplum to illustrate the importance of prayer, stressing the need for prayer proceeding from a pure life. The *thema* is again repeated.

It is at this point after the *thema*'s repetition that Legat announces the *processus*, the summary development plan, of his sermon. The *processus* is worth detailing here, for its method of construction encapsulates a characteristic structural procedure of some of the other sermons in the mooted Legat corpus; he even consciously identified his procedure as a *particularum nexus*, a 'binding together of particulars'.[52] The *processus* of *Estote sicut filii* (lines 203–12) is articulated as follows. Three types of children are announced: first, those diverse and dissolute in their condition; second, those wild and wanton in their affection; and third, those wise and wary in their conversation. The first type shows us that old nature is gone; the second type, that friend turns foe; and the third type, that wealth is woe. Old nature is gone by the withdrawing of worship and reverence; friend turns foe by the reforming of great offence; and wealth is woe by sudden alteration and common experience. This constitutes the substance of the *processus*. The nature of the treatment of its various components can be seen very clearly in the sentence that immediately ensues, where Legat introduces the first of what will

---

[52] Paraphrasing Horner in his edition, *A Macaronic Sermon Collection*, p. 33, line 140. Indeed, if the method in which the *processus* of this MS Bodley 649 sermon is articulated is compared with that of *Estote sicut filii*, whose *processus* will be described shortly, both methods will be seen to be remarkably similar.

be a series of three 'principals' in the manner of 'modern' sermon form (the third 'principal' has been lost because the sermon is atelous): 'Ffyrst than Y sey and prinspaliche that chylder diuerse and dissolut in condyciun schewun that holde nurtur ys agoo be withedrawy<n>g of dew worschep and reuerense' (lines 213–15). It is clear here how three components announced in the *processus* have been agglutinated (the *nexus particularum*) to form the basis for a further substantial disquisition (lines 215–447) in which reminiscences of the *thema* recur at opportune intervals (at lines 228, 236–37, 299, 332, and 447). Compare, too, the announcement of the second 'principal' which is handled similarly: 'I seyde the secunde tyme prin<s>palyche that chyldere wyld and wanton in here affecciun deme that frende ys foo be dew reformynge of greus trespas and gret offens' (lines 448–50). Like the first 'principal', so too this agglutinates the next three components of the *processus* as a basis for another disquisition (lines 448–533), although this one is cut short because folios of the next quire are wanting. These missing folios can be assumed originally to have contained a third 'principal' and the sermon's conclusion.

Thus Legat's eloquence also had its structural dimension. The whole sermon is thoroughly organized, though that organization seems rather to have been placed at the disposal of the sermon's content than to have existed conspicuously as an end in itself. This is a sermon whose 'modern' form supports its content rather than overpowers it by a form that is ostentatiously self-advertising; the form is executed with a certain degree of self-effacement. Contrast the Legat sermon in Worcester, Cathedral Library, MS F.10, which flagged its structure by signalling each respective part of the sermon in advance with an elaborate banner heading: it begins with an 'Introductio Thematis Ante Orationem'; follows with an 'Introductio Thematis Ante Partipationem [*sic*!]'; then a 'Trimembris Particio Thematis Pro Processu Totius Sermonis'; next a 'Primum Membrum Principale'; and so on.[53] It is clear from such showcasing that structure was an important aspect of Legat's eloquence and that it could be isolated, foregrounded and contemplated in its own right. But for whose benefit? Not, presumably, for that of his audience. They were more likely to have experienced his sermon and its carefully understated symmetry simply as consumers secure in their foreknowledge of where the discourse was taking them and what they should expect. As well as playing for their imaginations, fostering that security amongst the members of his audience was perhaps one of Legat's subtlest strategies for keeping them in their proper place.

---

[53] *Three Middle English Sermons*, pp. 1, 4, and 5.

A Sermon for the Third Sunday in Lent from Oxford, Bodleian Library,
MS Laud misc. 706

|fol. 144ʳ|

'Estote sicut filij', ad Ephesios 5. Sextus Iulius, *De bello Cesaris*, refert quod
fuit venerabilis princeps in antiquis temporibus nuncupatus Cleomus qui
habuit ciuitatem infra suum regnum obsessam cum inimicis. Iste princeps,
affectans multum confortare suum populum qui erat in miseria et discrimine
5   animare et prouocare illos fortiter ad resistendum suis inimicis, armauit
militem de suis, precipiens sibi vt iret ad predictam obsidionem, et similis
alijs inimicis, inuaderet eandem ciuitatem, habens in omnibus suis iaculis et
sagittis ista verba artificialiter sculpta et scripta: 'Estote sicut filij fideles
obsidionem vestram. Ego Cleomus in proximo venio remoturus.' Summa
10   istorum verborum est ista: 'Beth ȝe as gode childur oghe to be, and I schal
cum and remove the sege fro ȝoure cite.'

Be thys worthy prince I vndurstond at this tyme Crist, Godis son of heuen,
lord and emperoure of alle thys wyde world. This graciouse prince has
withein his reme a cite þat he loues tendurliche, Holy Chirche, greuusliche
15   beseget withe errowrs and heresis that be werryng amonge vs cristen pepul
in this days. Querfore he desyret gretliche to strenthe vs in the fyȝt of Holy
Chirche, send his knyȝt, the prechwr of þe word of God, to comfort and hert
vs myȝtiliche to withestond the perlus sawtes and soden inuasiouns of thes
curset enmys. This prechur schuld be sureliche armet withe the helme of
20   witte and discrecion, strongliche hertet withe boldnes of truthe and gode
entencion, and truliche famet be vertuus leuyng and honest conuersacion.
For as seth Seynt Ione Crisostoune, *De opere inperfecto*, omelia vj de laude
Pauli, he that takes on hym the offys of prechyng, hym behoueth noȝt to be
febyl and freel in leuyng, but bold and myȝty in wyt and konyng, redy as a
25   gode knyȝt to suffur dethe for the truthe and al maner of mychief. But
nowadays þer be mony princys, knyȝtis that con not wele decline hor owne
name, the qwyche vsurpe on hom the ministracion of prechyng, onliche be
ordinans of Holy Chirche comittyt to clerkys and curatis, as wyttenes law
canoun, xvj q. j, 'Adicimus', et extra de hereticis, 'Excommunicatus', qwer
30   euery lewman, woman, and religius witheout a generall priuylege or a speciel
leue of the dioscan be suspendit fro the offys of prechyng for diuerse perellys
and inconuenientis that wold sew of suche lewde suffrans. Thys prechurs be
wondir bold and presumptuus in prechyng, but sepius they medle falsnes

|fol. 144ᵛ| withe truthe and vicys withe vertuus for faut of wyt and ig<no>rans

35 of conyng.

Hit fares be al suche as hit ferde be the emperoure of Rome, Iulius Cesar.
This emperoure, as Valerius ad Rufinum telles, receyued in his goyng to the
Capytoly letters of contriuyng and ymaginacion of his dethe, but for gret
pryde and presumpciun that he hade of his owne persoun, lust and likyng in
40 wordliche worschepe, hym list not to breke his letres and ouerse hom, but
bare hom forthe closed in his hond to the Capytoly quere his enmys fel on
hym and wondyt hym to the dethe withe 24 wondis. Truliche, thus hit farus
be thes prentys prechurs. They presume so meche of hor owne wytte that
hom deynes noȝt to vnclose to ouerloke any doctor of Holy Chirche to be
45 enfourmed and know how and what þei schuld preche, but onely to be hold
wyse, and for priuy envy that thay haue to be subduit to the laws of Holy
Chirche, preche and renew errours and heresys that ware repreuet and
dampnet in old tyme, and so wylfulliche wond homself withe as mony
gostliche wondys as they fauir and mayntene errowrs and fals opyniouns.
50 Thes be noȝt the knyȝtis þat be sende fro oure graciose prince Crist Ihesu
to strenthe and comfort vs in oure beleue, but rather þe vntrew childur that
þe prophet Ysaye spekus of, Ysaye 30, sayng on this wise, 'Hij sunt filij
mendaces, nolentes audire legem, qui dicunt audientibus, nolite audire, et
aspicientibus, nolite aspicere que recta.' 'Thes be', sethe thys profit, 'fals
55 and vntrew childur, noȝt wele wyllyng to here of the lawys of God', but stir
and tyse tru pepyl to wyt hor inward seyt and affecciun fro al truthe and
riȝtwisnes. The fals doctrine and singler opynioun of al such charget ȝow
Seynt Poule be the wordys of my teme to eschew and fle when I sey, 'Estote
sicut filij', 'Bethe ȝe as gode childur oghe to be'.

60 Other ther be also that be conyng and wyse in prechyng, but lewde and
mysrewlet in hor owne leuyng, to the qwyche may resonabliche be reherset
the conclusioun that was ȝowyn in old tyme of þe clerge of Parys. Lincolne,
De oculo morali, tellus that qwen the clerge of Parys were assemblet in hor
scolys and biseliche occupiet in disputsons abowt hor lernyng, sodenliche þer
65 come in a |fol. 145ʳ| fole among hem askyng solucyuun of thys questioun:
qweþer hyt were beter to do þat man kowde and kew, or elles to lere þat he
kowde nawȝt. Thes philosophi, musing gretlych of þys questyoun, arguit pro
and contra to heiþer party. Thys fol stode style, alwey heryng after solucioun
of thys questioun. So at þe laste yt was diffinit and determit amonge hem

70　that hyt was beter and more meritorie to do that man kowde and kewe than
　　to lere that he knode naw3t. 'Qwerefore semyt me', quod thys fole, '3e be
　　more lewdyr and vnkonyng than I, in that 3e besy so gretlyche abow3t þat 3e
　　can now3t, nat fulfyllyng in dede that 3e haue y-leryt and can'. Trewly, gode
　　men, so semyt me suche that per gret bysynes prechyn clergeal and dewouut
75　sermouns, no3t suyng here oune doctrine in that, buthe wonder lewde and
　　repreuabyl. Ffor as sethe Seneca in hys boke þat he made, *De moralibus*,
　　ther ys no thyng so fowle, so wysyus in the repreue of vicis, as to be fownde
　　gulty in þe same paciuns that he repreuit. Qwerefore, 3eue the prechwr of
　　þe worde of God desyryt to saue ys name witheoute repreue, he moste haue
80　þe condycioun of a kocke, fyrst bete hymselue withe ys wyngus or he begyn
　　to crowe, ffyrst bete and scorge hys oune body withe dedys of penawns and
　　gode conuersacioun or he take on hym þe offys of prechyng. Ffor 3eue he
　　otherwyse do, he ys naw3t worthy amang the discyplys of Crist, bot rather
　　among the chyldryn that þe profyt Ieremye, of Trenorum primo, seyng on
85　þis wyse, 'Ffilij sunt perdicionis, quoniam inualuerunt contra eos inimici.'
　　Thes buþ bote forsake forlorne chyldryn, in that thei haue suffrit her
　　enmy the delue wylfullyche mayster and ouerlede hem. Bot 3it, gode men,
　　naw3twhytstondyng scuch su naw3t the stepys of Crist in that þey corforme
　　na3t here dedys to here thechyng, 3yt do 3e as he betaw3the and buthe as
90　gode chyldrun ow3t to be, as Y seyde at þe bygynnyng.

　　Thus maner of doynge haþe Sey3t Poule, as whytnyshit wylle hys pystylys,
　　Prima ad Corinthiorum ix°, qwere he seyde on thys wyse, 'Castigo corpus
　　meum et in seruitutem redigo, ne forte cum alijs predicauerim, ipse reprobus
　　efficiar.' 'I chastys my body', seyt Synt Poule, 'and kep yt in trale subieccioun,
95　anawnter Y be funde fawty an repreuit qwene Y schal preche to þe pepul
　　of al.' God men, al to fewe nowadayes, so seyþe Poule, in thys condy- |fol.
　　145ᵛ|cioun. 3it as many as kepe þe forme of trew prechyng herith lawlych and
　　buthe as gode chyldrun ow3t to be, as Y seyde at þe bygynnge.

　　The iij maner of prechwrs ther ys, and be they that byn sende fro almy3ty
100　God to strenth and to comford vs in owre beleue. Tales be surelyche armit
　　withe wyt and dyscreciun, and trulych famit withe feiful doctrine and honest
　　conuersacioun. But for as miche as they wyl sadlych and witheoute any
　　flatrynge reherse þe defawthes of here degre and condycioun, the be demit
　　for enmys of diuerse pepil, and so here harowys of scha<r>pe rebukyng
105　be enterlyche refusit and despusyd. Talis populus may wel be lykened to

a serpent that hys cleped abanes. Thes best, as Philosophus rehersit, *De animalibus*, aȝens þe kynde and condycioun of al oþer bestis berythe hys gal in hys here wondurlyche bytter, a myche lyche to a gal of a mon. Truli, so do talis pepul, for as sone as they ȝere here vicys and here defautys rehersyt in
110 special, they haue þe beter gal of whreth, of indynacioun in the ȝere of here hert, ymagyn and conseue malycyus wordus aȝens þe prechwre, and so be rather aperyd than amendyd be here beter herynge. Tales be nawȝt as gode chyldrun obedient, bote rather suynge þe condycyun of steppe childer, withe risu and grochyng reseyuyge vnderni<m>hi<n>ge and rebukynge for here
115 trespas. To heuery man of swche condycioun may resonabullyche the wordus that I fynde wretyn in holy wrete, Actuum 8, 'Fili, non est tibi pars neque sors in sermone isto, ... quia in felle amaritudinis video te esse.' 'Sone, thu hast no part no profyȝt of thys sermon, for Y se the in the gal of whreþe and bitturnes.' Qwerefor, ȝe that desyrþe to be edyfyt be worde of God, herit
120 withe deuoyt and meke spyryt that hy<s> spoken for ȝowre profyt and honeste. 'Et estote sicut filij,' and but as gode childrun owȝt to be.

The ij pepul ther ys also qui dicunt the prechwure spekyþe so hye diuinite, so depe clerge, no man may conseyue what he talkyt. Wherefor hem semyþe bot a spendyng and wastyng of tyme to ȝeue hym any audyens. Truly, god
125 men, talia verba be lewed and vnwytty, for as Origen seyt, super iudicium, ȝeue hyt so be that wrettys and charmys that diuerse pepil berun abowt here neckys, of the wyche they con ful lytyl scille or ryȝt noȝt, be of suche vertu to saue men fro bodylyche sykenes, myche more þe worde of God ys to the lowe herer of swche vertu that hyt wol kepe hym fro gostelych sykenes, of al hit be
130 nawt fullyche conseyut.

I rede in *vitas Patrum* that an holde fadyr askyd on a tyme a ȝonge man |fol. 146ʳ| what was the cause that he ȝaue hym to pley and ydul ocupacioun whyle þe word of God was a prechynge. He respondit and seyde ys whyt was so dul and so hard that he knew hymselue vnhabul to conseyue þe prechur.
135 This hold fadyr askyd hym qweþer he knew nawȝt how a harde stone whas perchyd whyt softe watur be ofte drepyng of reyne. This ȝong man grantyd that he knew yt welle. 'Truly on this same whyse', quod thys hold fadyr, 'the ardnes and the dolnes of manys whyt be ofte herynge of the word of God ys perchit and derkenes of ignorans excludyd be preuus of lyȝt, konyng, and
140 vndurstondynge.' Thus, than, seth ȝe se wyle that ȝe may nowȝt be excused be lackynge of conyng noþer dulnes of whyt, sekyt no suche ocacionse to be

myche absent fro Holy Churche prechyng, bote buþe as gode childrun oȝute
to be, as Y seyde at the bygynnynge.

The thred pepil ther ys also, that sone is schetyn withe deuocioun and stered
145 to do penauns for here senne, liche in condicioun to the whale. Autors that
tretyn of kynde telleþ that whanne fysscheris haue asspyed the plas qwere the
whale howyt and abydyth, they asaythe al the melody, al the mynstracy that
they can ymagyn and deuise. These fysche, delytyng gretlyche in here swete
noyses, natand so nye here schepis that he ys percusus and wondun withe
150 here arowes. Bote for as myche as hys scyn ys fatty and tyke, in þe begynnynge
he feluþe bote lytul desese. Bote afturwarde, be rumbi<n>g aȝens the cragis
of the see, ys wondis encresyn and smertyn sore be entryng of salte watur.
And so for cause he wil naȝt abyde thes deseses, he natat to the londe and
perychit. Thys condicioun haue they that sobe and syhe at sermouns, and for
155 the tyme be wondur dewout and in foul will do penawnse for here syn, bot
for cause they be nawȝt wondyd depe ynowe withe the arow of deuocyon,
they sclakyd al to sone of here purpos. Ffor as sone as the flesche begynnythe
anythynge to gruche aȝenste penaw<n>sce doynge, be hyt fastynge or eny
other priuey deuocyoun, they natant to the londe of lustus and lygyngis ther,
160 bote the more grace be to perce both body and sowle. Qwerefore, gode men,
sethe |fol. 146ᵛ| ȝe se wyle that swche deuociun ys bote lytul to prese, my
cunsel ys that ȝe more abydynglyche and withe stedefast intencyoun dysspose
ȝowresilfe to receyue the arowe of scharpe prechyng, for ȝyf ȝe take god hede
to the scripture that ys wretyn therin, ȝe schal wele know that yt ys nowȝt
165 schot to wonde ȝow bodylyche, bot onelyche to hele ȝow gostelyche.

In a narow as ȝe know wylle be 3 prin<s>pal partys: the hede scharpe and
presynge; the ryȝt schaft fedryd for fleynge; and the nocke opyn for reseuyng.
In the hede ys wretyn *timor et amicia*, loue and drede. In the schaft, *equitas
et iusticia*, equite and ryȝtwesnusse. In the fedrus, *bonitas, pietas, et clemencia*,
170 godenes, pyte, and mekenes. And abowȝt the nocke, *gracia et misericordia*,
grace and mercy. Fyrste in ʿþeʾ hede of thys arow ys wretyn *dileccio et timor*,
loue and drede, for the prechwre of the worde of God in the begynnge techyt
and informet heuery crystyn creature to sette ys loue on God of qwom he
hathe reseyuid ys beynge and many oþer benefectis bothe of fortune and of
175 kynde, haui<n>g wyt this lowe a gret fere and drede any wyse to defende
hym. Ferthermore, he schewyt ȝow how be equite and ryȝtwessenusse dome
of Gode, heuerey man gulty in any dedly syne fallythe into the sentens of

heuerlastynge dampnaciun. Bote for as myche as ryȝtwusnes ys fedryd wyt al
godnesse, pete, and mekenes, he steryt and cumfortyt heuery synful creature
180   to offyre vp ys preyre and aske grace and mercy.

Bote here and ȝe wele knowe how ȝe schal moste plese God withe offeryng
vp ȝowre preyre, ȝe moste take hede of the ordinans and custum that was
vsyd in holde tyme amonge the Romaynys. I rede in the storyse of Rome that
whenne the Romaynys were nawȝt herde of here askynge and here godes
185   whytdrew here anschers other wyse than they were wont to do, they anon by
one asent, one acorde offert vp a fayre ymage, gay and craftyliche depeyntyd
in the worschepe of here godes, the wyche was clepyd *viriplaca*. And anon
here goddis were plesed and ȝaue hanschers as they dede byfore. Truly on
thys same wyse, and ȝe wyle be herde and spede witheouȝt any fayle of ȝowre
190   asckynge, ȝe moste be of one acorde in ful loue and charite, for witheout thys
vertu no god dede, no prere, |fol. 147ʳ| may be herde. Ȝowre hert and ȝowre
tonge moste be of one asent. Ffor be decreys, de consecracione, distinccio 5,
'Non mediocriter', Good ys more y-plesed whyt the seyng of the vij psalmys
withe god deuocyoun of hert than whyt al the hole sawter seyd withe desidia
195   and vnlust, ȝe, moste thys ymage. Ȝe most also take god hede that ȝowre prere
be gaylyche depey<n>tyd withe clennus of lyfe and besy perseuerans and
withe god byleue and ful hope to spede of ȝowre askynge. Offere vp ȝowre
preyre to almyȝty God, seynge on thys whyse withe the profyt in the sawter
boke, Ps lxxxv, 'Miserere mei, Domine, et saluum fac filium ancille tue.' 'Thw
200   mercyful lord', he seyth, 'haue ruthe, pyte, and compassyun of me, and saue
the chyld of thy anmayd' otherewhyse gouer<n>t than he owȝt ‘to’ be. And
in thys prere ȝe schal haue recomende, et cetera.

'Estote sicut filij,' vbi supra. Bethe ȝe as gode childrun owht to to be, as Y
seyde before. Ffor the prosces of thes schort sermone, in thes wordis ȝe schal
205   vndurstonde 3 maner of chyldrun. The furste be childer diuerse and desolute
in condyciun, the secun<d> wilde and whanton in here affecciun, and the
thred be chylder whys and whar in here conuersacyun. The fyrste schewth vs
that wholde nurtur ys agoo, the secunde demethe that frende ys foo, and the
thyrde preueth that welthe ys woo. Holde nurtur ys agoo be whytdrawynge
210   of dewe worschepe and reuerense. Ffrende wexit foo be reformyng of gret
offens. And welthe ys woo be sodeyne chanchyng and comyn experiens, et
cetera.

Ffyrst than Y sey and prinspaliche that chylder diuerse and dissolut in
condyciun schewun that holde nurtur ys agoo be withedrawy<n>g of dew
215 worschep and reuerense. A gret clerk Walerius, *De dictis et factis memorabilibus*,
as hym rehersit Ianuens, *De opere quadragesimali*, sermone 43, tellit that
whene the kyng of Pers, Darius, hade wastud and destrued muche of the
contrey of Barbari, he purpost hym fullyche in confusiun and despute of the
same pepyl to dispule and furdo al the dede mens grauys that myȝt be founde
220 in the cuntre. Thes Barbarynys whondurlych agrised and elne apayde whyt
thys cruel purpos, sende for the |fol. 147ᵛ| inbassetowrs or messangers,
chargyng hem to telle and informe the kyng that of al they bare heuyliche
and suffred for a tyme the waste a<n>d depopulaciun that he hade y-do in
cuntrey, ȝyt that they had leuer as men dye bodylyche in the felde than suffer
225 hym haue hys purpos and suche disworschep, suche vylenye be do to here
progenitowrs. Be thes Barbarynys Y vndurstonde at thes tyme al temporal
men of trew crystyn feythe, whyche scholde rather reseyue dethe, and they
were gouerynt as gode childrun howȝt to be, than suffer any disworschep,
any vnreuerence be do to here moder Holy Churche. Bote for men nowadays
230 for the more parte buthe of the newe nurtur and dissolut in here condyciun,
prelaci and prystewhod, that schold be prinspal and as here gostlyche modere
be hade in dew worschepe and reuerence, in thes days ys so muche subduit
and despused that almoste heuery temporal mon, heuery seculer hae scorne
and indynacyun to do any membur of Holy Churche any worschepe or
235 reuerens, bote heuermore redy to reuyle hem whyt wordus of vngentry other
than were syttyng in here persons, and they were nurturde as gode chyldrun
owȝt to be. Suche pepul haue lytil meynde of the stori that Y fynde wretyn
in holy wret, iiij Regum, secundo capitulo, where Y rede that because the
ȝong c`h´yldere of Iericho rewylid and scornid the holy profyt Helyse, God
240 toke vengens on hem and were deuowrud 40 and mo withe wylde berys. Bote
perauenter tow that art of thys nurtur, to ascuse the of thys vngentri, seyst to
me o this wyse, 'Syre, the philosophus techyt vs, 4 Ethicarum, that onelyche
a god man and a uertuus owȝt to be worschep. Bot sethe hit ys so that men
of Holy Churche be bote as dede mens grauis — gay and glorius owȝtward,
245 bote witheine, ful of rotun vyses and stynkynge synne — they haue a name
of gostelyche conuersaciun, bote no temporal mon so worldeliche in here
werkys, in here dedys as they be, yt semeþe me that hit is leful to withedrawe
fro hem dew worschep and reuerens.' |fol. 148ʳ| Hic respondeo to thy scyle
and sey thu art deseyuid, and for thys reson ther the more ascused. For as
250 Doctor Holcot rehersyt vpon Sapiens, capitulo 75, and also decres acordit

therwyht, distinccio 93, 'Dominus', ȝe be hold to worschepe and reuerens
ȝowre gostelyche curat, of al he be mysgouernt, fro 23 scylis. Ffyrst he
repreueth the stat and the degre of Cryst whom euery crystyn creature ys
bow<n>de to worschep withe al ys hert, for he ys hed and prynspal of al the
255 comynte, the wyche owt alwey to be proferid, and also for he ys autor and
rewlowr of al vertu that ys vsed, ys suggetis that askyt alwey worschep to hys
rewarde. Bot ȝyt, notwhytstondynge al thys, hyt hofte tymes ys sene that the
clerge be here one mysgouernance ȝeue the comyn pepyl gret occasyun to
haue the les at reputaciun, and can nowȝt auoyde hyt that we ȝeue hem gret
260 occasiun to whytdraw dew worschepe and reuerens. And so who audiret
dicere veritatem, the defaute cleuit sumwhat on vre syde, and also in party on
hers in ȝowre, be grete neclygens of gostelyche charge and wor `l´delyche
ocupaciun in ȝowre, be hy pride that regnith amonge ȝow and scor<n>ful
indynaciun.

265 Ffyrst, than, Y sey that the clerge thorow here houne necligens ȝeue gret
occaciun to withedraw fro hem dew worschep and reuerens. Seynt Augustinus,
5ᵗᵒ *De Ciuitate Dei*, capitulo 13°, tellyt that the Romaynis, reuerensyng in
holde tyme gretlyche vertu and worschep, byldyd ij solempne templus in the
worschep of here nammys, made be suche ordinans, be swche crafte that no
270 man myȝt enter into the Tempyl of Worschep bot by the Tempyl of Vertu,
in tokyn that no mon scholde haue no worschep and reuerens amonge hem
bot ȝeue he were worthy be manhode and vertuus leuynge. Thys Tempyl of
Worschep ys nowȝt ellus bote thys ordur of prestehode, in the wyche by
manny hy status, hy degreus, ys gretlyche desyred of diuerse pepul. Bot many
275 ther be in, Y sey noȝt alle, that leue and declyne fro the ryȝt wey that to thys
tempul, and sue bypathys of loȝ- |fol. 148ᵛ| schep and ypocrisye, so rather to
enter than be habulte of conyng or vertuus lyuynge. What pepil nowadays
berst in maysterfullyche at the wyndowys of thys tempyl, be autorite `and´
be warante of lordschyp, vrenschype and cursyd symony? How may thow
280 vndurmyne also sclelig the wallys of thys tempul? And so be sclept of fals
flatryng and fenynge ypocrisye. Trulych, no fewur than be neclygent in here
gostlyche charge and for fawȝt of dew correcciun suffer here sogettys sue the
bypathus of vycyus leuynge. Thys tempyl ys noȝt ellus bot the ordur of
presthode, the wyche in hymsylue ys more of dyuynte, more of worschep
285 than regaly, kynhode, or eny other astat of temporal power. Into thys tempyl
no man schulde presume to entur bot he were in ful purpos, in ful wyl to
leue al wordlyche ocupacyun and gouerne hym be vertu lyche hys ordur

askyt. Ffor as seth Sey<n>t Orygen, super Leuiticum, heuery preste, heuery
membur of Holy Churche scholde so demene hymsylf in worde, in dede, in
290 port, in chere, among the pepyl that be no mysgouernans of person ys ordur
were dysworschept and les of reputaciun. Bot treulyche, sum ther be, Y sey
now3t alle, that entryn into thys tempul, reseyue the ordur of presthode
rather in hope to be encresyd 3ere efter to hyer degre, to hyer worschep, and
so to leue more at hese than they do now in thys sympyl astat. Werefor suche,
295 because they be naw3t set on perfecciun and grounde in vertu, be owt tymes
to wor`l´dlyche in here conuersaciun and take al to lytyl hede to gouerne
hem efter þe condyciun of here ordur. Thus because the pepyl seyth that they
be necligent and naw3t fullyche so besy to fulfylle here gostlyche charge as
gode chyldrun of Holy Churche ow3t to be, they take gret occasiun of
300 whytdrawynge dew worschepe and reuerens. Werefor, 3eue suche pepyl that
knowe hemselfe defectyue in thys condyciun desyre to exclude al suche
occasiun and fullyche put the fawte fro here syde, they most lere to lepe
vnder the |fol. 149ʳ| <.>awys that were y-vsed in olde tyme wen any man
sulde enter into the Tempyl of Worschep. Doctor Holcot rehersyt on
305 Sapiens, capitulo 165, and Ysydere towchyt the same, 18 Ethicarum, that
when a prins of Rome or kny3t sulde be led into the Tempyl of Worschep
efter a gret victory of ys enmys, be law and ordynans of the same cite he sulde
suffer pacienlyche on of sympyl degre that sat withe hym in hys schare to
smy3t hym in the necke, seynge to hym the wordus, *Nothi celicos*. Thes be
310 wordus of Greu and as myche for to saye as know thesylfe and be naw3t to
prowde, haue no3t to myche waynglory of thy worschep. Also for that tyme
what wordus of scorne, of repreue were spoke to hys persun, he schulde take
godlyche witheout any gruchyng of chere. O thys same wyse heuery membyr
of Holy Churche, and he wyl gouerne hym be vertu lyche hys degres askyt,
315 he moste haue the drede of God settynge contynuelyche in the chare of
mynde, the wyche schulde, as ofte as he were any thyng steryd or temdyd to
offende and breke the maundement of God, make hym to haue mynde of the
solempne of the wylful bout that he hathe profest hymsylfe to, and so
refreyne hymsylfe be vertu. Also, 3yf he saw ys one conuersaciun vnlyche
320 other mens, set neuer the more by hymsylfe nor the bolder to deme other
mens dedys, bot haue alwey a god eye to ys oune frelte, and thyng how abul
he ys to fal hereafter, bot 3eue he be preseruyd be specyal grace, and in so
myche haue the more rewthe and compassiun of hem that trespas and
offende. What wordus of scorne or of repreue be spoke to ys persoun, suffer
325 hem pacyenlyche for ys howne mery3t and for gode ensampul geuyng, and

ȝeue he thus do, than schal the wordus be veryfyde of hym that Y fynde y-
wretyn in holy wrette, Genesis 49, 'Laudabunt te fratres ... et adorabunt filij
patris tui', 'Thy brethryne schal preyse and comende the, and thy fadur
chyldur', that ys to sey, the comyn pepyl do the dew worschep and reuerens.
330　O thys wyse that ȝe may withedraw al helue occasiun and be gouer<n>de
vertulyche lyche ȝowre degre, I cunsel ȝow take hede to the wordus that I
toke to my teme and buthe as gode chyldrun oȝte to bee, et cetera.

I seyde also fyrthermore that dew worschepe and reuerens |fol. 149ᵛ| ys
gretlyche whytdraw fro the clerge be hye pride and scor<n>fu<l> indygnaciun
335　that regnith among the layfe. I rede that in the cyte of Athene prid was
depey<n>dyd al on hy a ymage of diuerse colouris, powdrid withe wylde
bestis hauynge ij hornes on here hede and bot oo fote to stonde on. Lord
God, whether thys ymage be naȝwt pey<n>dyd in the cyte of thys reme! Ȝes
truly, and hathe in so gret reuerens and worschep that Y der wel sey, and alfe
340　so myche worschep were do to ymagis that be depey<n>dyd in Holy Churche,
we schulde haue bot a fewe Lollardis in thys reme at the lest wey of that
opynyun than nowȝ thys onelyche of my worde. Bote conseyud and bewolde
withe ȝowre inwarde syȝt how dyuerse, how dyssolut the pepyl hys in here
aray, how hye of beryng and lordlyche in here chere, and late ȝowre oune eyin
345　be iuge whether Y sey soth or Y do nowȝt. And trulyche, Y dowt yt nawȝt,
ȝeue ȝe be wel sette, ȝe wyl acorde withe me and sey ther ys more ydolatrie,
more maumetri do to thys cursed ymage of pride than dew worschep or
merytory pylgrymage to howre Lady of Walsyngham, owre gloryous patroun
Synt Albone, or to the holy martyr Synt Thomas of Caw<n>terbury. For
350　nowadays almost euery person, he<ue>reyman be he come of neuer so lowe
lynage, nere so deformid in kynde and in condyciun, ȝyt he schal perche
hymsylfe so hy be lordlyche chere and hy beryng that hym deynyt nowȝt ouns
to loke dunward on hys beter. He depey<n>th hys body fro day to day withe
soleyne colowrs and diuerse schap of garmentis, nowe he husche oo colowre,
355　now anothere, now ys garmentis be iacgyt, now reuelyd, now colowreles.
Thus he ys so changeabyl, so varyant in hys aray that he not were he may
abyde. Al suche pepil may wel be lykynd to a serteyne beste that holy wrette
makyt menciun of, Leuitici xj, and ys cleped camelyon. Thys best, as Ysyder
rehersyd, 12 Ethicarum, hathe thys properte, that what colowre he beholdþe,
360　anon he turnit into the same and leuþe hys holde. Truly, thys hyt faryth be
thys mys- |fol. 150ʳ| prowde men, for ȝeue they may know or beholde any
solene aray that ys browȝt newe into thys reme, be hyt neuer so lewde, nere

so vnsytty, ȝe, more acordyng to a iaper than to the stat of a gentylman, ȝyt
they moste change here olde schappe into thys newe or ellus al whar nowȝt
365   worth an hawe. Thus because they wolde be holde diuerse and syngle in here
aray, they dysfugure and dysgysyn hemselue so nyslych fro day to day that
they be in repreth to heuery god mon and as scorny<n>g stokys to al the
comyn pepul. What man desyryt to here a hanscher of the newe nurtur, late
hym reherse to suche pepul how the holde nurtur and the holde maner was
370   ful gode, and consel hym to leue al suche nys dysgysyng for honeste of hys
owne person, and witheowȝte any fayle he schal be seruyd of hys desyre. Ffor
they schal onsuer and sey, 'What carest the of myn aray? Yt coste the nowȝt,
Y do the wel to wetyn. I chyl vse myn owne gode efter myn owne deuise and
aske the no leue.'

375   Truly, as me semyt, thys anschere may resonablyche be inpuignit for diuerse
scylys. Furst, for as myche as yt dyscordyt fro the holde curtesy, the holde
nurtur. Ffor as Seynt Bede tellyt, *De gestis Anglorum*, libro 3°, capitulo xxvj,
the pepyl in holde tyme was so nurturd, so gentyl in here condyciun that
nawȝt onelyche weresoeuere they met a relygyus man or eny clerke, they
380   wolde fal on kneys afore hym and aske ys blessynge, bot also as ofte as they
were spok to and repreuyd of here mysgouernawns, lowlyche to anschere
and profer a ful mendys. Also yt ys aȝenste the lawe of God, Leuitici 19,
Deuteronomij 22, were yt ys forbode that garmentis of dyuerse whyngis, of
dyuerse schappe schul be vsyd, and also for yt ys contrary to the law of the
385   empyre, and also that no man schuld were the schape of wommans aray nor
wommans mans. Bot nowadays thys law ys nothynge kepte. Wherefore, yt ys
for to drede that God do the same correcciun on al suche that he dede on
hym that browȝt vpon furste suche soleyne araye amonge the Romaynys, the
wyche, as Ianuens tellyt in a sermoun that he makyt, et incipit 'Homo
390   quidam erat diues', whas smetyn withe a lyȝtny<n>ge and kylde. Ffor ryȝt as
be lawe cyuyle in case that thu suldust anythinge |fol. 150ᵛ| defole thy neybur,
as be reuy<n>g 'or stopyng' of hys lyȝt, yt ys nowȝt to the to bylde, to plante
no treys on thy owne crow<n>d. Oo 'the' same vyse be al god law, al god
reson yt ys vnleful to heuery man to spende ys god so that wyse werby he
395   myȝt withedraw fro hymselfe the lyȝt of grace, and deses hys neybur be hele
ensampul ȝeuy<n>g. Ffor as seyth Seynt Gregori in ys omelijs, and suche
dissoluthe aray wer leful, Crist wolde nawȝt a presyd Seyt Ione Baptyst for
ys sympul clothyng nor, spekyng of the ryche mane that was greuuslyche

turmentyd withe peynys of helle, made any menciun how he was clothyd
400 withe bys and purpur.

Thys ymage of prude was powdrud withe wylde bestus. For w<e>resoeuere
thys synne reynyt, ther the pepul ys so ylle manert and vse so prauos tacchys
that ther ys no wolfe so gredy on raueyne, so bysy abowt ys pray, as they caste
and ymagyn how be fals extorsyun redy therwhyt, ʒeue any man wolde
405 withestonde hem, to les hym, to devoyre hem as any dragynnys withe here ij
hornys. Also of bodely strenthe, that withe a lytyl sekenes ys sone withedawe,
and temporal powere, be yt offys that ys bote a sympyl herytage of lordschepe,
or of frenschep that sone fadyt and passyt awey, ouerlede and subdew al the
cuntrey abowt hem. Suche, because they holde hemsylfe so strong, so myʒty
410 that they may o no wys fol bot scorne and indynaciun of mene of Holy
Churche, and in as myche as they dure and mowe, labur and trauel to here
hyndrynge — bot ʻtoʼ here owne confusiun. Ffor treulyche, and suche myster
men had here ful seyʒt and were nowʒt ble<n>dyd withe thys cursed syn of
prid, they schuld wel wete that witheowʒte Holy Churge they had bot oo fot
415 to stond on, an in soden puy<n>t to fal.

I rede that ther was in holde tyme a worschepful kyng and wys that had vj
chyldrun. Thes kyng in hys holde age clepyt al ys chyldrun afore hym and
seyde to the heldust, ʻTake that rod that thow hast in thy hond and brek yt.ʼ
Thes chylde dede as ys fadur bad hym and brak hyt. Anon whyt |fol. 151ʳ|
420 <e>sy streche wen hys was y-broke, ys fadur bad hym take ij togedur of the
same myche and breke hem also. Thys chylde dede as he whas bode and brake
hem, bot nowrun so hesylyche as the on alone. Wen they were broke, he bad
hym eftsonys take 4 and breke hem also. Thys chylde bysyud hym to fulfyl ys
fadur byddyng, bot onnethe he myʒt breke hem withe al the myʒt he had. At
425 the last, wene they were broke he bad hym put 6 togedur and breke hem ʒyf
he myʒt. Thys chyld assayde to fulfylle ys fadere desyre, bot yt wolde nowʒt
be; he wolde nowʒt breke hem withe alle the streche he hade. ʻO thys same
wyse yt wyl fare withe ʒowe efter my deses, for ʒyf ʒe fal at dyscord and be
disseueryd in party, truly, ʒe wyl sone be broke, ʒe schul nowʒt endure. Bot
430 ʒyf ʒe be al on and holde togedur as gode chyldrun sulde do, ʒe schal be
strong ynow and haue suffycyent powere to whytstonde al ʒowre enmyse and
leue euermore in ese and gret prosperyte.ʼ

Truly, o thys same wyse as longe as the clerge and the temporal be al on as
membrys of oo body kynt togedur be god loue and charythe, so long they
435 schal mowe stonde on here fete and withestonde al maner of enmys. Bot ȝeue
temporal men of gret prwde and presumciun presume to dysmembur thys
body and part the hed fro the renaunt, triste hyt wylle, they schal nowȝt
longe indure nor stonde in prosperite, bot as o body hedles rot and wast wey.
Thys preuyth wel the wyse man Salomon, Ecclesiastici 41, seynge o thys wyse,
440 'Superbyencium filiorum peribit hereditas, et cum semine eorum assiduitas
inproperij', 'The herytage of alle prwde chylder schal perche and wast awey,
and here scor<n>ful indynaciun schal cese withe al here posteryte.' Thus,
than, sethe ȝe se wel that suche prud, suche presumciun dothe nowȝt ellus
bot makythe dyseuerynge betuxt stat and stat and ˋfor theˊ moste party
445 bryngyth a mon to hys confusiun, cunsel ys that ȝe fullyche forsake al suche
syn, worschep ȝowre moder Holy Chyrche in god loue and charithe, and
buthe as gode chyldrun oȝte to be.

I seyde the secunde tyme prin<s>palyche that chyldere wyld and wanton in
here affecciun deme that frende ys foo be dew reformynge of greus trespas
450 and gret offens. I rede in holy wret, primo Regum 14, that when Kynge Saul
had fowȝt |fol. 151ᵛ| wyth the Phylesters and put hem at flyȝt, he chargit
al ys <..>e in general that no mon schuld be so bolde to taste eny mete tyl
he had ful avengyd hym of ys enmys. Whene he folowyd the chase and
pursuyd ys enmys a gret dele of the day fastyng, ys owne sone, Ionathas,
455 nawȝtwithestondynge the general precepte of ys fadur, withe a ȝerde that he
bere in hys honde tastyd of a honycombe that he fonde lychyng in hys wey,
and so refreschyd hymsylfe. Thys Kyng Saul ys euery crystyn creature that
leuythe in thys worlde, the wyche hathe a gret host, a myȝty, ys 5 wyttus, of
suffycyent power to ouercome al ys enmys and put hem at fleȝt and they be
460 gouernt as they owȝt to be. Bot truly, than they moste be vndur a general
precept: they most haue in charge no thyng to beholde that myȝt be occaciun
of inordinat luste or dyshonest, ne here her nothynge that myȝt turne any
man to velany or repreue, and the tonge kepe silens fro al maner of vicyus
comunycaciun and speke onlyche that were profyt and edyfycaciun to
465 manys sowle. Bot truly, many men nowadays hauit a sone wonder wylde and
whanton, the wyche ys clepyt Ionathas. Ionathas ys as myche to sey thys
chyld, thys flesly lust bowyt and inclynit man now to oo syne, now another,
now to taste of the suethe hony of lechery, now of glotenye, and so makyt
hym to breke ys general precept and ȝeue hym to febul company, steryt to

470   hante tauernys and placys that be susspectyf, and so gretlyche be defamyde
withe dyshonest lyuynge. When suche pepyl be accused how they be
mysruled and offende gretlyche aȝenst the lawe of Holy Churche, ȝeue the
ordynari wolde reforme hem be dew correcciun and bryng hem into honest
lyfe, anon frende wexyt foo, ffor as mony as be ther abowȝt they hade
475   dedlyche and holde hem here moste enmys. Ȝeue any frend of her`y´s of
god wylle and of god loue wolde theche hym howe he schulde mowe to
leue al suche wantoun gouernans and be- |fol. 152ʳ| come a chyld of honest
conuersaciun, hym he holdyt bot a seyntrol and bot a ypocryȝt, and take no
hede of hys wordus. Thus, because they wyl nawȝt lere how they myȝt
480   amende here synful lyfe, when they come thys holy tyme of Lentun to
confessiun, the lacke speche and fare as dombe men. A dumbe mane as ȝe
know wyl makyt oftymes a gret noyse withe hys mowth, bot what he wolde
mene, no man knowth nor may conseyue. Trulyche, thus hyt fareth be suche
pepyl. When they cum to confessiun, they crye the prest here and seye, 'Syre,
485   I haue synnyd in the vij dedly synnes, brok the 10 comaundementis of God,
mysspendyd my 5 wyttis, and nawȝt fulfullyd the vij dedy<s> of mercy to
my powere.' Thys ys an horebul noyse and gret, bot ȝyt hys ys confessor
nere the nere what he wolde mene, nor conseyuyt ner the more ys maner of
leuynge to telle hym how and of what wyse he hathe synned, where and what
490   tyme, withe al the cyrcumstans. Be he neuer so copyus amonge hys howne
felyschepe, ȝyt hereto ys tunge fayleth hym and lackyth speche.

  Al suche be opynlyche fyguryd in the gospel of thys day, the wyche techyt
vs that anon as Cryst had caste howȝt a dele of a dombe man, he spake
reua`s´lyche that al the pepyl wondred aȝen. Thus dombe man that thus
495   was trauelt withe the deuele betak<n>ythe heuery synful creature that ys
ouertrauel withe lustus and lykyngus of ys flesche, for as longe as he ys nawȝt
ful contryt of ys synnes, bot hathe a maner of inclynacyun of inordynat lust
dwellynge withein hym, so longe he ys dumbe and hath no grace to opyn ys
here and pu<r>ge ys consyens. Bot treulyche, as sone as he hathe declyned
500   hym of thys inordinat lust be dew repentans and terys of contryciun, hys
mowthe ys opunnyd and can schryue hymsylfe opunlyche of alle thys synnys
withe alle here circumstans. Therfor, god men, buthe |fol. 152ᵛ| wele ware
that the deuele haue no fot witheinne ȝow be suche inord<in>at lust, for
trust wele, as besy as the prechure of the worde of God ys to sowt ȝowre
505   hertus be ful ope of the mercy of God and so to stere ȝow opynlyche to
schewe ȝowre lyf to ȝowre confessowre, so besy ys he on hys syde in that he

can and may to harde ʒowre hertus be dyspayre and close ʒowre mythis be
schame and fere of penans fro vocal confessyoun.

Ianuensis, *De opere quadragesimali*, 46, tellyth that ther was on a tyme a man
510 wexyd whyt the deuele browʒt to an holy lyuere to be holpe and delyuerde
of ys deses. Anon as thys holy man sawe the person that was desesede, he
coniuryd the deuele to leue hym and to telle hym ys name and what powere
he hade to wexe me<n> o thys wyse. Thys deuele anon respondyd and seyde,
'How, Y am clepud *claudens*, 'closynge', for my offys ys to harde mens hertus
515 and close that they reseyue no contrysyon for here syne. And ʒyue so be that
be god prechynge and thechynge men haue remors of conciens and be
contryt for here synnes, I haue felaw asociat to me ys clepud *os claudens*,
'closer of manys muthe', that trauelyth and laborth withe al ys powere to
withedraw men fro vocal confessiun. And ʒeue any man ouercomehyt hym
520 be grace of God and for helthe of hys sowle confitetur seipsum clene of alle
ys syn, ʒyt haue we the thryd felow clepyd *claudens marsupium*, 'the closere
of the bage', withe gode dedys alwey besy to withedawe men fro here
deuocyon and let hem to do penans and satysfaccyon of here syn.' Wherefor,
god men, sethe ʒe see the deuele ys so bysy abowʒt to dyseyue ʒow, takyth
525 hede to ʒowre oune sowle helth and lete no schame, no fere ouercome ʒowe,
both rather as yt doth in many man cause in ʒow a general suet, and suetti
owt of ʒowre synnes on heuery party. Physyg thechyt vs that ʒeue a man be
syke and suet generalyche in alle the partys of hys body, ys opyn tokyn that
he ys couerynge and habyl to be holpe, bot and thys swette be bot in syngler
530 partys of hys body, hyt ys a uery euydens that ys sykenes ys glowynge on him
and he nothynge couerynge. Trulyche, o thys same wyse thow that hart syke
gostelyche, ʒeue hyt so be that thow confitearis the generallyche when thow
comyst to confessiun of all thy synys [...].

Critical Notes and Glosses

10 oghe] 'ought'.
11 sege] 'siege'.
14–15 greuusliche beseget] 'grievously beseiged'.
15 werryng] 'warring'.
16 fyʒt] 'fight'; prechwr of] prechwr MS.
18 perlus sawtes] 'perilous assaults'.
24 freel] 'frail'.
24 konyng] 'understanding'.

29 excommunicatus] excomunicamus MS.

30 lewman] 'layman'.

32 sew of] 'follow from'; lewde suffrans] 'base tolerance'.

34 faut] 'lack'; conyng] 'understanding'.

40 wordliche] 'worldly'.

40 ouerse hom] 'read over them'.

41 quere] 'where'.

43 meche of hor] 'much of their'.

47 ware repreuet] 'were reproved'.

55 here] 'hear'.

56 tyse] 'entice'; wyt hor inward seyt] 'turn their inner vision'.

58 teme] 'theme'; fle] 'fly from'.

62 ȝowyn] 'given'.

63 qwen] 'when'; scolys] 'schools'.

63 hor] 'their'; fole] 'fool'.

66 qweþer] 'whether'; kowde] 'knew'.

66 kew] 'knew'; lere] 'learn'.

68 style, alwey heryng after] 'still, all the time listening for'.

69 deffinit and determit] 'defined and determined'.

70 kewe] 'knew'.

71 he knode] knode MS; knode] 'knew'.

72–73 ȝe can] he can MS.

73 y-leryt] 'learned'.

74 clergeal] 'scholarly'; suyng] 'following'.

76 sethe] 'says'.

77 wysyus] 'vicious'; repreue] 'reproof'.

78 paciuns] 'passions'; ȝeue] 'if'.

80 bete] bete bete MS.

85 inimici] inimicos MS.

87 delue] 'devil'; ouerlede] 'oppress'.

88 scuch su nawȝt] 'such do not follow at all'.

89 thechyng] 'teaching'; betawȝthe] 'taught'.

91 This line seems to suffer from some syntactical ellipsis; whytnyshit wylle] 'well witnesses'.

94 trale] 'thrall'; anawnter] 'in case'; funde] 'found'.

95 an] 'and'.

97 herith lawlych] 'listen humbly'; lawlych and] lawlych as MS; owȝt] *om.* MS.

102 miche] 'much'; sadlych] 'soberly'; defawthes] 'faults'.

103 here¹] 'their'.

105 despusyd] 'scorned'.

106 Philosophus] phes' MS; my suggested expansion is hesitant.

107 berythe] 'carries'.

109 here] 'ear'; myche lyche] 'much like'.

109 ȝere here] 'hear their'; in special] 'in particular'.

110 beter] 'bitter'; whreth] 'wrath'; ȝere] 'ear'.

112 aperyd] 'worsened'.

112 be here] 'by their'.
114 grochyng] 'complaining'.
114 vnderni<m>hi<n>ge] 'reproaching'; swche] 'such'.
116 I] *om.* MS.
120 withe] *om.* MS; deuoyt] 'devout'.
123 clerge] 'scholarship'.
125 vnwytty] 'witless'; seyt] 'says'; ȝeue] 'if'; wrettys] 'letters'.
129 gostelych] 'spiritual'; of al] 'although'.
133 a prechynge] 'being preached'.
135 nawȝt] naw MS; perchyd] 'pierced'; drepyng] 'dropping'.
138 and the] and the and the MS.
139 preuus] 'experiences'.
140 seth ȝe se wyle] 'since you well see'.
144 thred] 'third'; sone] 'straightway'; schetyn] 'shot through with'.
145 senne] 'sin'; tretyn of kynde] 'discuss nature'.
146 fysscheris] 'fishermen'; howyt] 'dwells'.
149 schepis] 'ships'.
150 tyke] 'thick'.
151 rumbi<n>g] 'rubbing'; cragis] 'rocks'.
154 perychit] 'perishes'; syhe] 'sigh'.
155 foul] 'full'.
156 ynowe] 'enough'.
159 lygyngis] 'desires'.
161 ȝe se] ȝe so.
161 prese] 'praise'.
167 presynge] 'pressing'.
167 nocke] 'nock'.
174 ys beynge] 'his being'.
175 lowe] 'love'.
175 defende] ? *read* offende.
176 and] 'if.
185 anschers] 'answers'.
186 craftyliche] 'artfully'.
187 clepyd] 'called'.
189 spede] 'reap the advantage'.
194 than] that MS; sawter] 'Psalter'; vnlust] 'distaste'.
199 Thw] 'Thou'; he seyth] sey MS.
202 recomende] 'recommend'; this unfinished sentence may have cued prayers before the 'prosces' (line 204) was explained.
204 prosces] 'development (of a sermon)'.
208 wholde] 'old'.
208 frende ys] frende MS.
211 chanchyng] 'changing'.
217 Pers] 'Persia'.
219 dispule] 'rob'; furdo] 'destroy'.

220 agrised] 'upset'.

220 elne apayde] 'ill pleased'.

222 of al] 'although'.

224 they] *om.* MS.

230 buthe of] buthe of of MS.

232 subduit] 'borne down'; despused] 'despised'; hae] 'has'.

234 membur] menbur MS.

235–36 wordus of vngentry other than were syttyng in here persons] 'uncivil words of a sort unsuited to their persons'.

236 than] that MS.

237 meynde] 'mind'.

239 Helyse] 'Elisha'.

241 tow] 'thou'.

244 so that] so than MS.

248 scyle] style MS; scyle] 'reasoning'.

252 of al] 'although'; scylis] stylis MS.

253 creature ys] creature and MS.

255 comynte] 'community'; owt] 'ought'; proferid] 'promoted'.

256–57 ys suggetis ... rewarde] the syntax here is not entirely clear.

257 tymes ys] tymes MS.

259 reputaciun] 'esteem'.

261 cleuit] 'inheres'.

262 charge] 'responsibility'.

265 houne] 'own'.

269 nammys] 'idols'.

272 amonge hem] amonge MS.

274 degreus ys] degreus MS; degreus] 'ranks'.

279 loȝschep] 'baseness'; be habulte] 'by ability'.

279 vrenschype] 'friendship'.

280 sclelig] 'slyly'.

280 be scleþt] 'cunning'; fenynge] 'feigning'.

282 fawȝt] 'lack'.

284 tempyl] templys MS.

285 regaly] 'royalty'; kynhode] ? *read* knyȝthode.

288 seth] *om.* MS.

293 ȝere efter] 'afterwards'.

294 leue] 'live'; hese] 'ease'.

295 owt] 'oft'.

297 the] be MS; seyth] 'since'; they] *om.* MS.

302 lere] 'learn'; <.>awys] ? 'saws'.

304 sulde] 'should'.

308 pacienlyche] 'patiently'.

308 schare] 'throne'.

310 Greu] 'Greek'.

315 settynge] 'sitting'; chare] 'throne'.

316 he] *om.* MS; temdyd] 'tempted'.

318 bout] 'happiness'.

321 haue] haue haue MS.

321 frelte] 'frailty'; thyng] 'think'.

323 rewthe] 'pity'.

330 helue] 'evil'.

332 teme] a reference to the sermon *thema*.

335 layfe] 'laity'.

338 reme] 'realm'; hathe] 'held'.

342 than] that MS; now3 thys onelyche of my worde] the syntax here is uneasy; conseyud and bewolde] 'conceive and behold'.

344 eyin] 'eyes'.

346 3eue 3e] 3eue MS; well sette] 'well disposed'.

347 maumetri] 'idolatry'.

354 husche] 'requires'.

355 iacgyt] 'jagged'; reuelyd] 'folded'.

356 not were] 'does not know where'.

360 leuþe hys holde] 'leaves off his old [colour]'.

363 vnsytty] 'unsightly'; iaper] 'jester'.

364 schappe] 'shape'; al whar now3t worth an hawe] 'everything wouldn't be worth a straw'.

366–67 nyslych] 'foolishly'; repreth] 'reproof'.

367 scorny<n>g stokys] 'laughing stocks'.

368 hanscher] 'answer'.

370 nys] 'foolish'.

372 onsuer] 'answer'; carest] careyt MS.

373 I chyl] 'I will'.

374 leue] 'permission'.

375 inpuignit] 'assailed'; scylys] 'reasons'.

377 capitulo xxvj] capitulo xxv MS.

381–82 lowlyche] 'humbly'; a ful mendys] 'a full amendment'.

383 whyngis] 'epaulettes'.

391 thu suldust] 'you should'; defole] 'hinder'.

392 reuy<n>g] 'depriving'.

393 crow<n>d] *sic* MS for grownd; be al god law] 'according to all good law'.

394 so that wyse werby] 'in a manner whereby'.

395 hele] 'wicked'.

400 bys and purpur] 'linen and purple'.

401 powdrud] 'scattered over'.

402 prauos] praues MS; the reading is problematic, and I have attempted to resolve it by assuming that the word is a macaronically introduced Latin adjective; tacchys] 'habits'.

403 on raueyne] 'ravening'.

405 les] 'injure'.

405 devoyre] 'devour'.

407 sympyl] symplil MS.

408 ouerlede] 'oppress'.

410 o no wys fol] 'in no way feel'.

411 dure and mowe] 'dare and can'; trauel] 'work'.

412–13 suche myster men] 'men of such a kind'.

413 seyȝt] 'sight'.

414 that] that withe that MS.

415 puy<n>t] 'point'.

421 myche] 'size'.

422 nowrun] 'nothing'.

424 onnethe] 'barely'.

428 deses] 'death'.

429–89 disseueryd in party] 'in part split up'.

431 haue] om. MS.

433 temporal] 'temporal estate'.

434 kynt] 'knit'.

439 Ecclesiastici 41] Ecclesiastici primo MS.

441 perche] 'perish'.

444 dyseuerynge betuxt] 'separation between'; party] partyng MS.

445 cunsel ys that] 'it is advisable that'.

449 greus] 'grievous'.

450 primo Regum 14] primo Regum 24 MS.

451 Phylesters] 'Philistines'.

452 mete] 'food'.

455 ȝerde] 'stick'.

456 lychyng] 'lying'.

459 at fleȝt] 'to flight'.

462 dyshonest] 'dishonesty'; ne] the MS.

467 bowyt] 'sways'.

468 suethe] 'sweet'.

470 be] add. placys et canc. MS.

473 ordynari] 'ordinary (in this case, ecclesiastical)'.

474 hade] 'hate'.

475 her`y´s] 'theirs'.

478 seyntrol] 'saintling (contemptuous)'.

481 the] 'they'.

485 10 comaundementis] 10 ten comaundementis MS.

488 nere the nere] 'never the nearer'.

493 dele] 'devil'; reua`s´lyche] 'grievously'.

495 trauelt withe] 'worked upon by'.

496 ouertrauel] 'oppressed'.

497 ful] ful ful MS.

499 here] 'ear'.

504 sowt] 'soften'.

507 mythis] 'mouths'.

510 wexyd] 'tormented'.

511 deses] 'disease'.

513 wexe] wexe *add.* hym *et canc.* MS.
523 let] 'hinders'.
526 suet] 'sweat'.
526–27 suetti owt] 'sweat out'; thechyt] 'teaches'.
530 glowynge] 'growing'.
531 couerynge] 'recovering'.

Apparatus fontium and Commentary

1   Estote sicut filij: Ephesians 5. 1 (the first verse of the epistle for the third Sunday in Lent, Ephesians 5. 1–9); Sextus Iulius, *De bello Cesaris*: a reference to the story of Cleonymus in Sextus Julius Frontinus, *Stratagemata*, III.VI.7 (see *The Stratagems and the Aqueducts of Rome*, ed. by Mary Belle McElwain, with trans. by Charles E. Bennett, LCL, 174 (London: Heinemann; and New York: Putnam's, 1925), pp. 224–26).

22–23 Seynt Ione Crisostoune, *De opere inperfecto*, omelia vj de laude Pauli: a reference to one of the sermons of the *Opus imperfectum* of the pseudo-Chrysostom; compare Oxford, Bodleian Library, MS Bodley 709, fol. 42ʳ cols a–b (in a sermon on the *thema Vos estis sal terre*, running between fols 42ʳ col. a–44ᵛ col. a, and numbered as homily 10 in this manuscript). How the reference to *omelia vj de laude Pauli* applies I have not been able to determine. On the *Opus imperfectum* (MS Bodley 709 belongs to what has been designated the Family 4 textual tradition), see *Opvs Imperfectvm in Matthevm: Praefatio*, ed. by Joop van Banning, CCSL, 87B (Turnhout: Brepols, 1987), here p. 304.

28–29 law canoun, xvj q. j, 'adicimus', et extra de hereticis, 'excommunicatus': a reference to canon law. See *Corpus iuris canonici*, I, 765 and I, 967 (respectively Secunda pars, Causa XVI, qu. 1, cap. 19, and Secunda pars, Causa XXIV, qu. 1, cap. 4).

36–42 This account of the assassination of Julius Caesar on the Capitoline Hill appears to depend upon Valerius Maximus (see *Valerii Maximi factorvm et dictorvm memorabilivm libri novem*, ed. by Karl Kempf (Leipzig: Teubner, 1888), p. 195, lines 19–25).

52–54 Hij sunt filij ... que recta: Isaiah 30. 9–10 (cited here with some variation).

62–73 This narrative of the fool and the deliberating clergy of Paris is said to derive from *De oculo morali*, a work commonly but spuriously attributed, as here, to Robert Grosseteste (see Samuel Harrison Thomson, *The Writings of Robert Grosseteste Bishop of Lincoln, 1235–1253* (Cambridge: Cambridge University Press, 1940; repr. New York, 1971), p. 256). Evidently popular, this narrative was used also by John Mirk in his *Manuale sacerdotis* (see Oxford, Bodleian Library, MS Bodley 549, fol. 129ᵛ).

76–78 While I have not noticed anything in Seneca that matches closely what is found here — that nothing is as bad as to be taken with the same vices that one reproves — the sentiment that words and life should correspond is certainly Senecan; see, for example, *Seneca ad Lucilium epistulae morales*, ed. by Richard M. Gummere, 3 vols, LCL, 75–77 (London: Heinemann; Cambridge, MA: Harvard University Press, 1917–25), II, 138/4–6: 'Haec sit propositi nostri summa: quod sentimus loquamur, quod loquimur sentiamus; concordet sermo cum vita.'

85 Filij sunt ... inimici: Lamentations 1. 16 (cited here with some variation).

92–94 Castigo ... efficiar: I Corinthians 9. 27.

106 While Aristotle (perhaps the *Philosophus* referred to here, but see the critical note above on this line) was known amongst other things for his work on animals, I have not found the account of of the serpent 'abanes' (lines 105–08) there, nor in other important writers on animals (for example, Pliny, Isidore, and Bartholomaeus Anglicus).

116–17 Fili ... video te esse: Acts 8. 21 and 23.

121 Et estote sicut filij: Ephesians 5. 1.

124–30 Origen super iudicium: These details about people who carry portions of Scripture about their persons for talismanic uses, even though they do not understand the meanings of the words, may ultimately derive from Origen, homily 20 *In Jesum Nave* (see PG, XII, col. 919): 'Quemadmodum igitur carmina vim quamdam habent insitam, utque imprudens aliquid a carmine accipit, qui incantatur, ea nimirum est natura sonorum carminis, sive in damnum, sive ad sanitatem corporis vel animi sui: sic velim existimes omni carmine potentiorem esse significationem nominum divinae Scripturae. Sunt enim quaedam in nobis virtutes, quarum quae meliores sunt, per haec veluti carmina, quibus cum cognate atque affines sint, aluntur, nobis non percipientibus virtutes intelligentes ea quae dicuntur, potentiores in nobis fieri ad vitae nostrae subsidium atque adjumentum.'

131–40 This story of the old man who asks the young man why he devotes himself to idleness during sermons is said to derive from the *Vitae Patrum*, but I have not been able to locate it.

183–88 This story of how the Romans propitiated their gods when the latter ceased answering is said to derive from the 'storyse of Rome', which probably intends some version of the *Gesta Romanorum*.

192–93 decreys, de consecracione, distinccio 5, 'Non mediocriter': the reference is to canon law, *De consecratione*, distinctio V, cap. 24 (*Corpus iuris canonici*, I, 1418).

199 Miserere mei ... ancille tue: Psalm 85. 16 (cited here with some variation).

215–16 This story, attributed to Valerius, *De dictis et factis memorabilibus*, seems most proximately to have been derived from sermon 43 of the *Sermones quadragesimales* of Jacobus de Voragine; compare Oxford, Bodleian Library, MS University College 109, fol. 36ᵛ, col. a, in the sermon on the *thema Accesserunt a Ierosolimis scribe et pharisei dicentes*. However, it may be that the sermon author (Legat) also checked the original source in Valerius Maximus, because the story is not immediately attributed to this authority in this manuscript of the *Sermones quadragesimales*. (The full sermon here runs from fols 35ᵛ, col. b–36ᵛ, col. a.)

242 A reference to the *Nichomachean Ethics* of Aristotle, Book IV, Chapter 3. Compare *Ethica Nichomachea, Translatio Roberti Grosseteste Lincolniensis sive 'Liber Ethicarum' B. Recensio Recognita*, ed. by René Antoine Gauthier, Aristoteles Latinus, XXVI, 1–3, Fasciculus Quartus (Leiden: Publications universitaires, 1973), p. 441/9–10: 'secundum veritatem autem bonus solus honorandus'.

250 Robert Holcot on Wisdom, Chapter 75 (compare Oxford, Bodleian Library, MS Bodley 279, fols 91ᵛ, col. a–92ᵛ, col. a; especially fol. 92ʳ, col. b).

251 Distinccio 93, 'Dominus': the reference is to canon law, Prima pars, distinctio XCIII, cap. 25 (*Corpus iuris canonici*, I, 329–30).

266–72 This account of the two temples is said to derive from St Augustine, *De civitate Dei*, Book V, Chapter 13. However, nothing at that location in the work is pertinent, and a general search of Augustine's work has yielded nothing pertinent either.

288 The reference to Origen on Leviticus is to canon law, Secunda pars, Causa VIII, qu. 1, cap. 15 (*Corpus iuris canonici*, I, 594–95).

305   Derived from Isidore's *Etymologiae*; see *Isidori Hispalensis Episcopi Etymologiarum sive originum libri XX*, ed. by W. M. Lindsay, 2 vols (Oxford: Clarendon Press, 1911; repr. 1966), II, lib. 18, cap. 2 (*De trivmphis*); PL, LXXXII, cols 641–42.

327–28   Laudabunt ... patris tui: Genesis 49. 8.

341   Lollardis: see the discussion above.

348–49   Each of these (Our Lady of Walsingham in Norfolk, St Alban, and St Thomas Becket) represents a famous pilgrimage saint. The mention of St Alban may be significant for the provenance and auspices of this sermon; see the discussion above.

358   Leviticus 11. 30.

358   camelyon: 'chameleon'; the nature of the chameleon is derived from Isidore, *Etymologiae*; see *Isidori Hispalensis Episcopi Etymologiarum sive originum libri XX*, II, lib. XVII, cap. 2 (*De bestiis*); PL, LXXXII, cols 436–37.

377   The reference to Bede is to Book III, Chapter 26 of the *Ecclesiastical History*; see *Bede's Ecclesiastical History of the English People*, ed. by Bertram Colgrave and Roger A. B. Mynors (Oxford: Clarendon Press, 1969), p. 310: 'Vnde et in magna erat ueneratione tempore illo religionis habitus, ita ut, ubicumque clericus aliqui aut monachus adueniret, gaudenter ab omnibus tamquam Dei famulus exciperetur. Etiam si in itinere pergens inueniretur, adcurrebat, et flexa ceruice uel manu signari uel ore illius se benedici gaudebant; uerbis quoque horum exhortationis diligenter auditum praebebant.'

382–83   These references are to Leviticus 19. 19 and Deuteronomy 22. 5 respectively.

389–90   Jacobus de Voragine, in a sermon on the *thema*, *Homo quidam erat diues*, tells story of a man struck by lightning and killed. Compare Oxford, Bodleian Library, MS Bodley 320, fol. 104ʳ, col. b, in the second sermon for the first Sunday after Trinity in the *Sermones dominicales* of Jacobus de Voragine (which in full is found on fols 103ᵛ, col. b–105ʳ, col. b).

396–400   This reference to a discussion in one of the homelies of St Gregory of Christ commending the simple attire of St John the Baptist, and noting the purple and rich clothing of the man tormented in hell pain, follows immediately on from the account of the lightning-struck man; compare Oxford, Bodleian Library, MS Bodley 320, fol. 104ʳ, col. b–104ᵛ, col. a. The Gregorian homiletic source is similarly unspecified there.

416–32   I have as yet found no source for this exemplum about the king who provided to his children this lesson about unity (it is not recorded in Frederic C. Tubach, *Index exemplorum*, FF Communications, 86, no. 204 (Helsinki: Suomalainen Tiedeakatemia, 1969)).

439   Ecclesiasticus 41. 9 (cited here with some variation).

440–41   Superbyencium ... inproperij] Ecclesiasticus 41. 9 (cited here with some variation).

450–57   The account of the illicit tasting of the honeycomb paraphrases that in I Samuel 14. 24–27.

492   The gospel of the day referred to here (for the third Sunday in Lent) is Luke 9. 14–28.

509–23   This account of the three devils that impede confession derives from sermon 46 on the *thema*, *Socrus autem Symonis tenebatur magnis febribus* in the *Sermones quadragesimales* of Jacobus de Voragine; compare Oxford, Bodleian Library, MS University College 109, fols 38ᵛ, col. b–39ʳ, col. a; the full sermon is found on fols 38ᵛ, col. a–39ʳ, col. b.

THE REGULAR CANONS:
TWO ANONYMOUS SERMONS
FOR LENT AND FOR EASTER

Introduction

I n this chapter we turn from examples of the preaching of the regulars to consider now two examples of sermons most probably collected under the aegis of the Canons Regular that survive in an impressive anthology assembled in the first third of the fifteenth century (though probably after 1409) and now preserved in Hereford, Cathedral Library, MS O.iii.5.[1] The manuscript, a near contemporary of MS Laud misc. 706 reviewed in the previous chapter, thus makes a chronologically appropriate point of comparison with the work of the regulars in the moment that it also provides a transition from the regulars towards the preaching efforts of members of a different wing of the Church; this wing maintained regular life in a community, but also its members often might routinely undertake the cure of souls. It was here that some of the most influential contributors to preaching in Britain and Ireland during this period were fostered, as Chapter 2 earlier indicated. The salient aspects of the composition of MS O.iii.5 were also briefly described there, but a few further observations seem appropriate in the present context.

The manuscript comprises two parts, each by a different though near contemporary scribe. The second part is a Latin *Gesta Romanorum*, a work popular

---

[1] Mynors and Thomson, *Catalogue of the Manuscripts of Hereford Cathedral Library*, p. 20, date the first item in the manuscript (the sermons) to *c.* 1400; *LSCLME*, p. 158 n. 1, considers the date to be a little later than that, a view with which I agree.

with many a medieval preacher of orthodox outlook, and its appearance here may suggest that MS O.iii.5, as well as directly serving its readers in the first part with sermons ready made, may also have been conceived more generally as a preacher's resource, one that offered a potential supply of material for the composition of sermons of his own. This second part need detain us no further, however. The first part, our present concern, comprises forty-two sermons.[2] As was already mentioned in Chapter 2, this first part probably represents the fruits gathered from a number of sermon booklets, here presented more formally and consistently in the house style of one presiding scribe.[3] Given the likely booklet nature of the scribe's exemplar(s), it follows almost as a matter of course that the content of this first part of the manuscript is likely to have a random aspect, and this is indeed what we find,[4] yet, like MS Laud misc. 706 discussed in the previous chapter, so too MS O.iii.5 has clearly identifiable thematic centres of gravity: apart from its cluster of sermons destined for either visitations (five in total) or synods (eight in total, with a ninth that merely duplicates one of the eight), several of the rest congregate within the same period of the Church year: Lent (four in total), Passiontide (two in total, and both for Palm Sunday), and Easter.[5] Easter fares especially well, for at least nine sermons are devoted to the feast and a tenth is offered for use either at Easter or at Corpus Christi.[6] Further, the duplicated synodal sermon seems also to have been intended for an Easter delivery.

---

[2] The forty-second sermon of which merely duplicates the eighth. For a list of the sermons, see *LSCLME*, pp. 461–65.

[3] Whether he may also have been the author of some of these sermons seems indeterminable. However, there are some that he cannot have authored, since they are known elsewhere and in much earlier manuscripts. See further below.

[4] Compare *LSCLME*, p. 159.

[5] Of the remainder, the bulk belongs to various times in the Temporale: one is probably for the fourth Sunday of Advent (*LSCLME*, p. 161, simply classifies it as an Advent sermon); two are for the Ascension; one is for Pentecost; one is for the fifteenth and another for the sixteenth Sunday after Trinity. These sermons are not presented in any logical order, but distributed haphazardly through the collection. A couple of sermons are from the Sanctorale: one is for St Stephen; and another is possibly for the common of a martyr (or perhaps for some dead person). Two sermons are either for funerals or for anniversaries, and two more are of indeterminable occasion.

[6] *LSCLME*, p. 462 (no. 10).

While the forty-two sermons in the O.iii.5 sermon anthology are demonstrably not all the responsibility of one single author, certain groups of them may be.[7] For example, cross-references between some of the synodal sermons suggest that common authorship for certain members of this particular group is possible,[8] and on the basis of internal references within three of the five visitation sermons, the author of these three at least is likely to have been an Augustinian canon.[9] (Indeed, it is on the basis of these Augustinian references that the case for considering MS O.iii.5 in general an Augustinian compilation rests.) Some parts of the sermon collection also appear to have been worked over by a redactor who characteristically shows his hand in his interest in canon law.[10] Whether this redactor was also the author of those sermons that cannot otherwise be attributed and that exhibit this canonistic interest is undeterminable, but he clearly had a stake in guiding the shape that the collection was taking at a stage not long before it finally cohered in its O.iii.5 form.

The Sermons and their Audiences

Like MS Laud misc. 706 in the previous chapter, so too MS O.iii.5 contains sermons catering to a variety of audiences. Some were intended for audiences of clerics, the synodal and visitation sermons just mentioned being cases in point, and others, ones found among the Temporale sermon items, seem to have been intended for preaching *ad populum*, even though they have been committed to the page chiefly in Latin.[11] This *ad populum* element is an unsurprising eventuality in a sermon collection with a likely provenance amongst the Augustinian

---

[7] Eight sermons appear in one or more other collections; see *LSCLME*, pp. 161–62.

[8] Although not all; one is a redacted version of a synodal sermon of William Rimington delivered in 1373; see *LSCLME*, pp. 161–63.

[9] Explained in detail in *LSCLME*, pp. 159–60.

[10] *LSCLME*, pp. 162–63.

[11] Certain words appear in English in both of the sermons edited below, but the circumstances of their use, being different in both, are perhaps further reasons for believing that the sermons are the work of different authors. The Lent sermon uses English: a) to render its structural parts in rhymed form; b) for lyric utterance; c) very occasionally for actual sermon prose; and d) for proverbial utterance. The Easter sermon, conversely, uses English: a) very occasionally to translate Latin expressions; and b) for certain legal terms. The use of English in the latter is less extensive than in the former, though both sermons may have been delivered or intended for delivery in English.

canons.[12] Two sermons of this popular cast have been selected for presentation below, one for Lent and the other for Easter.

Noticeable differences in the style of the organization of both suggest either that one author who had cultivated different organizational styles is at work in them, or perhaps the more likely alternative explanation, that the two sermons represent the efforts of two different authors. The first, on the *thema, Penitenciam agite* (Matthew 4. 17), announces in a rubric its general serviceability throughout the whole Lenten season, and is, of the two, much the more rigorously and systematically structured according to traditional principles of the 'modern' sermon form.[13] It operates a *divisio extra* of its *thema*, whereby a key idea suggested by the *thema* (the idea is expressed as a fourfold principal rhymed vernacular *distinctio* on the four things that move each Christian to penitence) is introduced immediately after the announcement of the theme. Out of this initial and principal fourfold classification the sermon's basic structure is then generated. The first element of the classification is pressed to yield another, secondary, fourfold rhymed vernacular distinction, each element of which is discussed in order to fill out the sermon's substance. The second element of the initial classification is treated in exactly the same way, being made to produce another, secondary, fourfold rhymed vernacular distinction with discussion of each of its four elements. The third element of the initial classification indulges this style of subdivisional composition further still, for, after repetition of the initial classification's third element, another, secondary fourfold rhymed vernacular distinction of that is introduced, and then each of the four elements of this is subjected to yet further divisions: the first element of the secondary distinction is dilated with a further fourfold distinction; the second element with another; the third with another; and lastly the fourth with a threefold distinction. As if these procedures are finally running out of steam, or as if the author's enthusiasm has been suddenly dampened by his anticipation of an audience by now grown restless, the fourth and final element of the initial classification receives very brief treatment indeed by comparison with the preceding three. This description of the sermon's complex branching structure may perhaps be most conveniently represented diagrammatically:

[12] Pastoral work seems to have been undertaken by many of them from the earliest days of the existence of their order; see John Compton Dickinson, *The Origins of the Austin Canons and their Introduction into England* (London: S.P.C.K., 1950), p. 58.

[13] See Chapter 3, p. 45 and n. 16.

Thema: Penitenciam agite

Four things move each Christian to penitence
- A) Reason
- B) Treason
- C) Dread
- D) Meed

A) Reason explained. If you wish to know what man's life is, he is
- a) a mirror
- b) a flower
- c) a tree
- d) a reeve

a) a mirror explained (including three vernacular couplets, a vernacular Signs of Death quatrain, and a six-line vernacular death lyric)

b) a flower explained (including a vernacular couplet)

c) a tree explained (including a vernacular quatrain)

d) a reeve explained

B) Treason explained. There are four kinds of perdition
- a) fair promises not lasting
- b) the devil promises freedom and binds fast
- c) the devil breaks truce in time of peace
- d) the devil slays a man lawlessly

Exemplum about a pact made with the devil

C) Dread explained. There are four kinds of dread that prompt penitence
- a) of living
- b) of dying
- c) of deeming
- d) of pining

a) Of living explained. Living is compared to four things
- i) a bird singing
- ii) a blossom springing
- iii) a fish swimming
- iv) a sun shining

:

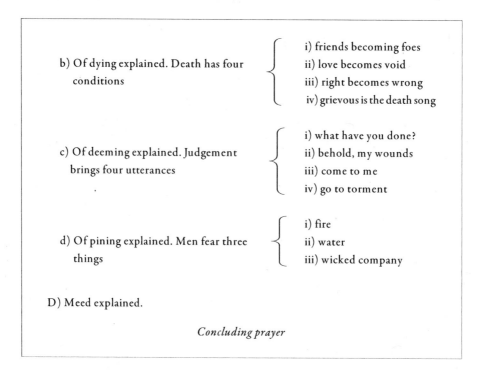

b) Of dying explained. Death has four conditions
  i) friends becoming foes
  ii) love becomes void
  iii) right becomes wrong
  iv) grievous is the death song

c) Of deeming explained. Judgement brings four utterances
  i) what have you done?
  ii) behold, my wounds
  iii) come to me
  iv) go to torment

d) Of pining explained. Men fear three things
  i) fire
  ii) water
  iii) wicked company

D) Meed explained.

Concluding prayer

The sermon's structure, thus, is artful and conspicuous. Whether in its day this aspect of its composition would have struck its audience quite as forcefully is less clear because, as previously noted, the sort of structure adopted and pursued rigorously here, the 'modern' form, ran in well-worn grooves; it may be suspected that then, as now, familiarity could work its familiar magic, rendering the familiar object routine and somewhat the less striking on that account. Nevertheless, whatever the contemporary impact of its structure, the preacher of *Penitentiam agite* has engaged with tradition diligently, and with some dexterity has made the traditional branches of the 'modern' form efficient pegs from which to hang his artfully sombre Lenten message of penitence.

To a large extent, the season would have dictated the consistently serious and reflective note that his preaching strikes. Penitence must even more than usually be the theme now, for the preacher's chief aim at this time had to be the stirring up of the penitential disposition of his audience. In responding to seasonal requirements, our preacher has especially inclined to select from penitence's rhetorical armoury one notable weapon: vernacular verse. Compared with the second (Easter) sermon that will be considered shortly, this Lenten one bristles with rhymes to help enable its message. Some are automatic in being structural, since they are summoned to help articulate the nodes of the discussion at points where *distinctiones* are introduced; the presence of others, introduced as amplifications of the preacher's matter, is far less predictable, and some seem as if they may originally have been independent entities, drafted in for his local purposes from a verse tradition already in existence outside his sermon.[14] Signs of Death motifs and other similarly gloomy reflections on man's lot form these verses' staple, yet the imaginative handling of them, along with the use of a number of other devices that help to rein in the audience's attention around themes that are often chilling,[15] show the preacher's committed understanding of his Lenten task and reveal what some of the resources that he could marshal in its service were.

At first sight, the sermon appears to offer a comprehensive account of what might either actually have been delivered from the pulpit, or have been intended for delivery, but in reality what it offers is only a very full ground plan of the sermon event. The sermons of Hugh Legat considered in the previous chapter might be contrasted in this respect: there, a much more absolute sense prevailed that the words on the page expressed a detailed record of the words of the discourse as the preacher would largely have delivered it. The anonymous author of *Penitenciam agite*, on the other hand, while he certainly went a long way towards scripting the complete performance, did not go the entire way. Notes like 'Pro processu sermonis est breuiter aduertendum [...]' (For the sermon's development it should briefly be mentioned; line 5), and more self-evidently, his injunction 'Nota vt placet' (Note [about this] as you please; line 179), reveal that there was an improvisatory element to his sermon, an element that existed beyond the page and that was prompted by cues like these. That the preacher could recommend such improvisation would also seem to testify to his confidence in his addressee's ability to draw on the resources of a mind well enough stocked with material to allow him to improvise adequately (if, indeed, the preacher was writing for others, and not simply inserting memoranda to himself). There is another injunction, however, that envisaged the addressee, whether the author himself or someone else, as having access to a library of some sort, so the onus did not need to rest solely upon

---

[14] Alternatively, of course, others might be the preacher's own compositions based on traditional lyric motifs. For further discussion of ways in which vernacular verses were used in sermons, see Chapter 9, below.

[15] In this regard note, for example, the insertion of the exemplum about the rich man fallen on hard times who made a pact with the devil (lines 101–15).

the resources of memory. 'Quere in Bruto' (Consult the Brut [Chronicle]; line 134) seems to refer the preacher to a chronicle source in which he could consult the story of King Lear and his three daughters in its full form.

Another feature of his sermon that contrasts strikingly with the work of Legat reviewed in the previous chapter is its comparative paucity of learned reference; here, apart only from citations of Scripture — and of these there are only four — there is absolutely nothing by way of overt allusion to *auctoritates* of any kind, not even to ones that are commonplace, let alone ones recherché. Instead, proofs are repeatedly drawn from everyday experience, and it may be suspected that the nature of this proof repertoire is another index of the sermon's popular pitch.[16] Its audience was not being reminded of its elevated status through being treated to an impressive array of authorities; indeed, it may have been of the kind to find such a display forbidding.

The second O.iii.5 sermon, on the theme *Alleluia*, is for the feast of Easter, and in it (Lenten) austerities are consciously set aside by the preacher in favour of catching an entirely different liturgical mood, one joyful and celebratory even to the point of indulging laughter to buoy up the occasion. *Alleluia* cites more scriptural passages than did *Penitenciam agite*. Although longer than that sermon by about a third again, its twenty-six biblical citations are proportionally rather more. It also cites a few familiar authorities (Isidore twice, Jerome once, and Valerius once). A more conspicuous difference, however, registers between the two sermons in the structure that *Alleluia* has adopted. Whereas *Penitenciam agite* followed a variety of 'modern' form, *Alleluia*, although it also uses sequences of *distinctiones* such as 'modern' form might employ, does not key them to any systematic branching structure. Consequently, its *distinctiones* are free to proliferate, and seem to accumulate associatively.[17] They collaborate with yet others which are prompted by a paraphrase of a section of the Book of Daniel (Daniel 8. 2–10), each *distinctio* group suggesting another group, as the themes that they contain ramify in the preacher's mind. A systematic account of this sermon might be expressed diagrammatically as follows, and the contrast of its structure with that of *Penitenciam agite* seen at a glance.

---

[16] One might compare the pitch of the sermon published from Oxford, Bodleian Library, MS Hatton 96, as Text D of Chapter 7, below.

[17] This associative sermon style might be compared with that sometimes adopted by the contemporary preacher John Felton in his *Sermones dominicales*; see *PPPLME*, pp. 71–74.

Thema: Alleluia

St John heard two songs, A) and B)

A) of sorrow and weeping ('Ve, ve, ve'), heard from the damned at the Last Judgement

B) of joy and laughing ('Alleluia'), heard from the saved at the Last Judgement

B) is sung with three voices
{
- a) that of a trumpet
- b) that of water
- c) that of thunder
}

a) is the voice of the tenor or burden part in music

b) is the voice of the mean or middle part in music

c) is the voice of the treble part in music

a) the voice of the trumpet/tenor part is that of clerics (some will sing 'Ve', some 'Alleluia')

b) the voice of water/the mean part is that of simple men (sometimes they will sing 'Ve', sometimes 'Alleluia')

c) the voice of thunder/the treble part is that of magnates (sometimes they will sing 'Ve', sometimes 'Alleluia')

B) 'Alleluia' is sung with three voices in four contexts
{
- i) [at victories; this element of the *distinctio* has been omitted, either by the scribe or already in his exemplar]
- ii) at marriages
- iii) at feasts
- iv) at judgements
}

A Christian must sing 'Alleluia' in these four contexts.

Paraphrase of Daniel 8. 2–10

The castle in which Daniel was is man's heart, and it is the Castle of Love.

A castle has three defences
{
- a) its leader
- b) its wall
- c) its ditch
}

In the castle of man's heart are three defences/chambers for three soldiers
{
- a) God
- b) one's neighbour
- c) one's enemy
}

a) Christ has the first chamber; he opened the chamber of his side and heart, whence flowed blood and water. Give him in return water in the form of two tears: i) of contrition for sins; ii) of compunction for Christ's suffering

b) one's neighbour has the second chamber

c) one's enemy has the third chamber

Man must not love the world more than God, nor his flesh more than his soul.

Concerning God's love, the world's love, and the flesh's love, consult the story of King Lear and his three daughters in the Brut Chronicle.

King Lear is anyone ruling the kingdom of the five senses. The three daughters are

- a) the flesh
- b) the world
- c) Christ

a) the flesh urges love of her above everything

b) the world professes great love for man

c) Christ says, I love you for yourself

a) the flesh (i.e., your wife, sons, daughters) receives you with five soldiers (i.e., with four planks and a winding sheet at your burial)

b) the world receives you with one soldier (i.e., with the single penny offered for you at your burial)

c) Christ loves you for yourself

Daniel 8. 3: 'I saw a ram with lofty horns standing on a river bank.'

The ram is the devil.

Three kinds of things in Scripture have horns

- a) rational (like Moses)
- b) irrational (like rams or oxen)
- c) inanimate (like an altar)

a) Moses was horned, his horns signifying: i) the front horn of a bishop's mitre; ii) the rear horn of a bishop's mitre

The devil is made a bishop, with a mitre whose i) front horn is pride and whose ii) rear horn is envy.

The devil married Iniquity, and begat upon her eight daughters

- a) Simony
- b) Usury
- c) Rapine
- d) Idleness
- e) Sacrilege
- f) Perjury
- g) Pomp
- h) Falseness

The devil marries each of these to eight types of men

- a) Simony to prelates
- b) Usury to townsmen and peasants
- c) Rapine to soldiers
- d) Idleness to chaplains and clerks
- e) Sacrilege to farmers
- f) Perjury to merchants
- g) Pomp to noblemen and heirs
- h) Falseness to lawyers

Noblemen are like birds of prey who live off rapine. They have on their seals: i) an ape; ii) an owl; and iii) an ass (summed up in a vernacular couplet).

- i) ape-like people adapt themselves to all men
- i) owl-like people only fight in their own nests
- iii) ass-like people are stolid

The ram is the devil, who has two horns: i) assizers; ii) pleaders.

Four things have sworn together

- a) fire
- b) water
- c) wind
- d) earth (the Truth)

- a) fire was asked where it might be found (in a flint)
- b) water was asked where it might be found (in plant roots)
- c) wind was asked where it might be found (in an aspen leaf)
- d) Truth was asked where it might be found (hold Truth fast, or else it will depart)

a) fire is greed

b) water is tribulation

c) wind is falseness

d) Truth is not found, but races away

Daniel 8. 4: 'The ram tossed its horns west, north, and south.'
'A word is but wind.'

Wind signifies the three languages of England {
    a) English
    b) Latin
    c) French

a) is spoken by simple men

b) is spoken by clerics

c) is spoken by noblemen

The devil tosses his horns of falseness against three estates of men {
    a) clerics are ignored
    b) noblemen are ignored
    c) simple men are ignored

a) if clerics preach to noblemen and simple men, these do not listen for two reasons:
    i) on account of their malice; ii) on account of shortcomings in the preacher

b) if noblemen ask clerics and simple men for subsidies, they are not willingly listened to

c) if simple men ask alms of noblemen or clerics, they may receive reproaches from noblemen, and the clerics may incline to relieve them of their money

Daniel 8. 5: 'Daniel saw a buck coming from the east, having a great horn between its eyes.'

The buck is God, having a great horn between his eyes, that is, the memory of vengeance taken before his son's Incarnation.

The buck, that is, Christ incarnate, broke up the two horns of the ram, that is, the pride and envy of the devil. The great horn of the buck was broken, that is, of vengeance.

As a result, four horns of mercy sprang up {
    a) longsuffering
    b) patience
    c) benignity
    d) goodness

The incarnate Christ was longsuffering, patient, benign and good after his Incarnation.

Seek mercy and you will find it because: i) Christ does not flee (his feet are transfixed); ii) he does not strike (his hands are outstretched); iii) he does not curse (he lowers his head to kiss); iv) he does not refuse (his heart is open in pardon).

Four horns sprang up because of four winds.

The four winds are the four ages of man: i) infancy; ii) youth; iii) middle age; iv) old age.

Daniel 8. 9: 'A horn of moderate size came out and was made great.'

The horn of moderate size is the vengeance exacted on the saved.
The horn of great size is the vengeance exacted on the damned.

Daniel 8. 10: 'He cast down some of the host of the stars and trampled them.'

Stars are clerics.

The devil was made a bishop, as said before, and bishops ordain { a) subdeacons
b) deacons
c) priests

a) his subdeacons who receive offerings are usurers, false merchants, taverners
b) his deacons who read the gospel are detractors, perjurers, false witnesses
c) his priests are such as frequent taverns (the devil's chapel) day and night

The devil-bishop has promoted his clerics, giving each a chapel, that is, a concubine.

They will be cast down at the Last Judgement and sing 'Ve, ve, ve', while the just will sing 'Alleluia'.

Concluding prayer

The turns in direction that this sermon takes would certainly have surprised its audience, because they are not anticipated in any opening statement, the sort of statement, for example, that the previous Lenten sermon provided. Part of the impact of *Alleluia* would therefore doubtless have consisted in a certain element of surprise. In escaping the gravitational structural pull of 'modern' sermon form, although having helped itself to some characteristic techniques of that form in its reliance upon *distinctiones* before getting airbourne, *Alleluia* leaves itself freer to drift at the preacher's will. While the paraphrase of Daniel 8. 2–10, introduced a little under a third of the way into the sermon (at lines 90–99), acts as a fixed point of reference to which the rest of the sermon repeatedly appeals and is recalled (these recapitulations are often heralded by the formulas 'Sequitur in auctoriate ...', or simply 'Sequitur ...', repeated with refrain-like insistence), this Old Testament visionary text readily lends itself to any number of allegorical interpretations. In addition to the liberty he can already avail of in the freer sermon form he has adopted, the preacher has additionally availed of the freedom of interpretative opportunity afforded by his visionary matter, choosing to erect his sermon around a biblical passage that he has, in essence, read as an allegory of the perennial struggle between Christ and the devil.[18] This allegorical account is embroidered with a variety of threads of social criticism and comment that sometimes reach for comically satirical and picturesque effect (as does, for example, the anti-matrimonial satire at lines 47–48, or the chestnut of the wondrous tree on which wives had a habit of hanging themselves at lines 49–56). Thus the sermon respires in a certain atmosphere of license both of form and of content.

When it occurs, the sermon's social criticism is meted out in an evenhanded way, and no one group becomes the preacher's especial bugbear, as, by contrast, the Lollards were wont to become for Hugh Legat, as was seen in the previous chapter. In the present sermon, all three estates of society are equally cited as culpable, and this broad traditional threefold paradigm for conceiving society's structure is given further definition when some of the specific component classes of the estates are listed and their sins discussed, as happens notably in the section on the eight daughters of the devil and their respective husbands (at lines 181–206).[19] What with all the social critique that absorbs the preacher's attention in *Alleluia*, little time is left for reflection on the feast of Easter itself, and in fact, this is an Easter Day sermon that is not really about Easter at all, although its touches of levity might be thought appropriate to the traditional *risus paschalis* and the Easter mood of rejoicing. Something similar may be said of the general Lenten sermon *Penitenciam agite*, where Lent itself was not the ostensible topic, although the Lenten ethos certainly was, as the preacher sought to instil the appropriate state of mind and receptive Lenten disposition in the members of his audience.

Between them, *Penitenciam agite* and *Alleluia* map a range of preaching strategies and moods as members of the Canons Regular of St Augustine were capable

---

[18] His allegorical reading need not have been original, but may have been prompted by existing exegesis.

[19] For a survey of the use of the motif of the three estates in late medieval preaching, see *PPPLME*, pp. 145–69.

of evoking and deploying them, now respectfully observing familiar protocols of 'modern' sermon form, now treating them lightly; now eliciting reflections on mortality as a prelude to penitence, now twinkling with a smile at the expense of the lot of married men. In their way, both leave the impression of having been deft in their efforts at dressing the spirit of their respective seasons within the minds of their audiences, and they support what other evidence has consistently suggested about this order within the Church, namely, that it was heedful of its long and distinguished tradition of service to preaching, and that it took that tradition very seriously.

A Sermon for Lent from Hereford, Cathedral Library, MS O.iii.5

|fol. 48ʳ, col. a|

Sermo communis pro tota Quadragesima

'Penitenciam agite', Matthei 4.

> ȝe þat singhyn bewar of gyle,
> Doth now penaunce a lyttyl qwyll.

5 Pro processu sermonis est breuiter aduertendum quod quatuor sunt que mouere debent quemlibet Christianum facere penitenciam. |fol. 48ʳ, col. b| Et sunt ista, videlicet, reson, treson, dred, and mede. Reson, for man has trespasde aȝayns his God vnkyndlych. Treson, for þe deuill is aboute to begyle vs wykydly. Dred, of payn þat is comyng. And mede, of blys þat is withouten endyng.

10 Primo dico quod primum quod debet mouere hominem facere penitenciam est reson. Si enim consideraret quantum delinquit qui peccat mortaliter, certe, reson moueret ipsum ad penitendum de peccatis suis. Ista enim causa est quare homines peccant quia se ipsos non cognoscunt. Si igitur vis scire quid est homo, ecce docebo te et dico quod

15   A man is a mirrour of soro and of wo.
    A man is somer flour <þ>at sone vill goo.
    A man is a tre of tenefull tylyng.
    And a man is a reue of ruful rekynynge.

Primo dico quod homo est a mirrour, et cetera. Si vis scire hominem, respice
20 ad eum quando venit in mundum, quando exit mundum per senectutem, et

quando de mundo transit per mortem. Et inuenies quod ipse est speculum meroris. Si enim respicis ad suum ingressum in mundum, videre potes quod talis est:

> He is a bird þat syngis of soro,
> 25 He is a best þat leuis in boro.

Et quid plus?

> Pore þ<i>ng is mans brode,
> Ffor vnmith and synne is all his gode.

Ipse enim quando ingreditur is a byrd, et cetera, quia prima nota quam cantat
30 is welaway and welawo. Ipse eciam is a best, et cetera, quia nullus secum defert cum quo iuuari potest, sed omnia habet ex mutuo, vt panem de terra, vestes de oue, et cetera. Ergo bene potest dici þat

> Pore þing is mans brode,
> Ffor vnmyth and synne is all his gude.

35 Sic inicium sue vite est speculum meroris, quia ecce tot infortuna ipsum sequitur:

> His myrthis slaket,
> His colour blaket,
> His hed aketh, |fol. 48ᵛ, col. a|
> 40 Hys body quaketh.

Et quid plus? Vere, euerimore þat hethen he wald þat his fete were colde. Si respicis quid sit post mortem, pro certo tunc scire potes quod est speculum meroris. Nam de hominibus mortuis sic solet dici:

> When þu lyes vnder þe stone,
> 45 And þi flesch is turnede to none,
> Qwhen þi here is waxin grene,
> Of þi fairnes is noȝt syne.
> Qwha so wold þan to þe go,
> He myght telle of soro and wo.

50 Et sic homo in omni tempore suo nihil aliud est quam speculum meroris.

Secundo, a man is a somer flour þat sone will go. Et comparatur bene flori propter quatuor. Nam flos, vt videmus, habet istas condiciones:

Qwen it is ȝong, it has no myht;
When it eldyt, it is fair in syght.

55 Þe fairer it is, þe les it lesteth. Vere, ita est de homine. Nam dum iuuenis
est, est impotens; quando bene creuit, pulcerrimus aspectu est. Sed quid?
Vere, quanto pulcrior est, tanto breuius durat, quia et quanto pulcrior est,
tanto senior est, et sic tanto morti propinquior. Et sic per senectutem perdit
pulcritudinem, ita quod nullus curabit de ipso. Vnde legitur, 'Dies hominis
60 tanquam flos agri; sic efflorebit.' Si vis igitur scire quid sit homo, ecce, he is
a somur flour, et cetera.

Tercio, a man is a tre of teneful tylyng. Nam quanto melius et melioribus
cibarijs pascitur et vestimentis induitur, tanto minoris valoris est, et minus
de co<m>modo faciet, for

65   If þu fest hym deliciously, þan he will sclepe;
      If þu ȝefe him defaute, þan he will wepe;
      If þu ȝefe hym pouerte, he conne do note;
      If þu make him rich, þan he will doute.

Ecce quanto maiorem solicitudinem circa ipsum facis, tanto ipsum rebelliorem
70 inuenies. Igitur si queris quid est homo, certe, he is a tre of tenefull tyllyng. |fol.
48ᵛ, col. b|

Sed quarto si vis scire quid est homo, certe, he is a reue of reufull rekynyng.
Numquid credis quod quantumcumque diues hic fueris quin, velis nolis,
alibi computabis. Sic enim dicit Apostolus, 'Oportet vos omnes manifestari
75 ante tribunal Christi vbi vnusquisque accipiet siue bonum siue malum pro
vt hic in corpore gessit'. Si ergo homo consideraret de isto compoto et quid
ipsemet est et quantus est ille quem offendit, vere reson moueret ipsum ad
penitenciam et hoc est primum verbum.

Secundo dico quod tresoun moueret ipsam tresoun iniquam diaboli, qui
80 semper solicitus est per suam maliciam homines defraudare. Quatuor enim
sunt genera perdicionis, et omnia illa in nobis diabolus exercet. Nam primum
genus perdicionis est fair beheste and euul lastyng. Secundo he hete fredam
and byndit fast. Tercio he brekis trus in tym of pes. Et quarto he sleth a man
laghles. Hec omnia diabolus facit.

85 Ipse pulcre promittit homini quando ipsum temptat ad peccandum. Sed
modo contingat quia quando penitere vellet et surgere, non eum permittit.

Secundo promittit libertatem peccantibus, quia consolacio et misericordia
Dei numquam possunt deficere. Sed nimis dure ligat assuetos ad peccata per
duo ligamina, scilicet per vericundiam et desperacionem, ita quod non modo
90 possunt confiteri et penitere.

Tercio he brekis trews in tym of pes. Trenga enim fuit accepta inter Deum
et hominem in die Parasceues pro pace perpetua, et tamen hoc non obstante,
ipse hodie trengam frangit dum homines per peccatum erga Deum erigit.

Sed quid? Vere, tandem he sles a man lawles. Homo enim rubet vt si fideliter
95 homo seruiat magistro suo, ipsum respicere deberet et remuniare et non
occidere nec flagellare. Tamen mos diaboli est quod si homo per totum
tempus |fol. 49ʳ, col. a| vite sue sibi seruierit, perpetue morti ipsum adducet.
Pro secundo quicquid ergo diabolus suggerit homini, hoc totum perdicio est,
et ideo si homo bene prospiceret quanta esset cum eo malicia et decepcio,
100 certe, tresoun moueret ipsum ad penitenciam.

Vnde pro treson diaboli nota bonam fabulam de diuite qui cum deuenisset
ad paupertatem, obuiauit ei diabolus, dicens, 'Si vis meus esse, ad omnes
honores te extollam'. Cui homo dixit, 'Libenter', et addidit homo, 'Vnum,
tamen, est quod rogo, quod ter me preminuas ante mortem.' Respondit
105 demon quod libenter fieret. Igitur hodie exaltato ad honores pristinos
vel maiores, quadam die obuiauit sibi diabolus in forma pauperis dicens,
'Domine, cogita de morte et quod multum incipis senescere'. Et homo, quasi
indignatus de verbis, pertransijt non curando. Iterum obuiauit ei diabolus in
forma alterius pauperis et dixit, 'Domine, diues es, bonum est quod pro
110 anima tua aliquid des pauperibus'. Cui ipse derisione respondens pertransijt.
Non multum post apparuit sibi diabolus ipso solo sedente dicens, 'Iam
premunio te quod sine fine morieris'. Cui homo, 'Nonne pepigi tecum
quod ter me ante mortem premunires?' Cui demon, 'Hoc feci'. Et recitauit
sibi tempora, vt supra. Ergo inquit diabolus, 'Fui. Et iam tercio veni ad te et
115 iam mecum ibis ad tormenta'. Et accepit et portauit ad infernum. Ecce,
karissimi, qualis perdicio sic certe tresoun vt predixi moueret quemlibet ad
penitenciam, et hoc est secundum verbum.

Tercio dred moueret quemlibet ad faciendum penitenciam. Est quartus timor, quorum quilibet moueret ad penitenciam: drede of leuynge; drede of

120 de- |fol. 49ʳ, col. b| yng; and drede of demyng; and dred of pynyng.

Primo, dico quod dred of leuing, quia labilis est vita hominis, quia quatuor rebus breuissimis comparatur. Comparatur enim vita hominis to a fowle syngyng, and to a blossom sprynging, and to a fysch swymyng, to a sonne schynyng.

125 Primo, comparatur to a foule synghyng. Quantumcumque auis cantat suauiter et dulcissime, si aliquis faciat sibi signum ad percuciendum, statim fugit et cantus amplius non auditur. Vere, sic est de homine. Quicumque iocundus sit, cum sibi factum fuerit signum de morte, statim de mundo anelat et cantus siue iocunditas amplius non auditur.

130 Comparatur enim vita hominis to a blossom. Videmus enim quod si hic fuerit arbor plena floribus, modicus ventus superveniens omnes flores euellit et arbor postea stat vt nvda floribus euulsis. Vere, ita homo quantumcumque habundet amicis (quos per flores intelligo), statim vt ventus sue vite et mortis priuatus est, velud vite sue floribus nudus, sine auxilio corporis in terra, et

135 forte anima in purgatorio iacebit.

Tercio, comparatur vita hominis to a fysch, et cetera. Videmus enim quod piscis natans in aqua, statim cum vmbram hominis viderit, fugit et nescitur amplius quo deuenitur. Vere, eodem modo est de vita hominis, quodque quantumcumque diues vel fortis seu pulcher fuerit, statim cum vmbra,

140 que est mors, venerit, affugit de stagno huius mundi et nescitur amplius quo deuenitur.

Sed quarto, comparatur vita hominis to þe sonne, et cetera. Videmus enim quod sol quantumcumque clarus sit, si modica interuenerit nubecula et ipse operiatur, amplius non lucet, sed omnes eius radij recedunt de terra. Vere, sic

145 est de vita hominis, quantumcumque enim iocundus sit vel clarus |fol. 49ᵛ, col. a| in genere et radians in potestate, statim cum nubicula mortis venerit et ipse coopertus fuerit terra putrida, amplius non lucebit, sed tollitur de terra memoria eius. Vnde propheta, 'Perijt memoria eorum cum sonitu', et cetera. Et sic concludo quod si aliquis de benignitate cogitaret, vere, drede of

150 leuyng ipsum moueret ad penitenciam.

Secundo, dred of deyng moueret quemlibet hominem ad faciendum penitenciam. Quando enim mortuus est, homo nescit quos amicos habet. Mirabiles enim sunt mortis condiciones, videlicet, iste:

> Deth of frendis maketh fone.
155 > Deth þer was loue maketh none.
> Deth of ryth maketh wrong.
> And rufull is þe dede songe.

Primo, deth of frendis, et cetera. Videmus enim quod illi in quibus confidebant homines in vita sua et quibus familiares extiterint, statim post mortem vix
160 vnum bonum verbum de eo dicere possunt, quantumcumque in vita fuerint optima et simplices quare homo, quia est condicio mortis þat deth of frendis, et cetera.

Secundo, deth þer vas loue, et cetera. Quantumcumque sit homo dilectus in vita sua, post mortem cito obliuiscitur. Nulli enim vel valde pauci sunt
165 amici quorum amorem mors non dissoluit. Nam quondam fuerunt duo, quorum vnus dilexit alium sicut se ipsum. Tamen post mortem vnius alius superuiuens superueniens dixit:

> 'When þu myght no lengur speke,
> And þi body is in erth reke,
170 > No force is woder þu wende,
> Bot grete hym wele at þe londis ende.'

Quia post mortem homines deligere desinunt. Nam hec est condicio mortis, þat deth þer was loue, et cetera.

Tercio, deth of ryght makis wrong. Videmus enim quod si homo |fol. 49ᵛ, col.
175 b| dum viuit haberet centum libros, statim cum mortuus fuerit, dicetur fuisse pauper si nihil habuisse; ymmo illud quod prius iuste fu<i>t suum, nunc iniuste efficitur alienum. Quare hoc? Quia est condicio mortis. Moraliter, deth of right makis, et cetera.

Quarto, rufull is þe deth song. Nota vt placet. Vere, karissimi, qui cogitataret
180 de hac morte, drede of deing moueret ipsum ad penitenciam.

Tercio, drede of demyng moueret ipsum ad penitenciam. Sed certe, multi sunt qui de isto in die non cogitant, et causa est quia nesciunt quid ibi

audituri sint. Ideo quid ibi auditurus es dicam tibi. Nam primo, 'What has
þu doyn?' Secundo, 'Lo, wondis myne'. Tercio, 'Come ȝe to me'. Quarto, 'Go
185 ȝe to pyne'.

Primum, 'What hast', et cetera. Vbi nullus erit aduocatus qui pro te
respondebit, nihil siletur, et videbitur palam in fronte tuo nisi prius de ipsis
confessus fueris, et cetera. Coram toto mundo iudex interrogabit, 'What', et
cetera.

190 Secundum verbum erit, 'Lo, wondis', et cetera. 'Ecce, tu peccator miserrime,
quod ego pro amore tuo istam carnem suscepi, triginta tres annis in angustijs
tecum fui, tandem in cruce pro te moriens, ista vulnera pertuli vt te per hec
ad faciendum penitenciam allicerem, et noluisti. Ideo lo, wondis myne qui
clamant vindictam sumi de te.'

195 Tercium verbum est 'Come ȝe to me'. Sed quomodo audituri sunt illud?
Certe, illi qui pro peccatis suis hic penitenciam fecerunt et confessi sunt.

Sed quartum verbum erit, 'Go ȝe to pyne'. 'Vos inquam peccatores qui per
confessionem et cordis contricionem peccata vestra michi aperire noluistis,
cum ego pro vobis cor meum aperiri permisi cum lancea. Ideo go ȝe to |fol.
200 50ʳ, col. a| pyne sine fine.' Hec, karissimi, erunt verba que audiet quilibet in
die iudicij. De quibus si homo bene cogitaret, credo quod drede of demyng
moueret ipsum ad penitenciam ante illum diem.

Sed quarto, dico quod drede of pynyng moueret ipsum ad penitenciam.
Dicitur enim communiter quod propter tria solent homines timere: for fire,
205 for watyr, and for wikked company. Sed pro certo, timor pene future multo
magis deberet mouere eos timere, vbi ignis est interminabilis et immensurabilis,
vbi aqua semper erit currens de dampnatorum occulis, et vbi pena erit sine
fine, gaudio, et sine solacio. Si ergo cogitaret homo de pena illa, vere, timor
of pynyng moueret eum ad penitenciam.

210 Quarto et vltimo, dico quod mede of blys, et cetera, moueret hominem ad
penitenciam. De quo mede siue blys loquitur quidam deuotus et dicit sic, 'Si
omnes masculi et femine essent scriptores velocissimi, et tota aqua recens et
salsa esset incaustum, et tota terra et firmamentum essent membrana, et
omnes arbores et rami essent penne, omnes isti cum istis non sufficerent

215 scribere modicum siue minimum gaudium'. Ex quo ergo si penitenciam
        feceris pro peccatis tuis, potes habere non solum minimum gaudium sed
        eciam maximum, et omnia ista gaudia. Racionabiliter, mede of blis schuld eg
        ye to do penaunce pro peccatis tuis. Igitur Deus det nobis sic penitere quod
        ad illud gaudium poterimus peruenire. Quod nobis concedat qui sine fine
220 viuit |fol. 50ʳ, col. b| et regnat. Amen.

Critical Notes and Glosses

2   Matthei 4] Matthei 3 MS.
3   singhyn] 'sing'.
4   qwyll] 'while'.
16   vill] 'will'.
17   teneful tylyng] 'difficult cultivation'.
18   reue of ruful rekenynge] 'reeve of grievous reckoning'.
25   best þat leuis in boro] 'beast that lives in a lair'.
27   brode] 'offspring'.
28   vnmith] 'febleness'.
38   blaket] 'grow pale'.
41   euerimore ... were colde] The anacoluthon here seems hard to resolve. The reference to cold
        feet suggests that it is still following through on the Signs of Death sentiment of the preceding
        lines, but exactly how remains unclear.
46   here] 'hair'.
48   Qwha so] 'Whoever'.
54   eldyt] 'grows old'.
56   aspectu] aspectus MS.
65   fest] 'feast'.
66   defaute] 'lack'.
67   note] 'nothing'.
68   doute] 'be fearful'.
82   hete] 'promises'.
84   laghles] 'unlawfully'.
94   sles] fles MS.
120   demyng] 'judgement'; pynyng] 'torment'.
122   comparatur[1]] *om*. MS.
154   fone] 'foes'.
156   ryth] 'right'.
157   dede songe] 'dirge'.
159   extiterint] exteterint MS.
163   vas] 'was'.
167   superuiuens superueniens] superueniens superuiuens MS.
169   reke] 'buried'.

170 No force ... wende] 'It matters not where you go to.'

172 deligere] the spelling of this word with an *e* rather than an *i* here constitutes a recognized medieval variant of *diligere*.

175 libros] libri MS.

181 demyng] deyng MS.

184 Quarto] Quinto MS.

Apparatus fontium and Commentary

2   Penitenciam agite: Matthew 4. 17.

37–40 This quatrain lyric from the Signs of Death tradition (on which see Rosemary Woolf, *The English Religious Lyric in the Middle Ages* (Oxford: Clarendon Press, 1968), pp. 67–113 and 309–55) is currently known to exist in one other version (*NIMEV*, p. 84, item 1220/2).

44–49 This six-line lyric, published here for the first time and again from the Signs of Death tradition, is not currently known to exist anywhere else.

59–60 Dies hominis ... efflorebit: Psalm 102. 15.

74–76 Oportet vos ... in corpore gessit: II Corinthians 5. 10 (cited here with some variation).

101–15 I have not noticed any close analogue to this particular story of the rich man who fell on hard times and made a pact with the devil, and no exemplum closely matching it is recorded in Tubach, *Index exemplorum*. Stories about pacts made with the devil are common enough in themselves, however.

148 Perijt ... cum sonitu: Psalm 9. 7.

153–57 See also below Chapter 9, pp. 298–300.

154–57 This quatrain lyric, published here for the first time, is not currently known to exist anywhere else. It evidently belongs within the tradition of death lyrics, although the full meaning of the final line, 'Greet him well at the land's end', remains mysterious. See further Chapter 9, pp. 298–300.

195–200 The thought behind the third and fourth utterances of Christ in this passage is much influenced by Matthew 25. 34–46.

A Sermon for Easter from Hereford, Cathedral Library, MS O.iii.5

|fol. 90ʳ, col. b|

Sermo in die Pasche

'Alleluia', Apocalypsis 19. Et ibidem scribitur quod Iohannes audiuit duos cantus cantari in celo: vnus erat of sorow and off weping, et alter of ioy et of laȝyng. Primus cantus erat 'Ve, ve', 'Wo, wo'. Vnde dicit ibidem Iohannes
5   quod audiuit vocem aquile volantis per medium celi voce magna dicentis, 'Ve, ve, ve' hominibus habitantibus in terra et diligentibus terrena plusquam

diuina. Quia tales terrenorum diligentes cantabunt in die iudicij 'Ve, ve, ve'
cum viderint iustos saluari et seipsos condempnari ignibus eternis. Cantus
eorum tunc erit dolor, id est, 'Ve', quia sicut dicitur Apocalypsis 8. Qui
10 manducabunt linguas pre dolore et maledicent parentibus qui eos genuerunt
et mulieribus que eos lactauerunt, et blasfemabunt Deum viuentem in secula
seculorum qui eos creauit. Secundus cantus erat of ioye and of laȝyng. Hec
enim magis est ad propositum in isto sacro tempore et ad loquendum et
pertractandum, et iste cantus erat 'Alleluia'. Quem quidem cantum cantabant
15 omnes sancti in signum quod omnes saluandi cantabunt 'Alleluia' in die
iudicij, cum viderint se saluatos et liberatos a penis eternis et in eterna gloria
cum Deo esse collocatos. Tunc enim laudabunt Dominum et dicent 'Alleluia'.

Istum cantum tribus vocibus et vicibus canitur. Primo, dico quod beatus
Iohannes audiuit istos 'Alleluia' cantantes tribus vocibus, scilicet voce tube,
20 voce aque, et voce tonitrui. Sic enim dicit beatus Iohannes, 'Audiui vocem
quasi tube magne, et quasi vocem aquarum multarum, et quasi vocem
magnorum tonitruum dicencium Alleluia'. Vox tube erat in loco tenorum,
id est, burdoun. |fol. 90ᵛ, col. a| Vox aque in loco medij, id est, meyn. Vox
tonitrui in loco tercio, id est, trebyll. Iste autem tres voces signant tria
25 genera hominum cantancium 'Alleluia' (scilicet clerici et presules, diuites et
principes, simplices et pauperes).

Prima vox quam audiuit beatus Iohannes fuit quasi vox tube, per quam
signa<n>tur clerici et presules et alij prelati ecclesie. Scitis enim quod ad
ministrallos pertinet portare tubas. Clerici et prelati boni sunt ministralli
30 Dei, qui portant ora sua ad predicandum verbum Dei. Nam clericis dicit
Deus per prophetam Ysaiam 58, 'Clama ne cesses, quasi tuba exalta vocem
tuam.' Dicit enim Ysodorus quod tuba canitur in festis et in bellis: in festis
pro solempnitate, in bellis pro necessitate. Sed isti clerici promoti cantant
cum tuba sua 'Alleluia' pro suis pinguibus promocionibus. Si enim promoti
35 fuerint ad ecclesiam vel prebendam centum librarum vel episcopatum,
cantabunt 'Alleluia', canticum gaudij et leticie atque risus. Sed in die iudicij,
quando exigetur ex eis compotus de receptis et de expensis, et quomodo
intrauerunt et vixerunt et rexerunt, inuenti sunt minus habentes, et quod
male expendiderunt bona ecclesie, tunc cantabunt et vlulabunt 'Ve, ve, ve',
40 qui est cantus off sorow and wepyng. Quia tunc optabunt se fuisse pastores
ouium pecorum suorum magis quam gregis Dei. Iuxta illud Ezechielis 34 de
pastoribus Israel, et cetera.

Secunda vox fuit aque que signat simplices, sicut dicitur communiter simple
men. Vnde Apocalypsis 5. Aque multe populi multi sunt. Vox ergo aquarum
45 est vox simplicium. Dicit enim Ysodorus, libro 13, capitulo 9, quod est lacus
quidam in Iudea qui in die sit ter amarus et ter dulcis. Sic simplices cantant
ter in die 'Alleluia' et ter 'Ve, ve, ve'. Cuius enim vxor moritur, cito simplex
homo maritus eius cantat 'Alleluia', canticum gaudij et risus. Sed cum peior
vxor succedit, tunc cantat 'Ve, ve, ve', canticum doloris et fletus. Narrat enim
50 Valarius quod quidam homo venit ad vicinum suum conquerens ei cum fletu
et dixit, 'Arborem habeo in orto male- |fol. 90ᵛ, col. b| dictam, in qua tres
vxores mee suspenderunt se successiue.' Cui vicinus eius ait, 'Miror te in
tantis bonis successibus, goud happis, lacrimasse. O quam gloriose arbor!
Illa liberauit te a multis dispendijs et doloribus. Rogo, da michi de illa
55 surculos tres, id est, grasses, quos feram in orto meo. Timeo quod oportebit te
surculos huius arboris mendicare, cum non poterunt inueniri.' Moralizacionem
istius quere quare. Secundo, cum simplex homo inuenerit amicum diuitem
cantat 'Alleluia'. Sed si eum perdiderit, potest cantare 'Ve, ve, ve'. Karissimi,
inuenistis diuitem amicum, id est, Christum. Caueatis ne perdatis.

60 Terciam quam audiuit beatus Iohannes fuit vox tonitruorum multorum.
Que quidam vox signat diuites et magistratus et magnates. Tonitruum
terribiliter sonat, modo superius, modo inferius. Sic diuites modo cantant
canticum leticie et risus, habentes omnia prospera, modo aduenientibus
aduersitatibus cantant 'Ve, ve, ve', canticum doloris et fletus. Nam si post
65 infortunium, id est, malam fortunam, succedit bona fortuna, vt si de
pauperibus fiant diuites, tunc cantant 'Alleluia'. Sed si post bonam fortunam
succedit mala fortuna, vt si de diuitibus fiant pauperes, tunc cantant 'Ve, ve,
ve'. Sed si fuerit quantumcumque seleratus, cantabit et dicit 'Alleluia'. Sic
pro toto mundo est vel erit de uobis: iam estis in fortuna gracie, et potestis
70 narrare de infortunio culpe et cantare 'Alleluia'.

Post ergo quod cantabant 'Alleluia' tribus vocibus in quatuor vicibus, et
hoc propter raciones quatuor que scribuntur Apocalypsis vltimo. Thema.
Dixerunt 'Alleluia' omnipotenti Deo regi qui '...' vindicat sanguinem
servorum suorum.

75 Secundo, cantabatur 'Alleluia' pro conubijs, vnde vbi supra. Audiuit Iohannes
voces dicencium 'Alleluia', quia venerunt nupcie Agni et vxor eius. Preparat
se iam in Pascha. Fuerunt nupcie filij Dei. Disponsat vero Christus vxorem,
|fol. 91ʳ, col. a| scilicet animam cuiuslibet boni Christiani.

Tercio, cantabatur 'Alleluia' pro conuiuijs. In die Pasche fecit conuiuium
80 omnibus Christianis. In quo conuiuio dedit carnem suam nobis ad edendum
et bibendum. Vnde beati sunt qui vocati ad cenam Agni vel nupciarum, vbi
thema.

Quarto, cantabatur 'Alleluia' pro iudicijs. Habetur enim vbi thema quod
Iohannes audiuit voces cantancium 'Alleluia, laus, et gloria, et virtus Deo
85 nostro, quia vera sunt et iusta iudicia eius'. Nam post factum bellum in die
Pasche, dedit Deus Pater iudicium quod Filius eius Christus iuste lucratus
est hominem de manu diaboli.

Istis quatuor modis debet Christianus cantare Christo 'Alleluia': primo pro
victorijs; secundo conubijs; et tercio pro conuiuijs; et quarto pro iudicijs.

90 Sed forte 'aduersarius noster diabolus tamquam leo rugiens querens quem
deuoret', et cetera. De primo exponi post. Visio Danielis 8, 'Videbam', inquit
Daniel, 'in castro quodam arietem vnum stantem ante palludem, habentem
cornua excelsa, ventilantibus cornibus contra occidentem, aquilonem, et
meridiem; et ircus caprarum veniebat ab oriente et non tangebat terram,
95 et habebat cornu magnum inter oculos suos cum quo comminuit duo
cornua arietis, et cum creuisset ircus, fractum est cornu magnum, et orta sunt
quatuor cornua subtus illud propter quatuor ventos. De vno ex eis egressum
est cornu vnum modicum, factum est grande contra meridiem, et contra ₁
orientem. Et eiecit de stellis et conculcauit eas.' Moraliter. Per castrum in
100 quo Daniel erat, intelligo cor hominis, et est castrum amoris. Et bene potest
cor comparari castro, quia sicut bonum castrum habet tres custodias, scilicet
ducem, murum, et foueam, illas cor hominis tres habet custodias, scilicet
tres cameras in quibus debent esse tres milites, scilicet Deus, proximus, et
inimicus.

105 Interiorem custodiam |fol. 91ʳ, col. b| huius castri, scilicet cordis, habebit
Deus. Vnde illud, 'Dilige Dominum Deum tuum ex toto corde tuo'. Christus
enim apperuit tibi cameram lateris sui et cordis quando fuit lancea
perforatus, et uide, effluxit fons in quo faces accense extinguntur miri licoris.
Dicit enim Ysodorus, libro 13, capitulo ix *Ethicarum*, quod in Egipto est
110 quidam fons in quo faces accense extinguntur, et faces extincte accenduntur.
Talis nature est fons qui decurrit de latere Christi, vbi decurrebant duo
licores, scilicet sanguis et aqua. Si igitur amor extinctus est erga Deum, pone

cor tuum in predictum fontem, cogitando de sanguine rubro qui exiuit de
latere Christi, et inflammabit cor tuum ad deligendum Christum. Cum sit
115 cor tuum inflammatum amore inordinato erga temporalia, pone cor tuum in
predictum fontem, cogitando de aqua que effluxit de corde Christi, et
extinguit illum amorem sine mora. Ecce, Christus dedit tibi sanguinem
et aquam; des sibi modicum de aqua. Vnde in euangelio Iohannis 4, quod
Christus petiuit aquam de vna muliere ad refrigerandum sitim suam, et quod
120 fecit tunc temporaliter, fac nunc spiritualiter. Quando, vero, aliqua sintilla
gracie vel aliquis instinctus Spiritus Sancti descendit in cor tuum, tunc stat
Christus ad ostium cordis et petit a te aquam, scilicet duas lacrimas: vnam,
scilicet de contricione pro peccatis, et aliam compunccionis pro Christo
iniuste paciente.

125 Secundam custodiam siue cameram cordis tui habeat proximus tuus, quia
diliges eum sicut te ipsum. Sed terciam custodiam siue cameram habebit
inimicus tuus, iuxta illud, 'Diligite inimicos vestros, beneplacite hijs qui
oderunt vos.' Et sic debetis ordinare |fol. 91ᵛ, col. a| amorem vestrum. Absit
quod homo plus diligeret mundum quam Dominum suum creatorem, et
130 carnem plusquam animam suam, quia amor mundi est falsus et periculosus,
et amor carnis est nequam et viciosus, quia vterque promittit bene et durat
male.

Est enim de amore Dei, mundi, et carnis sicut olim accidit de amore trium
filiarum regis Anglie qui vocabatur Leyr. Quere in Bruto. Moraliter. Per
135 istum regem potest intellegeri quilibet qui habet regere regnum, scilicet
quinque sensuum suorum. Per tres filias possunt intellegeri caro, mundus, et
Christus. Caro suadet vt diligat eam super omnia. Mundus dicit quod diligit
eum summe. Sed Christus dicit quantum habes siue vales tantum dilige,
et quando expulsus eris de regno, scilicet quinque sensuum tuorum, id est,
140 de vita tua, tunc experieris dileccionem istarum filiarum, scilicet trium —
carnis, mundi, et Christi. Post mortem vna filia, caro, scilicet recipiet te cum
quinque militibus. Per carnem intelligo vxorem et filios et filias, quia filij et
filie de carne tua, et vir et vxor vna caro sunt. Cum enim fueris mortuus,
vxor, filij, et filie tradent te sepulture cum quinque militibus, id est, cum
145 quatuor tabulis ad custodiam tuam, et cum vno linthiamine ad inuoluendum
te. Secunda filia que est mundus et diuicie recipiet te cum vno milite, quia
executores tui, qui habent omnia bona, offerent pro te vnum denarium in die
sepulture tue. Sed tercia filia, scilicet Christus, diligit te quantum vales. Non

potes restitueri in regno tuo et in celo nisi per Christum et bona opera tua
150 que te perducent ad regnum quod perdisti.

Sequitur, inquit Daniel in auctoritate predicta, 'Videbam arietem vnum
stantem ante palludem, habentem cornua excelsa'. Iste aries est diabolus qui
stat continue in huius mundi |fol. 91ᵛ, col. b| palude, contra nos tendens
insidias, et habet cornua excelsa. Legimus in sacra Scriptura quod tria genera
155 rerum habent cornua: racionale, et irracionale, et inanimatum. Racionale vt
Moyses, irracionale vt aries, bos, et habemus inanimatum vt altare. Legimus
virum cornutum vt Moysen. Sed numquam legimus mulierem cornutam.
Nec racionem scio quare mulieres habent cornua, nisi vt pro amasijs suis
pugnent vt arietes faciunt adinuicem frequenter, vel nunc vt prouocent
160 animas Christi sanguine redemptas facilius ad peccandum cum eis, vel nisi
vt appareant habere maiora capita quam sue simplices vicine. Caueant tales,
quia dicit Ieronimus de talibus que sic se ornant vt pulcres hominibus vel
pulcriores appariant quam sunt et ab hominibus appetentur. Quociens, inquit,
ita faciunt, peccant mortaliter. Sed Moysen legimus cornutum. Fuit enim
165 legislator, et cornua sua signabant duo cornua in mitra episcoporum, scilicet
anterius et posterius. Et ista cornua in mitra signant quod episcopi debent
scire tam nouam legem quam antiquam. Sed nota quomodo ministrallus
respondit cuidam regi Anglie de istis cornibus. Requisitus quid signant
ista duo cornua in mitra episcopi, et respondit vt predictum est. Requisitus
170 vlterius quid signant ista duo que pendunt in scapulis annexa mitre. Respondit
quod neutrum testamentum sciunt. Sed absit quod ita sit. Sed diabolus
iam factus est episcopus, et fecit sibi vnam mitram cum anteriori cornu et
posteriori cornu. Anterius est superbia, et posterius est inuidia. Superbia est
antiquius et dignius, quia facta erat in celo antequam Adam primus noster
175 parens erat creatus, et ideo cor- |fol. 92ʳ, col. a| nu expulsi erant angeli
innumerabiles de celo. Ideo expulsus erat ipsemet diabolus cum cornu suo
superbie, et sic venit in paradiso et succreuit sibi ibidem aliud cornu, scilicet
invidie, cum quo expulit Adam et Euam de isto nobilissimo loco paradisi
terrestris in hanc vallem miserie et doloris, et cum eis totam progeniem
180 eorum, et inter eos adhuc traxit et adhuc trahit moram, et inter nos ad
faciendum omne malum quod potest. Et in hac valle lacrimarum diabolus
disponsat Iniquitatem, et genuit ex ea octo filias, quarum primam maritat
octo generibus hominum. Quarum nomina sunt hec: Symonia et Vsura,
Rapina, Ocium, Sacrilegium, Periurium, Pompa, Falsitas.

185 Istas octo filias diabolus maritat istis octo generibus hominum, scilicet Symonia maritat prelatis ecclesie Dei, qui emunt et vendunt promociones ecclesiasticas sicut vaccam yel bouem. Secundam, scilicet Vsuram, maritat diuitibus burgensibus et campestribus, qui mutant bona sua sub pacto lucri et lucrandi. Terciam filiam, scilicet Rapinam, maritat multis ex hijs

190 militibus qui rapiunt bona subditorum suorum cum iniustis extorcionibus et amerciamentis. Vnde Ecclesiastici 13, 'Venacio leonis onager in heremo; sic pascua diuitum sunt pauperes'. Quartam filiam, scilicet Ocium, maritat capellanis et clericis et alijs religiosis qui nesciunt post officium Dei se occupare, nec studendo, nec legendo, nec orando, nec contemplando, nec

195 scribendo, nec libros respiciendo, sed dant se venacioni, et cetera. Quintam filiam, scilicet Sacrilegium, maritat istis agricolis qui false et male decimant Deo bona sua. Sextam filiam, scilicet Periurium, maritat istis marcatoribus qui iurant cotidie false vt carius vendant. Septimam filiam, scilicet Pompam, maritat istis generosis, heredibus, et alijs qui vellent reputari generosi et

200 nobiles, prout apparet in eorum apparatu, et cetera. Octauam filiam, scilicet Falcitatem, maritat istis aduocatis, inplendours, et assysours |fol. 92^r, col. b| qui pro pecunia de falso faciunt verum, et econtra. Et diu fuit antequam potuit maritare istam filiam propter suum turpe nomen. Ideo diabolus pater eius mutauit nomen eius et vocat Falcitatem Prudenciam. Et mutato sic

205 nomine, iam habet multos maritos et plures quam Salomon vmquam habuit concubinas, et tamen habuit trecentas. Sed que est causa quare sic multi agunt falsitatem? Vere, quia plus lucrantur falsitate quam veritate. Vnde in Psalmo, 'In quorum manibus iniquitates sunt, dextra eorum repleta est muneribus.' Propter quod Deus inprecatus talibus malediccionem suam,

210 dicens, 'Ve vobis, diuitibus', et cetera. Deus conqueritur per prophetam, 'Quare atteritis populum meum, et faciem pauperum destruitis, et rapina eorum pauperum est in domo vestra, vt multi existis.'

Generosi possunt assimilari miluo. Miluus habet istam naturam, quod viuit de rapina et insidiatur auibus domesticis, et eas rapit et siluestribus

215 numquam insidiatur. Sic multi generosi et diuites spoliant suos vicinos, id est, domesticos, sed siluestres et extraneos vel tales volunt resistere numquam vel raro, et hoc solum propter verecundiam. Vnde possent racionabiliter habere tales sculptum in sigillis suis: simea, bubonem, et asinum. Et girum scribe per ista verba,

220   'Here is none more ne lasse
    Bot an ape, an owle, and an ase.'

Sunt enim tales simie, quia similant se ritibus omnium hominum. Sunt enim
bubones, quia non audent alicubi pugnare nisi in nidis, id est, nisi in propria
villa vel domo. Sunt enim asini propter stoliditatem, quia prouerbialiter
225 dicitur, 'Put þe asse, beet þe asse — þu sall neuer of ase make gude rede
horse.' Sic enim multi de istis generosis, quantumcumque per sermones vel
increpaciones percuciuntur, numquam tamen corriguntur. Habent enim
boues et capre cornua, sicut aries. Vnde per arietem intelligitur diabolus, qui
habet duo cornua. Qui sunt assyssours et playdours. Et cum istis cornibus
230 corrumpunt et expellunt vbique. Super cornua arietis pendet frequenter
campana que est os eorum, |fol. 92ᵛ, col. a| id est, claper vel lingua. Hec
campana numquam pulsatur, nisi ad offretorium misse; offeras istis
playdours, quod sic et statim pulsabunt campanam suam. Et sic per totam
istam patriam, et sic per cornua vel campana<m>, vbique clamant contra
235 veritatem, in tantum quod veritas in valde paucis locis inuenitur.

Sed notari potest quatuor sibi inuicem coniurauerunt, scilicet ignis,
aqua, ventus, et solium (veritas). Isti quatuor mutuo sibi obuiauerunt. Ignis
requisitus vbi deberet inueniri in magna necessitate. Respondit quod in
silice. Aqua requisita, respondit quod in radice m<.>cti vel alarpi. Ventus
240 requisitus, respondit quod in folio of aspe. Veritas requisita, respondit, 'Teneatis
me firmiter dum poteritis, quia si semel recessero, vix redibo, et vbi me
inuenietis, dicere nescio vobis.' Moraliter. Per ignem intelligo cupiditatem,
quia si ignis eo quod est in auaro magis crescit, sic cupidus quanto magis
habundat in temporalibus. Ideo dico quod iste ignis cupiditatis inuenitur in
245 silice, id est, in auaro, quod est durum sic silex. Per aquam possunt intellegeri
tribulacio et angustia, quia sicut aqua crescit et decrescit, ita tribulacio et
angustia in mundo. Hec aqua inuenitur in radice m<.>cti vel alarpi, id est,
ad finem mundialium. Qui crescit et decrescit sicut aqua. Per ventum potest
intellegeri falsitas, quia sicut ventus instabilis est et mutabilis, sic multi
250 homines instabiles sunt, et cetera. Non tamen admiror de vento si verificatur,
cum ipse dominus cunctorum sic velit. Sed admiror minus vaga corda virorum,
cur tociens mutant se prohibente Deo huius venti; id est, falsitas inuenitur sub
folio aspe, id est, sub lingua adulatoris. Qui mouetur ad modum folij per
ventum ad omnem partem, sed certe, veritas nullicula inuenitur, discurrit
255 per omnia.

Sequitur in auctoritate quod aries iste ventulabat contra occidentem,
aquilonem, et meridiem. Dicitur vulgariter quod verbum non est nisi ventus.
Per istum ventum possunt intellegeri tria genera yd<i>omatum que vtuntur

in Anglia, scilicet Anglicum, Latinum, et Gallicum. Anglicum locuntur
260 simplices et pauperes; Latinum, clerici et scolares; Gallicum, isti generosi, id
est, nobiles. |fol. 92ᵛ, col. b| Et contra ista tria genera hominum diabolus
ventulat cornua sue falsitatis, in tantum quod sicut post deluuium Dominus
diuisit linguas hominum propter superbiam in edificacione turris Babilonis,
ita quod nullus intelligeret alium, isto modo propter falsitatem et malam
265 concupiscenciam et superbiam vestram diuise sunt lingue vestre, ita quod nullus
intelligit alium cum effectu. Si loquantur clerici et predicent magnatibus et
simplicibus, non audiunt eos saltem cum effectu. Et hoc potest esse propter
duplicem causam, unam propter maliciam audiencium. Multi enim sunt ita
mali quod non merentur recipere graciam vt proficiant audita. Alia racio
270 potest esse defectus predicancium, quia 'cuius vita despicitur, restat quod
eius predicacio contempnatur'. Modo vident homines quod prelati et multi
ecclesiastici, qui deberent de iure predicare contra luxuriam et auariciam et
cetera huiusmodi vicia et peccata, reputantur ita viciosi vel magis in omnibus
miserijs, fore si quis alius de populo et communiter in omni vicio, ita mali
275 sunt quod audientes eos predicare contempnunt eorum predicaciones.
Tamen sic non debent esse. Sed si communiter principes isti et magnates
locuntur clericis et simplicibus et peta<n>t ab eis subsidium pro guarra
siue pro alijs causis, pro certo, non audiunt eos libenter, quamuis propter
metum et timorem dent eis de temporalibus. Sed si simplices laici loquantur
280 principibus, magnatibus, siue prelatis et clericis alijs, vt simplices petant
elimosinam a diuitibus, post quod raptabunt fore dura verba vel in causa
duriora verba. Si autem simplices loquantur sacerdotibus, patet quod
frequenter proniores sunt operaciones ad extorquendum ab eis eorum
pecunias quam ad dandum eis salutarem medicinam, ammonicionem a
285 multo forciori. Estimo quod ex quo nolunt dare simplicibus spiritualia que
Dei sunt, non libenter dabunt eis temporalia que mundi sunt, quia omnes
tales plus diligunt mundum quam Deum.

Sequitur in auctoritate quod Daniel vidit ircum caprarum venientem ab
oriente, qui habebat cornu magnum inter oculos suos. Moraliter. |fol. 93ʳ,
290 col. a| Per ircum istum potest intellegeri Deus omnipotens, qui habebat
cornu magnum inter oculos suos, id est, memoriam vindicte quam assumpserat
ante incarnacionem Filij sui, quia ante incarnacionem ordinabatur quod
mulier adultera lapidaretur, et ita de alijs peccatis capiebat duram vindictam.
Sed post incarnacionem suam mulieri adultere dixit, 'Mulier, ego te non
295 condempnabo, sed vade et amplius noli peccare'.

Sequitur, iste hircus, id est, Christus incarnatus, comminuit duo cornua
arietis, id est, diaboli superbiam et inuidiam, per suam humilem caritatem et
dileccionem. Sed cum creuisset ircus, scilicet Christus, cum in carne fuit
manifestus, comminutum est cornu magnum, scilicet vindicte, et orta sunt
300 quatuor cornua misericordie, scilicet longanimitas, paciencia, benignitas, et
bonitas. Ecce quam longanimus erat Christus post incarnacionem. Expectat
enim peccatorem vsque ad finem vite sue. Ecce quam paciens — non capit
vindictam quamdiu homo viuit vsque ad mortem. Ecce quam benignus —
contulit enim latroni confitenti paradisum, dicens, 'Hodie mecum eris in
305 paradiso'. Ecce quam bonus — 'Pater', inquit, 'ignosce illis qui nesciunt quod
faciunt.' Ecce quatuor porte aperte sunt volentibus ingredi, nec ante diem
iudicij claudentur. Quere, igitur, peccator misericordiam et inuenies, quia a
querente non fugit Christus, quia pedes habet fixos ad exspectandum, nec
peccatorem percutit, quia manus habet extensas ad amplexandum, nec
310 maledicit, quia caput habet inclinatum ad osculandum, nec negabit se,
quia habet cor apertum ad conferrendum peccatori veniam. Et ista quatuor
cornua orta sunt propter quatuor ventos. Scitis enim quod vita hominis non
est nisi ventus. Per quatuor ventos intelliguntur quatuor etates hominis,
scilicet infancia, iuuentus, senectus, et senium. In quacumque istarum etatum
315 veneris, inuenies portam semper apertam.

Sequitur in auctoritate, 'post hec egressum est cornu modicum et factum est
grande'. Istud cornu modicum vocat vindictam modicam, quam modo sumit
de peccatoribus saluandis; que erit grandis quo ad peccatores dampnandos
|fol. 93ʳ, col. b| in die iudicij contra meridiem et contra orientem, id est,
320 contra infideles et Christianos, quia de vtroque sumet vindictam in die
iudicij.

Sequitur in auctoritate, 'et eiecit de stellis et conculcauit illas'. Per stellas
intelligo clericos et viros ecclesiasticos qui deberent lucere mundo per
exemplum bonorum operum. Dixi prius quod diabolus factus erat episcopus.
325 Solium episcopi est ordinare subdiaconos, et diaconos, et presbiteros. Officium
subdiaconi est stare iuxta episcopum in missa et recipere oblaciones. Illi enim
subdiaconi qui recipiunt oblaciones sunt vsurarij, falsi mercatores, et falsi
tabernarij, et omnes tales. Fecit enim diaconos ad legendum euangelium suum
qui non valent minorem epistolam in missali. Sed qui sunt euangeliste
330 diaboli? Certe, detractores Deo odibiles, periuri, mendaces, et falsi testes, qui
non erunt inpuniti. Ordinauit eciam sibi sacerdotes. Et qui sunt isti? Certe,

illi qui frequentant tabernas nocte et die. Que igitur capella diaboli, vbi
diabolus facit sua mirabilia talia qualia pertinent ad eum. Non dico quod
sacerdotes frequentant tabernam. Absit. Sed si fecerint, verius nunccupantur
335 sacerdotes diaboli quam Dei. Et episcopus diabolus promouit clericos de
capella sua, et dat cuilibet eorum pro ecclesia capellam, id est, concubinam,
vt dicitur communiter de istis stellis, id est, de istis clericis. Cornu vindicte
deiciet et conculcabit eos in die iudicij, quia tunc mittentur in caminum ignis
ardentis et cantabunt, 'Ve, ve, ve', canticum doloris et fletus. Iusti autem in
340 regno eterno cantabunt 'Alleluia', canticum gaudij et risus. Quod nobis
concedat Ihesus Christus, qui cum Patre et Spiritu Sancto viuit et regnat.
Amen.

Critical Notes and Glosses

4   laʒyng] 'laughing'.
7   diligentes] dilecciones MS.
11 que] qui MS.
12 laʒyng] halwyng MS.
18 canitur] *om.* MS.
23 burdoun] 'burden'.
23–24 meyn] 'mean'; id est, trebyll] id est *om.* MS; trebyll] 'treble'.
31 Ysaiam 58] Ysaiam 18 MS.
32 et] *om.* MS.
36 leticie] leticij MS.
41 pecorum] perriii' MS.
45 libro 13] libro 19 MS.
53 goud happis] 'good fortunes' (translating the preceding words *bonis successibus*).
55 grasses] 'shoots' (translating the preceding word *surculos*).
73 The word marked for insertion here is illegible.
83 Quarto] 4^{or} MS.
94 meridiem] merediem MS.
97 ventos] ventus MS.
99 conculcauit] *add.* eos et canc.
103 esse] *om.* MS.
108 extinguntur] extinguitur MS.
109 *Ethicarum*] ethenic<..>zarum MS.
135 intellegeri] the spelling of this word with a medial *e* rather than an *i* here and elsewhere
     in the sermon constitutes a recognized medieval variant of *intelligeri*.
137 vt] *om.* MS.
149 restitueri] restui MS.
150 te] *om.* MS.
150 perdisti] a contracted form of *perdidisti*.

174 facta] factum MS.
177 in] *om.* MS.
182 octo] 9 MS.
190 iniustis] inustis MS.
191 13] 5 MS; Venacio] veneracio MS.
192 scilicet Ocium] *om.* MS.
201 inplendours] 'plaintiffs'; assysours] 'jurymen'.
219 scribe] scribi MS.
221 ase] 'ass'.
225 Put] 'shove'.
225–26 gude rede horse] 'a good eager horse'.
228 arietem] aries MS.
229 assyssours] 'jurymen'; playdours] 'plaintiffs'.
231 claper] 'clapper (of a bell)'.
232 offretorium] an orthographic variant of *offertorium*; cf. Ronald Edward Latham, *Revised Medieval Latin Word-List from British and Irish Sources* (Oxford: Oxford University Press, 1965; repr. 1983), p. 321.
240 aspe] 'aspen'; in radice m <.> cti vel alarpi] (and again at line 247) the two doubtful nouns may be plant names.
243 auaro] aura MS.
266 si] *om.* MS.
283 proniores] pronicores MS.
285 dare] *om.* MS.
294 adultere] adulterij MS; dixit *om.* MS.
325 Solium] Solius MS.
327 subdiaconi] diaconi MS.

Apparatus fontium and Commentary

9   Revelation 8. 13.
20–22 Audiui ... dicencium Alleluia: Revelation 19. 6 (cited here with some variation).
21–24 The comparison of society's three estates to the three voice parts of medieval improvised polyphony is an unusual comparison, though not without parallel in other contemporary sermon literature; see, for example, the sermon for the twentieth Sunday after Trinity edited in *PPPLME*, pp. 160–67, where the comparison has been worked out with particular elaboration.
23 burdoun: 'burden', the bottom or holding part of three-part improvised polyphonic music, and often a plainsong melody. It is appropriately the part sung by the clerics.
23 meyn: 'mean', the middle part of three-part polyphonic music.
24 trebyll: 'treble', the upper part of three-part polyphonic music.
31–32 Clama ... vocem tuam: Isàiah 58. 1.
41–42 Compare Ezechiel 34. 1–31.
44 While Revelation 5 is referred to in the text, Revelation 19. 6 may be more applicable (although Revelation 5. 11–12 does refer to the voices of many angels around God's throne, the voices of the animals and the elders).

45–46 Isidore's *Etymologiae* says that the lake referred to here is 'In Troglodytis', not in Judea; see *Isidori Hispalensis Episcopi Etymologiarum sive originum libri XX*, II, lib. XIII, cap. 13 (*De diversitate aqvarvm*); PL, LXXXII, col. 483.

49–56 For a version of this popular and widely circulating story of the tree on which wives hanged themselves, compare, for example, that in the *Gesta Romanorum* (*Gesta Romanorum*, ed. by H. Oesterley (Berlin: Weidmann, 1872, repr. Hildesheim: Olms, 1963), no. 33). It is attributed in the sermon to one 'Valarius', that is, to one Valerius (possibly Valerius Maximus was being thought of, though the story is not found in his works). The change of the medial vowel in 'Valarius' from the more usual *e* to an *a* probably reflects a vocalic lowering induced by the succeeding liquid *r* consant; this particular phonological change seems attested elsewhere in this scribe's usage, as for example in line 197 below, where *marcatoribus* is found for *mercatoribus*).

84–85 Alleluia ... iudicia eius: Revelation 19. 1–2.

90–91 aduersarius noster ... deuoret: I Peter 5. 8.

91–99 Videbam ... conculcauit eas: Daniel 8. 2–10 (cited here as a paraphrase with extensive variation).

106 Dilige ... corde tuo: Mark 12. 30 (cited here with some variation).

109–10 Isidore's *Etymolgiae* says that the fountain is 'In Epiro', not in Egypt, as the sermon does; *Isidori Hispalensis Episcopi Etymologiarum sive originum libri XX*, II, lib. XIII, cap. 13 (*De diversitate aqvarvm*); PL, LXXXII, col. 483.

118 John 4. 5–29.

126 diliges ... te ipsum: cf Mark 12. 31.

127–28 Diligite ... oderunt vos: Matthew 5. 44 or Luke 6. 27 (cited here with some variation).

133–34 A Brut Chronicle reference to the well known story of King Lear and his daughters. The instruction *quere in Bruto* seems to imply that the sermon author imagined that its preacher (whether that was himself or someone else) would have access to such a chronicle. It may be that the sermon author foresaw his sermon being supported by the resources of some specific library, perhaps that of the house in which the sermon author may have been working, where such a chronicle may already have been to hand. It is interesting to compare the use of the *quere in* cross-referencing formula, for example, in the late fifteenth-century library catalogue of the Augustinian Canons of Leicester (see *The Libraries of the Augustinian Canons*, ed. by Teresa Webber and Andrew G. Watson, Corpus of British Medieval Library Catalogues, 6 (London: The British Library, 1998), p. xxiii).

151–52 Videbam ... excelsa: Daniel 8. 3.

157–61 Women's dress was a favourite topic for sermon censure. The 'horned' headdress, as here, was especially vulnerable to attack, for not only was it one of those superfluous, and highly conspicuous, personal adornments which, according to preachers, was worn in pride to incite lechery, but it also gave its wearer the appearance of an irrational animal, thus seeming to negate the reason which was held to be a distinguishing mark of humanity. For further examples of clerical attack on the headdress, see Owst, *Literature and Pulpit*, pp. 390–404. On the garment itself, particularly fashionable between the reigns of Henry IV and Henry VI, see Herbert Norris, *Costume and Fashion*, II: *Senlac to Bosworth* (London: Dent; New York, Dutton, 1924), pp. 437–44.

167–71 I have not found a source for the story of the jester's interpretation of the bishop's mitre.

191–92 Venacio leonis ... pauperes: Ecclesiastes 13. 23.

201 inplendours: 'plaintiffs' is neverthess not recorded as a substantive in MED.

208–09 In quorum manibus ... muneribus: Psalm 25. 10.

210 Ve ... diuitibus: Luke 6. 24.

211–12 Quare atteritis ... existis: Isaiah 3. 15 and 14 (cited here with some variation).

225–26 Put þe asse ... gude rede horse: the expression seems proverbial, but it is not recorded in Whiting and Whiting, *Proverbs, Sentences, and Proverbial Phrases*.

256–57 aries ... meridiem: Daniel 8. 4.

270–71 cuius vita ... contempnatur: although unattributed here, this famous maxim of St Gregory had a sturdy afterlife in medieval preaching, becoming something of a watchword; for further discussion of its origin and circulation, see *PPPLME*, p. 296.

288–89 Daniel vidit ... oculos suos: Daniel 8. 5.

294–95 Mulier ... noli peccare: John 8. 11.

296–97 comminuit duo cornua arietis: Daniel 8. 7.

304–05 Hodie ... in paradiso: Luke 23. 43.

305–06 Pater ... quod faciunt: Luke 23. 34 (cited here with some variation).

307–11 These lines on the disposition of Christ towards the sinner are much influenced by the affective tradition of Christ as lover from the Cross; compare an early instance of this tradition in one of the passages of the *Liber meditationum*, attributed to St Anselm (PL, CLVIII, col. 761). The characteristic motifs of the tradition were commonly employed in orthodox preaching (compare, for example, the appearance of the tradition in a vernacular sermon for the first Sunday of Advent in Cambridge, University Library, MS Gg.6.16, fol. 35ᵛ).

316–17 post hec ... est grande: Daniel 8. 9.

322 et eiecit ... illas] Daniel 8. 10.

THE SECULAR CANONS: A SERMON OF
THOMAS CYRCETUR FOR GOOD FRIDAY

Introduction

C orporations of secular canons staffed some of the most important
ecclesiastical establishments of Britain and Ireland in the later Middle
Ages. A clockwise sample of the cathedrals quickly establishes this point
for medieval England: beginning in the south-west with Exeter Cathedral, the
sample would include the cathedrals of Wells, Hereford, Lichfield, York, Lincoln,
London, Old Sarum (ceasing between 1220 and 1227 after the move to Salisbury),
and Salisbury.[1] In Ireland, the tally of secular cathedrals was, if anything, even
more impressive. The Irish Church could boast cathedrals run by secular canons
in Cashel, Cork, Dublin, Emly, Kildare, Kilkenny, Leighlin, Limerick, Lismore,
Tuam, and Waterford. Within this Irish circuit, the secular cathedral of St Patrick
in Dublin seems to have aspired to a place of especial eminence, for recent research
has revealed an extraordinary architectural alignment, unprecedented amongst
cathedrals in these islands, that must have been consciously devised between it and
Old Sarum. St Patrick's, Dublin, wrote in stone and architectural ground plan
what its historical record also suggests, namely, that it regarded itself as Sarum
transplanted to Ireland, 'a light to lighten the Gentiles' who lived under English
lordship on a neighbouring shore.[2] No medieval sermons delivered by the secular

---

[1] For a general study, see Kathleen Edwards, *The English Secular Cathedrals in the Middle
Ages*, 2nd edn (Manchester: Manchester University Press, 1967).

[2] See Alan J. Fletcher, 'The Liturgy and Music of the Medieval Cathedral', in *St Patrick's
Cathedral, Dublin: A History*, ed. by John Crawford and Raymond Gillespie (Dublin: Four
Courts, 2009), pp. 120–48 (p. 126).

canons of St Patrick's are known to survive, although to judge by the provision made in the late medieval cathedral accounts that sermons should be delivered at least on profile occasions like the feast of Pentecost, as well as by the notoriety that one St Patrick's preacher managed to achieve through the incendiary quality of his sermons (and whose case will be reviewed further in Chapter 8), the cathedral certainly had its share of *ad populum* preachers and took their office very seriously. Given the special relationship between St Patrick's, Dublin, and Old Sarum/Salisbury, it might almost be guessed that what went on in the one place in matters of procedure and liturgy would equate with what went on in the other,[3] and what we know of preaching in Salisbury would bear this equation out: *ad populum* sermons were delivered here too, and from the earliest years of the Salisbury foundation.[4] It is a much later example of one of these, and the man responsible for it, that will occupy this chapter.[5]

Thomas Cyrcetur and his Manuscripts

The man in question was Thomas Cyrcetur († 19 February 1453), canon of Wells (from 1426) and then of Salisbury (from 1431).[6] Born *c.* 1376, he became a fellow of Merton College, Oxford, either in 1395 or 1396, and held that post until at

---

[3] In matters of procedure and liturgy, Salisbury by the thirteenth century was establishing itself, of course, as a centre of liturgical excellence; the Sarum Use would become one of the most widely followed sets of liturgical prescription throughout both Britain and Ireland. See Nigel Morgan, 'The Introduction of the Sarum Calendar into the Dioceses of England in the Thirteenth Century', in *Thirteenth Century England: Proceedings of the Durham Conference 1999*, ed. by Michael Prestwich, Richard Britnell, and Robin Frame (Woodbridge: Boydell and Brewer, 2001), pp. 179–206.

[4] From at least as early as the time of Richard Poore (bishop of Salisbury from 27 June 1217 until 14 May 1228 when he was transferred to Durham), *ad populum* preaching had been conducted in Salisbury and the Salisbury diocese; see *Councils and Synods with Other Documents Relating to the English Church*, ed. by Frederick M. Powicke and C. R. Cheney, 2 vols (Oxford: Clarendon Press, 1964), II, 61.

[5] Indeed, there seems to have been a culture of *ad populum* preaching at the secular cathedrals generally, although the records are not extensive (see Edwards, *The English Secular Cathedrals*, p. 216). At Lincoln, for example, an *ad populum* sermon was delivered each Sunday; see *Statutes of Lincoln Cathedral*, ed. by Henry Bradshaw and Christopher Wordsworth, 2 pts in 3 vols (Cambridge: Cambridge University Press, 1892–97), I, 284–85; II, 25, 32, and 96; III, 301.

[6] The following paragraphs are much indebted to the thorough study of Ball, 'Thomas Cyrcetur'. Cyrcetur's work is omitted from *LSCLME*.

least 1401.[7] Having graduated BD by 1417, he seems to have left the university shortly afterwards for residence and parish duties at Wellow, a few miles to the south of Bath in Somerset.[8] His Wells and Salisbury canonries followed in due course, and having combined both in the 1430s, he resided alternately between the two places. Eventually in the 1440s he settled at Salisbury where he stayed for the remainder of his life.

To this day, Salisbury Cathedral preserves in its library some fourteen (possibly fifteen) manuscripts that Cyrcetur once owned, and in many of these his distinctive hand can be found copying texts either in whole or in part, or annotating others. Most of the texts copied or annotated by him were the work of other authors. However, some — and they are mainly sermons — seem to have been his own compositions. Before turning to the sermons themselves and the particular specimen of Cyrcetur's preaching chosen for edition in this chapter, this clutch of manuscripts and their content is worth considering as a group, for they afford an entrée to Cyrcetur's professional preoccupations and allow us to form some preliminary impression of where his intellectual investments lay. In short, some measure of the man can be estimated from the books that he owned. It therefore seems appropriate to begin by providing a list of them and brief summaries of their principal contents (not all the authors of the items in these manuscripts are either specified or specified correctly; I have added, or if necessary substituted, correct names where these are identifiable). Unless otherwise indicated, the contents listed below are in Latin.

Manuscripts formerly owned by Thomas Cyrcetur, now housed in Salisbury, Cathedral Library

MS 13: (i) a short tract on the observation of Sunday, and another attributed to St Bernard in praise of the psalms; (ii) a tract on prayer and on the *Pater noster*; (iii) dominical and feast day sermons; (iv) a tract attributed to St Augustine in praise of the psalms; (v) dominical and feast day sermons; (vi) a short meditation attributed to St Jerome; (vii) the tract *Speculum peccatoris* by the pseudo-Bernard; (viii) a short introduction to an exhortation on the works of mercy; (ix) a letter of St Augustine to his sick nephew; (x) a meditation of

---

[7] Emden, *A Biographical Register*, I, 531.

[8] He was also presented to the church of Sutton Veny in Wiltshire in 1421; for further details, see Ball, 'Thomas Cyrcetur', pp. 206–07.

St Anselm; (xi) a tract lamenting lost virginity; (xii) a short item concerning good and bad priests; (xiii) a tract on prayer to the saints; (xiv) a short item on man's ingratitude.

MS 36: The *Floretum*, an alphabetically arranged Wycliffite *florilegium* for preachers.[9]

MS 39: (i) Meditations of the pseudo-Bernard; (ii) the tract *Speculum sacerdotum*; (iii) treatises on the *Pater noster*, the *Ave Maria*, and the Apostles' Creed, by John Waldeby; (iv) the Middle English translation by John of Trevisa of the Gospel of Nicodemus (copied by three scribes, the last of whom was Cyrcetur).

MS 40: The *Legenda aurea* by Jacobus de Voragine.

MS 55: (i) the *De virtutibus* from the *Summa de vitiis et virtutibus* by William Peraldus; (ii) a tract by St Anselm on the Assumption; (iii) a letter by St Anselm to a monk; (iv) St Gregory's *Homiliae super evangelia*; (v) a short item concerning man's cause against God and the devil; (vi) a short item on sacraments; (vii) a short item on confession; (viii) a short item on penance; (ix) Nicholas de Lyra's postils on Proverbs.

MS 81: *Biblia sacra*.

MS 84: The *Historia scholastica* by Petrus Comestor.

MS 87: The *Secunda secundae* of the *Summa theologiae* by St Thomas Aquinas.

(?)MS 97: (i) Latin sermons; (ii) the *Expositio super orationem dominicam* by Serlo of Wilton; (iii) the *De conflictu vitiorum* by Ambrosius Autpertus; (iv) a tract on contempt for the world, *incipit: Si predicator vult invitare auditores ad mundi*; (v) the *Miracula beatae Virginis Mariae* by William of Malmesbury. MS 97 was used by Cyrcetur, but is not known certainly to have belonged to him.

---

[9] The *Floretum*, compiled between 1384 and 1396, is of uncertain authorship; see the introduction to *The Middle English Translation of the Rosarium Theologie*, ed. by Christina von Nolcken, Middle English Texts, 10 (Heidelberg: Universitätsverlag Winter, 1979); also, Anne Hudson, 'A Lollard Compilation and the Dissemination of Wycliffite Thought', in Anne Hudson, *Lollards and their Books* (London: Hambledon, 1985), pp. 13–30 (first publ. in *JTheoS*, n.s., 22 (1972), 65–81).

MS 113: (i) the *Boece* by Geoffrey Chaucer (with opening chapters of Boethius's Latin original copied by Cyrcetur into the margins); (ii) a tract *Tribulaciones cum consolacionibus earundem*; (iii) Meditations on the Passion by St Bonaventure; (iv) a 'carmen lugubre', *incipit: Omnes huius seculi dilectores in terrenis rebus.*

MS 126: The *Pupilla oculi* by John de Burgh, with several additions by Cyrcetur in English (namely, on fol. 5^r, four lines of verse on the Seven Deadly Sins and ten on the Decalogue, plus an Apostles' Creed; on fol. 5^v, eight lines of verse on the spiritual works of mercy and six on the bodily works of mercy; on fol. 198^v, the Seven Deadly Sins, each followed by a selection of their circumstances), and also by him in Latin (for example, on fol. 3^r, notes for a sermon on the Decalogue; on fol. 3^v, notes for sermons on the Virgin and on St Juliana; on fol. 5^v, an exhortation 'denuncianda laicis in die pasche'; on fol. 198^v, a form of confession).

MS 166: (i) a work by Nicolas de Byard, *incipit: Duplex est abstinentia*; (ii) *Adaptaciones omnium capitulorum in hoc libello contentorum prout competunt sabbatis dominicis et festis totius anni.*

MS 167: (i) a tract *De peccato originali* by Egidius de Columna; (ii) a *tabula* for the *Legenda aurea*; (iii) the *De doctrina theologica* by John Maudith; (iv) theological notes in Latin and English, partly in the hand of Cyrcetur. (Part of MS 167 is now extant in Oxford, Corpus Christi College, MS 222; fols 57^r–81^v of this manuscript contain a copy of the *Philobiblon* by Richard of Bury.)

MS 170: (i) the *Compendium theologice veritatis* by Hugo Ripelinus; (ii) the *De secretis nature*, a compilation from various authors on the natural world; (iii) the *De regibus et modo eorum*, a tract largely excerpted from the pseudo-Aristotelian *Secretum secretorum*.

MS 174: (i) a collection of Latin Temporale and Sanctorale sermons (the latter both for the *commune* and *proprium sanctorum*), including some sermons for special occasions (for example, for a synod, for a church dedication), and with a list of contents in what may be Cyrcetur's more formal hand (fol. 340^r); (ii) an extract of the *Speculum christiani* (on fols 346^r–48^r) in Cyrcetur's hand.[10]

[10] Noted by Ball, 'Thomas Cyrcetur', p. 218 n. 84.

In addition to places in the manuscripts noted above where Cyrcetur's more substantial additions are to be found, all contain marginal annotations by him.[11] These demonstrate not merely that he read the texts annotated, but also indicate the nature and level of his engagement with their content. The manuscripts constitute a coherent ensemble, one that may in general be characterized as ideally suited to the needs of the medieval preacher and priest with cure of souls. Indeed, comparable bibliographical preference and coherence can be noticed amongst the book collections of some of Cyrcetur's contemporaries who were similarly shouldering pastoral duties. For example, when in 1445 Roger Celle, secular chaplain of the parish chapel of St Andrew adjoining the abbey of St Albans, died, he left to another of the abbey's secular chaplains a large book collection. Much of the content of Celle's collection either overlaps directly with Cyrcetur's, or overlaps in terms of the nature of the texts owned by both men. Thus like Cyrcetur, Celle also had a copy of the meditations of the pseudo-Bernard and of the *Historia scholastica* of Peter Comestor; equally, he had a *Speculum curatorum*, a work whose title necessarily implies that it was directed at curates, as Cyrcetur's *Speculum sacerdotum* may similarly have been.[12] Where Cyrcetur's collection appears to have been different from Celle's is in terms of its greater range and depth of theological and pastoral material, something to be expected from a man of university training and whose career path had, moreover, connected him with secular canonical establishments known for their commitment to learning and its pastoral application.[13] Among the early and late Fathers he owned copies of works by Jerome, Augustine, Gregory, and Anselm; among the later theologians he owned copies of works by Aquinas (that part, incidentally, of the *Summa theologiae* most suited to pastoral use), by Hugo Ripelinus, and by John Maudith. Moral theology and catechetical exegesis are represented respectively by William Peraldus and John Waldeby. Scripture and scriptural commentary are present in Cyrcetur's library, as are hagiographical materials of various sorts, including the

---

[11] Indeed and as indicated, some of those texts, either in whole or in part, were also copied by Cyrcetur.

[12] Hertford Record Office, ASA/AR1 (Stoneham Register, 1415–70), fol. 50ᵛ. Celle also had a copy of the *Horologium divinae sapientiae* of Henry Suso, and of the *Stimulus amoris* (probably the pseudo-Bonaventuran work of that name), along with *plures tractatus perutiles valde*.

[13] Wells Cathedral was notable in this regard, for example. Here, Cyrcetur made the acquaintance of Canon John Orum, a man whose unpublished theological lectures in Wells still survive (in Oxford, Bodleian Library, MS Bodley 859, fols 261ʳ–276ᵛ); on Orum, see further Ball, 'Thomas Cyrcetur', pp. 209–10.

Legenda aurea by Jacobus de Voragine and William of Malmesbury's collection of Marian miracles. A number of meditations attributed to different authors may be found, and a significant number of works with a pastoral application — items on penance and confession, for example, or the *Pupilla occuli* of John de Burgh. Chaucer's *Boece* makes an interesting addition, and Cyrcetur's careful attention to it is witnessed in his marginal annotation of its opening chapters with the Boethian Latin original. But the epicentre of all this collection seems nevertheless to consist in sermons and sermon aids, the latter being represented by Nicholas de Byard's *distinctio* collection and also by the *Floretum*. Incidentally, the appearance of the latter, a Wycliffite preacher's *florilegium*, should not come as too much of a surprise. The *Floretum* was to a large extent capable of being turned to orthodox purposes, containing as it did a majority of extracts from sources which were perfectly respectable and without the least taint of heresy. These could be used profitably by the orthodox preacher once such quotations as derived from the reprobated *doctor evangelicus* had been identified and quarantined.

It is furthermore clear that Cyrcetur personally regarded his library as being well adapted to a preacher's needs. His *ex libris* inscriptions, attached to various of the manuscripts in his possession, provide proof of this. That in Salisbury, Cathedral Library, MS 39, fol. 147^r, is one case in point:

> Liber Thome Cyrcetre, post cuius decessum liberetur alicui deuoto sacerdoti qui vtitur predicare Dei verbum, vt celebret et oret pro anima eius et pro quibus tenetur et omnibus fidelibus, et cetera, continue dum liber durauerit; semper disponatur post obitum ocupantis vt ocupans oret pro vltimo possessore et possessoribus precedentibus, nec non et omnibus fidelibus viuis et defunctis.
>
> (A book of Thomas Cyrcetur, after whose death let it pass to some devout priest to use for preaching God's word, to celebrate [Mass] and to pray for his [Cyrcetur's] soul and for [the souls of] those he is obliged [to pray for] and for all the faithful, et cetera, continually as long as the book shall last; let it always be the arrangement that after its owner's death the [new] owner will pray for its previous owner and for antecedent owners, as well as for all the faithful living and dead.)

Another of his *ex libris* inscriptions, in MS 174, fol. 342^v, is couched in similar formulas (though attempts to efface this inscription render it obscure in places):

> Liber Thome Cyrcetre, post cuius decessum liberetur alicui seculari clerico sacerdoti et predicatori, vt celebret et oret pro anima eius et pro precedentibus possessoribus ac pro quibus tenentur et omnibus fidelibus, et cetera, continue dum liber durauerit; semper disponatur post obitum [...]
>
> (A book of Thomas Cyrcetur, after whose death let it pass to some secular priest and preacher, to celebrate [Mass] and to pray for his [Cyrcetur's] soul and for [the souls of] antecedent owners and for [the souls of] those he is obliged [to pray for] and for all the

faithful, et cetera, continually as long as the book shall last; let it always be the arrangement that after [its owner's] death [...])

Here, the 'devout priest' envisaged as the beneficiary in the *ex libris* of MS 39 is
exchanged specifically for a 'secular priest and preacher'. Cyrcetur had different
plans for certain other of his books — MS 55, for example, was donated on the
condition that it 'be chained in the [cathedral's] new library' (cathenandus in
libraria noua).[14] In general, however, future generations of preachers were what
he had in mind.

Cyrcetur's Preaching and his Sermon for Good Friday

From these more oblique testimonies to Cyrcetur's provision and regard for
preaching, we may now turn directly to the written evidences of his own preaching activity. These suggest that this was far more extensive than we are now
permitted to appreciate, and that it stretched over many years. Some of his
earliest sermons to the laity were probably delivered before he was installed in his
canonries and while still vicar of Wellow: Wellow's parish church was dedicated
to St Juliana, and at least one *thema* and a set of notes for a sermon on St Juliana
survive in the Cyrcetur corpus.[15] He listed the *themata* of several sermons in some
eight manuscript collections that he owned, although only one of these collections
is now extant (Salisbury, Cathedral Library, MS 174, in which the Good Friday
sermon edited below may be found).[16] In addition to these eight manuscript
books, Cyrcetur owned a large number of unbound *quaterni* of sermons written
on paper. This is clear from a note in MS 174, fol. v[r], as was demonstrated in
Chapter 2.[17] One forms the impression of a man whose personal library, already
heavy as has been seen with volumes that preachers would value, comprised a
substantial sub-library of sermons proper, some bound but many others not, and
who took care that compositions by their nature so easily prone to scatter as so
many *membra disiecta*, especially those preserved in unbound form, should be
corralled together, conveniently co-ordinated, and indexed (at least to the extent

[14] The new library referred to here was probably that which the Salisbury chapter decided on
15 January 1445 to have built; see further Ball, 'Thomas Cyrcetur', pp. 208–09.

[15] Salisbury, Cathedral Library, MS 126, fol. 3[v].

[16] One of the missing collections included *quaterni* formerly owned by one Richard Stabul,
a former colleague of Cyrcetur's at Merton; see Ball, 'Thomas Cyrcetur', p. 220.

[17] See above, pp. 26–27.

of having their *themata* listed in one central point of reference). Cyrcetur evidently brought the advantages of a tidy, academically trained mind to this corner of his ministry, and the fact that he took the trouble that he evidently did is a further implicit expression of his esteem for preaching in the clerical scale of things, an esteem which, as has already been noted, was also expressed explicitly in the inscriptions of ownership that he added to a number of the manuscripts in his possession.

Today, out of all of these indications of a personal library well stocked with preaching matter, only three Salisbury Cathedral manuscripts containing sermons some of which appear to have been Cyrcetur's own work survive: MSS 126, 170, and 174. In the main, his sermons in these manuscripts exist as notes. The most rudimentary among them consist of skeleton sermon plans or outlines.[18] (Schemata of this sort may be found across a range of late medieval sermon manuscripts and are, of course, not restricted to the secular canons.)[19] Then there are a number of other sermons cast in *distinctio* form that occupy a page or two.[20] Just a few are more substantially developed as fully-fledged sermons, although even these may not be quite entire: Cyrcetur's Good Friday sermon given below is such a case, for it suddenly stops short with an instruction *Nota alibi*, presumably Cyrcetur's personal memorandum telling him to find the rest of the sermon in some other place that he was familiar with and to which he could turn as and when needed. Nevertheless, for all that there is something inchoate about the way in which his sermon corpus has been recorded, by that same token it brings us closer to a medieval preacher and his processes of sermon composition than can any of the sermons preserved in a more complete state that previous chapters of this book have surveyed, or indeed, than can any to be visited in the chapters that lie ahead. The reason for this is that Cyrcetur's sermons are holographs. We can therefore more nearly track his literary activity as he worked out his sermon drafts or crafted his more finished performances.[21]

---

[18] For example MS 126, fol. 3ᵛ or MS 174, fol. 349ʳ⁻ᵛ.

[19] To take but one example, the original label of Worcester, Cathedral Library, MS Q.53, reads: 'in isto volumine continentur themata cum eorundem inductionibus et divisionibus [...] pro toto anno tam pro dominicis et aliis diebus temporalibus quam pro festifitatibus sanctorum'. See Greatrex, 'Benedictine Sermons', p. 275 n. 79.

[20] For example MS 174, fols 305ᵛ–311ᵛ or fols 344ʳ–345ᵛ.

[21] Insights of this order are largely unavailable from the other sermon manuscripts so far considered, or the ones to be considered in later chapters, since all of these seem to have been not holographs but scribal copies. The only sermon text that could conceivably stand outside this

Like Hugh Legat, whose preaching was considered earlier in Chapter 4, Cyrcetur, also an Oxford man and Legat's close contemporary, belonged to the second generation of anti-Wycliffite preachers. Yet, while consciousness of the Lollard heresy provoked Cyrcetur to respond on more than one occasion, his response, as far as the record permits us to determine, was neither as persistent as Legat's nor as detailed as Legat's was sometimes capable of being.[22] By contrast, Cyrcetur's characteristic sermon concerns seem to have centred upon the nature of the pastoral office and the duties of the good pastor, as well as upon human suffering and affliction in general.[23] While typically his, these concerns were of course also traditional, and so it becomes difficult to estimate the extent to which his investment in them may or may not have been prompted by private personal preference. However, in one characteristic area of his approach to preaching, his investment does seem more suggestive in this regard: he appears to have taken sides over an issue that is likely to have been exercising orthodoxy at the time, the question of how proper preaching should be constituted. His adopted position here would necessarily have set him at odds with Legat's approach and with that of other members of the contemporary Benedictine 'school' of preaching. Marginal annotations in Cyrcetur's hand in MS 167 (its content was summarized above) proclaim in a number of places the supremacy of Scripture, remarking Scripture's superiority, for example, to 'ineptis fabulis poeticis et aliis secularibus scienciis'.[24] Cyrcetur, then, would evidently have had some reservation about the terms in which the preaching efforts of Legat and Legat's confrères were

---

generalization is that edited in Chapter 3 from Oxford, Bodleian Library, MS Bodley 26, but this is by no means certain. The sermons edited in Chapters 4 and 5 (respectively from Oxford, Bodleian Library, MS Laud misc. 706, and Hereford, Cathedral Library, MS O.iii.5) are highly unlikely to have been authorial holographs, because the incidence of textual error in them seems too high to have been the responsibility of an author; the errors suggest scribal rather than authorial incomprehension. Equally, none of the sermons edited in Chapter 7 was a holograph (perhaps only with the exception of the sermon edited as Text D, and even that is most unlikely).

[22] Cyrcetur's anti-heretical or specifically anti-Wycliffite remarks may be found in Salisbury, Cathedral Library MS 174, fol. 349r: 'triplex est fructus hereticorum [...] quomodo heretici sunt lupi et quomodo cognoscuntur ab agnis et ouibus per tria'; in a sermon for the eighth Sunday after Trinity, appropriately enough on the *thema*, *Attendite a falsis prophetis* (Matthew 7. 15); and also on fol. 357v: 'filij diaboli sunt omnes superbi [...] Item filij diaboli sunt omnes heretici et lolrardi [*sic*] et omnes infideles' (in a series of notes).

[23] As Ball, 'Thomas Cyrcetur', p. 218, has pertinently noted.

[24] Salisbury, Cathedral Library, MS 167, fol. 51r.

cast; at the very least, it seems that Cyrcetur would not have chosen to follow these men down their particular 'classicizing' path. In view of his stated disregard for 'poetic fables and other secular sciences', one wonders what he would have made of many of the other characteristic products of members of Legat's St Albans 'school' — of John Wethamstede's *Pabularium poetarum*, for instance, a reader's companion to the fables of the classical poets, or of Thomas Walsingham's *Prohemia poetarum*, an *accessus* to the authors and texts set for the curriculum of the Latin schoolroom.[25] This Benedictine 'classicizing', and an avidity for the literary products of non-Christian culture, had also seeped into the order's preaching, as they had also and perhaps more famously into the preaching of some of the friars of a century or more earlier. The friars had set precedents, had the Benedictines wished to appeal to them.[26] In Cyrcetur, then, we see an alternative position staked out within orthodoxy itself over what constituted appropriate *materia predicabilis*; distrust of 'poetic fables and secular sciences' in sermons was evidently not confined exclusively to preachers of the radical reformist party, although, to be sure, such distrust was their hallmark. It seems that orthodoxy at this time harboured a range of views on what the ingredients of acceptable preaching might be. Furthermore, Cyrcetur's statement of principle regarding the supremacy of Scripture is something borne out by the practice of his surviving sermons and sermon notes. Here we find for the larger part a Bible-based orientation and simplicity, where concessions to a more popular taste, whenever they occur, seem mainly to be cast in terms of appeals to everyday experience, rather than to imposingly learned authorities, in order to prove points of the argument.[27] Exempla, by contrast, whose nature it commonly was to favour fictions, have been avoided.[28]

---

[25] For these works of Wethamstede and Walsingham, see, respectively, *A Handlist of the Latin Writers of Great Britain and Ireland*, pp. 344 and 690.

[26] Beryl Smalley, *English Friars and Antiquity in the Early Fourteenth Century* (Oxford: Blackwell, 1960). Indeed, there is a possibility that Thomas Walsingham had read work by John Ridevall, one of the friars of the 'classicizing' school; see Clark, *A Monastic Renaissance*, pp. 182 and 196.

[27] Cyrcetur's Ash Wednesday sermon (MS 174, fol. 340ᵛ) is characteristic: *Karissimi, vt docet experiencia [...]*.

[28] At least in terms of what the extant corpus permits us to determine. While Cyrcetur, to be sure, refers to proofs from experience as exempla (at least three are adduced in his Ash Wednesday sermon on fol. 340ᵛ), Cyrcetur's exempla are nevertheless appeals to common experience, not fable narratives of the sort that the exemplum is most usually associated with.

Cyrcetur's Good Friday sermon on the *thema, Egressus Ihesus cum discipulis suis trans torrentem Cedron* (John 18. 1) runs true to Cyrcetur's form in these respects. It may have been preached before a mixed congregation of men and women who had gathered 'cum magna deuocione vt audietis passionem Saluatoris nostri' (lines 7–8), perhaps in Salisbury Cathedral itself, or wherever else Cyrcetur faced such a congregation.[29] The sermon's pitch, in keeping with the liturgical moment, is emotional — should he preach or should he weep, he wonders (lines 2–3) — and it captures some of the typical moods and characteristic techniques for their projection inherited from the tradition of affective piety.[30] At the same time, the sermon's emotional charge is contained within the rehearsal of a Passion narrative methodically synthesized by Cyrcetur from the accounts that he found in the four Gospels. His self-effacement about the way he put his sermon together ('modo meo incomposito et rudi'; lines 28–29) may perhaps also be taken to imply that he did his comparative collation of the Gospels himself, without the assistance of some work, for example, as the *Unum ex quatuor* of Zacharias Chrysopolitanus, the *Concordia quatuor evangelistarum* of Clement of Llanthony, or some other such like biblical concordance. Certainly, he owned a Bible manuscript (Salisbury, Cathedral Library, MS 81) in which the primary sources for his collation were all readily to hand.

Given that *Egressus Ihesus* stops short with a simple *Nota alibi* instruction to its reader, it is finally impossible to gauge the full range of this sermon or the sources on which it drew. Nevertheless, the signs are that it delivered neither more nor less than Cyrcetur's Passion-narrative synthesis, one whose length he was conscious might weary his congregation (lines 29–31; if they were attending his sermon in the context of some longer Good Friday liturgy, his apprehensions were doubtless justified). He began the narrative with events immediately prior to Good Friday, opening with Christ in the house of Martha at Bethany, then moving on to Christ's entry on the following day into Jerusalem, where the chief priests were plotting how best to contrive his death. The narrative continues until the events of Maundy Thursday and Christ's washing of his disciples' feet before it suddenly breaks off. What has been deferred by the *Nota alibi* instruction presumably centred on the Crucifixion and the circumstances surrounding it.

---

[29] Note lines 4–6 of the sermon edited below, which perhaps might be taken to indicate that men and women were in attendance.

[30] For example, compare the list of emotive questions at lines 20–23.

Although the beginning of the sermon, with its announcement of a *thema*, followed by a preamble or *prothema*, and a prayer asking for aid before the repetition again of the *thema*, is reminiscent of sermons organized according to the 'modern' form of sermon composition, the rest of it, in comprising an edited synthesized biblical narrative accompanied by selected exegesis of that narrative, seems by contrast a little more reminiscent of sermons organized according to the 'ancient' mode, *secundum ordinem textus*.[31] Hence *Egressus Ihesus* appears as something of a hybrid in terms of its chosen form.[32] Possibly the hybridity had been encouraged by the particular circumstances of the delivery of this sermon. If, as seems likely, it occurred in a liturgical context on Good Friday, Cyrcetur may have found it opportune to elaborate on what was being presented liturgically, amplifying and clarifying it for the people, as it were, by also connecting them with the foundational narratives that drove that day's distinctive liturgical display. Thus his sermon might be thought at once elucidatory and emotive, designed to evoke an informed memory of Christ's Passion, a memory which, if evoked adroitly, would in turn stimulate devotion, devotion that might itself in turn precipitate penitence (lines 16–20). Preaching could therefore play an important part in setting off this affective chain reaction: members of the congregation, once set successfully in penitential mood, would not only be considered to be in a potentially salvific state of mind, but also to have been rendered receptive to the invitation to confession, the required preliminary to their mandatory Easter communion in two days time.

Egressus Ihesus cum discipulis suis trans torrentem Cedron thus collaborated in its complementary way with the wider Church-sponsored event of the day, and shows, or at least gives a flavour of the way in which, one particular and highly educated secular canon in the first half of the fifteenth century tuned his preaching to the circumstances of that event accordingly.

---

[31] Although the sermon is incomplete, and therefore we cannot technically presume to speak of what it may or may not have contained, it seems highly unlikely that in its original complete state it would have subsequently followed through with a sermon in the 'modern' form after having presented so lengthy a Passion narrative.

[32] Ball, 'Thomas Cyrcetur', p. 212 nn. 39 and 40, says Cyrcetur used both 'ancient' and 'modern' sermon form, which seems right, but his classification of the Good Friday sermon as showing 'ancient' form cannot be left quite so straightforward as that. For a comprehensive discussion of ancient and modern form, see *EPLMA*, pp. 228–68.

A Sermon for Good Friday from Salisbury, Cathedral Library, MS 174

|fol. 344ʳ|

'Egressus Ihesus cum discipulis suis trans torrentem Cedron', et cetera.
Iohannis 18. Considerando diem hodiernam, nescio cogitare quid sit melius
facere, quam plorare vel predicare. Quia quando cogito quod Dominus
noster, Salvator noster, pater noster, frater noster, hodie mortuus est, videtur
5 mihi quod non est aliqua creatura que non debet hodie plorare secundum
modum suum, et specialiter homo et femina deberent, pro quibus mortuus
est filius Dei. Sed cum iam video quod estis congregati cum magna deuocione
vt audiatis passionem Saluatoris nostri, mihi videtur conueniens non solum
plorare sed eciam predicare. Vnde nos facimus vtrumque. Ore predicabimus,
10 aure audiemus quod in corde et in oculis plorabimus passionem Saluatoris
nostri. Sed illud non possumus facere |fol. 344ᵛ| sine adiutorio Virginis Marie
matris sue, que hodie super omnes alias creaturas plorauit stando iuxta
crucem. Et ipse eciam plorabat clamando, 'O vos omnes qui transitis per
viam', et cetera. Vnde in principio nostri sermonis et predicacionis nostre
15 rogemus eam toto corde, et cetera. 'Egressus Ihesus', et cetera.

Ego nescio quomodo hodierna die facerem vos magis conuenientem et magis
deuotam predicacionem quam reminiscare vos de Christi passione, hoc est
dicere quam facere vel mouere vos ad habendum memoriam et remissionem
et deuotam cogitacionem de Christi passione. Nam quicquid de ea dicitur,
20 totum trahit nos ad deuocionem et penitenciam. Quid enim debent lacrime?
Quid dolos? Quid vulnera? Quid brachia in cruce? Quid claui tam grossi?
Quid lancea? Quid corona de spinis tam acutis? Quid verba benedicta que
in cruce pertulit, nisi deuocionem et penitenciam? Vocant enim nos ad
penitenciam verbo, sed multo magis, et cetera.

25 Debetis intelligere quod passio Christi scribitur ab omnibus quatuor
euangelistis et ideo legitur quatuor diebus, vt Christiani audiant quid
quisque eorum dicat. De ista mirifica passione nullo modo discordant in
sentencia, sed quod vnus dimittit, alius suplet. Vnde modo meo incomposito
et rudi, vidi quatuor euangelia de quibus congregaui hic sermonem, et licet
30 historia fuerit longanimis debet accediare eam audire et deuote attendere
amore illius qui non fuit accediatus eam sustinere in corpore suo amore nostri.
Et ideo debetis scire quod ordo passionis Christi fuit per istum modum.

Sciendum fuit die Martis, Dominus noster fuit Bethanie in domo Marthe
quindecim stadijs a Iherusalem, et omni die ibat in Iherusalem et redibat
35 Bethaniam. Et ideo die Martis dixit in Bethania illa verba, 'Scitis quia post
biduanum Pascha fiet,' scilicet quinta |fol. 345ʳ| feria ad vesperam. Christus
die Mercurij venit in Iherusalem cum discipulis suis. Quo die principes
sacerdotum cum senioribus congregati fuerunt in atrio Caiphe querentes
quomodo possent Christum occidere, dicentes, 'Non in die festo, propter
40 rumorem populi', nam autem congregabat<ur> totus populus propter diem
festum, et populus multum diligebant Christum. Et ideo principes timebant
capere Christum propter populum. Et ideo dixerunt, 'Non in die festo,
ne forte tumultus fieret in populo', et cetera. Iudas vnus de duodecim,
qui disposuerat in corde suo quomodo posset se vindicare et recuperare
45 illam pecuniam quam reputabat se perdidisse de affusione vnguenti quod
Magdalena super caput Christi effuderat quando senebat in domo Simonis
leprosi. Sed fuit die Sabbati vltimo preterita, sciens principes sacerdotum
cum alijs congregatos in palacio Cayphe ad tractandum de morte Christi,
occulte statim iuit ad eos et pepegit cum eijs tribuere eijs Christum sine
50 aliquo tumultu populi pro triginta argenteijs. Perdiderit enim tantum de
effusione illius vnguenti, quia estimauerit illud valere 300 denarios et decima
trecentorum d sunt 30 d, quia ipse erat proditor et fur et latro, et portabat
pecuniam, et semper decimam partem furabat. Et ideo voluit recipere quam
perdiderat. Ista vendicio facta fuit die Mercurij vltimo preterito, et hoc
55 inuenit propheta Ysaias, qui legit eo die dicens, 'Ecce, merces eius cum eo.'
Eodem die Christus redijt Bethaniam, et more solito hospitatus est in domo
Marthe. Sequenti die, scilicet die Iouis, Christus, sciens horam mortis sue
propinquare, assumptis discipulis |fol. 345ᵛ| suis venit Iherusalem, et
veniendo discipuli dixerunt sibi, 'Magister, vbi vis paremus tibi Pascha?' At
60 dixit Petro et Iohanni, 'Ite in ciuitatem et occurret vobis homo lagenam
aque baiulans, sequimini eum.' Prevenerunt, igitur, illi Domino discipuli
ante, et inuenerunt omnia secundum dixerat illis Ihesus, et parauerant
omnia necessaria pro cena. Veniens autem Ihesus cum alijs discipulis, et
reperiens cenam paratam, posuerunt se omnes ad cenam.

65 Nota hic bene Bonauenturam de cessione in cena et vultu Christi et
discipulorum et quod ille hic fecit, scilicet cito surrexit, vestimenta deposuit,
lintheo se precinxit, aquam in palium misit, et pedes discipulorum lauit.
Nota alibi.

Critical Notes and Glosses

11 possumus] possimus MS.

31 fuit] fuit fuit MS.

43 forte] fore MS.

46 senebat] i.e. cenebat; this orthography probably represents the medieval pronunciation.

50 triginta] triginti MS.

53 semper] *add.* sm *et canc.*

60–61 homo lagenam aque baiulans, sequimini eum] *om.* MS.

61 Prevenerunt] Invenerunt MS.

66 ille] illi MS.

Apparatus fontium and Commentary

1 Egressus Ihesus ... Cedron: John 18. 1.

55 Ecce, merces eius cum eo: Isaiah 40. 10.

59–61 'Magister, vbi vis paremus tibi Pascha?' At dixit Petro et Iohanni, 'Ite in ciuitatem et occurret vobis homo lagenam aque baiulans, sequimini eum': a conflation of Matthew 26. 17–18 and Mark 14. 12–13.

59–61 A reference to Bonaventure, Meditations on the Passion. This work was owned by Cyrcetur (Salisbury, Cathedral Library, MS 113, with annotations in his hand).

THE SECULARS: FOUR SERMON VARIATIONS ON A THEME ATTRIBUTED TO ROBERT HOLCOT

Introduction

We come in this chapter to our final group of preachers, the seculars, that large and largely anonymous company for whom the majority of the surviving English prose Sunday sermon compilations of the later Middle Ages, with occasional exceptions, were probably produced,[1] as indeed were also many Latin sermon compilations belonging to this period.[2] It is therefore not wholly inappropriate that this chapter should bulk larger than any of the rest.

All *materia predicabilis* was potentially eligible for a wide circulation and currency within the late medieval Church, no matter in which branch of the Church it had originated. The culture of the preachers was in principle a common property with common rights of access, even though, as was seen in the previous chapter, certain preachers found some parts of its terrain more congenial than others, depending upon their point of view, and even though, from the year 1409 onwards, some preachers found official limits set upon what they could

---

[1] See for example Spencer, 'Middle English Sermons', p. 621.

[2] Perhaps the most extensively copied among which being the *Sermones dominicales* of John Felton; see *PPPLME*, pp. 58–118; to the twenty-nine manuscripts, in part or in whole, of this dominical collection currently identified (ibid., pp. 62–63) should now also be added the following: Cambridge, University Library, MS Ii.3.22, fols 43ʳ–144ʳ (a manuscript formerly owned by the Benedictines of Norwich); Cambridge, Jesus College, MS 13, booklet 5, fols 126ᵛ–128ᵛ (Felton's Corpus Christi sermon on the *thema, Qui manducat hunc panem, vivet in eternum*); and Oxford, Bodleian Library, MS Bodley 687, fols 74ᵛ–76ᵛ (Felton's Easter Day sermon on the *thema, Acceperunt corpus Iesu*).

legitimately aspire to preach about.[3] Nevertheless, a state of affairs essentially communal and open to all is suggested in each of the cases edited below in this chapter, four sermons for various occasions whose kernel ultimately derived from the same motif, the story of an allegorized castle attributed to the Dominican friar Robert Holcot († 1349). The authors of these sermons wove variations on the motif, however, and produced four specimens of preaching whose overall effect, when each is compared with the other, is very different. Yet, all of these sermons are likely to have been produced by seculars; certainly, three out of the four manuscripts in which they are severally contained suggest that it was seculars whom their copyists had in mind when they were being made.[4]

The Latin Bedrock of Late Medieval Vernacular Preaching

These sermons of likely secular auspices also help to focus another set of issues that have a wide application to medieval sermon studies. In recent years it has become increasingly clear to students of late medieval English preaching how heavily reliant much of the extant vernacular sermon corpus is on a Latin substratum. Something similar might be said of the other medieval vernacular covered by the terms of this book, Irish, although far more work remains to be done on preaching conducted in this particular vernacular than will be offered in these pages.[5] This reliance on Latin is more, or less, pronounced: some sermons are extensively dependent upon Latin sources, while in others the dependence is more local and intermittent. Yet in most cases a reliance in some degree is to be found.

The magnetic pull which the Latin centre exerted upon its orbiting vernacular sermon texts is, of course, hardly surprising. Much of the material out of which preachers in the vernacular forged their preaching was first codified in Latin, even if sometimes — as indeed may have been the case with the theme attributed to Robert Holcot whose later (secular) reception will be investigated here — this

---

[3] The limits were set by Archbishop Thomas Arundel in his Oxford Constitutions of that year; for further details, see Chapter 4, n. 14 (p. 71, above).

[4] The sole notable exception being Lincoln, Cathedral Library, MS 133; see the headnote to Text C, below.

[5] A beginning has been made by Brian Murdoch, 'Preaching in Medieval Ireland: The Irish Tradition', in *Irish Preaching 700–1700*, ed. by Alan J. Fletcher and Raymond Gillespie (Dublin: Four Courts, 2001), pp. 40–54.

codifying was done half with an eye to the material's rendition in English when
eventually uttered in the pulpit. After all, theological reading and writing, relatively elite practices, were one thing, while preaching, delivered to all sorts and
conditions, was another, and typically both inhabited different, if contiguous,
linguistic terrains. Thus, especially in the early days of the flowering of the written
production of late medieval English vernacular preaching, a period whose beginning dates approximately from the 1380s, vernacular sermon authors in search of
materia predicabilis often had little option but to return to the Latin centre
and to quarry it.[6] As yet there circulated relatively few substantial sermon collections in English that might meet the prospective preacher's needs and thus be
liable to compete successfully against Latin for his attention. At the beginning of
this period of manuscript efflorescence, an interesting example of one vernacular
preacher's enforced recourse to Latin rather than to English source material is
afforded in John Mirk's *Festial*, compiled probably *c.* 1382–90.[7] By the fifteenth
century, when this work was enjoying immense popularity in scribal (and from
1483, printed) copies, it was also lending itself to precisely the sort of editing
and recycling that wide textual accessibility made possible: once a substantial and
relatively comprehensive vernacular sermon cycle like Mirk's had come into being
and had been well circulated, sermon compilers and redactors had every opportunity to use it as the point of departure for their own preaching efforts.[8] But
when Mirk himself wrote, the option of consulting major sermon collections in
English does not seem to have been open to him, or at least, it may not have been
a viable option, perhaps because no collections suiting his purposes as yet existed.[9]
Latin seems to have been Mirk's constant companion as a source because, given
the time of his writing and his particular requirements, it was an inevitable one.
Indeed, one copy of the *Festial* betrays how close to the surface of Mirk's English

---

[6] Sermons existed in English well before the 1380s, but only from about this time does their
bulk in manuscripts become noticeable.

[7] Fletcher, 'John Mirk and the Lollards'.

[8] An interesting case is studied in Alan J. Fletcher and Susan Powell, 'The Origins of a
Fifteenth-Century Sermon Collection: MSS Harley 2247 and Royal 18.B.XXV', *LeedsSE*, n.s.,
10 (1978), 74–96, where the sermon compiler of the particular sermon sequence witnessed in
these manuscripts used Mirk as a basis but then looked again for material in some of Mirk's
original Latin sources as well as in yet other Latin sources that Mirk did not use.

[9] Fletcher, 'Unnoticed Sermons from John Mirk's *Festial*', pp. 514–15. The proposition made
there that heterodox Wycliffite preaching may have stimulated Mirk's endeavours now seems
quite compatible with a date around 1389–90 suggested for the composition of the vernacular
Wycliffite Sermon cycles (*English Wycliffite Sermons*, IV, 8–20).

prose the current of his Latin source could flow. London, British Library, MS Cotton Claudius A.ii, a particularly early *Festial* manuscript and the one linguistically nearest to Mirk's base at Lilleshall Abbey in Shropshire, occupies a unique place in the *Festial*'s textual tradition.[10] In the course of its sermon for the feast of St Thomas the Apostle, Mirk's principal source, the *Legenda aurea* of Jacobus de Voragine, erupts in undigested Latin directly into the Middle English: 'Also in hys prechynghe taghte xij gradus virtutum assignare [...]', says Mirk of St Thomas, and so the written text of his sermon proceeds to rehearse the Latin of Jacobus for several lines before reverting once more to the vernacular.[11]

One of the main ancillary purposes of this chapter will be to illustrate an important corollary to the tendency of vernacular sermon authors to congregate around the vast Latin reservoir of *predicabilia*, however less essential that reservoir may have become during the course of the fifteenth century as the quantity and currency of vernacular sermon collections steadily increased.[12] Since this reservoir was not filled solely by Latin sermons (witness Robert Holcot's *Moralitates* discussed below — not actually sermons themselves although devised by him to be exploited by preachers), it followed that some of the materials siphoned off were not already organized according to the forms that typically prevailed in much late medieval Latin preaching. These are the forms perhaps most famously set out and recommended in the *artes predicandi*, and they are also to be deduced (though with the exercise of due caution) from observing the implicit principles of composition followed in actual sermon texts. What emerges from many sermons in English — and it is something that each successive Middle English sermon published in this chapter as Texts B to D makes increasingly clear — is that not only were many vernacular sermon authors seldom concerned to arrange material from

---

[10] Tentative localizations of the written dialects of twenty-six *Festial* manuscripts are given in Wakelin, 'The Manuscripts of John Mirk's *Festial*', p. 103. Given its early date and the linguistic fit of its language, Cotton Claudius A.ii could conceivably be an authorial holograph.

[11] London, British Library, MS Cotton Claudius A.ii, fols 14ᵛ–15ʳ; compare *Iacopo da Varazze, Legenda Aurea*, ed. by Giovanni Paolo Maggioni, 2nd edn, Millennio Medievale 6, Testi 3, 2 vols (Florence: SISMEL, Edizioni del Galluzzo, 1998), I, 58–59. In all other *Festial* manuscripts containing this section, this substantial Latin passage has been fully digested into Middle English. Also, note in MS Cotton Claudius A.ii the appearance of the occasional undigested word in Latin (for example, *multitudo*, for English 'multitude', on fol. 43ʳ, etc.).

[12] The increase is evident notwithstanding an apparent lull post-1409 when Archbishop Thomas Arundel's Constitutions were promulgated. This lull in activity has been observed in *EPLMA*, p. 320; for a general account of the consequences of the Constitutions on English prose compositions, see Watson, 'Censorship and Cultural Change in Late-Medieval England'.

Latin sources according to notions of sermon form promoted by the *artes* when they disposed it in English, but also in many cases they would not have been so inclined when several of their sources, like the *Moralitates*, were not already cast in sermon-ready form.[13] However, it is by no means the case that this inevitably led preachers in the vernacular simply to replicate whatever form their Latin material had when they translated it into English. Nevertheless, the translated material's arrangement into a sermon form fit for vernacular preaching might be achieved by applying the lightest of preaching protocols. For example, the simple addition to the translated material of an opening biblical *thema*, or of terms of address acknowledging the presence of a congregation, might be sufficient, as might be the provision of bidding prayers or a formulaic concluding prayer, all these being routine components of many a medieval sermon, whether in Latin or in the vernacular. Such touches were evidently adequate in themselves to frame the translated material within a sermon form that was reckoned acceptable, at least to the translators. Thus it becomes abundantly clear from inspecting a range of Middle English sermon texts that many vernacular preachers, facing their task of turning Latin *predicabilia* into English preaching, did not additionally feel themselves constrained by ambient conventions of sermon form of the more exacting sort: for such men, an acceptable form was something that could be accomplished in English with relative ease, and the result would be of a kind that might not typically have been prescribed by the grammarians of sermon form, the authors of the *artes predicandi*; indeed, it would in some cases have been proscribed. If this was already so in the period when vernacular preachers were obliged to draw substantially on Latin sources, how much more so when they would be able to avail increasingly of the English ones that were beginning to circulate and in which less constrained forms of sermon construction had already become acceptable?[14]

This is one of the lessons that the Middle English treatment of the narrative of the Castle of Prudence in the sermons published in Texts B to D below also teaches, and if the sermon in Text E — preserved mainly in Latin — was nevertheless intended for preaching in English, as seems most likely, the lesson is

---

[13] Such comparative nonchalance is noted in *EPLMA*, p. 267, and *PPPLME*, pp. 252–60.

[14] Whenever these English sources were themselves sermons, the simplification in them of traditional sermon form may already have occurred. We have examples of English sermons, originally dependent on Latin sources but on which no exacting standard of sermon form has been imposed, themselves becoming available for further cannibalization by yet other preachers. A good case in point is investigated in Fletcher and Powell, 'The Origins of a Fifteenth-Century Sermon Collection'.

repeated. To be sure, it has already been learnt in other contexts than these,[15] but the present sermons make a particularly arresting case in that they witness to highly contrasting recyclings by four very different authors of an ultimate and predominantly Latin text. Each author incorporated his derived matter into the form of his sermon in a unique way, for each sermon's form exhibits its own distinctive emancipations from norms characteristic of the *artes*: we pass from a comparatively formal, though by no means traditionally systematic, sermon for the first Sunday of Advent found in Oxford, Bodleian Library, MS e Museo 180, to three compositions that are freer still, one possibly for the same occasion in Lincoln, Cathedral Library, MS 133, another for an unknown occasion in Oxford, Bodleian Library, MS Hatton 96, whose form is so free that it might perhaps more appropriately be thought of as 'preachable material' than 'sermon', and the last for Passion Sunday in Dublin, Trinity College, MS 75. In the following discussion, these texts, edited below in a series of appendices as Texts B, C, D, and E, will be referred to respectively as e Museo, Lincoln, Hatton, and Trinity.

The Castle of Prudence

But we must begin with the kernel of each of these, the Castle of Prudence motif, in order to see what these subsequent redactions have done to it. In its simplest form, as an independent unit, the moralized 'picture' of the Castle of Prudence is to be found among the *Moralitates* of Robert Holcot. To date, however, I am aware of its existence in this context only in a single manuscript copy, London, British Library, MS Arundel 384, where it appears towards the end of the *Moralitates*.[16] Although there are therefore grounds for suspecting that the Castle of Prudence motif was a later addition to the *Moralitates* by another author, the question cannot be finally settled one way or another; indeed, the treatment of the

---

[15] *EPLMA*, p. 267, and *PPPLME*, pp. 252–60.

[16] *Catalogue of Romances in the Department of Manuscripts in the British Museum*, ed. by J. A. Herbert and H. L. D. Ward, 3 vols (London: Trustees of the British Museum, 1883–1910; repr. 1961–62), III, 106–13, provides a full list of the *Moralitates* in this manuscript. A conspectus of manuscripts of the *Moralitates* is given by Nigel F. Palmer, 'Das "Exempelwerk der englischen Bettelmönche": Ein Gegenstück zu den "Gesta Romanorum"', in *Exempel und Exempelsammlungen*, ed. by W. Haug and B. Wachinger, Fortuna Vitrea, 2 (Tübingen: Niemeyer, 1991), pp. 137–72 (pp. 168–72). No other manuscript of the *Moralitates* extant in the British Isles contains the Castle of Prudence motif; it has not been practicable, however, to check all the Continental European manuscripts.

motif certainly makes it resemble other of the canonical *Moralitates*, nor would its occasional use of English have been out of character when English also features occasionally in Holcot's preaching.[17]

The Arundel Holcot version of the Castle of Prudence motif runs as follows. A certain king built a castle and decreed that none should enter unless he could construe the three shields hanging in the entrance. The first was silver with three red roses in which was written the word 'Vita'; the second black with three silver swords in which was written 'Mors'; and the third blue with three gold trumpets in which was written 'Iudicium' (see Figure 1 for this and the other shield arrangements as the texts seem to describe them). A philosopher happened along, asked admission of the porter, who told him the law concerning entry to the castle. The philosopher scrutinized the shields and declared that the castle was appropriately named the Castle of Prudence. He interpreted the first shield as signifying that a man in his lifetime must love God in three ways, with all his heart, mind, and strength. This he must do with a pure mind, and that is what the silver on the shield signified, the red of the roses signifying love. The philosopher interpreted the second shield as all-conquering death, and the third, as the three possible judgements of a sinner — either bodily pain for his sins, or the pain of purgatory, or the eternal pain of hell. He interpreted the silver of the swords and black of the shield as signifying that death separates a man from his life and deposes him; and he interpreted the third shield as signifying the Last Judgement at which a triple trumpet will sound, the first of 'Rise, you dead, and come to Judgement', the second of 'Come, you blessed of my Father', and the third of 'Depart, you cursed ones, to the fire'. The philosopher finally summed up the shields in a verse quatrain. Then follows a moralization. The castle is heaven, which none enters unless he loves God with his whole heart, mind, and strength, and fulfils the commandments as the king of the castle decreed. A man should also fear the threefold trumpet and the sword of divine vengeance against the reprobate. The inscriptions of 'Vita', 'Mors', and 'Iudicium' on the shields urge men to consider these three things and to perform them. The English equivalents to these three contain in all nine letters, three in the first word, 'Lyf', three in the second, 'Ded', and three in the third, 'Dom'. The three letters of each of these words reveal the properties or *membra* of what has been understood. Thus *L* reveals that 'Lyf' is 'Litel', *I* that 'Lyf' is ''Yuel', and *F* that 'Lyf' is 'Fykel'. Similarly, *D* reveals that 'Ded' is 'Dolyng', *E* that 'Ded' is 'Endyng', and *D* that

---

[17] Out of his 119 sermons witnessed in Cambridge, Peterhouse, MS 210, four contain English divisions of their *themata* (see fols 1ʳ, 32ʳ, 128ʳ, and 139ʳ).

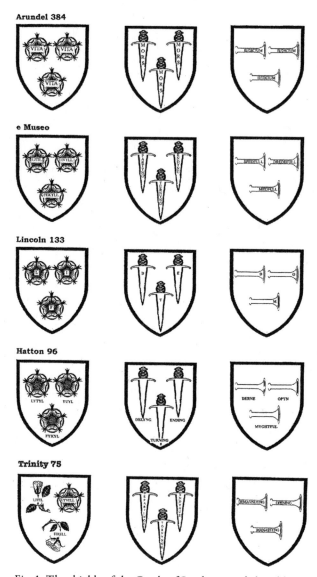

Fig. 1. The shields of the Castle of Prudence and their blazons.

'Ded' is 'Deyng'. Finally, *D* reveals that 'Dom' is 'Dome', *O* that 'Dom' is 'Oppynly', and *M* that 'Dom' is 'Myghtfully'.

It should be noted that the Arundel manuscript readings of the English words are not entirely perfect, however. The second term, 'Ded' (Modern English 'Death'), doubtless read 'Det' in the original, since without a final -*t*, it is not possible to derive the third *membrum*, 'Turnyng', and this is the reading that comparison with the other texts confirms the original to have had. Arundel's 'Deyng' is thus erroneous. Also, Arundel's 'Dolyng', given as the first *membrum*, must be a misreading of 'Delyng', for this is the word required by context and established as original by comparison with the other texts. Finally, the first *membrum* of the third term, 'Dom', which is given in Arundel as 'Dome', is very likely a misreading of 'Derne', a *difficilior lectio* that only the Hatton manuscript has retained intact. The Arundel misreading is explicable in terms of a scribal misapprehension: Anglicana *e* can easily resemble an *o*, and Anglicana long-tailed *r*, before the two minims of *n*, could easily have been read as a third minim to produce an *m*, hence 'Dome' here.

The symbiosis between Latin and English in the concluding moralization of the 'picture' of the castle and its three emblazoned shields is suggestive, and perhaps it also discloses an attitude to the relation between Latin and English that was prevalent amongst at least some contemporary preachers at the time the *Moralitates* were written, after *c*. 1334 and before 1342.[18] The Castle of Prudence author betrays a little self-consciousness about his linguistic change of gear when explaining that 'in Anglicana lingua', the words 'Lyf', 'Ded' (*recte*, 'Det') and 'Dom' each contain three letters. In what he was doing here we have a reverse instance, if for rather different reasons, of what was to happen in John Mirk's sermon on St Thomas the Apostle a generation or so later: there, as was seen, Latin ran close to the surface of Mirk's English necessarily, since a Latin text was his immediate primary source; the Castle of Prudence author, conversely, although he used no immediate primary source in English that we know of, was aware of the possible value of the vernacular, and evidently this awareness ran close to the surface of his Latin while he composed.[19] In fact, only through lapsing

---

[18] For the dating of the *Moralitates*, see Smalley, *English Friars and Antiquity*, p. 146; and on the use of 'pictures', see ibid., pp. 165–83.

[19] If the Castle of Prudence author was in fact Holcot, then we know from other evidence that Holcot had time for the vernacular. He seems to have known the early Middle English poem *The Owl and the Nightingale*; see Alan J. Fletcher, 'The Genesis of *The Owl and the Nightingale*: A New Hypothesis', *ChauR*, 34 (1999), 1–17.

into English could he conveniently construct the scholastic, ternary symmetry that he imposed at the end of the moralization of his 'picture', since English alone provided the requisite three-letter words that made the moralization possible. This moralization was patently not in all respects structurally complete: 'Quere confirmacionem pro membris diuisionis', he advised (see Text A, line 40–41). That is, the reader or preacher consulting his material still had work of his own to do: he had to adduce confirmatory proofs for each *membrum* of the threefold *divisio* applied to each of the words 'Lyf', 'Ded' [*recte* 'Det'] and 'Dom'. So the Castle of Prudence author had provided readers with no more than the bare essentials. Amplification of those essentials fell to whoever used his 'picture'. We will see shortly that at least one subsequent vernacular preacher did precisely what was recommended.[20] As earlier suggested, by introducing the vernacular, the Castle of Prudence author may have anticipated the eventual requisition of his motif by preachers whose sermons would be delivered in the vernacular extensively. Certainly, he did nothing to discourage them from further Englishing his work when he chose to use the vernacular himself, even if only locally. Be that as it may, any preacher operating in Latin and drafting in the Castle of Prudence motif would necessarily have imported into his Latin sermon an English leaven, though this would not in itself have seemed especially innovative or remarkable, given that already well before the middle of the fourteenth century English was making guest appearances in Latin preaching, especially in the guise of proverbs.[21] If we may so interpret his use of the vernacular, the Castle of Prudence motif was conceived, therefore, in what was by now a tolerant, indeed collaborative, borderland between Latin and English, the languages respectively of clerical and demotic discourse. Without question, the motif drew its existence from the linguistic rapprochement of the two, even if we abstemiously insist on limiting this rapprochement to the author's mind alone and refuse to discover in it signs of a wider cultural trend. Nevertheless, a temperate climate in which the commerce between Latin and English might develop and grow is suggested here, and consequently it comes as no surprise to find the Castle of Prudence motif soon being turned fully into English, as Texts B, C, and D will illustrate (and even

---

[20] This is γ on the *stemma codicum* (see Table 1). The status of γ is further discussed below.

[21] See Wenzel, *Verses in Sermons*, pp. 61–100. He notes that proverbs were among the first vernacular items to appear. In the Castle of Prudence, however, the English was used at structural points (for the headwords of each *divisio* and their threefold members), as it would similarly and more commonly be used from the mid-fourteenth century on in many sermons whose language of written record was substantially Latin.

Text E, though committed to parchment largely in Latin, is very likely to have been preached substantially in English by the mysterious Doctor Curteyse to whom it is assigned). However, as will also be seen, the net effect of each sermon is very different from that of the other.

The e Museo 180 Version

We turn now to the first of the sermons, e Museo (see Text B), thus named after its most textually accurate copy in Oxford, Bodleian Library, MS e Museo 180. This manuscript belongs to a group of three other related sermon manuscripts, all copied for the most part by the same scribe.[22] The e Museo sermon contains an important clue that its author may not have encountered the Castle of Prudence motif in a copy of Holcot's *Moralitates* such as Arundel 384 witnesses to, but knew it in some intermediary version (the dependence of Lincoln, Hatton, and Trinity on the Castle of Prudence motif was similarly indirect, as will become clear in due course). The intermediary has been designated as γ in the *stemma codicum*. The e Museo sermon is the only one studied here that declares its source (Text B, line 30). Its author claimed to have found his *Castrum Sapiencie* not in the *Moralitates*, but in the *Gesta Romanorum*. The substantive variant *Castrum Sapiencie*, opposed to *Castrum Prudencie* in the Arundel text, a variant shared also by Lincoln, Hatton, and, with a small difference, Trinity,[23] may help justify the *stemma* proposed in Table 1. While the reading *Castrum Prudencie* could theoretically be explained as being specific to the Arundel manuscript's textual tradition, with e Museo, Lincoln, Hatton, and Trinity more accurately reflecting the original at this point, there are no grounds for believing that the Arundel text is defective anywhere other than in certain of its vernacular elements earlier discussed. Indeed, a *Castrum Prudencie* would seem a *difficilior lectio* than a *Castrum Sapiencie*. But grounds for believing in an intermediary state of the motif represented by γ do not consist solely in this; witness, for example, the fact that the

---

[22] The others are: Lincoln, Cathedral Library, MSS 50 and 51 (originally one manuscript now in two modern bindings); Gloucester, Cathedral Library, MS 22 (which does not, however, contain the sermon under present consideration); and Durham, University Library, MS Cosin V.IV.3. For further details, see *PPPLME*, pp. 154–59; a full edition of the sermon cycle in these manuscripts is currently being prepared by Stephen Morrison for EETS. On the sermon in e Museo 180 see also *A Repertorium of Middle English Prose Sermons*, III, 1884–86.

[23] The Trinity sermon does not actually refer to a *Castrum Sapiencie*, but it is clear that its castle was thought to embody *sapiencia* (see Text E, lines 14–15), and thus the Trinity version shares in the tradition lying behind the others (and see also n. 28, below).

three sermons preserved extensively in English (e Museo, Lincoln, and Hatton) all share variations on the conversation between God and the damned at the Last Judgement, and other points of substantive overlap will become clear later in the course of this discussion.

Table 1. *Stemma codicum* **of the manuscripts witnessing to the Castle of Prudence motif.**

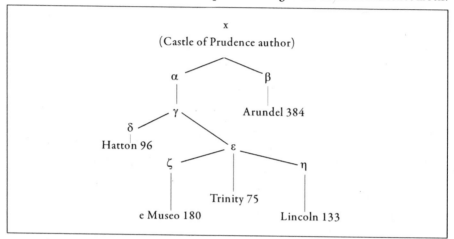

The *Gesta Romanorum*, a popular composition existing in various recensions, is known to have drawn on Holcot's *Moralitates* extensively,[24] but the Castle of Prudence 'picture' has not been noted amongst the material that the *Gesta Romanorum* incorporated.[25] Therefore, if the ascription of e Museo is to be trusted, and always assuming that the Castle of Prudence motif was indeed Holcot's work and not someone else's subsequent addition, there evidently existed a tradition of another of Holcot's *Moralitates* having entered the *Gesta Romanorum* that has been overlooked. Whence also the beginning of the view developed here that at least one intermediary redaction intervened between the Latin Castle of Prudence source in its original form and the four sermons. In fact, there are additional reasons for believing in the intervention of an intermediary (for example, as earlier

---

[24] Smalley, *English Friars and Antiquity*, p. 146.

[25] *Catalogue of Romances*, III, 112–13, no. 53, does not note the exemplum in the early printed editions of the *Gesta Romanorum* or in the edition of the *Gesta Romanorum* by Hermann Oesterley (Berlin: Weidmann, 1872; repr. Hildesheim: Olms, 1963). Nor does it appear in early printed editions of the *Moralitates*.

noted, all the sermons agree against the Arundel Holcot's Castle of Prudence in referring to a Castle of Wisdom). So whatever the truth of the e Museo author's precise ascription of his source to *Gesta Romanorum*, one thing at least seems clear, and that is the existence of some intermediary redaction coming between himself and the original form of the Castle of Prudence. We will return to questions about the nature of the intermediary later.

In starting with an account of the day's gospel, the beginning of e Museo is reminiscent of a venerable tradition of sermon form, and in this is quite unlike Lincoln, Hatton, and Trinity. Its gospel account is a liberal paraphrase, subsequently expounded after one of the higher levels of exegesis, the allegorical level, as the nature of the exegesis, Text B, lines 23–29, makes clear, and the word *moraliter* that introduces the exegesis evidently here means 'allegorically'.[26] *Moraliter* was one of the words commonly inserted into sermon texts to signal the start of any level of exegesis, whether literal, moral, tropological, or anagogical. Its wide range of senses therefore makes it a difficult word to render, but the meaning in this case seems evident from the context. Similarly, the 'moralle understondyng' of the gospel (Text B, line 23) is to be understood as intending the allegorical rather than the moral significance.[27] For many orthodox sermons, as for e Museo, the gospel paraphrase simply provided a point of departure for an exposition which is largely independent of the gospel text.[28] Nevertheless, the procedure of e Museo remains most nearly akin to the 'ancient' form of preaching, a form that

---

[26] See Latham, *Revised Medieval Latin Word-List*, p. 304 ('Moralitas').

[27] See OED, s.v. 'moral' adj., sub-sense 3b. For another example from a contemporary sermon of 'morally' meaning 'allegorically', see the first Advent sermon of Oxford, Bodleian Library, MS Bodley 806, fol. 2ᵛ. Here, the translated English 'morally' introduces an exegesis that is allegorical (and compare the practice of the sermons discussed in Chapter 4, above, of Oxford, Bodleian Library, MS Bodley 649; see, for example, fol. 14ᵗ).

[28] What is of particular interest about the e Museo gospel paraphrase is that it appears to have been drawn from the Later Version of the Wycliffite Bible; see Stephen Morrison, 'Lollardy in the Fifteenth Century: The Evidence from Some Orthodox Texts', *Cahiers Élisabéthains*, 52 (1997), 1–24. The Bible-based sermons of the Lollard cycles are perhaps the most conspicuous example in late medieval England of the tradition of sermon composition which repeatedly refers to the scriptural text of the day throughout the course of the sermon. The Middle English translation of the French *de tempore* cycle of Robert of Gretham provides an orthodox instance of this method: Thomas G. Duncan, 'A Transcription and Linguistic Study of the Introduction and First Twelve Sermons of the Hunterian MS Version of the "Mirror"' (unpublished B.Litt. thesis, University of Oxford, 1965). For further cases of an orthodox preference for sermon exposition *secundum ordinem textus*, see Owst, *Preaching in Medieval England*, pp. 309–12, and especially the comprehensive survey of the 'ancient' (and 'modern') forms of English preaching in *EPLMA*, pp. 228–68.

had never been lost from sight in the later Middle Ages in England, even though
the 'modern' form, much in favour since the thirteenth century, had tended to
eclipse it. Thus in respect of deploying a sermon form with a traditional lineage,
the form of e Museo, in the beginning (Text B, lines 1–29), is the most familiar
of the four. After the gospel paraphrase, the sermon author announces its moral
interpretation, 'after þe seyng of docturs', and concludes with the statement that
the castle to which the gospel refers is the castle of heaven. This then prompts the
introduction of the *Castrum Sapiencie* motif from '*Gestis Romanorum*'. First
comes the shield with its three roses gules on a ground argent, in the first of which
is written 'Litil', in the second 'Ivyll', and in the third, 'Fekyll' (contrast the
Arundel Holcot, where 'Vita' seems to have been written in each; see Figure 1 and
Table 2). So the sermon author's immediate source has bypassed the headword of
the *divisio* (that is, 'Lif' or, as the Arundel Holcot proposed it, 'Vita') and gone
straight to the three *membra* (*membra* inasmuch as, without a headword, they
may only be loosely so described).[29] Second comes the shield with its three swords
argent on a ground sable, in the first of which is written 'Partyng' (contrast in
Table 2 the Arundel Holcot's different word but essentially similar meaning),
in the second 'Endyng', and in the third 'Turnyng'. Here, the *P* of 'Partyng'
damages the possibility of ever being able to link these three *membra* with some
such headword as 'Det' as in the Arundel Holcot (see Table 2).[30] Third comes the
shield with its three trumpets or on a ground azure, in the first of which is written
'Spedfull', in the second 'Dredefull', and in the third 'Medefull'. Here more
decisively still, the possibility of linking these *membra* with some such headword as 'Dom' is done away with. It may be suspected that since all the *membra*
in the e Museo sermon enter a symmetrical, and hence mnemonically serviceable, rhymed partnership with their associates ('Lit*il*', 'Ivy*ll*', 'Feky*ll*'; 'Part*yng*',
'End*yng*', 'Turn*yng*'; and 'Sped*full*', 'Drede*full*', 'Mede*full*'), this partnership
may have been the supervening consideration for the sermon author or the
redactor represented in his immediate source, more important than observing
headwords or the satisfactory derivation from them of the various *membra*. Next,
the clerk interprets the meaning of the shields generally, encapsulating it in a
Latin rhyme whose first line is worded a little differently from that found in the
Arundel Holcot, and whose second line, 'Hec tria scuta sciat quisquis celicola fiat',

---

[29] It must have been in this particular sermon author's immediate source that this had already
happened, because the other sermons behave similarly (see Figure 1 and Table 2).

[30] As will be seen, the Trinity sermon, to which e Museo seems closest, retains the *D* in
'Departinge'.

is not found there at all, and which may therefore either be an elaboration introduced into the postulated intermediary between the original form of the Castle of Prudence and the sermons (γ on the *stemma codicum*), or one introduced at some stage subsequent to the intermediary (ε or ζ).[31] The moral explanation of the *Castrum Sapiencie* then follows. The castle is the kingdom of heaven, and the ensuing commentary weaves in two references to the day's epistle (Text B, lines 71–72 and lines 76–77). The first shield is interpreted as the shield of man's life, the second that of his death, and the third that of the Last Judgement.

Table 2. Headwords/headletters (as applicable) and their *membra* appearing in the different redactions of the Castle of Prudence motif.

Arundel 384			
Vita – Lyf	Litel	Yuel	Fykel
Mors – Ded [Det]	Dolyng [Delyng]	Endyng	Deyng [Turnyng]
Iudicium – Dom	Dome [Derne]	Oppynly	Myghtfully
e Museo 180			
	Litill	Ivyll	Fekyll
[No headwords or headletters]	Partyng	Endyng	Turnyng
	Spedfull	Dredefull	Medefull
Lincoln 133			
L, I, F	Lyfe	hyt ys schorte	Fals/Fekell
D, E, T	Delys	Endus	Turnus vp so done
D, O, M	Dredfull	Opon	Myghtfull
Hatton 96			
	Lytyl	Yuyl	Fykyll
[No headwords or headletters]	Delyng	Ending	Turning
	Derne	Opyn	Myȝtful
Trinity 75			
	Litel	Yvell	Fikell
[No headwords or headletters]	Departinge	Endynge	Tornynge
	Demavndyng	Opening	Manassyng

[31] Or it may conceivably be a more authentic witness to what was in the original form of the Castle of Prudence, but which appears shortened to one verse only in MS Arundel 384. However, the fact that this second line of verse is not in the Trinity version perhaps weighs in favour of some late addition to the e Museo textual tradition, perhaps at stage ζ in the diagram, not something original to the Castle of Prudence author.

Over the first shield the clerk writes two Latin verses (the first of which, 'Vita qua vivis, lex mortis, iudicii vis', is not in the Arundel Holcot).[32] These verses are then rendered in English. The sermon proceeds to claim that it may be demonstrated that man's life is the 'law of death' mentioned in the verse, and goes on to adduce proofs. While recourse to proof texts at precisely this point of the narrative is not quite what the Castle of Prudence author had envisaged, it certainly consorts with his scholastic turn of mind as witnessed, for example, in his tell-tale instruction, 'Quere confirmacionem pro membris diuisionis' (Text A, line 40–41). Another portion of the day's epistle is woven into the sermon's commentary (Text B, lines 103–04 and 105–07), and the appropriateness of comparing man's life to the three degrees of the life-cycle of the rose (a motif found also in Hatton and Lincoln, though in the latter with considerable substantive variation, and very succinctly in Trinity), is rounded off with yet another citation from the day's epistle (Text B, lines 24–25).

Over the second shield the clerk writes a Latin verse, 'Mors habet excerto tria: divido, termino, verto', which this time bears little resemblance to its counterpart in the Arundel Holcot. There are various possible explanations for this. The variation may once again indicate a redaction entering somewhere into the textual tradition, either at the stage of the intermediary γ, or at some stage subsequent to the intermediary, at ε.[33] Alternatively, the Arundel Holcot may itself not be representing the Castle of Prudence author's original faithfully, although this is perhaps a less likely explanation, given the lack of internal rhyme of the e Museo verse, whereas all the Arundel Holcot verses rhyme internally. A third possibility is that both verses, each only singly present respectively in e Museo and in the Arundel Holcot, were together present in the Castle of Prudence author's original (that is, the e Museo textual tradition retained one verse and the textual tradition of Arundel 384 retained the other).[34] A commentary follows which once more and for the last time works in part of the day's epistle (Text B, lines 158–60).

Over the third shield the clerk writes a Latin verse, 'Monstrant tube qualis iudex veniet generalis', that is approximately comparable to that in the Arundel

---

[32] This verse must have entered the tradition earlier than ζ, since it is present in Trinity.

[33] This verse is also present in Trinity and therefore could not have been introduced by ζ.

[34] This is conceivable, though I believe less likely. There is a strict consistency to the internal rhymes of the Arundel Holcot that vanishes in the verses reported in the e Museo (and Trinity) witness.

Holcot.[35] A commentary follows which illustrates how the Last Judgement will be 'spedefull'. This is followed by illustration of how it will be 'dredfull', and this section introduces the Doom dialogues — an extended, dramatic passage, based on Matthew 25 — between Christ as *iudex mundi* at the end of time and the souls of the damned and the saved (in that order, taking its cue from the Castle of Prudence in reversing the saved-damned order found in the gospel). Comparable dialogues, which similarly reverse the gospel's order, are also to be found in Lincoln and Hatton (though in Trinity, as will be seen, the telegraphic lemmata *Venite, benedicti Patris mei*, and *Ite, maledicti*, restore the gospel order). A short final commentary on how the Last Judgement will be 'medefull' concludes the sermon.

The Lincoln 133 Version

We pass now to the second sermon, that in Lincoln 133 (see Text C). Although our sense of its form is impaired because it is both acephalous and atelous, it does not seem unlikely that much text has been lost. Notwithstanding this, it is unlikely that even in its pristine state would its form have had an ancestry as recognizable as that of the first part of the e Museo sermon, and this despite the fact that the Lincoln sermon stands alone among the sermons in explicitly referring to its *theme* (Text C, line 138), a term characteristically, though not exclusively, associated with sermons cast in the 'modern' mould of preaching.[36] It is clear from what survives that the Lincoln sermon cannot in fact have been thematic in any systematic sense that the 'modern' preaching mode typically comprehends, for there are no apparent divisions of the sermon's *thema* (*Timor mortis conturbat me*), let alone any subdivisions of it. The sermon as extant starts with a comparison of the seven properties of a dead body to the Seven Deadly Sins: the body's stiffness betokens pride; coldness, envy; hideousness, anger; heaviness, sloth; swelling, gluttony; putrescence, lechery; and grasping (that is, the convulsively snatching hands of a dying man), avarice. The narrative continues by observing that when a wicked man dies, he is in dread for four reasons: first, for

---

[35] Trinity is a little closer here to the Arundel Holcot, one of the reasons for its location relatively closer to ε.

[36] Though the Trinity sermon implicitly has a *thema* inasmuch as it begins with a line from the day's epistle. On the Lincoln sermon see also *A Repertorium of Middle English Prose Sermons*, I, 346–48.

memory of his sins; second, for dread of pain; third, for dread of damnation; and fourth, for bitterness of everlasting death. This observation immediately leads into the Castle of Wisdom motif.

A 'phylosephur', contemplating the feebleness of mankind and mankind's inclination to sin, made three gates, each surmounted by a shield, as an example to all. On the first shield, in each of three roses gules on a ground argent, was written a letter, respectively *L*, *I* and *F*; on the second shield, in each of three swords argent on a ground sable was written a letter, respectively *D*, *E* and *T*; and finally on the third shield, in each of three trumpets or on a ground azure, was written a letter, respectively *D*, *O* and *M* (see Figure 1 and Table 2, and compare the contrasting way the words are treated in the Arundel Holcot, e Museo, Trinity, and Hatton). A second 'phylosephur' came along, asked the castle porter to let him in, and declared that if he were to enter, he would first have to heed what life, death, and Judgement were.

The moral of all this is then introduced with a sermon formula especially frequent in the second half of the fifteenth century: 'Now gostely, frendes, as to owre purpose'.[37] The castle is the castle of heaven. The first shield is man's life. A commentary on this then follows which includes four quotations from Job, three of which are also found in the Office for the Dead. (Two of them were also used in a similar context in the e Museo sermon, in the commentary on the first shield.) The commentary concludes by saying that we should have in mind the three letters on the shield, *L*, *I* and *F*, but the value of the mnemonic acronym is damaged, since *L* is made to stand for 'lyfe' rather than the adjective 'Litil' that the shield has in the other texts, *I* stands for life's brevity, 'hyt ys schorte' (though how, precisely, is not clear, so that here the value of the 'LIF' acronym is lost utterly), and *F* stands for 'fals' and 'fekell', which although it retrieves possibilites for moral interpretation comparable to that introduced by the Arundel Holcot and more fully exploited by e Museo, does so too late to retrieve the general

---

[37] Alan J. Fletcher, 'The Meaning of "Gostly to owr Purpos" in *Mankind*', *N&Q*, n.s., 31 (1984), 301–02, though there are occasional earlier appearances; compare, for example, 'So goostly in þis purpose', in Richard Alkerton's Easter week sermon of 1406; see *A Study and Edition of Selected Middle English Sermons: Richard Alkerton's Easter Week Sermon Preached at St Mary Spital in 1406, a Sermon on Sunday Observance, and a Nunnery Sermon for the Feast of the Assumption*, ed. by Veronica O'Mara, Leeds Texts and Monographs, n.s., 13 (Leeds: Leeds Studies in English, 1994), p. 60, line 105. The collocation may also be found outside sermons proper. The earliest instance I know to date is in Walter Hilton's *Scale of Perfection*; *Walter Hilton: The Scale of Perfection*, ed. by Thomas H. Bestul (Kalamazoo: Medieval Institute Publications, 2000), p. 176, line 1129. *EPLMA*, p. 410 n. 159, has observed the collocation in the Middle English poem *Pearl*, a text approximately contemporary with the *Scale*.

integrity of the sequence.[38] The second shield is man's death, with the letters D, E and T. D signifies that death 'delys' (separates), E that it 'endus' (ends), and T that it 'turnus vp so done' (turns upside down). Here, the mnemonic acronym works (compare the Arundel Holcot and e Museo in Table 2). A commentary, approximately comparable to an outline discussion also found in the Trinity sermon discussed below, proceeds to describe three strokes of Death's sword: first, kindred and friends are cut away; next, worldly goods; and last, oneself. The three aforesaid letters, D, E and T, reveal three things. D signifies that one should 'deal' one's soul to God and one's goods to the world. To illustrate this, an exemplum is introduced from the *Alphabetum narracionum* of a dying rich man who is urged to make a will by his friends. When the clerk noting down his will asks what he is to write, the dying man replies with the verse 'Terram terra tegat [...]' (Text C, lines 113–16). This is said to illustrate all three propositions, how death 'separates', 'ends', and 'turns upside down'. The third shield is man's Last Judgement, with D standing for 'dredfull', O for 'opon' and M for 'myghtfull'. Here, the mnemonic acronym works within its own terms, and nearly corresponds to the Arundel Holcot *membra*, though it does not fully correspond to the e Museo *membra* (see Table 2). A commentary follows on D, O and M.

The last part of the sermon begins by saying that if anyone wants to enter the castle, he must think upon its three shields, that is, upon what life, death, and Last Judgement are. The preacher then repeats his *thema*, *Timor mortis conturbat me*, and the Doom dialogues follow, an eschatological gospel narrative popular with medieval preachers and based ultimately on verses from Matthew 25 but taking its lead from Holcot in addressing the damned first. Christ's judgement of the damned souls, 'Ite, maledicti, in ignem eternum qui preparatus est diabolo et angelis eius' (Text C, lines 141–42), is split into six individual utterances (*Ite, Maledicti*, etc.), each a rebuff to the damned souls' petitions. The sermon ends with a description of hell, and although no formal ending is given, the concluding 'et cetera' perhaps served as a cue to the preacher to supply one.

The Hatton 96 Version

The third sermon, or perhaps it might more circumspectly be called *materia predicabilis*, is from Hatton 96 (see Text D). It launches straight into the Castle of Wisdom motif without any preamble. A lord built a beautiful castle, and had set

---

[38] It appears that in Lincoln, the usual headword 'Lif' has been transferred to the first *membrum* ('lyfe') in place of 'litil', which in turn appears to have been transferred to the second *membrum* ('hyt ys schort') in place of 'ivyll'.

over its gate the three shields now familiar. (There is a small departure from all the other sermons in that the words on the Hatton shields are written around the devices, not inside them; see Figure 1.) The words on the shields are respectively 'Lytyl', 'Yuyl', and 'Fykyll'; 'Delyng', 'Ending', and 'Turning'; and 'Derne', 'Opyn', and 'Myʒtful'. The words around the devices correspond to the Castle of Prudence author's familiar *membrum* trios — in Hatton the most closely, in fact, of all the sermons — including the shield word 'Derne' ('Dom' in the Arundel Holcot, though since this should properly read 'Derne', Hatton seems to be witnessing here to the Castle of Prudence author's original reading). And like the presentation of the trios of e Museo (and, as will be seen, also of Trinity), some of which differ from Hatton's, those in Hatton bypass the first, second, and third headwords (the Arundel Holcot's 'Lyf', 'Ded' (*recte* 'Det') and 'Dom') to proceed directly to the headwords' three *membra*. A philosopher comes along, seeks entry, and the porter tells him that he must first construe the shields hanging over the gate. He does so, explaining that the shields symbolize man's life, death, and the Last Judgement.

Hatton then proceeds to unveil the allegory in a commentary. The castle is heaven. The shield with roses represents man's life. Man's life, with its stages of childhood, manhood, and old age, is comparable to the three phases of the life cycle of the rose, an idea also developed in e Museo (Text B, lines 108–23), in Lincoln (Text C, lines 77–88, though here with considerable substantive variation), and also, though very succinctly, in Trinity (Text E, lines 23–30) discussed below. The commentary then explains why life is 'Litil', 'Yuil', and 'Fikil' and includes one of the scriptural lemmata (Job 14. 5) used at a comparable point in the narrative of Lincoln (Text C, line 78).

The shield with swords represents man's death, and the swords represent the three strokes that Death strikes when he comes. A similar idea of Death's three strokes also occurs in note form in the Trinity sermon discussed below, and in Lincoln at a similar narrative juncture, in the commentary on the second shield (Text C, lines 97–103). The three strokes in Hatton compare with those in Trinity, as will be seen, but differ somewhat from those in Lincoln. In Hatton (and in Trinity), Death first removes man's wit; second, his goods; and third, his friends. What Death has to do with 'Delyng', 'Ending', and 'Turning' is next explained. Death 'delyþ' (separates) everything bound together by law, love, and nature. These categories are illustrated. Death 'endiþ' well and woe, friend and foe, meat and drink, rest and 'swink' (toil). These rhymed dyads are illustrated. And finally Death 'turniþ' fair into foul, rich into poor, and king into carrion. These dyadic transformations are also illustrated.

The shield with trumpets represents the Last Judgement, and the trumpets represent the three sets of words that God will speak at it. They are 'Arysiþ, ded men, and comiþ to þe dome', 'Goþ, corsid gostis, into fur þat euir schal last', and 'Comiþ, my blessyd chyldryn, to þe blysse þat my Fadir aþ y-dyȝt to ȝow of þe bygining of þe world' (Text D, lines 127, 128–29, and 147–48 respectively). Of the four versions, Hatton here corresponds the most closely to the Arundel Holcot, and probably, indeed, to the Castle of Prudence author's original. Also, Hatton is probably closest in most respects to the intermediary, γ, in the *stemma*. The first set of words is illustrated by the quotation from St Jerome that also appears in Lincoln (though there misattributed to St John). The second is illustrated from God's dialogue with the damned from Matthew 25, an excerpt used by both Lincoln and e Museo, and also by Trinity, though noted there only vestigially. And the third is illustrated from God's dialogue with the saved from Matthew 25, briefly alluded to in e Museo and Trinity, but not at all in Lincoln. Each of the three conditions of the Last Judgement, as 'Derne', 'Opyn', and 'Myȝtful', is then illustrated in turn. Hatton concludes in a familiar, formulaic way with a rhymed prayer.

The Trinity 75 Version

Paradoxically our last sermon (Text E), whose form, of the four, is the least readily discernible on account of the particular circumstances of its record, nevertheless lays greatest claim to having actually been preached. The original form is obscured chiefly because the sermon exists now only as a set of notes, but also because its actual delivery may have been in the main via English, not via the macaronic Latin and English mixture that the notes are written in. It is also the only sermon with an attribution to a specific preacher. Evidently it was preached, or had been intended for preaching, by the mysterious 'Doctor Curteyse', the 'Courteous Doctor', on some Passion Sunday in an unknown year.[39] Palaeography would suggest that the scribe entering the Courteous Doctor's sermon notes was working *c.* 1440, so it seems reasonable to suppose that the Passion Sunday for which the sermon was composed fell either in the latter part of the fourteenth or in the first part of the fifteenth century.[40]

---

[39] On the mysterious 'Doctor Curteyse', see further the notes given below in the *Apparatus fontium* and commentary to Text E, line 1.

[40] Compare Malcolm B. Parkes, *English Cursive Book Hands 1250–1500* (Oxford: Clarendon Press, 1969, repr. with minor revisions, London: Scolar, 1979), pl. 10 (i). What palaeography suggests can be further narrowed by internal evidence; see the headnote to Text E, below.

Although, then, its form is obscured, enough still remains to permit a tentative, if partial, view of what that form was like. An opening *thema* lifted from the Passion Sunday epistle is announced (Text E, lines 1–2), but the subsequent notes do not suggest that the sermon generated from this theme was to be thematic in the sustained way that the 'modern' preaching mode typically comprehended, because no apparent division of the *thema* occurs, let alone any subdivision of it (compare the Lincoln sermon in this respect, where a *thema* is referred to, but has no structural consequences). Immediately after the *thema*, two gates are announced, one in the east, of those who enter, which is baptism, and the other in the west, of those who depart, which is penitence.[41] The announcement introduces an architectural conceit in which is pictured an edifice (a castle or fortified building, presumably, since it has a drawbridge) of theological significance: between this castle's gates are found all the sacraments of the Church. Thus this castle of the sacraments makes an appropriate prelude to the castle and its symbolic shields that follow immediately upon it and that is introduced briskly as a 'Narracio poetica' (Text E, line 10).

A philosopher, looking for rest, visited many regions. Finally he rested on his staff in a deserted country near a byway and saw a heavenly tower, painted and adorned most elegantly, and arrayed all about with shining shields. Asking the gatekeeper for information about the edifice, he was told that it was one of divine wisdom, and that he would not enter it unless he could explain the shields with perfect clarity. Moved by a love of wisdom, the philosopher inspected the three shields above the gate (now familiar to us but with one small innovation: the three roses on the first shield were depicted respectively as a bud, a mature rose, and a withered rose, according to the stage of man's life that each represented; see Figure 1). The words on the shields are respectively 'Litel', 'Yvell', and 'Fikell'; 'Departinge', 'Endynge', and 'Tornynge'; and 'Demavndyng', 'Opening', and 'Manassyng'. And like the presentation of the trios of e Museo and Hatton, those in Trinity bypass the first, second, and third headwords (the Arundel Holcot's 'Lyf', 'Ded' (*recte* 'Det'), and 'Dom') to proceed at once to the headwords' three *membra*.

Essentially, the remainder of the Trinity sermon draws parallels between the (Old Testament) time of the law and the (New Testament) time of the perfection of the law. God in the Old Testament gave Moses 614 laws to convey to the people, of which 366 were negative and 248 positive. On account of the fragile

---

[41] Self-evidently, the association here of baptism and penitence with the beginning and the ending of the seven sacraments is not fortuitous; baptism is the first sacrament that the Christian soul receives on entry into the world, and penitence, which seems here to stand in for extreme unction, a sacrament closely connected with the penitential system, the last on going out of it.

nature of human memory (Text E, lines 61–63), God distilled this multiplicity of injunctions into the Decalogue, and in the (New Testament) time of the perfection of the law, further distilled them into the two Dominical precepts, which were in their turn further conflated in the Pauline maxim, 'Plenitudo legis est dileccio' (Text E, line 68). The sermon then proceeds to draw parallels between the action of Moses in Exodus 24 when he consecrated the people and the altar of God with the blood of birds and bullocks, and the actions of a Christian priest who in present times ministers at the altar the sacrament of the paschal bullock of the Christians (the 'vitulus Christianorum in die Passche'; Text E, line 72), Christ. Moses called the blood that he sprinkled over the heads of the people the blood of the covenant, and this blood (presumably now being understood as the blood of Christ) will accuse people at the Last Judgement unless they shall have observed it. Concluding sermon formulas were no doubt uttered in the original delivery, but were not recorded.

The Versions Compared

Apart from the shields, inherited — if with assorted permutations en route — from the Castle of Prudence author, all the sermons share various topics and citations which, while not present in the Arundel Holcot, and indeed probably not in the original ultimately lying behind it, were nevertheless anticipated there with the instruction 'Quere confirmacionem pro membris diuisionis'; the user must seek out confirmatory proofs on his own account. The most economical explanation for this state of affairs is that someone took the Castle of Prudence author at his word, expanded his skeletal 'picture' as he had recommended, and produced the intermediary γ from which it is reasonable to suppose that all four of the sermons have descended (see Table 1).

The Castle of Prudence copy which the compiler of the γ intermediary used, α, seems in certain respects to have been a superior witness to the Castle of Prudence author's original than Arundel 384's copy, β; note, for example, the greater adequacy of some of the vernacular components of the Castle of Prudence 'picture' appearing on the α side of the textual tradition and witnessed in Hatton. Yet for all that the sermons share sufficient amplificatory material in common to suggest their mutual origin in a common source, γ, that shared material only broadly agrees: while many of the sermons' topics are, to be sure, comparable in general terms, in terms of the *detail* of their substantive variation their divergences are very extensive indeed. The most likely explanation for this is that the intermediary γ was compiled in Latin (excepting, of course, the minimal vernacular components that were already inherited from the Castle of Prudence author), and that the sermons represent independent translations and/or reworkings that have ultimately stemmed from the γ intermediary. Possibly this γ intermediary was found in a *Gesta Romanorum*, as the declaration in the e Museo text might lead us to suspect; alternatively, it could have been a Latin sermon or some other such compilation offering suitable *materia predicabilis*. In the case of Hatton, an English translation of γ has been postulated in the *stemma* at δ, when the Latin shield verses present in γ were perhaps also jettisoned. Another recension of γ has been postulated in the *stemma* at ε in which the shield verses were retained and which generated the English translations represented by ζ and η. A further reason for postulating the translated recension ζ between e Museo and ε is that the Latin shield verses which e Museo shares with Trinity, and which have enough in common to unite these two witnesses against the Arundel Holcot, nevertheless diverge further from the Arundel Holcot's verses than do Trinity's. The postulated translated recension η between Lincoln 133 and ε is also presumed to have dropped the shield verses. Independent translations arising from γ would go some way towards explaining why the substantive variation of the three sermons recorded in English is so wide: the latitude of translation choices open to independent translators of a common ultimate Latin source would easily account for it. The differences between the three sermons that had necessarily arisen as a by-product of their independent translation, ultimately, of γ (in Hatton's case) and of ε (in the cases of e Museo and Lincoln) were then further complicated by the individual interests, additions and stylistic idiosyncrasies of each sermon compiler, and the net result amounted to a unique composition in each instance. While each sermon was essentially similar to the others since all had ultimately derived from γ, each became strikingly different in terms of its relative balancing and integration of the Castle of Prudence component within its general structure and in terms of the overall effect that each sermon makes.

What are these overall effects? Another lesson for late medieval English preaching that the variations on the theme of the Castle of Prudence teach is implicit in their sheer variety. The motif was delivered into the vernacular by men of varied stylistic competences, resources, and aims.[42] As has already been stated, none of the sermons can be satisfactorily classified according to any of the stricter

---

[42] As was assumed earlier, Trinity 75 too was delivered in English but recorded on the page in Latin. However, the condensed and abbreviated state of preservation of this sermon unfortunately prevents close assessment of the capabilities of its preacher, the Doctor Curteyse.

contemporary formulations of what acceptable sermon form should be, and this includes even the e Museo sermon, which comes closest to adhering to a form traditionally sanctioned. What we are dealing with, therefore, is a group of sermons which have been largely liberated from the constraints of theory and tradition into a more telling arena of practice, practice which may itself in due course become a new tradition. How does each very different writer harness in his own unique way the Castle of Prudence motif to accomplish the common aim of drawing minds towards the Last Judgement in which the motif finally comes to rest? Let us first examine each sermon's structure, using 'structure' here to refer, not to any theoretical standard ordained by the *artes predicandi*, but to the actual organization of the texts as they have been recorded. How central is the Castle motif to each?[43]

In the e Museo sermon, the image of a castle first appears in the gospel pericope from Matthew 21. 1–9, 'Ite in castellum quod contra vos est' (Text B, lines 5–6). The gospel passage ends, 'Blissed is he that commethe in þe name of the Lorde' (Text B, lines 21–22). If we pass on to the ending of the sermon we find that the opening command of the gospel pericope, 'Ite', has reversed into 'Venite', the eschatological invitation of Matthew 25. 34 (Text B, lines 204–05), as the historical *castellum* of the opening gospel pericope is displaced by the heavenly one implied by St Matthew four chapters later. The sermon concludes with the image of the blessed, 'Venite benedicti [...] Blissed be he þat commethe in the name of God [...] blissed be he þat governethe hym so that he may come to þat ioye [...]' (Text B, lines 204–09), entering God's castle at the end of time. The structure of the e Museo sermon is therefore nearly circular, to the extent that its ending repeats its beginning in transfigured form. The transitions from idea to idea throughout the text are achieved smoothly, mainly by the varied repetition of particular lexical items: the *castellum* of the gospel pericope leads to its allegorical interpretation as the castle of heaven, which in turn provides a link to the Castle of Wisdom; the 'labor' of the people of Israel to reach the Promised Land connects with the 'grete labor and grete disese' that people experience in this world, and so on. Thus in e Museo the Castle motif is organically worked into the whole. As with the other three sermons, e Museo towards its conclusion indulges in the dialogue between God and the damned inspired ultimately by Matthew 25,

---

[43] Where appropriate, the discussion which follows takes due, but silent, consideration of the fact that two of these sermons, Lincoln 133 and Hatton 96, are structurally incomplete (Lincoln certainly and Hatton conceivably), and that Trinity is incomplete by virtue of the circumstances of its record, as a set of sermon notes. These various kinds of incompleteness, however, should not detract from the validity of the general observations made.

but the final note struck by e Museo here is, as has been noted, one of promise and optimism.

Compare Lincoln 133, where the introduction of the Castle motif is far more workmanlike. We are straight into a sermon obviously darker in tone, understandably, given that its (non-biblical) *thema* is discovered to have been *Timor mortis conturbat me* (Text C, line 138). The focus throughout the opening section, as much of it as survives, is on the properties of a dead body, and on their allegorical equivalence to the Seven Deadly Sins. Again turning to the end, it will be seen how the sermon concludes with reflections on the pains of hell, embodied in the familar, sensory images: 'Þer schall be stynk orrebell. Þer schall be merkenys-felyng. Þer schall be crying, and seyng of deuells' (Text C, lines 167–68). The sermon therefore ends as it began, sombrely. The last lines directly address an audience, asking 'qwerto, þen, luf3e so mekull þe vanyte3 of thys worde, and luste3 to ocubye þe lyfe aftur þe lust and þe lykyng of þi flessche?' (Text C, lines 171–73). Perhaps the section missing from the beginning of the sermon may be imagined as having struck a note similar to this — the writer, as earlier mentioned, must have announced his gloomy theme and would presumably have followed it with some comment on its substance — but leaving aside the Lincoln sermon's tonal consistency, we do not otherwise find in this sermon the same sense of an evolving and circular connectedness such as is evident in e Museo.[44]

The Lincoln 133 dialogue with the damned (Text C, lines 138–62; compare its e Museo and Hatton treatments at Texts A, lines 181–96, and D, lines 128–42 respectively) sees God's address to the damned broken down into six numbered parts, each of which is individually translated. The Lincoln writer displays throughout a penchant for the enumerated catalogue. As well as the 'picture' of the three shields, each with its own subdivisions, which is common to all four sermons, we find additionally in Lincoln the seven properties of a dead body and their equation with the Seven Deadly Sins, and the four reasons why a wicked man is in dread of death. The connections between Lincoln's sets of ideas are far less carefully crafted than the connections in e Museo are. The link to the Castle motif, for example, is tenuously contrived. Its stages might be paraphrased as follows: avoid the Seven Deadly Sins; a wicked man suffers much dread in death; therefore a philosopher, mindful of the wickedness of man, made three gates and placed a shield above each. The connecting 'therefore' here is perfunctory and

---

[44] The Lincoln sermon, moreover, is left hanging on a Latin quotation attributed to Solomon ('Fatui non poterunt diligere nisi ea que eis placent'; Text C, line 173), which is untranslated and which could potentially lead into pastures fresh.

quite unconvincing. Equally unconvincing is the way in which the comparison of the life cycle of man to that of the rose is brought in: 'For ryght as þe rose florys are fayre to þe syʒt, ryght so monnes lyfe in thys world hyt ys schort and lytyll' (Text C, lines 78–79). The rose image is treated at greater length and somewhat more convincingly later, but its brusque initial introduction is maladroit. The Castle motif in Lincoln, like many of the sermon's other component parts, could be detached without Lincoln's general organizational plan sustaining any serious damage. The structure of Lincoln, then, is much more episodic.

The Hatton 96 sermon begins without preamble, starting immediately *in medias res* with the Castle motif: 'Hit wes somtyme a lord þat let makne a castel' (Text D, line 1). The body of the sermon thereafter is devoted entirely to the description and explication of the three shields, right up to the final section which ends on a short rhymed prayer that we might escape punishment and win eternal bliss. Thus, unlike the use to which the other sermons put it, the Castle motif in Hatton is its sufficient cause. Conceivably, Hatton may have been devised as an adjunct or ancillary text of some sort, preachable matter written to be annexed to a larger discourse if the themes with which it deals were found appropriate to the occasion. In that case, it could then have been elaborated and meshed into some other, wider treatment, just as the Castle motif has been in the e Museo, Lincoln and Trinity sermons, with varying degrees of success. Yet since there is no clear evidence of such a purpose, it seems simplest to assume that the Hatton text as it stands is self-sufficient.[45] It appears that the Hatton writer was at liberty simply to move from one description to the next as the Castle motif, mediated through the δ recension, dictated. Within its various sections, he managed transitions between images and ideas with great skill and fluidity. Compare, for example, the relative seamlessness of this associative sequence: the second shield is sable with three silver swords; sable is black, the colour of sorrow; men wear black as a sign of sorrow in time of death; and the three swords betoken Death's three strokes (Text D, lines 61–64).

For the reasons noted earlier, the original form of the organization of the Trinity sermon must be spoken of more cautiously. This granted, it would seem that its organization was in part produced by a process of associatively connecting ideas, as the Doctor Curteyse's opening castle of the sacraments seems to have

---

[45] While no indication in Hatton's layout, such as the insertion of a heading, might suggest such a conclusion, the structure of the piece nevertheless has an integrity that its absorption into a larger discourse may well have destroyed. Perhaps, therefore, what we see today is as much as its early readers or audience originally got.

flowed into his treatment of the Castle motif.[46] But thereafter, it is not fully clear how he connected the rest of his sermon, the series of parallels between the (Old Testament) time of the law and the (New Testament) time of the perfection of the law, to what had gone before. There are some apparent moments of connection: a mention of the sacrament of the altar (Text E, lines 69–70) makes another associative thematic link with the sacraments with which the sermon began; and a mention of the Last Judgement late in the sermon (Text E, lines 75–76) then leads the Doctor Curteyse into the shield verses, which are set out en bloc, with a final note that the philosopher placed the verses over the gate so that the meaning of the shields would be apparent to anyone who happened to come by. In this sermon, it would seem that the Castle motif was distributed between two major narrative units. First came the castle of the sacraments, then followed the first narrative unit in which the Castle motif made its debut. Next came the reflection on the times of the law and of the perfection of the law, followed by the second narrative unit in which the Castle motif featured again.

Having illustrated the sheer variety of treatments to which the Castle motif was submitted, I will finally look a little more closely at how its introduction has been managed in each of the three sermons recorded substantially in the vernacular (if not quite entirely, the Trinity sermon nevertheless being largely disqualified from such consideration on the basis of its telegraphic state of record).

Christ 'bowȝte man with his precius Pascion to bryng al mankynde to þe castel of heven. Ensampil of this castel we have, in *Gestis Romanorum*' (Text B, lines 28–30). Thus e Museo 180. Here, the identity of the castle of heaven with the Castle of Wisdom is established from the inception of the image. After the writer has described the shields in brief and told of the arrival of a 'rial and a notabyll clerke' to solve the riddle of their meaning, he proceeds at once to spell out an allegorical explanation: 'be this castell is vnderstonde þe kyngdome of heven [...] ther is all maner of welthe and ioye, ever lyȝte and never nyȝte, and more gretter murþe and ioye then hert can þinke or mowþe can speke' (Text B, lines 55–58). The allegory is already firmly installed, and the wealth, joy, and mirth that are mentioned are at once understood to be not of this world, but of the kingdom of heaven.

The lead-in to the motif in Lincoln 133 has already been noted. The philosopher, beholding the 'febulneȝ of monkynd', made 'thre ȝateȝ and abofe ych ȝate

---

[46] For an outstanding example of contemporary sermon development generated by the associative flow of ideas, see the sermon by the Oxford preacher John Felton analysed in *PPPLME*, pp. 71–74.

a schylde of diuers colors' (Text C, lines 57–59). The shields are then briefly
described before we hear that a second philosopher visits the castle. After the
porter has explained the law of the castle to him and he has studied its shields, he
offers the opinion that the place may be called 'a wyse castell' (Text C, line 71).
Here, the sermon writer's narrative grasp is relatively weak. First we have what
seem to be three disembodied gates; then a 'castell' is mentioned in passing;
finally, and with some delay, it becomes 'a wyse castell'. Two lines later the writer
states: 'By thys castell I vnderstond þe castell of heuen', but the allegorical punch,
delivered with such determination in e Museo, is here pulled completely.

As mentioned above, Hatton 96 gets straight to business:

> Hit wes somtyme a lord þat let makne a castel in a place þat he loued more þen anoþer
> and let ordeyne þerin al manere delicys þat ben ymaginyd oþer by þoȝt of man his
> herte — mete, drinke, golde, siluyr, perri, preciouse stonis, mirþis, ministracy wiþout any
> cesing — and ȝef þis castel a nome: þe Castel of Wisdome. (Text D, lines 1–5)

> (Once upon a time there was a lord who had a castle made in a place that he loved more
> than any other, and he arranged for there to be in it all manner of imaginable delights
> conceivable by the heart of man — food, drink, gold, silver, jewels, precious stones,
> mirth, minstrelsy without any ceasing — and he gave this castle a name: the Castle of
> Wisdom.)

The shields are described summarily and the law of the castle stated; we hear that
many come who fail of entry before a philosopher arrives.

Let us compare this moment of the philosopher's arrival in each of the three
vernacular texts. In e Museo it runs:

> And at the firste there cam to þis castel a rial and notabyll clerke, and he sadly and
> discretely understode be his discrescion and notabil connyng, þat þere was direct in these
> scheldis aforeseyde grete lurnyng of sowle-hele. (Text B, lines 42–45)

> (And first there came to this castle a royal, notable clerk, and by his discretion and notable
> ability he fully and discreetly understood that a great message salutary for the soul was
> indicated in these aforesaid shields.)

And in Lincoln:

> And so hyt befell þer come another phylosephur by thys castell a way and asket entre
> in [...] [*the castle porter then explains the law of the castle to him*] [...] And þen þis
> phylosophur lyftand up hys hed and beheld þus thre schyldes and sayde þat þis may be
> cald a wyse castell. (Text C, lines 65–71)

> (And so it happened that another philosopher came his way by this castle and asked
> admission ... And then this philosopher, lifting up his head, looked upon these three
> shields and said that this may be called a wise castle.)

And in Hatton:

> Þys phylosofre byhuld bysylyche þyse scheldis þat noʒte ne schold astert hym, and at þe last he was warre of þulk dox, dasow lettrys þat were aboute þe rosis, swerdis, and trompis, and saide to þe porter, 'Bewe sire, þise ne beʒ noʒt scheldis of armis, bot hit beʒ scheldis þat bytokyniþ manis lyf, deþ, and dome'. (Text D, lines 15–19)

> (This philosopher beheld these shields intently so that nothing should escape him, and he finally understood those same obscure and dim letters that surrounded the roses, swords, and trumpets, and said to the porter, 'Good sir, these are not military shields, but are shields that signify man's life, death, and judgement.')

In these short extracts the narrative strategies of each of the three vernacular sermon writers, their strengths and weaknesses, stand neatly epitomized. The dignified authority conveyed by the vocabulary of e Museo's doublets is complemented in their formal syntactical balance — 'rial'/'notabyll', 'sadly'/'discretely', 'discrescion'/'connyng' — and they progress confidently towards the conclusion: the shields blazon 'grete lurnyng of sowle-hele'. The impression created is that it is the message to be relayed by this 'rial and notabyll clerke' that will be all-important, not the events leading to it. The sermon's audience, it will be recalled, has already been primed to expect an allegory on the kingdom of heaven; much of the mystery of the castle has previously been dispelled.

The writer of the Lincoln sermon does not achieve anything like this. That someone chances by and is then told about the law of the castle is less effective in terms of narrative suspense than e Museo's management of the episode (and Hatton's and, for that matter, the Arundel Holcot's and Trinity's).[47] The Lincoln writer fails to capitalize on the potential here. For the rest, his is a bare description of events. While it might be argued that here, too, the ultimate interest is the message, not the narrative, contrast e Museo where, as was seen, the message is lent advance weight by the way in which its bearer, announced as a 'rial and notabyll clerke', is presented.

The two extracts from Hatton 96 quoted above suggest a similar conclusion: this was also a writer who, like that of e Museo, invested in the art of narrative, though he distributed his investment somewhat differently. Hatton's compara-

---

[47] In Trinity, the philosopher's chancing upon the castle is also picturesquely realized (see Text E, lines 11–15), and suggests comparison with the sudden fabulous appearance of castles to wayfarers in medieval romance; compare, for example, the appearance of Castle Hautdesert to Sir Gawain in the Middle English romance *Sir Gawain and the Green Knight*, ed. by J. R. R. Tolkien and Eric Valentine Gordon, 2nd edn, rev. by Norman Davis (Oxford: Clarendon Press, 1967; repr. 1985), pp. 22–23, lines 763–810.

tively lengthy description of the castle itself is absent from the other treatments, and note in what the castle's delights consist: food, drink, gold, silver, mirth, and minstrelsy. A castle for a lord indeed. Thus far, Hatton's seems an alluringly palpable earthly castle, until the moralizing philosopher solves the riddle. Contrast e Museo, where we were aware from the start that we were dealing with a figure for the kingdom of heaven, and where the 'welthe and ioye' of the castle were of a different order, spiritualized and immaterial. Even the name of the castle in Hatton gives no real clue that the text will ultimately be religious. The sermon writer, through his philosopher, acknowledges the potential for misinterpretation: 'Bewe sire, þise ne beȝ noȝt scheldis of armis' (Text D, line 18–19). Both the theme and mode of address here might have been lifted from romance, as might the reference to the 'lord' (Text D, line 1). These details produce a genre resonance absent from the other texts.[48] (In fact, yet again the writer of the Lincoln sermon misses an opportunity by having a philosopher build the castle in the first place. No maker is mentioned in e Museo.) Unlike e Museo and Lincoln, Hatton makes a preliminary effort to tease and then confound audience expectation. Its narrative strategy in this respect seems as important as the message it seeks to convey.

One further noteworthy point arising from the last-quoted Hatton extract is that, unlike the 'rial and notabyll clerke' of e Museo who seems certain of the answer to the riddle from the outset and has no need even to look at the shields, and the philosopher in Lincoln who simply lifts his head, beholds the shields, and pronounces his verdict at once, the philosopher in Hatton, 'byhuld *bysylyche* þyse scheldis *þat noȝte ne schold astert hym*, and *at the last* he was warre of þulk *dox, dasow lettrys*' (Text D, lines 15–17). The italicized words here function on two levels: most immediately, they draw matters out, heightening the suspense; and secondarily, they send out a message, as surely as did the description of the clerk in e Museo, though here in Hatton to different effect, about the value of clerkly learning. In Hatton the answer to the shields does not come pat. Effort is required, even from those who might be expected to know the answer already. This, of course, has an interesting corollary: it takes a 'notabyll clerke', to use e Museo's phrase, or a philosopher to uncover and expound the hidden meaning of veiled and symbolic text. Hatton has chosen its own way to dramatize and so reaffirm education and clerkly authority as the prerequisites of trustworthy exegesis.[49]

---

[48] Except perhaps in the Trinity version; see the preceding note for discussion.

[49] This ideological charge is noticeably present, if in varying extents, in all of the sermons, and may be taken as a sign of their profound orthodoxy.

The Question of Audience

Aside from the varying competences manifest in each of the three vernacular sermon authors' respective handlings of the introduction of the Castle motif, also to be reckoned with is a variety that may have arisen as a function of considerations of audience. Important determinations here are each sermon's original provenance and date, and these, as far as they can be fixed, have been presented in the headnotes to Texts B, C, and D (also to E, though for reasons earlier explained, this sermon is precluded from any extended stylistic discussion). Suffice it to say here that the evidence yielded by the sermon manuscripts — perhaps with the exception of Hatton 96 — is disappointing. The manuscript copies are too far removed from the original moment of their sermons' birth to afford any reliable indication of whom their sermons may first have been intended for.[50] It is therefore necessary to look to the sermons themselves for any internal clues they can provide about the four men who created them and about the possible audiences those men had in mind.

The search for this information obliges some reflection on the implications of linguistic choice, including the choice of Latin or the vernacular, in e Museo, Lincoln, and Hatton (the linguistic choices of Trinity constitute a special case unavailable for discussion in this respect since its text is largely in Latin). At the most basic level, there is the question of how Latin is used. It may be observed that the use of Latin steadily decreases from e Museo to Lincoln to Hatton. The e Museo sermon has no fewer than thirty-five separate instances of Latin items or quotations, mainly biblical; in Lincoln the number falls to twenty-one, again mainly biblical; and Hatton dwindles to a mere two, one from Job, the other from Solomon. As the vernacular sermons are all of approximately similar length, these are interesting statistics. One particularly noteworthy feature of e Museo is its inclusion of the Latin verses which the clerk wrote over each of the gates in the castle. These are found, with more or less variation, in the Arundel Holcot, but not in either Lincoln or Hatton (their near kinship to the verses appearing in Trinity, discussed above, providing one of the bases for postulating ε ultimately lying behind e Museo and Trinity in the *stemma*). The e Museo writer provides English verse translations for these rhyming Latin couplets, though admittedly the

---

[50] It is nevertheless true that the manuscript copies may contain clues to the nature of *subsequent* audiences that the sermons came to cater for. Three out of four of them may have been intended for secular priests (though indeed, all four of the original sermon authors are likely themselves to have been seculars). The sole exception is Lincoln 133 which, surprisingly, was owned and copied by a draper.

meaning of the translation for the verse over the roses of the first shield is a little opaque:

> Vita qua vivis lex mortis, iudicii vis,
> Vita notata rosis brevis est, mala, plena dolosis

This is rendered:

> Thy lyfe it is a law of dethe,
> A strengþe of dome the to begyle.
> Fygurde be these rosis redd
> It is full ivill and lastythe but a whyle.
> (Text B, lines 89–92)

Niceties of translation aside, can the use of such verses give any indication of the type of audience for which this sermon was intended? After all, verses were commonly used in late medieval preaching, even if more austere preachers frowned upon them as an adulteration.[51] Might verses indicate a more popular pitch on the preacher's part and a concession to his audience's relative lack of education or sophistication? Fortunately, the e Museo sermon may elsewhere shed some light on this question, for its author has characterized his audience by opening with the formulaic address, 'Good men and women'. His sermon was evidently designed for a mixed audience, and therefore probably not one evenly educated to the same altitude. Although some members of an audience like this, perhaps the majority, might not have understood the Latin used in the sermon, they might nevertheless have understood the Latin's general purpose.[52] In the e Museo sermon, then, it may be that the use of Latin reveals more about the sermon writer than it does about his target audience. As already suggested, in a sermon concerned to surround its internal message-bearer, the philosopher, with an aura of authority, its use of Latin could only confer a similar advantage upon the external message-bearer, the preacher himself.

The writer of the Lincoln sermon was somewhat less sedulous in his attention to Latin and its handling. There are no English verses in this sermon. Quoted authorities are either Church Fathers (whether rightly or wrongly attributed) or biblical. The first biblical quotation, from 'Dauid' ('Mors peccatorum pessima'; Text C, line 24), is neither translated nor glossed, and in Text C, line 118, there

---

[51] For a thorough discussion of the use of verses in sermons, see Wenzel, *Verses in Sermons*, pp. 61–100. The topic is also considered below in Chapter 9.

[52] See *EPLMA*, p. 56.

appears to be a scribal error, precipitated perhaps by some indecision about how the translation should be conducted. The sermon ends, as mentioned earlier, with an untranslated quotation from Solomon: 'Fatui non poterunt diligere nisi ea que eis placent.' The reason why no translation or gloss is given is unclear. As the *et cetera* following the quotation suggests, the line may simply have been recorded for use as a cue, should subsequent expansion be required. Whatever the case, this dangling quotation adds to the Lincoln sermon's general air of incompleteness and episodic form.

On the question of the use of Latin, the Hatton sermon is perhaps the most interesting. It has already been noted that here only two Latin citations are to be found. One is a reference to Job 14. 2 which Hatton shares with Lincoln (Text D, line 28); the other is from 'Solomon' (Ecclesiastes 1. 11; Text D, line 100). Seven further authorities are invoked by the Hatton writer, among them Jerome, Bernard, and Gregory (whether rightly or wrongly attributed). In fact, the Hatton writer's range of *auctoritates* is wider than that of either of the other two vernacular sermons. Yet when he adduces these *auctoritates*, he either renders them already translated into English ('Iob saiþ þat "mannis days beþ sort and þe tal of is monþ is toward þe"'; Text D, line 52); or he paraphrases them ('Seint Gregori saiþ þat þe dome schal be ful grisful, wan man schal y-se aboue hym God wroþ þat is boþe domisman and party'; Text D, lines 164–65). A further notable example of his insistent vernacularity resides in the fact that his dialogue between God and the damned takes place entirely in English (contrast its e Museo and Lincoln treatments). Stylistically, the Hatton dialogue thus duplicates the unbroken flow of the original gospel narrative more nearly than does the corresponding dialogue section in Lincoln and e Museo, where the flow is interrupted by self-conscious exchanges between Latin and English.

The Hatton writer also employs vernacular verses but, unlike those of e Museo, his are neither translations of, nor in any way related to, the verses derived from the Castle of Prudence motif. The above-quoted English verse translation of e Museo may be compared with the following verses on old age found in Hatton, and the striking differences between the two poems in terms of their tone and register noted:

> Wan þat is wyte waxit falou
> And þat is cripse waxit calau,
> Wen þi neb ryveliþ as a roket
> And þin hein porfilin as scarlet,
> And þi nose droppiþ as a boket,
> Þan þou beon y-clipid kombir-flet.
> (Text D, lines 43–48)

> (When what is white grows yellow,
> And when curly hair becomes bald,
> When your face wrinkles like a rochet,
> And your eyes are rimmed with scarlet,
> And your nose drips like a bucket,
> Then you'll be called 'space-waster'.)

Hatton's homely imagery (caught especially in the cluster of similes in lines 3–5) is completely at odds with the metaphorical texture and stately tone of the e Museo verse. If the vernacular verses of e Museo bear the hallmark of an authority that they have redacted from their Latin models, no comparable *gravitas* is cultivated by Hatton's verses. Even so, the Hatton writer could also be said to have had some concept, if one more broadly based, of literary authority. Apart from providing wonted fare from the Bible and Church Fathers to prove his point, and offering verse like that just quoted, he also distils proverbial wisdom (Text D, lines 87–88), and appeals to what common sense should make self-evident: 'Þys dom schal be myȝtful. Wat schold mor myȝt þan wiþ a blast of is mowþe gadyr togedyr al eorþe and heuen and helle and al þat is þerin?' (Text D, lines 171–73). Thus poetry, proverbs and appeals to common sense seem raised to a virtual parity with *auctoritates* of the more familiar sort.

Were the presence of Latin taken as the benchmark of education and authority, the Hatton writer might seem on the face of it the least imposing of the three vernacular sermon authors. But what does the lack of Latin reveal about him and his audience? In fact, it is not possible to infer from this absence any reciprocal lack of education on his part, for his avoidance of Latin is hardly in itself evidence of his inability to use it. Since it appears that the essentials of his sermon were ultimately translated from a Latin text in the first place, the Latin recension γ postulated in Table 1, he obviously knew his Latin. It may be more profitable to look to the sermon's putative recipients for an answer to why its authorities were offered almost entirely in English. Here arises the question of the 'implied audience' that the sermon may suggest. Yet any attempt to uncover an implied audience must be aware that what is actually being traced is the phenomenon that Walter Ong has termed the 'created audience', that is, the audience created by the writer in the act of writing.[53] While we try, at this remove, to conjecture from a sermon its original contemporary audience, we have to reckon with the possibility

---

[53] Walter Ong, *Interfaces of the Word: Studies in the Evolution of Consciousness and Culture* (Ithaca: Cornell University Press, 1977), pp. 53–81.

that the sermon writer composed for an audience that he anticipated, not for one that he actually had. The distinction, though nice, needs to be made. As will be seen, it may well be that the implied audiences of e Museo, Lincoln, and Trinity were similar, yet as a result of their writers' respective skills (or lack of them), the sermons are stylistically very different.

What, then, is the implied audience in the case of the e Museo sermon? It has already been noted that e Museo points the way to an answer in its 'Good men and women' formula, for this suggests a mixed, lay congregation, in all likelihood one innocent of clerkly learning. However, other aspects of the sermon seem to tend in a different direction. Its overall structure, its comparatively generous use of Latin, its poised prose occasionally decked in doublets and alliteration (for example, 'we so fekill and so feynt in feythe and so freyle and so fals in oure lyvyng'; Text B, lines 134–35), along with its references to the *Gesta Romanorum* (Text B, line 30) and the *Poetria nova* (Text B, line 61), may all imply an audience whose intellectual capacity, if uninformed according to narrowly clerical standards, was nevertheless not to be slighted or patronized. The sermon writer created a text whose main argument was understandable by an audience with an educational formation that was modest enough, but at the same time, the argument could also have been appreciated by an audience not insensible to its niceties of dress and manner of conduct; that is, if his audience's members were not actually sermon connoisseurs, then at least they may have been people of educated sermon tastes.

On the surface, Lincoln shares some of the features of e Museo. There is use of Latin (if less frequently), use of an exemplum attributed to the *Alphabetum narrationum* (Text C, lines 105–18), and a hint of academically respectable structure in the marshalling of various numbered divisions and in the mention of a sermon *thema*. However, the abiding impression left by Lincoln is that while its writer was someone who had an inkling of how sermon theory should in principle guide preaching practice, he was simply not very adept in translating that theory into being. If his target audience was of similar calibre to that conjectured for e Museo, its members may well have found the less-than-pristine form into which he pressed his matter disappointing.

The implied audience in Hatton's case would seem, on the face of it, to have been rather different. As noted earlier, although several recognized *auctoritates* are referred to, only two are quoted in Latin and both are then translated. In Hatton there is by contrast an equally great investment in 'homely', vernacular authority: in vigorous English verses, proverbs, and appeals to common sense. Of a piece is the introduction of such practical information as rosewater being 'holsum to manis heyn' (Text D, line 24; see the note on this), or advice that when a man is dead, one must at once 'turne im out of is bed on þe colde erþe and leþ a torf on is womb for swelling' (Text D, lines 73–74; see also the note on this). The imagery here and throughout the sermon is vivid and concrete.

The manipulative narrative strategy of the Hatton writer has been noted earlier. He seems also to have had an interest purely in the language in which he chose to present his narrative. This interest was of a complexion somewhat different from that shown by the writer of the e Museo sermon. There, language displayed moments of impressive control and tight, formal balance, witnessed in such features as the repetition of certain words to link various thematic ideas, and in the use of alliteration and doublets. In Hatton the style is a little less mannered, though still by no means artless. Observe, for example, this anaphoric accumulation in Hatton: 'Ryʒt so mannis lyf waxit among þornis, now of worldelyche bysynisse, now of bodylyche secknisse, now heer, now sowe, now rype, now moue, now hole, now sek, now lyʒe, now wep' (Text D, lines 24–27); or these doublets: 'deþ endyþ weel and wo, frend and fo, met and drink, rest and swink' (Text D, lines 93–94). The first example, man's life growing among thorns, equips the 'life as a rose' image, also more rudimentarily present in the other two vernacular sermons, with an additional series of allegorical 'thorns';[54] and the second example, the things that Death brings to an end, shows the writer indulging not only his taste for doublets but also a fondness for casting them in rhymed dyads. While the language here and elsewhere in Hatton, then, may be playful, it is so in terms that nevertheless emphasize the domestic and homespun.

Because Hatton corresponds least of our three vernacular sermons to official ideals of received sermon form, it seems to offer proportionally more access to the mind of the man who wrote it, in as much as it reveals him to have been unconcerned by traditional expectations in this regard. Yet that nonchalance would not seem to have been the offspring of any unfamiliarity with those expectations; it is a safe assumption, for reasons mentioned earlier, that he had been educated to a reasonably high standard, and as such he was likely to have encountered received ideals of sermon form. He also betrays some acquaintance with and sympathy for the resources of secular literature in the quasi-romance opening discussed above (Text D, lines 1–4), and occasional touches elsewhere (references to a 'king and quene', Text D, line 120; to 'cloþis of gold', Text D, line 72; and to

---

[54] Though since such thorns appear in the Trinity sermon (Text E, lines 28–31), we should probably not regard them as an innovation on the part of the compiler of the sermon reflected in Hatton.

jousting 'of werre oþyr of pes', Text D, line 110) evince the sort of interest in a high-class secular milieu that the romance genre typically shares. Yet he was at the same time a man with a common touch, someone who could wear his learning and contact with those literary and cultural contexts lightly. Most importantly, perhaps, given the dedicated purpose of his text, he was a person aware of the need to capture the attention of an audience and of how to go about doing that, contriving his *captatio benevolentiae* deftly. What can be deduced about that audience? Given the characteristic strategies of the Hatton author, it may be that his implied audience was not itself highly educated, and his indifference, on this occasion at least, to received norms of sermon composition may indicate an audience for whom those norms, or even the paying of lip service to those norms, were not a *sine qua non* of acceptable preaching. The touches evocative of romance by no means necessarily imply a courtly milieu and they are, moreover, far outnumbered by images selected from life lived lower down the social scale.

So in sum, when all four sermons are gathered for comparison, it becomes apparent how very different their growths from the same Latin kernel are, growths whose differences are to be explained not only by the differing narrative competences of their authors, but also by possible differences in audience calibre. The sermons also demonstrate forcefully that by the fifteenth century, if not indeed already before, the sermon genre had become a relatively fluid discourse in which the application of regimented ideas of sermon form, so frequently the burden of the theorists, was no longer — even if it had ever once been — the overriding concern of sermon practice.[55] And once the conduct of actual practice had rendered the more rigorous theoretical forms negotiable, the boundaries of the discourse were prone to a striking variety of realignments, especially when sermons in practice were left free to absorb matter that more rigorous theoretical forms could less comfortably accommodate.[56] This was the more liberal and practical environment, then, in which all four sermons edited here were fostered, and in which they were also left free to develop in such very different directions. Somewhere tending towards the redundancy or in some cases the collapse of pristine theoretical ideals of sermon form must have been the imperative that

---

[55] This point may have implications for critics of Middle English literature who attempt to demonstrate a conformity to the rules of the *artes predicandi* in such literary works as they seek to persuade us are influenced by medieval sermon form. It may be that any influence from the medieval sermon genre will be rather more diffuse than narrow appeal to the *artes* alone can warrant.

[56] Compare, to cite but one example, the English lullaby around which a sermon, copied in the first half of the fourteenth century and formerly preserved in Fountains Abbey, Yorkshire, was constructed (see *PPPLME*, pp. 32–39).

clerical culture, at a pastoral level at least, conduct itself in the vernacular, in some cases using vernacular components ill suited to fulfilling the requirements of theories of sermon form that had been drafted with Latin preaching models chiefly in mind. The Castle of Prudence author's admission of English was symptomatic of his time, and prophetic of even more conspicuous consequences for the sermon genre as time went by. His tolerance foretold a flexibility, a pluralism, that came increasingly to characterize pastoral writing conducted, as inevitably much of that writing must be, at the Latin and English interface of clerical and lay culture. Through the very necessity of speaking English in pastoral circumstances, Latinate clerical culture would help lay a foundation for its own invasion through English. It unwittingly collaborated with the agenda of those English voices that would eventually be raised against the Latinate exclusiveness of clerical learning. However, before the latter years of the fourteenth century when those voices would become strident, the seeds of this paradoxical collaboration were quietly being sown in the very moment that the preaching clergy sought to fulfil their evangelizing and catechizing mandate.

Text A

London, British Library, MS Arundel 384, fols 93ᵛ–94ʳ

Refert Hermes Egipcius quod quidam rex condidit quoddam castrum quod vocabatur Castrum Prudencie, et precepit quod nullus intraret nisi sciret describere tria scuta que in foribus castri pendebant. Primum scutum erat de argento cum tribus rosis rubeis, quarum due fuerunt superius et tercia 5 inferius. Secundum scutum erat nigrum cum tribus gladijs de argento a singulis angulis pendentibus. Tercium scutum erat de azorio cum tribus tubis aureis. In tribus rosis rubijs primi scuti scripta erat 'Vita'. In gladijs secundi scuti scripta erat 'Mors'. In tubis tercij scuti scriptum erat 'Iudicium'. Contigit igitur quemdam philosophum venire illuc et petiuit ingressum, 10 cui ianitor respondit quod lex castri erat sic statuta, quod nullus intraret nisi sciret illa scuta describere. Et philosophus respiciens erectis oculis ad scuta, et statim intellexit ipsorum interpretacionem. Et ait ianitori, 'Vere, racionabiliter vocatur istud castrum Castrum Prudencie, et racionabiliter est lex posita castri, et ideo ut ego ualeam intrare, dico quod primum significat 15 quod homo debet in uita sua tripliciter diligere Deum, scilicet ex toto corde, tota mente, tota uirtute, et hoc ex mente pura, quod interpetatur per scutum argenteum et tribus rubeis |fol. 94ʳ| rosis, nam puritas interpretatur in argento et in rubedine amor. Secundum signat mortem quam omnes sustinebimus.

Triplex gladius signat triplex iudicium peccatoris, quia aut iudicabitur ad
20 penam corporalem pro peccatis faciendam, aut penam purgatorij, aut penam
eternam. Per hoc quod gladij sunt argentei, et scuta nigra signant quod mors
diuidit a uita et detrudit in ingredientem mortis. Tercium scutum signat
finale iudicium in quo sonabit triplex tuba. Prima sonabit 'Surgite, mortui,
venite ad iudicium'. Secunda erit sentencia beatorum que sonabit 'Venite,
25 benedicti Patris mei', et cetera. Tercia erit omnibus terribilissima que sonabit
aduersos reprobos, 'Ite, maledicti, in ignem', et cetera. Et continuo subiunxit:

'Splendor in hijs scutis monstrat documenta salutis.
Vita notata rosis breuis est et plena dolosis.
Mors datur a tergo tribus ensibus omnibus ergo.
30   Monstro tubis quale erit examen generale.'

Moraliter. Istud castrum est celum, quam mansionem nullus intrabit nisi
diligat Deum ex toto corde, et cetera, et impleat mandata sicut ipse rex
huius castri precepit. Si uis ad uitam ingredi, serua mandata. Et eciam ut
timeat triplicem tubam et gladium diuine vlcionis in reprobos. Et ad ista
35 consideranda et implenda incitaret triplex scriptura in scutis predictis que
est 'Vita', 'Mors', et 'Iudicium'. Vnde in istis vocabulis in Anglicana lingua
sunt nouem littere, scilicet tres in primo, tres in secundo et tres in tercio.
Sic: 'Lyf', 'Ded', 'Dom'. Vnde tres littere cuiuslibet indicant proprietates
rei intellecte. Per 'L' notatur quod uita est 'Litel'; per 'I', 'Yuel'; per 'F',
40 'Fykel'. Vnde vita hec est 'Litel', 'Yuel', & 'Fykyll'. Quere confirmacionem
pro membris diuisionis. Secundo mors est 'Delyng', 'Endyng', 'Turnyng'.
Et tercio, iudicium finale erit 'Derne', 'Oppynly' & 'Myghtfully', et cetera.

Critical Notes and Glosses

41 Delyng] dolyng MS
41 Turnyng] deyng MS 42 Derne] dome MS

Apparatus fontium and Commentary

1   This *moralitas* is headed in the MS: De iudicio; Hermes Egipcius: here the Castle of Prudence
    author seems to be referring to Hermes Trismegistus of the Hermetica, but what actual source
    he was using, I have not been able to determine. On the knowledge of the Hermetica in the
    later Middle Ages, see Thorndike, *A History of Magic and Experimental Science*, II, 219.
15–16 ex toto corde ... virtute: compare Mark 12. 30.
24–25 Venite, benedicti Patris mei: Matthew 25. 34.
26 Ite, maledicti, in ignem: Matthew 25. 41.

Text B

Oxford, Bodleian Library, MS e Museo 180, fols 177ᵛ–85ᵛ

Good men and women, ȝe schal vnderstonde that the Gospel of þis day
makethe mencion what tyme that owre soveren Sauiowre Criste Ihesu went
withe his discipyls here on erthe in þis present lyfe, and came nyȝe to the cite
of Ierusalem in the cuntre of Bethfage, at the mownt of Olivete. Then Ihesus
5 sent his tweyne discipyls and seyde to hem these wordis, 'Ite in castellum
quod contra vos est, et statim inuenietis asinam alligatam et pullum cum ea.'
Go ȝe into the castel þat is aȝenste ȝow and anon ȝe schal fynde an asse tyed
and a colt withe hyr. Vnbynde ȝe them and bryng hem to me. And if eny man
that seythe to ȝow enyþing, sey ȝe that the Lord hathe nede to hem, and anon
10 he schal leve hem. Truly al this was done that was seyde be the prophete
seyng þus, 'Dicite, filie Syon, ecce rex tuus venit tibi mansuetus, |fol. 178ʳ|
sedens super asinam et pullum filium subiugalis.' Sey ȝe to the dowȝter of
Syon, loo thi kyng commethe to the homly or mekely sittyng on an asse, and
a foole the sonne of a beest vnder ȝoke. Fforsothe the discipils went and dyd
15 as Ihesus commawnded to hem, and they browȝt an asse and the foole and
leyde there cloþis on hem, and made owre Sauiowre Ihesu to sitt above on
hem. And so þer was moche other pepil that leyde ther cloþis in þe way, and
some pepill dyd cutt braunchys of trees and strewyd in the wey. But the
company that went before and tho that sued behynde cryed and seyde,
20 'Osanna filio David; benedictus qui venit in nomine Domini.' Þat is to sey, we
pray the saue vs, þu þat art þe sonne of Dauid. Blissed is he that commethe in
þe name of the Lorde, osanna in hyȝeste thyngis.

Moraliter. The moralle vnderstondyng of this Gospell after þe seyng of
docturs, where as Crist commawnded |fol. 178ᵛ| tweyne of his discipils to go
25 to þe seyde castell, is to vnderstonde that þis precius Lorde Criste Ihesu cam
firste to make man, and after that gafe to hym a law to govern hym by.
Another tyme he cam to by man what tyme that he cam and toke flessche
and bloode of þe glorius virgyn our Lady, and after that bowȝte man with his
precius Pascion to bryng al mankynde to þe castel of heven.

30 Ensampil of this castel we have in *Gestis Romanorum*, that þer was in the olde
tyme a castell þat was calde 'Castrum Sapiencie', the Castell of Wisdom, and
in the entryng of this castell there was deput iij scheldis. The firste schelde

was of siluer withe iij rosys as it had ben gooldis, and in þe firste rose was
wreton 'Litil', in the secunde rose was wreton 'Ivyll', and in the therd rose
35 was wreton 'Ffekyll'. The secunde schelde was of sabyll withe iij swordis of
siluer, and |fol. 179ʳ| vpon the firste sworde was wreton 'Partyng', and in þe
secunde, 'Endyng', and in þe þerde, 'Turnyng.' The therde schelde was of
asure withe thre trompis of golde, and vpon þe firste trompe was wreton
'Spedfull', and on þe secunde, 'Dredefull', and vpon þe therde, 'Medefull.'
40 So the law was ordend at þat tyme that ther scholde no man enter into this
castell, but if case were that he kowde discerne and construw the cawse and
the intent whi they were so sett and so portrude. And at the firste there
cam to þis castel a rial and a notabyll clerke, and he sadly and discretely
vnderstode be his discrescion and notabil connyng, þat þere was direct in
45 these scheldis aforeseyde grete lurnyng of sowle-hele. And þen he wrote over
the ʒatis þese ij versis:

'Splendet in hiis scutis tibi gens doctrina salutis;
Hec tria scuta sciet quisquis celicola fiet.'
'In these scuchyns þat schynythe |fol. 179ᵛ| so bryʒt
50 There is doctrine to the pepyll of gostly well.
These thre muste he con aryʒt
That in heven desyrethe for to dwell.'

And after þis he wrote versis over [every] schelde conteynyng the mater in þe
schelde, as ʒe schall here more pleynlyer in the explanacion.

55 Moraliter. Gostly to owre purpose, be this castell is vnderstonde þe kyngdome
of heven, the whiche is a suer castell and a perfite plesaunt abidyng, for ther
is all maner of welthe and ioye, ever lyʒte and never nyʒte, and more gretter
murþe and ioye then hert can þinke or mowþe can speke, ever duryng worlde
withe owten ende. Now frendys, I can þinke that ʒe wolde feyne enter
60 into this castell, þat is to sey, the passyng ioyes of heven. But as Galfridus
Anglicus, in *Nova Poetria* seythe, 'Sunt alij qui scire volunt sed non operari.'
There bythe moche pepyll that wolde feyne haue heven but they |fol. 180ʳ|
kepe not ne they wyll not labor therfore. So we rede in holy Scripture of þe
pepil of Israell, when they herd of the plentowse contre of the londe of
65 promyscion, ffeyne they wolde haue ben þere. But when þei herde of the
grete bateyle þat þei scholde haue or they cam theder, þen þei were passyng
wery of there iurney and repentid them sore of there grete labor. So in like

wise moche pepill of the worlde wil not remember themselfe, how þei haue
grete labor and grete disese in this worlde, and how they schall procede and
70 passe owte of this worlde, ne they wot never how sone, whether to peyne or
to ioye. And therfore seythe the Apostil Paule in þe Pistill of this day,
'Scientes tempus quia hora est iam nos de sompno surgere.' We know this
tyme that the owre now is come that we owȝte to rise fro slepe. Þat is to sey,
now þe tyme is com þat we scholde |fol. 180ᵛ| ryse owte of synne and slepe
75 no lengar þerin. But as fast as we may, wake into vertues lyvyng becawse of
the commyng of Criste. As who seythe, þe tyme of his Natiuite. 'Nunc enim
propior est nostra salus quam cum credidimus.' Ffor now owre helthe is nere.
That is to sey, the tyme is commyng þat Criste wolde be borne for mans
redempcion. Therfore, and ȝe purpose to enter into this castell aforeseyde,
80 þat is to sey, into the perpetuall ioye, þe kyngdome of heven, then muste ȝe
haue ever in ȝowre remembraunce these iij scheldys aforeseyde. The firste is
the schelde of mans lyfe, the whiche was deput withe roses. The secunde is
the schelde of dethe þat was peynted withe iij swordes. And þe therde is the
schelde of the dredeful day of dome, þe whiche was figurde be þe tromppis.
85 The ffirst I sey is þe schelde of mans lyfe, and over þat scheld withe roses þis
clerke aforeseyde wrote these versis,

'Vita qua |fol. 181ʳ| vivis, lex mortis, iudicij vis;
Vita notata rosis brevis est, mala, plena dolosis.'
'Thy lyfe it is a law of dethe,
90   A strengþe of dome the to begyle;
Ffygurde be these rosis redd
It is full ivill and lastythe but a whyle.'

That mans lyfe is a law of dethe it may well be prevyd, and litil tyme
indurythe. Ffor like as ȝe see þat temporall law desisiþe and termynethe
95 debatis and stryvis and ȝeldythe every man his owne, so in like wyse dethe
endythe all thyngis betwene the body and þe sowle. Þerfore whyle þu haste
space to amende þi lyfe, it is grete wisdome for þe to cast awey the derke and
mystye spottis of synne, and grownde the in grace of good lyvyng. Ffor as ȝe
see that a rose florisschythe more and is more fresscher when the lyȝt of the
100 day is comen and þe nyȝt before 'is' past, so on the same maner wyse when
þe derkenes of synne is past, þen almyȝti God ȝevithe lyȝte into thi sowle,
and so cawsithe |fol. 181ᵛ| a vertues man or woman to increce more and
more in vertu and grace of good lyvyng. And so berithe witnesse þe Apostill

Paule in the Pistill of this day, 'Nox precessit, dies autem appropinquauit.'
105 The nyȝte went before but the day hathe nyȝhede. 'Abiciamus ergo opera
tenebrarum.' Therfore, seythe the Apostill, caste we awey þe werkis of
derkenesse. 'Et induamur arma lucis.' And be we clothed withe the armor of
lyȝte. Ffor mans lyfe may well be likened be roses in iij degreis. Ffirste there
is a bud in þe whiche the rose is closed in. And after owte of this bud
110 spryngethe a feyre rose, a swete and a delicius, and sone after withe wyndes
and weders the levis fadythe and fallythe to þe grownde, and so turnethe to
erthe. So gostly, in every man and woman of the worlde there bythe iij
ages. The firste age is childhode, in þe whiche the flowris of manhod and
womanhode ben closed in. Ffor ther is no man can |fol. 182ʳ| tell what schall
115 falle of a childe in tyme commyng, whethere he schall be riche or pore, good
or bad, wyse or vnwyse, riche or recheles. Ffor his flowris schall spryng, increce
and growe after governaunce. And after þis commethe ȝowthe; then hathe
he or sche lyȝtnes, swiftnes, wantonnes and many other ornamentis of
kynde. But þen at the laste commethe age; then schrynkethe his flessche,
120 then fadythe his colowre. His bonys be very sore, his lymmys wexythe febyll,
his yeesyȝte felythe and wexithe very dyme, his bake begynnythe to bow and
croke downwarde to the erthe þat he cam of. Then his flowris declynethe
and fallythe awey to þe grownde. And so man hathe none abidyng. Therfore
seythe the Apostill Paule in þe Pistill of this day, 'Sicut in die honeste
125 ambulemus.' As in a day walke we honestly. As who seythe, the tyme of owre
|fol. 182ᵛ| beyng here, dispose vs honestly in þe moste vertues wyse to the
plesure of God. Ffor þe dayes of owre beyng here ben full ivyll. 'Dies mali
sunt.' And when þu schalt passe owte of this worlde, þu schalt not take all thy
wordly gooddys withe the. 'Homo cum inter`i´erit non sumet omnia.' And
130 þe prophete seythe, he schall haue somwhat withe hym and þat is but smalle.
Ffirste he schall have vij foote of erthe to ley his body in and a wyndyng
schete. Thus þis maner of remembraunce of owre synfull lyvyng, and also of
owre litil abidyng here, and also the ivill `s´pendyng of owre tyme in þis
present lyfe, and then we so fekill and so feynt in feythe and so freyle and so
135 fals in owre lyvyng. All thys scholde cawse vs to vnbynde owre sowlis from
synne. And so scholde it be vntyed frome the devyll, and then browȝte into
the castell of heven. But in conclucion, of oure lyvyng here Iob seythe, 'Homo
natus |fol. 183ʳ| de muliere breui viuens tempore', pro primo; 'Repletur
multis miseriis', pro secundo; 'Qui quasi flos egreditur et conteritur', pro
140 tercio. A man is borne of a woman, lyvyng but a schorte tyme, ffor þe firste,

and he is fyllyd withe moche miseri and wrechidnes, ffor þe secunde, and we schall passe as a flowre and not long tyme indure here, ffor the therde.

The secunde schelde þat I spake of I seyde was þe schelde of dethe, the whiche was figurde be the swordes, and over that schelde þis forseyde clerke
145 wrote this verse:

'Mors habet excerto tria: Diuido, termino, verto.'

'I parte', seythe Dethe, 'I ende, I turne all new'. What trowiste þu that Dethe departiþe when he commethe? Ffirste he departiþe every man and woman frome all there good frendys in þis worlde, and he bryngethe mans lyfe to
150 an ende and turnethe þe sowle from þe body. And þen departythe the body to þe erthe þat he cam of, |fol. 183ᵛ| and the gooddis to the worlde, and þe soule to the wey of everlastyng dampnacion or els into the wey of everlastyng salvacion. As David seythe, 'Relinquent alienis diuicias suas et sepulcra eorum et domus illorum in eternum.' They schall leve þer riches behynde
155 them and there grave schall be þer howse witheowten ende. Therfore resist all maner of synne that commethe of þe flessche whyle þu art alyve, and not to haue a delyte in metis and drynkis and long liyng in beddis. Ffor so commawndythe þe Apostill Paule in the Pistill and seythe, 'Non in comessacionibus et ebrietatibus, non in cubilibus et inpudicicijs, non in
160 contencione et emulacione.' Þat is to sey, not in superflue of festis and dronkennessis, not in beddis and unchastiteis, not in strife and in envy, 'Sed induimini Dominum Ihesum Cristum', but be ʒe clothed in the Lorde Ihesu Criste, as who seythe, be ʒe indued withe mekenes and perfit lufe and charite, withe the remembraunce of dethe at the departyng owte of þis worlde. |fol.
165 184ʳ| And so schalt þu fynde occasions and cawse to ryse owte of synne into þe state 'of' vertu and grace, by þe whiche þu schalt haue þe more grace and help of God at thi departyng to passe and procede into the castell of heven, of þe whiche spekythe Criste in þe Gospell of Iohn seyyng thus, 'Hec est vita eterna vt cognoscant te verum Deum et quem misisti, Ihesum Cristum.' That
170 is to sey, this is þe lyfe that ever schall last that they know þe very God in Trinite and whome þu sendist, Ihesu Criste.

The therde schelde that ʒe schall haue in mynde is the schelde of the dredfull day of dome as I seyde was figurde be þe trompis. And over this schelde þis forseyde clerk wrote this verse:

175   'Monstrant tube qualis iudex veniet generalis.'

The trompis schewe the how and what wise þu schalt come to þe dome.
It schall be passyng spedefull, ffor all schall come to the dome þe whiche
toke cristendome. As the holy Apostill Paule rehersiþe and seythe, 'Canet
enim tuba et mortui |fol. 184ᵛ| resurgent incorrupti.' All tho that toke þe
180 sacrament of baptym schall ryse aȝene in þe lickenes as they were in þe firste
begynnyng. But it schall be passyng dredfull, ffor to all soche as at that tyme
stondythe in þe wey of dampnacion, almyȝti God schal sey þese wordys,
'Discedite a me maledicti in ignem eternum qui preparatus est diabolo et
angelis eius.' That is to sey, 'Go hens awey fro me ȝe cursed pepyll into the
185 endlesse fyre of hell, the whiche is ordend to the devyll and to all his aungels'.
Þen if case be þat þu myȝtiste sey vnto almyȝti God thus, 'Now good Lorde,
syn it is so þat þu commawndiste vs to go fro the, suffer vs nyȝe the', þen
seythe þe good Lorde as I seyde, ' Discedite a me', 'Go ȝe awey fro me'. 'Now
good Lorde, syn þu wilt not suffer vs ny the, ȝit grawnt vs þi blissyng.' He
190 seythe aȝene, 'Maledicti', 'ȝe schall departe fro me acursid'. 'Now good Lorde,
graunte us a comfortabyll place to abyde in.' He schal |fol. 185ʳ| sey aȝene,
'In ignem eternum', 'Into everlastyng fyre of hell'. 'Now good Lord, grawnte
vs þat owre peynes may have a schorte tyme.' He schall sey aȝene vnto hem,
'In eternum', 'everlastyng'. 'Now good Lorde, grawnt vs good compeny and
195 good felischip.' He schall sey aȝene, 'ȝe schall have non oþer but all the devyls
in hell'.

Now frendys, for the grete mercy of owre Lorde, remember þiselfe þu þat art
a synner, ffor now þu mayste vnbynde þi sowle frome synne and haue the
mercy of God. But when þe naturall lyfe is past frome the body, þen schall
200 the ryȝtwisnes of God procede and no mercy. And therfore seythe Criste in
þe Gospell of this day, 'Soluite et adducite michi'. 'Breke atwo the halter of
synne, aske mercy and þu schalt come to me.'

The therde I seyde it schall be passyng medefull. Þat is, to all tho þat schall
stonde in þe wey of saluacion almyȝti God schall sey, 'Venite benedicti Patris
205 mei.' Come ȝe blissed |fol. 185ᵛ| childern of my Fader to everlastyng blisse.
And then may I sey as it is in þe Gospell, 'Benedictus qui venit in nomine
Domini.' Blissed be he that commethe in þe name of God. As who seythe,
blissed be he þat governethe hym so that he may come to þat ioye and blisse
þat almyȝti God bowȝt vs to. To the whiche, et cetera.

Headnote

The three operative manuscripts for this edition are: Oxford, Bodleian Library, MS e Museo 180; Lincoln, Cathedral Library, MS 50; and Durham, University Library, MS Cosin V.IV.3. They have respectively the sigla *O* (e Museo), *L* (Lincoln), and *D* (Durham) in the apparatus. All these manuscripts are written on paper by the same scribe in a hand dating probably to the late fifteenth century (his hand also appears in Gloucester, Cathedral Library, MS 22, although Gloucester lacks the sermon edited here). Nothing is known about this scribe, other than the fact that he seems, on linguistic grounds, to have been writing a variety of Middle English whose orthography locates in southern Bedfordshire, towards the Buckinghamshire border. His multiplication of what is fundamentally the same vernacular *de tempore* sermon cycle suggests that he produced his manuscripts for retail.

Apparatus of Variants

Lines 1–19 Good ... cryed] *lac. L*
Line 1 Good ... women] Ffrendys *D*
Line 2 what] of the *D* Line 3 on] one *O*: in *D*; and] *add.* so when he *D*
Line 4 in] *add.* to *O*
Line 5 his tweyne] ij of hys *D*
Line 6 alligatam] alligatum *D*; et²] *add. canc.* pl *O*
Line 7 anon] þer *D*
Line 8 a colt] hyr foole *D*; them] hyr *D*; hem] hyr *D*
Line 9 that seythe] sey owȝt *D*; enyþing] *om. D*; to hem] to hyr *D*
Lines 9–10 anon ... hem] *om. D*
Line 10 al] *om. D*; that was seyde] *om. D*
Line 11 Dicite] Discite *O*
Line 13 homly] lovyngly *D*; on] vp on *D*
Line 14 of a] of *D*; Fforsothe] þen *D*
Line 15 to hem] þem to do *D*; an] the *D*
Line 16 on¹] vp on *D*; to] *om. D*; on²] vp on *D*
Line 17 other] *om. D*
Lines 17–18 and ... wey] *om. O*
Line 19 company] pepyll *D*; sued] folowyd *D*; seyde] *add.* þus *LD*
Line 20 Þat ... sey] *om. D*; we] I *O*
Line 21 is] be *LD*
Line 22 the Lorde] god *L*; osanna ... thyngis] *om. D*
Line 23 Moraliter] *add.* So gostly to owre purpose *LD*; The ... Gospell] by this gospell I vnderstonde *D*
Line 24 tweyne] ij *LD*

Line 25 seyde castell] castell afore seyde *D*; to vnderstonde] *om. D*; Criste Ihesu] almyȝti god *O*

Line 26 that] *add.* he *D*; to hym] hym *D*

Line 27 Another] The secunde *D*; he cam to] crist cam for to *L*; by man] make man free *D*; that]
   om. O

Line 28 þe] that *D*; Lady] *add.* Seynt Mary *LD*; that] *add.* he *D*

Line 29 to¹] for to *D*; to²] in to *D*

Lines 30–59 Ensampil ... heven] *om. D*

Line 33 of] on *L*

Line 34 Litil] *add.* And *L*

Line 36 the] *om. L*

Lines 36–37 in þe secunde] on þe secunde sworde was wreton *L*

Line 37 in þe þerde] on þe þerde swerde was wreton *L*

Line 38 þe firste] every *O*

Line 39 and¹] *om. O*; secunde] *add.* tromppe was wreton *L*; therde] *add.* tromppe was wreton *L*

Line 42 they] þat þese scheldys *L*

Line 45 hele] helthe *L*

Line 50 well] helthe *L*

Line 51 he] be *L*

Line 53 every] overy *O*; schelde] scheldys *L*

Lines 54–55 in ... Moraliter] aftyrwarde So *L*

Line 57 all] *add. canc.* of Ioye *O*; of] *om. L*; and¹] *add.* all maner of *D*; and more] more *O*

Line 58 ever] evermore *D*

Line 59 Now] But *L*

Line 60 þat ... heven] *om. L*; the passyng] in to the *D*

Line 62 moche pepyll] many *L*; wolde feyne] feyne wolde *D*

Line 63 kepe not ne they] *om. LD*

Line 66 þen] *om. D*

Line 67 sore] *om. D*

Line 68 wise] *add.* þere is *D*; worlde] *add.* wolde feyne haue heven but þei *L*: *add.* þat *D*

Line 69 and grete] and *O*

Line 70 whether] ne wheder *L*: other *D*; or] *add.* els *D*

Line 71 day] *add.* þus *LD*

Line 72 tempus] *om. OLD*

Lines 72–73 We ... come] knowe ȝe þat þe owre is now comyn *D*

Line 74 now ... com] þe tyme *L*: þe tyme is commyng *D*; scholde] owȝte to *L*; owte of] from *L*

Line 75 we] *add. canc.* make *O*

Line 76 his] cristis *D*

Line 77 propior] *om. D*; quam cum credidimus] *om. OL*; Ffor] fforsothe *D*; nere] nyȝe *L* Line
   79 to enter] for to enter *LD*; this] þe *D*; into] to *O*

Line 80 ioye] Ioyes of *D*

Line 81 ever] evermore *LD*

Lines 81–94 these ... indurythe] the departyng owte of þis worlde *D*

Line 85 The] *om. O*; þe schelde of] *om. O*; lyfe] *add.* withe rosys *L*; withe roses] *om. L*

Line 86 these versis] þis verse *L*

Line 87 Vita ... vis] *om. L*

Line 94 temporall] *om. O*; desisiþe and] *om. LD*; termynethe] determynythe and endythe *L*

Line 95 stryvis] *add.* bytwene one man and a noþer *L*; and²] *add.* so *D*; in like wyse] dothe *O*; dethe] *add.* in like wise *O*: when dethe commythe he *D*

Line 96 endythe] determynythe and endythe *L*; Þerfore] And therfore *D*; haste] *add.* tyme and *D*

Line 97 space] *add.* here *L*; lyfe] *add.* for *D*; for þe] and *LD*

Line 98 in] *add.* vertu and *L: add.* þe *D*; Ffor] *add.* lyke *D*

Line 99 more and is] and is more and *L: add.* and more and is *D*

Line 100 comen] come *L*: commyng *D*; before ` is´] *om. D*

Line 101 thi sowle] ʒowre sowlys *D*

Line 102 so] þat *O*; increce] be incresyd *D*

Lines 102–03 more and more] *om. LD*

Line 103 in] wythe *D*; so] þat *D*; witnesse] *om. D*

Line 104 day] *add.* and seyþe þus *L: add.* and seiþe *D*; precessit] precedit *D*; appropinquauit] appropinquabit *D*

Line 105 but] and *L*; Abiciamus] Abiciamur *D*

Line 106 Therfore ... Apostill] *om. LD*

Line 107 we] *om. O*

Line 108 Ffor mans lyfe] ffor þi lyfe *O*: Mans lyffe *L*: ffor the lyffe of man *D*; likened be] fygurde by *L*: lykened vn to *D*; in] ffor I conceyve in a rose *D*

Line 109 in] *om. D*; rose is] rosis ben *L*; in. And] and *D*; owte of] *om. O*; bud] *add.* in þe whiche the Rose is *O*

Line 111 fadythe and fallythe] fallythe and fadythe *O*; fallythe] *add.* awey *L*

Line 112 gostly] in lyke wyse þere is *L*: *om. D*; the] this *D*; there bythe] *om. L*; iij] *add.* degres of *L*

Line 113 age] *om. LD*; flowris] flowre *O*; and] or *D*

Line 114 womanhode] woman *D*; ben] is *O*; in] there in *D*; man] *add.* þat *LD*

Line 116 riche or recheles] *om. L*; Ffor] *add.* as *D*; schall spryng] ben spryngyng so schall he *D*

Line 117 þis] childhod *D*; ʒowthe] *add.* and *LD*

Line 119 þen] *om. LD*; age] *add.* and *LD*

Line 120 colowre] *add.* And *D*; very] *om. LD*; sore] *add.* and *D*

Line 121 his ... dyme] *om. L*; felythe] *add.* hym *D*; wexithe very dyme] *om. D*; to] for to *L*; bow] *om. L*; and²] or *O: om. L: add.* to *D*

Line 122 of] *add.* And *LD*; his] *add.* feyre *L*

Line 123 awey] *add.* and so fallythe *O*; none] no sure *L*; abidyng] *add.* here and *L: add.* and *D*

Line 124 day] *add.* thus *L*

Line 126 here] lete us *D*; honestly] *om. D*

Line 128 take] *om. L*; all] *om. D*; thy] maner of *O: add. canc.* ri *L*

Line 129 wordly] *add.* riches and þi *L*; inter` i´erit] interieret *D*

Line 130 þe] *om. O*

Line 131 in] there in *O*; and] *add.* ʒit he schall have *D*

Line 132 Thus *om. L*; and] *add. canc.* as *O*; also] *om. L*

Line 133 also] *om. L*; owre] *om. O*

Line 134 fekill] synfull *D*; and³] *om. D*

Line 136 so ... vntyed] *om. L*: also *D*; then] be *L*: so *D*; into] vn to *L*

Line 141 and he is fyllyd] it is here fulfylled *O*

Lines 141–42 we schall passe] *om. D*

Line 141 we] he *L*

Line 142   passe] *add.* awey *L*; flowre] *add.* fadythe and fallythe awey *D*; indure here] indurythe *D*

Lines 143–47 The ... new] *om. D*

Line 143 schelde] *om.* L

Line 147 ende] *add.* and *L*

Line 148 every] bothe *D*

Line 149 all] *om. O*; there] his *D*; good] *om. O*; þis] *om. L*; to] in to *LD*

Line 153 David] *add.* þe prophet *L*; alienis] alieni`a´s *D*; diuicias] *om. D*

Line 155 howse] *add.* worlde *L*; resist] *add.* þu *L*

Line 156 synne] *add.* from þe *L*; 000 flessche] fowle flessche *L*

Line 157 metis ... and] *om. O*; metis] delycate metis *D*

Line 158 þe] *add.* holy *L*; seythe] *add.* þus *LD*

Line 159 et¹] *om. O: add.* in *D*

Line 160 contencione] conntenttentacione *O*: contempcione *D*; superflue] superfluens *LD*

Line 161 dronkennessis] of dronkennessys *D*

Line 162 induimini] induemini *OL*: induamini *D*

Line 163 and¹] *add.* in *D*

Line 164 at] and *LD*; departyng] peynefull departyng *L*; worlde] present lyffe *LD*

Line 165 to] for to *D*; synne] *add.* up *L*

Line 166 state] *add. canc.* and *O*; and grace] *om. D*; grace and *om. L*

Line 167 to] when þu schalte *L*: And so for to *D*; procede] to procede *O*; into] to *L*

Line 168 of Iohn] of Seint Iohn *L*: *om. D*

Lines 172–96 The ... hell] *om. D*

Line 172 in] in ȝour *L*

Line 173 this] þat *L*

Line 174 forseyde] *om. L*

Line 176 The] þese *L*; wise] wyse that *L*; dome] dome and *L*

Line 177 all] all tho *L*; þe whiche] þat *L*

Line 178 Canet] canit *OL*

Line 179 incorrupti] primi *OL*

Line 180 lickenes] same lykenes *L*; were in] were at *L*

Line 181 soche] tho *L*

Line 184 ȝe cursed pepyll] acursid *L*

Line 185 endlesse] *om. L*; hell] *add.* everlastyng *L*; all] *om. L*

Line 186 almyȝi] *om. L*

Lines 186–87 þen ... seyde] he schal sey aȝene *L*

Line 188 awey] *om. L*

Line 189 ȝit] *om. O*

Line 190 seythe] schall sey *L*; Maledicti] *om. O*; ȝe schall departe] departe ȝe *L*; me] *om. O*

Line 192 eternum] *om. L*; everlastyng] þe *L*

Line 193 tyme] ende *L*; vnto] to *L*; hem] hem þus *L*

Line 194 In] *om. L*

Line 195 He] þe good lorde L; aȝene] *om. L*
Lines 195–96 all ... hell] þe devil and all his aungells L
Line 197 owre Lorde] god LD; þiselfe] ȝowre selffe and L
Line 198 ffor] *om. L*; the] *add.* grete L
Line 201 Breke] *add.* ȝe LD
Line 202 þu] ʼþenʼ ȝe D; schalt] schall D
Line 203 The ... is] And D; to] *add.* sey L; all tho] hem O
Line 205 blissed childern] childerne blessyd L: blessyd D; to everlastyng blisse] *om.* D; to] in to
    L; blisse] Ioye and blys L
Lines 206–09 And ... vs to] *om. L*
Line 206 it is] I seyde D
Line 207 be] is D
Line 208 þat] þe D
Line 209 cetera] *add.* Amen D

Critical Notes and Glosses

8–9 if eny man that seythe to ȝow enyþing] (The ellipsis noted here has been removed in the D
    reading. (The L text is wanting at this point.) The omitted item, if supplied, would at its
    simplest need to be the present subjunctive of the verb BE, whose subject would be 'eny man'.
    (This assumes that the presence of the word *that* is not an error. On the non-expression of
    the finite verb, see Tauno F. Mustanoja, *A Middle English Syntax*, Mémoires de la Société
    néophilologique, 23 (Helsinki: Société néophilologique, 1960), p. 510.)

17–18 and ... wey] The reading, adopted here from D, lacks a direct object pronoun, but it is
    clear from the preceding clause (see Mustanoja, *A Middle English Syntax*, I, 144–45). The use
    of the auxiliary DO in an affirmative declarative sentence is rare at this date (see A. Ellegård,
    The Auxiliary Do: The Establishment and Regulation of its Use in English, Gothenburg Studies
    in English 2 (Stockholm: Almquist and Wiksell, 1953), pp. 179 and 182).

19 sued] 'followed'.

22 thyngis] The word is redundant. The translator has thought it necessary to supply the Latin
    adjective *excelsis* with an explicit noun for it to govern. Compare the similar treatment as 'hiȝ
    thingis' in the Wycliffite translation (*The New Testament in English*, ed. by J. Forshall and F.
    Madden (Oxford: Clarendon Press, 1879), p. 44, verse 9).

23 opposite in left margin: Moraliter.

24 tweyne] 'two'.

31 opposite in left margin: Castrum Sapiencie.

32 opposite in left margin: .1.

32 deput] None of the recorded Middle English senses of the word *deput* will do here. The
    context requires a word with a sense similar to *painted*. Possibly the word is in some way a
    corruption of *depeinte* used often in the sense of emblazoning arms (see MED, s.v.
    'depeinten'), and this sense is the one particularly appropriate for *deput* here and throughout
    the sermon. The word also appears at line 82.

33 it] A singular pronoun but with the presumably plural antecedent of *rosys* (line 33).

34 opposite in left margin: .2.

34 opposite in left margin: .3.

42 portrude] 'portrayed'.

55 opposite in left margin: Moraliter.

81 opposite in left margin: .1.

82 deput] 'painted'.

82 opposite in left margin: .2.

83 opposite in left margin: .3.

86 opposite in left margin: versus.

112 opposite in left margin: Moraliter.

113 opposite in left margin: Primum principale.

118 ornamentis] 'attributes' (and see the further note below under *Apparatus fontium* and Commentary).

121 yeesyȝte] 'eyesight'.

132–35 A textual corruption may account for the anacoluthia of these lines, but they might equally be reflecting the ellipsis common to speech patterns. (The appearance of disjunctive rather than discursive syntax in speech is widely noted; see, for example, Barbara M. H. Strang, *A History of English* (London: Methuen, 1970), pp. 66–67.)

141 and he is fyllyd] Emendation of the *O* text in this line makes better sense, but it is conceivable that the *O* reading was the one taken from the exemplar.

143 opposite in left margin: Secundum principale.

172 opposite in left margin: Tercium principale.

181 soche] 'such'.

187 syn] 'since'.

Apparatus fontium and Commentary

1 Good men and women: This is a common opening for many vernacular fifteenth-century sermons *ad populum*, and here indicates that the text's intended congregation comprised both sexes. (If, as seems likely, the sermon author's intended congregation was parochial, there are signs that it was possibly one of greater than average sophistication; see the earlier discussion on the pitch of the e Museo 180 text.) 'Good men and women' is John Mirk's favourite opening throughout his *Festial*, at least some of which was destined for parish preaching in St Alkmund's, Shrewsbury (*Mirk's Festial*, pp. 1, 6, 11, 15, etc., and see Fletcher, 'John Mirk and the Lollards'). The words 'makethe mencion' (line 2) also coincide with an opening sermon formula. Compare John Wyclif's Latin usage at the start of some of his sermons, *Hoc evangelium facit mencionem [...]* (*Iohannis Wyclif Sermones*, I, 9, line 4). See also further Chapter 10, below.

5 Ite in castellum: Matthew 21. 2, part of the day's gospel (Matthew 21. 1–9).

11 Dicite, filie Syon: Matthew 21. 5.

20 Osanna filio David: Matthew 21. 9.

23–29 I have not been able to identify the source of this exegesis. Since the author refers to it as the 'seyng of docturs' (line 23–24), it would appear to exist somewhere in an *auctoritas*. (It also happens that the 'processe' of an unrelated sermon for the second Sunday of Advent in London, British Library, MS Royal 18.B.xxiii has practically identical contents; see *Middle English Sermons*, ed. by Woodburn O. Ross, EETS, o.s., 209 (London: Oxford University

Press, 1940; repr. 1960), p. 314, lines 16–20.) It is not to be found in either the *Catena aurea* or the *Glossa ordinaria*. Since it is composed of three main distinctions, it resembles many of the entries found in collections of *distinctiones*. One of these might provide a source, though again I have not located it in any of the more influential *distinctio* collections (such as Thomas of Ireland's *Manipulus florum* or the works of Nicholas Gorran and Nicholas Byard). Equally, however, the exegesis may derive from one of the fourteenth-century alphabetical compendia (themselves the direct descendants of the earlier *distinctio* collections) that were designed specifically for preachers. For a basic corpus of thirteenth-century English material, see André Wilmart, 'Un répertoire d'exégèse composé en Angleterre vers le début du XIIIe siècle', *Mémorial Lagrange* (Paris: Gabalda, 1940), pp. 307–46, and for a general discussion of the *distinctio* genre, see Richard H. and Mary A. Rouse, 'Biblical Distinctions in the Thirteenth Century', *Archives d'histoire doctrinale et littéraire du moyen âge*, 49 (1974), 27–37. See also Homer G. Pfander, 'The Medieval Friars and some Alphabetical Reference Books for Sermons', *MÆ*, 3 (1934), 19–29.

30–59 A stylistic change in the prose of this passage is registered in its increased use of two specific syntactic features. The existential 'there' construction (Mustanoja, *A Middle English Syntax*, I, 337) appears five times within a short space, at lines 30, 32, 40, 42 and 44. Doublets are also prominent, particularly between lines 55–59. The doublets help impart a rhythm to the prose, while existential 'there' allows the postponement of the subject to a final emphatic position in the prose unit. Such devices are appropriate to the language of the storyteller.

47 Splendet in hiis scutis: The Arundel Holcot reads for these lines simply, 'Splendor in hiis scutis monstrat documenta salutis' (fol. 94^r). Both lines of the sermon and the one of the Arundel Holcot, if in fact intended as dactylic hexameters, do not scan properly.

49–52 In these scuchyns ... dwell: These lines, like all other pieces of verse throughout the manuscript, are written as prose. They were probably noticed to be verse by the scribe, however, since he has separated each line by putting an oblique red dash at the end of it. The verses eluded the *NIMEV*.

55 Gostly to owre purpose: This expression is a formula of late medieval preaching discourse, and normally introduces an exegesis above the literal sense of Scripture (see Fletcher, 'The Meaning of "Gostly to owr purpos" in *Mankind*').

61 Sunt alij qui scire volunt: This line is taken from the *Poetria nova* of Geoffrey of Vinsauf (P. Leyser, *Historia poetarum et poematum medii ævi* (Halle: Sumptu novi bibliopolii, 1721), p. 273, line 2020). The sermon text is slightly corrupt; 'alij' reads 'aliqui' in Geoffrey. It is interesting to observe elsewhere how Geoffrey's works might find their way into the fifteenth-century clerical miscellany. One such example is contained in Oxford, Bodleian Library, MS Bodley 832, a paper production from the second half of the fifteenth century, which was owned by a parish chaplain and which contains excerpts of the *Poetria nova*.

63–67 The lines refer to the accounts of Numbers 14. 1–4.

72 Scientes tempus: Romans 13. 11, part of the day's Epistle (Romans 13. 11–14). None of the Vulgate variants on this text recorded in *Bibliorum sacrorum latinae versiones antiquae*, ed. by P. Sabatier, 3 vols (Paris: Didot, 1751), omits the noun *tempus*, as do all the manuscripts here. Since its presence is also implied in the vernacular paraphrase, it has been inserted. (Where possible, Vulgate variants in the *Biblia sacra iuxta Latinam Vulgatam versionem* (Rome: Typis polyglottis Vaticanis, 1926–) have been consulted.)

73–75 This tropological interpretation compares with the gloss of Haimo in the *Glossa ordinaria* (see *Biblia sacra cum glossa ordinaria*, 6 vols (Antwerp, 1617), VI, col. 117): 'Dicit ergo omnibus credentibus: Hoc scientes simus, quia tempus est nos de somno pigritiae et desidiae surgere: de somno quoque infidelitatis, vitiorum atque ignorantiae. Ille surgit, qui iacebat: et si.nos hactenus iacuimus in vitiis, et torpore vitiorum, surgamus ad bona opera agenda, et laboremus viriliter studioseque.'

76 Nunc enim: Romans 13. 11.

90 strengþe of dome: The Latin is adequately translated in this rendering, but the significance of the phrase remains unclear.

93 prevyd: The use of the word is interesting, suggesting as it does a scholastic turn of mind for which the necessity of proof texts was axiomatic.

96–97 whyle þu haste space to amende þi lyfe: The first instance of a change from the plural personal pronoun to the singular in this sermon. The second part of the sermon favours the use of the singular. The usage may be a stylistic device, a 'deictic' usage to impress the sermon's message more immediately upon the individual members of a plural congregation. Many contemporary sermons make use of this singular/plural alternation (and note this feature also, for example, in the Signs of Death lyric of John Bromyard's *Summa predicantium* (Alan J. Fletcher, 'A Death Lyric from the *Summa Predicantium*', *N&Q*, n.s., 24 (1977), 11–12). However, a further feature is also to be noted in that singular and plural number may be brought together within the same prose unit. The 'ȝe ... thi' alternation between lines 98–101 may be an example of this, although it is conceivable (if perhaps unlikely) that 'ȝe' may be an instance of the 'polite plural' usage, and bear a singular number (Mustanoja, *A Middle English Syntax*, I, 126–28). But in line 197, 'frendys ... remember þiselfe', the usage is unmistakable.

97–98 Alliteration is prominent in these lines (compare also lines 134–35). It is used as an ornament for local effect in the sermons of e Museo 180, but never in any sustained way. Sermons existed whose prose was by contrast consistently alliterative over long passages (for example, excerpts of the sermons contained in London, British Library, MS Additional 41321 and Oxford, Bodleian Library, MS Rawlinson C. 751, manuscripts which to a large extent contain overlapping collections (Cigman, *Lollard Sermons*). But amongst the corpus of fifteenth-century Middle English sermon manuscripts, few contain sermons quite so extensively comparable.

104 Nox precessit: Romans 13. 12.

108–23 The text here is printed from the *L* manuscript by Owst, *Literature and Pulpit*, p. 534. The theme of man's life as a flower is ultimately a biblical topos, figuring particularly in the sapiential books of the Old Testament. The simile was widely used and developed in religious literature, as in Richard Rolle's early work on Job: *Flos speciosus est in estate sed postea marcescit, et qui primo placidus erat oculis intuencium, subito redigitur in pulverem, et conteritur in nullum. Sic florescit homo in annis iuvenilibus, et transacto lacune tempore, cum iam senescere incipit, velut flos egrediens in mortem cadit* (Oxford, Bodleian Library, MS Laud misc. 528, fol. 61ʳ). The simile finds a natural place in this Advent sermon in helping to convey the message of the impermanence of life and its inevitable ending, a message liturgically expected at this time of the year, and which, when eloquently expressed, may help to wean affections from created things to things uncreated. (On the tradition of the graphic contemplation of the signs of Old Age, see Woolf, *The English Religious Lyric*, pp. 102–03, and for the use of such material in a sermon context, Alan J. Fletcher, 'Death Lyrics from Two Fifteenth-Century Sermon manuscripts', *N&Q*, n.s., 23 (1976), 341–42.)

113 The firste age: Opposite this line in the left-hand margin is written *Primum principale*. (The second and third *principale* divisions are found in the manuscript in the margins approximately opposite the words of lines 143 and 172 respectively.) Originally, the *principale* divisions were more strictly applied to the primary divisions of the theme before they were themselves subdivided (on this, the 'modern' mode of preaching, see Homer G. Pfander, *The Popular Sermon of the Medieval Friar in England* (New York: New York University, 1937), pp. 17, 45–66, and especially *EPLMA*, pp. 228–68). By the fifteenth century, *principale* divisions were being used to denote any multiple divisions of material, whether these occurred in a sermon with a strict 'modern' structure or not.

118 ornamentis: The two qualities of 'lyȝtnes' and 'swiftnes' mentioned in line 118 are at least morally neutral; the third, 'wantonnes', never appears to have had other than morally dubious overtones. The sermon author would hardly describe 'wantonnes' as an 'ornament' unless he were being ironic, and this is not likely here. Consequently, the word *ornamentis* might best be glossed as 'attributes' to cover all three qualities.

124 Sicut in die: Romans 13. 13.

127–28 Dies mali sunt: Ephesians 5. 16.

129 Homo cum inter`i´erit: Psalm 48. 18. The Vulgate does not read *Homo*, but *quoniam*. This might be a conscious, or unconscious, alteration of the Latin subordination to give the clause an independent status. As such it fits the context of the delivery better. The Psalm is used again at lines 153–54.

137–39 Homo ... conteritur: Job 14. 1–2. These lines are often repeated in the sermons of the period, and would have been widely familiar from their appearance in the fifth *lectio* of the second Nocturn of the Office of the Dead (Procter and Wordsworth, *Breviarium*, II, 276–77, and also *The Hereford Breviary*, ed. by W. H. Frere and L. E. G. Brown, Henry Bradshaw Society 26 and 40, 2 vols (London: Harrison, 1904–10), II, 44).

146 Mors habet excerto tria: The Arundel Holcot reads for these lines, 'Mors datur a tergo tribus ensibus omnibus ergo' (Text A, line 29). The line of the sermon, if in fact intended as a dactylic hexameter, does not scan properly.

147–51 The motif here of the three effects of Death is loosely comparable to the motif of Death's three strokes in Lincoln 133 (Text C, lines 99–103), Hatton 96 (Text D, lines 63–80), and Trinity 75 (Text E, lines 37–40).

153 Relinquent alienis diuicias: Psalm 48. 11–12. The Vulgate variants do not record an *et* between *eorum* and *domus*.

157 not to have a delyte in: This infinitive construction has an imperative force. Possibly the preceding and regular imperative construction sets a semantic 'tone' which an infinitive may be capable of bearing. (Compare the modern construction 'Not to worry'.) Conversely, the use of an infinitive as an imperative is found widely in Middle, as in modern, French, and perhaps the type of construction used here has originally been suggested by French precedent. (The use of the infinitive as an imperative has not been recorded by Mustanoja, *A Middle English Syntax*.)

158–59 Non in comessacionibus: Romans 13. 13.

160 superflue: The variant *LD* readings, which are both 'superfluens', give the earliest example of the word with this spelling as yet recorded (OED, s.v. 'superfluence'; first cited *c*. 1530).

161–62 Sed induimini: Romans 13. 14. The form normally found among the Vulgate variants is *induimini*, and the text has been emended accordingly. (The *OL* readings *induemini*, the second person plural future indicative passive of *induo*, make no sense.)

168–69 Hec est vita eterna: John 17. 3. The Vulgate readings normally have *solum verum* or *unum (et) verum* for the simple *verum* recorded here, but the text is not emended.

175 Monstrant tube: The Arundel Holcot reads for these lines 'Monstro tubis quale erit examen generale'. The line of the sermon, if in fact intended as a dactylic hexameter, does not scan properly.

178–79 Canet enim tuba: 1 Corinthians 15. 52. No Vulgate readings have the form *canit* which appears in *OL* (*D* omits the text of this section). Since the future tense is more apt, it has been inserted. Also, since the form *primi* makes less sense than the recorded Vulgate form *incorrupti*, it has likewise been emended.

183 Discedite a me: Matthew 25. 41. Excerpts of the same chapter and verse are used subsequently at lines 188, 190, 192 and 194. This interchange between Christ as *iudex mundi* and the souls of men between lines 181 and 196, here dramatically conceived in direct speech, is a favourite preaching theme, as not only the sermons edited here testify. A sermon for the tenth Sunday after Trinity in Oxford, Bodleian Library, MS Bodley 95, fol. 73^v, for example, employs a similar interchange. The usefulness of the Latin text *Discedite a me* to the medieval preacher is seen again in the first complete sermon of Oxford, Bodleian Library, MS Rawlinson C. 751, where individual parts of this chapter of Matthew become, metaphorically, the seven knots of the scourge of the Last Judgement; see Cigman, *Lollard Sermons*, pp. 207–40. It may also be noted that the Doom dialogues were a favourite element in the Judgement scenes of medieval drama. They are eloquently treated in the York play of the Mercers (*York Plays*, ed. by Richard Beadle (London: Arnold, 1982), pp. 406–15). Examples are also found in the Chester play of the Judgement (*The Chester Mystery Cycle*, ed. by R. M. Lumiansky and David Mills, EETS, s.s., 3 (London: Oxford University Press, 1974), I, 438–65), and the Towneley Judgement (*The Towneley Plays*, ed. by Martin Stevens and A. C. Cawley, EETS, s.s., 13 and 14, 2 vols (Oxford: Oxford University Press, 1994), I, 401–25). The dialogues of these sermons, however, are somewhat different in that they take place *after* the damned have accepted their doom, and are seeking for some mitigation of hell torment. The rhetorical balance of question with its uncompromising answer points up the grim finality of their sentence.

201 Soluite: Matthew 21. 2.

204 Venite benedicti: Matthew 25. 34.

206 Benedictus qui venit: Matthew 21. 9.

209 To the whiche, et cetera: A cue to the preacher to supply the remainder of the ending, probably the same as that written at the bottom of fol. 139^v in this manuscript. 'To the whiche Ioye god bryng bothe ȝow and me that dyed for us on þe Rode tre Amen'. Sermon endings were frequently rhymed, and some, as the one here, were widely current. Compare, for example, Oxford, Bodleian Library, MS University College 28, fol. 90^r, col. a, 'to yis kyngdom blissed ihesu bryng ȝow and me ye quilk dyed for us on ye rode tre'. And again, in a slightly different form in the same library, MS Ashmole 750, fol. 86^v, 'to þat ioyȝe brynge ȝow he þat with his blod bowt vus on þe rode tre'. Or again, in London, British Library, MS Harley 2383, fol. 81^v, 'to þe wyche Ihesu bryng bothe yow and me þat dyyd for us on þe Rode tree'.

Text C

Lincoln, Cathedral Library, MS 133, fols 98ʳ–101ʳ

[...] dedely synne ys because of seuen propurteʒ þat ys in a dede body þat are
lyke to þe Seuen Dedely Synneʒ. The fyrst ys, a dede body ys starke and styf
and noʒt plyant ne mendable. Ryght so a prowde mon ys styf and starke
agaynus almyghty God and wyll noʒt meke hym ne obey hym to almyghty
5   God ne to Holy Kyrke. And ryght as a mon ys ded to oure bodely syʒt, ryght
so a prowde mon ys dede in þe syʒt of God and all hys angellus. And þe
secunde propurte of a dede body ys qwen þe herte ys borston ʻand ' þe
kyndely hete passys away and þe body waxeʒ colde. Ryght so þe herte of
þe envious mon þat for deseʒ þe wrencheneʒ of charyte so fer forthe þat þe
10 hete of charyte wyll noʒt abyde in þe brest of a invious mon. And þe thryd
propurty of þe dede mon ys þis: he ys ferefull and vugly to loke apon. Ryʒt
so on þe same wyse an angre mon, wyll he ys in þe synne of wrathe and ys
sterede to styke or to kylle hys euen cristyn, he ys more vugly to loke apon
gostely þen ys þe dede body. The fourte propurte of a dede body ys þis: hyt
15 hys ponderant and heue in þe seruys of God and makes hym vnlusty to any
gode werkes worchyng. And þe fyfte propurte of a dede body ys þis: qwen þe
herte ys borston þe body rancles and bolneʒ. Ryght so þe synne of glotere hyt
makes a mon wgly, for qwy ryʒt als a mon þat ys in þe cumruus dropsy ys
bolne and swellande, and euer more drynkande and euer thrusty, so ys a
20 drokyn mon swellande full of all maner of synne, for then he ys redy to
bakbyte and to sle with hys tong and to do all þe harme þat he may. And
þerfore, frendes, as ʒe se a dede body ys swellant bodely aftur hys dethe, ryʒt
so schall a gloton be swellant aftur hys, gostely, in þe euerlastyng payne of
helle. For as says þe profet Dauid, 'Mors peccatorum pessima'. And allso þe
25 wyse mon says in a verse aʒaneʒ droken men þat sex thynges þay lesyn:

'Forma, genus, mores,
Sapientia, sensus, honores:
Morte ruunt subita,
Sola manent merita.'

30 Schappe, kynde and manerys |fol. 98ᵛ| and manes wysdam, wytt and honours
— all thys sex takys þe synne of gloteny for < ... > mon. The sexte propurte
of a dede body ys þis: yf he be kepet long aboue þe erthe he turneʒ to sty
ʻn 'ke and to corrupcyon. Ryght so þe synne of lechere ys vset in þis worde
and hyt turneʒ to stynke and to corrupcyon in þe syʒt of God and all hys

35 angellus. And þe seuet propurty of a dede body ys þis: qwen þe paynus of
    dethe comus owuer man or womon, quat thynke þay lay honde þer on þay
    holde hyt fast. Ryght so on þe same wyse þe groppe of couetyse hyt closeȝ
    mens hondes so nowondays, þat quat thynke þat þay lay honde on þay holde
    hyt fast, for þay wyll part with ryght noȝt wyll þay hafe lyfe in thys worde,
40 and aftur þayre dethe þay schall hafe lytyll nede for þayre kepyng. Here I
    fynde in Scripture qwere I in þis gospell of Sente Luce xij qwere I fynde of a
    ryche mon þat hade mech gode gedurt togedur and sayde to hymselfe on þis
    wyse, 'Body, þu hast goode ynoȝe. Ete fast and drynke fast and take þe nese
    at þine awne lyst'. And þen at þe last almyghty God apperyt vnto hym sayng
45 to hym on þis wyse, 'O stulte, anima tua hac nocte egrediatur a te. Que ergo
    congregasti cuius sunt?' Luce xiijᵒ. 'O yow fole, þis nyȝt þi soule schall be
    takyn fro þe. Quose godeȝ ar þos þat þu has gedyrt togedyr?' For þyn ar þay
    noȝt. For ryght noȝt broght þu with þe hedyr, ne ryght noȝt schall þu ber
    away with þe.

50 Therfore, frendes, þes Seuen Dedely Synneȝ þat are lyke to þe seuen propurtys
    of a dede body schall ȝe see and beholde, and þerfore be wrothe be hom and
    exchewe hom as meche as ȝe may, for as Scripture says, 'Mortuo homine
    impio, non erit vltra spes'. 'Of þe dethe of a weket mon ys no hope of
    forgyfneȝ'. For qwen a wyket mon deȝ he ys in mekyll drede, fyrst for mynde
55 of synne, þe secunde for |fol. 99ʳ| drede of payne, þe thryde for drede of
    damnacyon, þe faurt for bytturnys of dethe euerlastyng. Þerfore, beholdyng
    a phylosephur þe febulneȝ of monkynde, how febull hyt ys and how redy to
    syn, to gyf vus ensampull of oure lyffyng he made thre ȝateȝ and abofe ych
    ȝate a schylde of diuers colors. Þe fyrst schylde was of syluer with thre red
60 rosse, and in ych rose a lettur. In þe fyrst was a 'L', in þe secunde a 'I', in þe
    thryd a 'F'. And þe secunde schylde was of sabull with thre swordys of syluer,
    and in ych sworde a lettur. In þe fyrst sworde was a 'D', in þe secunde sworde
    a 'E', in þe thryde was a 'T'. And þe thryde schylde was of aser with thre
    trompus of golde, and in ych trompe a lettur. In þe fyrst trompe was a 'D', in
65 þe secunde trompe was a 'O', and in þe thryd trompe was a 'M'. And so hyt
    befell þer come another phylosephur by thys castell a way and asket entre in,
    and þe porter of þis castell vnswarede and sayde þat þe lorde of þis castell
    hade ordant syche a laghe þat þer schulde no mon entur into þis castell but
    yf he colde discrete þus thre schyldeȝ þat hengun ouer þe castell ȝateȝ. And
70 þen þis phylosophur lyftande vp hys hede and behelde þus thre schyldes and
    sayde þat 'þis may be calde a wyse castell'. 'Qwy?' sayde þe porter þen. 'For yf

I wyll entur into þis castell, me behoweȝ to take hede qwat my lyfe ys, and
quat dethe ys, and quat dome ys.'

Now gostely, frendes, as to owre purpose. By thys castell I vndurstonde þe
75 castell of heuen, into þe qwech no mon may entur bot yf he take hede quat
ys lyfe and quat ys dethe and quat ys dome.

By thys fyrst schylde þat was of syluer I vndurstonde ȝogh and mannes lyfe,
þe qwech þat ys fayre and fecull. For ryght as þe rose florys are fayre to þe
syȝt, ryght so monnes lyfe in thys worde hyt ys schort and lytyll, and þerfore
80 says Iob þat monnes lyf ys bott schort: 'Homo natus de muliere breui viuens
tempore.' |fol. 99ᵛ| 'Mon borne of a womon lyfus bott a lytyll qwyle'. For qui
noo mon con tell < ... > how long ne how schorte qwyle. Þerfore sayeȝ Iob,
'Breues dies hominis sunt'. 'The days of men ben schort'. No nowmbur of
thys wekys, mon, in þe, so þat mons lyfe ys bott schort and lytyll. And allso
85 hyt ys fals and fecull and lyke vnto wyntt, or elleȝ as a flore. And þerfore sayeȝ
þe Scripture, 'Memento mei, Domine, quia ventus est uita mea, nec aspiciat
me visus hominis'. 'Lorde, haue mynde on me, for my lyfe ys but a wynde,
for þe syȝt of a mon may nott beholde hyt'. 'Qui quasi flos egreditur et
conteritur, et fugit velut vmbra et vmquam in eodem statu permanet'. For
90 ryght as a flore ys fayre in þe mornyng and desolet in þe euen, and flys away
as a schado and neuer more schall be in þe same state, ryght so mons lyfe hyt
ys fals and fecull and full of mony desyese. Þerfore yf þu wylt entur into þe
castell, hafe these thre letturs in þi mynde þat are wrytyn in þe schylde, þat
ys to say, 'L', 'I', 'F'. 'L', ffor þi lyfe; 'I', for hyt ys schorte; and 'F', for hyt ys
95 fals and fekell. And yf þu take hede to theȝ thre well, schalt þu entur into þis
castell.

The secunde schelde was of sabull with thre swordeȝ of syluer and with hor
thre letturs 'D', 'E' and 'T'. 'D', for hyt delys; 'E', for hyt endus; and 'T', for
hyt turnus vp so done. Bott theȝ thre swordeȝ smytyn thre strokys. At þe
100 fyrst stroke þat dethe smyteȝ at þe with hys sworde hyt smytes away fro þe þi
kynraden and þi frende. The secunde smytes away þi wordly goodes. For þe
the thryde smytes a stroke þat ys for to drede sarest. Þat ys qwen he strykes
þi body fro þi soule. Bott þen þis thre letturs beforesayde telne þe thre
thynkes. 'D': how þu delys þi soule to God and þi goode to þe worde.
105 Acordyng þerto I fynde in a boke þat ys caltyt *Alphabetum narracionum*, how
þer was a ryche mon þat lay on deyng and hys fryndes come to hym and bade
hym dele hys goode and make hys testament. And þen thys ryche mon calde
a clerke and bade hym come and wryte hys testament. Aftur þe consell of hys

frendes þis clerke, because |fol. 100ʳ| he knew þat he was a ryche mon and
110 hade myche goode, he broȝt with hym a parchyment skynne. And qwen he
come to þe ryche mon he asket hym quat he schulde wryte, and þe ryche mon
vnswaret agayne and bade hym wryte:

'Terram terra tegat.
Demon peccata resumat.
115 Mundus res habeat.
Spiritus alta petat'.

'The erthe schall couer þe erthe. My synneȝ I beqwethe to þe deuell and my
goodes þe worde schall haue, and my saule to heuen schall craue.' And
þerfore by thys take ȝe emsampull how dethe delys and how hyt endus and
120 how hyt turnys vp so downe. And þerfore conselande vus þe wyse mon and
says euer þis wyse, 'Memorare nouissima tua et in eternum non peccabys'.
'Haue mynde', says þe wyse mon, 'on þe last ende', þat ys for to say, on dethe,
'and þu schalt neuer synne'.

The thryde schylde was of asure with thre trompus of golde. And in þe fyrst
125 trompe was wryton a 'D', for þe dome of almyghty God ys dredfull. In þe
secunde trompe ys wryton a 'O', and þat betokyns sygnifycacyon þat hyt ys
opon. And in þe thryde trompe was wryton a 'M', in signifycacyon þat hyt
ys myghtfull. Therto acordes well þe holy doctur Sent Iohn sayng on þis
wyse, 'Siue comedo siue dormeo, semper sonet in auribus meis vox tremendi
130 iudicij'. 'Qwether I ete or I slepe or quat thyng þat I do, euer hyt swoneȝ in
myne ere þe dredfull voyce of Goddes dome'. Therfore, frendys, syn þis
goode holy mon dredes þus mekull þe dome of God, mecull more aght vus
þat arun synners to dred þis dome.

Therfore, yf þu wylt entur into þe castell, þe behoueȝ to take hede and haue
135 in mynde þes thre schyldes, þat ys to say, quat ys lyfe, quat ys dethe, and quat
ys dome. For Sent Iohn says: 'Si mortuus fuerit, viuet.' 'Yf þu be ded, ȝet schall
þu lyfe'. And yf þu take no hede to goode lyuyng in thys worde |fol. 100ᵛ|
þou < ... > wordes in my tyme: 'Timor mortis conturbat me, et cetera.' The
thryd dethe, þat ys dethe of body and sawle togedyr, and þat ys most to be
140 drede, for in þat ys no redempcyon ne turnyng agayne qwen almyghty God
schall say to þe, 'Ite, maledicti, in ignem eternum qui preparatus est diabolo
et angelis eius'. 'Gose, ȝe curset, into þe fyre of hell qwech ys ordente to þe
deuell and all hys angellys'. Fyrst þis Lorde says, 'Ite', 'Go ȝe'. Ȝette þu may
aske grace of þi Lorde and say, 'Lorde, and we schall go fro þe and noȝte
145 abyde with þe, we beseche þe, gyf vus þi blesyng.' Then comus þe secunde

worde and forbarrus hom qwen he says, 'Maledicti', 'curset' or 'warede'. ʒette
may þu aske anoþer grace and say, 'Lorde, and we schall go fro þe in þi
cursyng and noʒte in þi blessyng, gud Lorde, putt vus in such a place qwere
we may be withowte desses or payne.' Þen comus þe thryde worde and
150 forbarrus hom, þat ys, qwen he says, 'In ignem', 'Into þe fyre'. ʒet may þu aske
anoþer grace and say, 'I besech þe, Lorde, þat þe oure may be schortutt and
sone haue ende.' Then comus þe furth worde and forbarres hom qwen he
says, 'Eternum', 'Into þe fyre euerlastyng'. 'A, Lorde, and we schall go fro þe
in þi cursyng to þe fyre þat ys allway lastyng because of oure cursyt lyuyng,
155 ʒett we besech þe, Lorde, of a bone, þat ʒe wyll put vus vndur a gouernanse
of sech a gouernore þat wyll be frendfull and ese to vus.' Then comus þe fyfte
worde of dyscomfort qwen he says, 'Qui paratus est diabolo', 'Qwych þat ys
ordent to þe deuell'. ʒett may þu aske anoþer grace and say, 'Lorde, yf we
schall go fro þe in þi cursyng to þe fyre of hell þat ys ordent for þe deuell,
160 goode Lorde, putt vus in such a company as wyll be abowte to schorton |fol.
101ʳ| and lesson oure payne.' Þen comus þe sexte worde and forbarrus hom
þat qwen he says, 'Et angelis eius', þat ys, 'to þe deuell and all hys angellus'.

By þese sex wordeʒ ben sayde, nawþer þe praer of Oure Lady ne of all þe
senttes of heuen may nott avayle þat tyme, bott þis sentens schall be gyfyn
165 and sayd to hom þat schall be dampnet, for þen þay go to dethe of payne. For
þer schall be gnascyng of tethe and wepyng of teres, sorow and ʒellyng, crying
and dred, and tremelyng and quakyng. Þer schall be stynk orrebell. Þer schall
be merkenys-felyng. Þer schall be crying, and seyng of deuells, and so mekull
soro þat na mon con tell, ne herte may thenke, ne ee see. Woo, woo, my
170 broþer, syn so mekull sorow and so mekull vgsumneʒ schall be to þe sawle
allonly for þe syʒt of þe deuels, qwerto, þen, lufʒe so mekull þe vanyteʒ of
thys worde, and lusteʒ to ocubye þe lyfe aftur þe lust and þe lykyng of þi
flessche? Salamon: 'Fatuj non poterunt diligere nisi ea que eis placent, et cetera.'

Headnote

Lincoln, Cathedral Library, MS 133 is written on paper, and much of it may have
been copied over a period of time. On the face of it, its theological and pastoral
content might suggest that it was owned by a parish priest; the more remarkable
truth, however, is that it appears to have been copied by Giles Wright, a draper, for
his personal use (the view expressed in Fletcher, 'Unnoticed Manuscripts', pp.
518–19, that Wright was probably in clerical orders and not a layman is now
superseded). On fol. 46ʳ appears the note indicating his ownership, 'Iste liber

constat Egidio Wry3t', written almost certainly in the hand which copied the first major item in the manuscript on fols 8ʳ–46ʳ, and perhaps much more of the manuscript subsequently. He appears again in a will on folio 47ᵛ, where he is referred to as 'Egidius Wryght de Flixton'. This information, together with a date recorded in a *probacio testamenti* on fol. 50ʳ, *quarto die mensis Marcii anno Domini Mᵒ ccccᵒ lxxxᵒ*, helps to locate the manuscript in place and time. The Flixton referred to is almost certainly Flixton in Lancashire (the written dialect of the manuscript locates in the north-west Midlands; *LALME*, I, 98, locates its linguistic samples from the manuscript in the adjacent county of Cheshire), and at least this portion of the manuscript appears to have been copied up in 1480. Apart from Flixton, Wright also had connections with Oxford (for details, see Thomson, *Catalogue of the Manuscripts of Lincoln Cathedral Chapter Library*, pp. 102–04). The first major work in Wright's manuscript is an acephalous collection of clerical statutes and *constituciones* in Latin deriving from William Lyndwood's *Provinciale* (fols 8ʳ–46ʳ). Then there follows a group of Latin wills and testaments, amongst which the names of various testators, including Wright's, are to be found (fols 47ʳ–50ʳ). After comes an excerpt from a Latin and English *Speculum Christiani* (fols 51ʳ–67ᵛ; this copy of its text was not noticed by Gustav Holmstedt in his edition for EETS). Then there follows a Latin tract *de officio Misse* (fols 68ʳ–97ᵛ), and finally, the group of eleven vernacular sermons of which all, except the first which is edited here, derive from John Mirk's *Festial* (they are itemized in Fletcher, 'Unnoticed Manuscripts', p. 522).

Critical Notes and Glosses

3   mendable] 'capable of improvement'.
4   hym²] blotted in MS.
5   to oure] blotted in MS.
7   qwen] 'when'.
8   kyndely] 'natural'; body] blotted in MS; so] followed by 'y' badly formed and abandoned.
9   dese3 þe wrenchene3] the meaning of this remains obscure.
11 he] followed by *h* crossed out.
13 sterede to styke] 'provoked to stab'.
15 ponderant and heue] 'lumpen and heavy'; vnlusty] 'out of sorts'.
17 rancles] the *l* of 'rancles' seems to have been corrected from *h*.
17 rancles and bolne3] 'festers and swells'; glotere] 'gluttony'.
18 cumruus dropsy] 'cumbrous dropsy'.
19 bolne] 'swollen'.
25 lesyn] 'lose'.
33 worde] 'world'.

35 seuet] 'seventh'.

36 owuer] 'over'; thynke] 'thing'.

37 groppe] 'grasp'.

39 wyll] 'while'.

41 qwere I] pleonastic, anticipating the following 'qwere' I on the same line.

42 gedurt] 'gathered'.

43 ynoʒe] 'aplenty'.

43–44 þe nese ... lyst] 'your ease at your own desire'.

50 Synneʒ] followed by an unclear letter crossed out.

51 wrothe be hom] 'be angry with them'.

53 weket] 'wicked'.

63 thryde[1]] thyde MS; And] *add.* in MS; schylde] sworde MS.

63 aser] azure.

68 ordant syche a laghe] 'ordained such a law'.

69 discrete] 'tell apart'; þus] 'these'.

69 ouer] oyer MS.

72 me behoweʒ] 'I must'.

77 ʒogh] 'youth'.

78 fecull] 'fickle'; florys] 'flowers'.

85 wyntt ... flore] 'wind ... flower'.

92 desyese] 'disease'.

94 ys[2]] *om.* MS.

97 hor] 'their'.

98 delys] 'separates'.

99 vp so done] 'upside down'.

99 theʒ] 'these'.

100 smyteʒ at þe] 'smites at thee'.

101 k ynraden] 'kindred'.

101 þi[2]] Originally 'þe' with 'e' superscript, then 'e' crossed out and 'i' inserted superscript.

101–02 For þe the thryde] the meaning is not clear; sarest] 'most grievous'.

103 telne] 'tell'; thynkes] 'things'.

105 caltyt] 'called'.

106 was] *om.* MS.

106 hym] followed by 'he a' *canc.*

117 beqwethe to þe deuell] 'bequeath to the devil'.

118 goodes] followed by to in the MS. There was a choice here of omitting either 'to' or 'schall haue'; the chosen reading reflects more faithfully the Latin original.

118 craue] 'long for'.

120 conselande] 'counselling'.

130 swoneʒ] 'sounds'.

134 þe behoueʒ] 'it is necessary that you'.

138 tyme] 'theme'.

142 ordente] 'ordained'.

144 and[2]] 'if'.

146 forbarrus] 'prevents'.

146 warede] 'accursed'.
149 desses] 'disease'.
151 oure] 'hour'; schortutt] 'shortened'.
152 hom] *om*. MS.
154 because] two words in MS, with an unclear letter crossed out after 'be'.
155 bone] 'favour'.
156 frendfull and ese] 'friendly and lenient'.
163 By ... nawþer] 'Once these six words are uttered, neither'.
164 be] followed by 'com' *canc*.
166 gnascyng] 'gnashing'.
166 ʒellyng] preceded by 'w' *canc*.; tremelyng] 'trembling'.
168 merkenys-felyng] 'palpable darkness'.
169 ee] 'eye'.
170 vgsumneʒ] 'ugliness'.

Apparatus fontium and Commentary

3 mendable: This usage antedates the first recorded instance in the OED (1533). It is not recorded at all in the MED.

24 Mors peccatorum pessima: Psalm 33. 22.

26–29 A common tag. See Hans Walther, *Initia carminum ac versuum medii ævi posterioris latinorum*, Carmina medii ævi posterioris latina, 1, 2 pts (Göttingen: Vandenhoeck and Ruprecht, 1969), I, 339, item 59.

45–46 O stulte ... sunt: *recte* Luke 12. 20.

52–53 Mortuo homine ... vltra spes: Proverbs 11. 7.

69 discrete: Not in the OED as a verb until 1646, and not in the MED at all.

74 Now gostely ... to owre purpose: a tag used to introduce one of the levels of exegesis or interpretation above the *sensus litteralis* in vernacular sermons, and especially noticeable in sermons of the second half of the fifteenth century.

80–81 *Homo natus ... tempore*: Job 14. 1. This lemma is used also in the e Museo sermon: see the note on Text B, lines 137–38. It is also found in the Sarum Breviary, Office of the Dead, Second Nocturn, Fifth Lection. See Procter and Wordsworth, *Breviarium*, II, 276–77.

83 Breues ... sunt: Job 14. 5. It is also found in the Sarum Breviary, Office of the Dead, Second Nocturn, Fifth Lection. See Procter and Wordsworth, *Breviarium*, II, 277.

86–87 Memento ... visus hominis: Job 7. 7.

88–90 Qui quasi flos ... permanet: Job 14. 2. This lemma is used also in e Museo 180: see the note on Text B, line 139. It is also found in the Sarum Breviary, Office of the Dead, Second Nocturn, Fifth Lection. See Procter and Wordsworth, *Breviarium*, II, 277.

99–103 The motif here of Death's three strokes, loosely comparable with the substance of the e Museo 180 text (Text B, lines 147–51), is more closely comparable with Hatton 96 (Text D, lines 63–80) and Trinity 75 (Text E, lines 37–40).

105 *Alphabetum narracionum*: The *Alphabetum narracionum* is a collection of tales for the use of preachers, alphabetically arranged according to subject. It was probably initially compiled early in the fourteenth century (see Herbert and Ward, *Catalogue of Romances*, III, 423–28).

I have not noticed this particular tale amongst catalogued and published versions of the *Alphabetum*, however.

113–16 Terram terra tegat ... alta petat: Walther, *Initia*, I, 1009, item 39.

121 Memorare ... peccabys: Ecclesiasticus 7. 40.

136–37 This quotation, erroneously attributed here to St John, is normally ascribed to Jerome in various *distinctio* collections. The *Manipulus florum* of Thomas of Ireland quotes thus: 'Quociens diem illum considero, toto corpore contremisco, sive bibo sive aliquid aliud facio, semper videtur michi illa tuba terribilis sonare in auribus meis, "Surgite, mortui, venite ad iudicium"' (Oxford, Bodleian Library, MS Oriel College 10, fol. 390ᵛ, col. a; here it is cited as Jerome *in epistola Heliodorum monachum*, but is not in fact to be found there). Simon of Boraston's *Distinctiones* ascribe the text simply to Jerome (Oxford, Bodleian Library, MS Bodley 216, fol. 68ᵛ, col. b). The *Speculum laicorum* also includes the quotation (Oxford, Bodleian Library, MS Bodley 474, fol. 56ᵛ), and again ascribes it to Jerome. The nearest parallel that I have been able to find anywhere in Jerome's works is in the pseudo-Hieronyman *Regula monacharum* (PL, XXX, col. 430, *De Consideratione extremi diei iudicii*), and runs as follows: 'Semper tuba illa terribilis vestris perstrepat auribus; Surgite mortui, venite ad iudicium.' This has possibly been conflated with another part of the same work, ibid., col. 387: 'sive leges, sive dormies, sive scribes, sive vigilabis, Amos tibi semper buccina in auribus sonat'.

136 Si mortuus fuerit, viuet: John 11. 25.

138 Timor mortis conturbat me occurs in the Sarum Breviary, Office for the Dead, Third Nocturn, Responsorium 7. See Procter and Wordsworth, *Breviarium*, II, 278. Responsorium 7 follows after the lection from Job 17 (incipit: *Spiritus meus attenuabitur*), and is as follows: 'Peccantem me quotidie et non poenitentem timor mortis conturbat me. Quia in inferno nulla est redempcio miserere mei Deus et salva me.'

141–42 Ite, maledicti ... angelis eius: Matthew 25. 41.

173 Fatuj ... eis placent: a version of Ecclesiasticus 8. 20; the sermon ends without any apparent formal conclusion of the sort often used to round off a sermon. Since many of these were formulaic (see the note to Text B, line 209), it may have been left to the sermon user to improvise one.

Text D

Oxford, Bodleian Library, MS Hatton 96, fols 193ʳ–97ʳ

Hit wes somtyme a lord þat let makne a castel in a place þat he loued more þen anoþer and let ordeyne þerin al manere delicys þat ben ymaginyd oþer by þoȝt of man his herte, mete, drinke, golde, siluyr, perri, preciouse stonis, mirþis, ministracy wiþout any cesing, and ȝef þis castel a nome: þe Castel of
5 Wisdome. He let depeynte ofir þe castel ȝate þre sceldis. Þat on wes of siluire with þre rosis of goulis; þe secunde sabile with þre swerdis of siluir; þe þridde asure with þre trompis of gold. He let wryte in huche schelde

þre wordis. In þe sceld wiþ þe ros þuse þre: 'Lytyl', 'Yuyl', 'Fykyl'. About þe
þre swerdis: 'Delyng', 'Ending', 'Turning'. About þe þre trompis: 'Derne',
10   'Opyn', 'Myӡtful'. And þan he ordeynid for lawe þat þer ne schulde no man
come in þe castel bot he couþe deuise þilke þre scheldis.

Biful þat moni come þat woldine in þat ne couþe noӡt diuisyn þe scheldis and
faylydine of entre. At þe last come an fyloӡofre and axide entre. Þe porter
told hym þat þe law of þe castel wes þat þer ne scholde no man come þerin
15   bot he couþe deuysyn þe scheldis ofyr þe ӡate. Þys phylosofre byhuld
bysylyche þyse scheldis þat noӡte ne schold astert hym, and at þe last he
was warre of þulk dox, dasow lettrys þat wer aboute þe rosis, swerdis,
and trompis, and saide to þe porter, 'Bewe sire, þise ne beӡ noӡt scheldis of
armis, bot hit beӡ scheldis þat bytokyniþ manis lyf, deþ, and dome'. Þise
20   Lorde God almyӡty.

Þis castel |fol. 193ᵛ| hys heuen, in wyche buþ al delycys. Þe scheld with þre
rosys bytokniþ mannis lyf, for acordaunce þat is bytwene þe cunde of man
and þe kunde of rosys. Þe rose waxit among þornis and also by defouling of
þe rose is makyd watyr þat is holsum to manis heyn. Ryӡt so mannis lyf waxit
25   among þornis, now of worldelyche bysynisse, now of bodylyche secknisse,
now heer, now sowe, now rype, now moue, now hole, now sek, now lyӡe, now
wep. So þat man nys neuer on houre of a day stabylich in o state. As Iob sayþ:
'Nunquam in eodem statu permanet.' Þat is to sugg, man lastyþ neuer in o stat.
And skylfollich mannis lif is tokind to þe rose for þre statis þat is in mannis
30   lif: þe furst is chyldhede; þe secund is manhed; þe þryd is held. By þe rose,
wan he comiþ vyrst hout and sonnyþ furst is red lemys in May, his bytoknyd
a chyld on is norice lappe of on ӡer old oþir tuo þat is fayre and lykful, for
ӡong þing is comunlich quemfol. Þan he schall be a person, a byssoppe, a
gret lord. But wel were is modir ӡiff he mowe boe a god sepherd, for to þe
35   sepherdys broӡt furst þe angel typingys of Goddis burþe, aftyr a fewe of
Goddis derlingys, Mary and a fewe oþir. Þe secund stat of þe ros is lems buþ
sprad abrod and is in most rode, and bytokniþ a man in is best stat with ful
rode and ful streynþe. And wiþ is long lokkus and oþir ioliftese a weniþ he
schal neuer be feblyr ne foulir þan he is þan. And þarfor me sayþ, he is in is
40   flouris. Bote it wol far of hym |fol. 194ʳ| as it fariþ of þe rose. Furst he vadiþ,
weltryþ, and welouþt, and wrynkeliþ, fallyþ to þe eorþe an rotiþ. So schal
man in held falouyn and weltrin and swyndin away. Wan:

Wan þat is wyte waxit falou,
And þat is cripse waxit calau,
45 Wen þi neb ryveliþ as a roket,
And þin hein porfilin as scarlet,
And þi nose droppiþ as a boket,
Þan þou beon y-clipid kombir-flet.

Bot nim heod. About þe þre ros verin y-writ þre wordis: 'Litil', 'Yuil',
50 'Fikil'. Þat bytokniþ þe condicion of mannis lif. Þat manis lif be litil
witnisiyit holy lore (Salomon) and sayþ: 'A litil and wiþ tene is þe tyme of
oure lif'. And Iob saiþ þat 'mannis days beþ sort and þe tal of is monþ is
toward þe'. Noȝt alon of monþis, bot of huch step þat of þi fot, huch þoȝt of
þin hert his y-wryte in Goddes bok. Manis lif is also yuil, for it waxit among
55 þornis of worldelich bisinisse, of sekniss, of onsykyrnes of lif, of sikyrnes of
deþ, and oncerteyne weþir he schal to wele oþir to wo. Hit is also fikil, for it
byhot pes and it is fol of werre, hit byhot sikyrnis, it is ful of falsnis. For a
man not wat deþ he schal deye, ne how, ne wenne, ne wer. Þus is mannis lif
litil, yuil, fikil. Tak of litil 'l', of ifil 'i', of fikil 'f', and þat wol make manis lif.
60 So þat lif of is kunde is litil, iuil, fikil.

Þe secund scheld wasse sabil with þre swerdis of siluir. Sabil, þat is, blac,
is colour of deol, for men in tyme of deþ buþ cloþed with blac in tokne of
deol. And sckylfolich is deþ bytoknid by þre swerdis for þre strokys þat deþ
smit whan he comiþ. Furst he bynemiþ a man al is wyttys. Wan is þat:

65 Wan is heyn turniþ, |fol. 194ᵛ|
And is breþ stynkyþ,
And þe fet coldeþ —
Þan farwel, wyt!
Farewel, wyf and child!
70 And weel is þan forȝet.

Þe secund strok he bynymyþ a man al is godis þatwan þe breþ is ago, for be
a man neuer so rych, þoȝ a lyg in a cloþis of gold, in tapitis ant cortenis of
gold and perri, as swyþe as he is ded, turne im out of is bed on þe cold erþe
and leþ a torf on is womb for swelling. He is a party pore þat noȝt ne haþ bot
75 herþe next im, ne noȝt hab ne may bot at oþir menis wyll.
Þe þrid stroke he bynymyþ a man al is frendis. Þat is, wan he is leyd in is
put and þe rof of is hous lyþ on is mouþ. Ȝut as long as he lyþ on ber is frendis

doþ hym som solace of massis, of diriges, of sauters. Bot wan he is leid in þe
erþe, farwel frend, farwel wyf and child. Þe wyf most habb an housbond, þe
80 heyr most habb a wyf, so þat þilk þat al houned noȝt nay. Þis beþ deþis þre
strokys. Bot ȝut þer wer þre wordis about þe þre swerdis and wer þise:
'Deling', 'Ending', and 'Turning'. Furst deþ delyþ al þilk þat but i-bound
togidir by lawe, by loue, and by cunde. By lawe buþ y-bound togidir þe man
and is wyf, þe lord and is bondman. Bot wan þe deþ comiþ, þan deliþ he þe
85 wyf fram þe housbond, þe lord from þe seruaunt. He delyþ al þilk þat buþ y-
bound togidir by loue, as wyf and child. Þat schold most loue, hy habbyþ
oftsonis forȝut. As me saiþ on hold Englis: 'Wan deþ haþ i-bite and is last
strok y-smite, þan ay loue ys lef forȝut'. He deliþ also |fol. 195ʳ| so þulk
þat buþ i-bound togidir by cund. By kund buþ y-bound in man þe foure
90 elemente, fur, watyr, eorþe, and eyr, also manis body and manis soul. But wan
deþ comiþ, habuþ to dreuid uchon is way. Þus deþ deliþ al þat beth y-bound
togidir by lawe, by loue, by kund.

Þe secund word was 'Ending', for deþ endyþ weel and wo, frend and fo,
met and drink, rest and swink. For ȝif a man be her in weel and go to heuen,
95 al þe weel of þe world nis bot a pine of deþ in reward of þe blisse of heuen.
Ȝife a be in pine and go to heuen, ȝut wol þe blysse þen seme more ioy. Ȝif he
be in pine and go to helle, al þe pine and þe wo of þe world wer a blysse in
reward of þe lest pine of helle. So þat deþ ondeþ weele and wo, frend and fo.
For haue a man neuir so god frend, be he ded, farewell frendssipe, for he is
100 forȝute. For Salomon saiþ, 'Non est priorum memoria', et cetera. 'Þer nis no
mynde of hem þat beþ ago'. He endiþ so. For be a man ded, ne recchwhym
neuir war he lygge no more þan a ston oþyr a clot of erþe. Þise silfe maner he
endiþ met and drink, rest ant swynk.

And also deþ turniþ fayr into foul, rych into pore, king into karoyne, for
105 he ne sparyþ no man. Furst he turniþ fayr into foul, for þer was neuir man by
way of kunde þat as swiþe as he wer ded, þat he nas gastful and lolich and
wondirlich abhominable to manis kunde. As Seint Austin sayþ, for loue of
wymmen men brekyþ hous, passiþ heggis, wall', and watris. Bot take þe
fayrist wyȝt þat euir wes, lat hir be an þre dayis ded, þulk þat woldin by hyr
110 lif iovst for hir of werre oþyr of pes, he nold þan |fol. 195ᵛ| for al þe good þat
he hauiþ onis kus hir mouþ. Manis kund nis noȝt eschu of ded ox oþir a cou,
bot me schal onneþ fynd ani so bold þat durst a nyȝt lig by a ded man, ne by
is dame, ne by is sire, so abhominable and so wlatsum is þo kund to þoþir.

Þus þan turneþ deþ fair into foul. He turniþ also rych into por, for deþ
115 bynymmyþ a man al is wittis and al is godis and al is frendis. Deþ castiþ is
caroyne to eorþe, þat is wormys met, for of þe brain kenniþ a tad, and of þe
marowe of þe eschin kenniþ a neddre, and of the þoþir del oþir wormis
inowe. He turniþ also manis soul God wot weþir, to rest oþir to trauail, to
blisse oþir to pine. He turniþ also king into karoine, for he ne spariþ no man.
120 For king and quene, lord and lady, por and rych, al hy habbyþ on maner
coming into þis world and going owt. Þus þan deþ deliþ, endiþ, an turniþ.
Tak of deling 'd', of ending 'e', of turning 't', ant þat wol mak deþ. So þat det
of is kund beriþ wiþ him þis þre: deling, ending, turning.

Þe þrid scheld was of asur with þre trompis of gold, and bytokniþ þe
125 dome, and skylfollich, for þre wordis þat God wol spek at þe dome. Of þe
furst spekyþ Seint Ierom and saiþ, 'Weþir I slep oþir waak, sitte oþir go, me
þinkyþ þat þilk tromp blowiþ in myn eer, "Arysiþ, ded men, and comiþ to þe
dome"'. Þe secund word þat God wol spek is, 'Goþ, corsid gostis, into fur þat
euir schal last'. Þan schal ben a chest bytwx þe damnud soulis and þe god.
130 And hy wolliþ sug, 'Leue Lord, ʒif we schol go fram þe in wom is al blis, |fol.
196ʳ| al weel, wolt ʒefe ous þi blessing þat we mowin go þe miryer?' Þan wol
God sig, 'Nay, goþ fram me. Mi cors go with ʒow'. Þan scholliþ hy syg, 'Lord,
we schol go fram þe þat art wele of lyf and rote of blys and ek hab þy cors.
Wodyr schol we go?' Þan wol he syg, 'Goþ into þe fur of helle.' Þan schollyþ
135 hy syg, 'Lord, we scholle go from þe wyþ þy cors into þe fur of helle. Woldist
do ous þilk grace þat þe fur hab sumtim end?' Þan wol he syg, 'Goþ from me.
My cors go wiþ ow into þe fur þat euir schal last'. Þan scholliþ hy syg, 'Wy
scholle we go fram þe and hab þy cors, and into þe endeles fur of helle?' Þan
wol God say, 'For Ich wes hongry and ʒe ne ʒef me no met. Ich wes þursty;
140 ʒe ne ʒef me no drink. Ich wes seek; ʒe ne confortyd me noʒt. Ich wes in
prison; ʒe ne vysityd me noʒt. Ich wes a gyst, and oncouþe, and pilgrim; ʒe ne
herborouid me noʒt. And þerfor ʒe scholle into endeles pine of helle'. Bot
now nym hed. Siþ þe Gospel saiþ þat hy scholliþ hab pine of helle þat ʒifeþ
noʒt her good for Godis loue, wat scholliþ hy hab þat beþ robberis and
145 mansleeris and lybbyþ in dedly sin to har liues end? Hy scholliþ al go to helle,
bot þulk robberis and þeuis scholliþ hab endeles mor pine þan þoþyr. Þe þryd
word þat God wol spek is, 'Comiþ, my blessyd chyldryn, to þe blysse þat my
Fadir aþ y-dyʒt to ʒow of þe bygining of þe world.' Þan hy syg as þoþyr þat
beþ y-damnid sayd: 'Lord, scholle we |fol. 196ᵛ| go wyþ þe þat art rote and
150 weele of al blysse and hab þy blessing and ioy bout end?' Þan God syg, 'ʒa, ʒe

scholle go with me and hab my blessyng and þe blysse of heuen day bout end'.
Þan hy scholl' syg, 'Wy?' and he wol ansuerr, 'For wan Ich wes hongri and
þursty and nakyd and in prison and sek ȝe fedd me and cloþyd me and
confortyd me, and þerfor ȝe scholl' hab þe blysse of heuen and be Godis

155 derlingys and lyb euir in weel with God and with is angelys'.

Bot ȝut about þe þre trompis wer þis þre wordis: 'Dern', 'Opin', 'Miȝtful'.
Þat is þe condicioun of þe dome. Þat þe dome be derne wytniswith Crist in
þe Gospel and saiþ þat day no man bot þe Fadir no Sone not it noȝt, in as
much as he is man. And þerfor Crist hymsilf saiþ in þe Gospel: 'But algat

160 aredy, for ȝe ne wytþ neuir þe day ne þe tyde'. Hit is also opin. Þe dome
schal be so opin as Seint Bernard sayþ, þat alþing þat euir God makid he
wol bryng with hym to þe dome, and þat oþir to ber wytnisse with man þat
he wel haþ despendid Godis creaturis, oþir to ber wytinis aȝeyins man to is
dampnacion. And Seint Gregori saiþ þat þe dome schal be ful grisful, wan

165 man schal y-se aboue hym God wroþ þat is boþe domisman and party, byniþe
hym helle opyn with endelese pine al redy, within hym is conscience gulty,
without hym deuelis accusing, and al about hym þe world al brenning. Ȝif
riȝtful man schal onneþ be saf, sinful þus y-kaȝt wydir schal he biturþin? He
schal say to þe dalys, 'Helie ous', and to þe hullis, 'Fal apon ous'. Hyd him

170 may he noȝt, and aperin darre he noȝt. He hys y-bound with pine in eche
halue. So þis dom is opin inow. |fol. 197ʳ| Þys dom schal be myȝtful. Wat
schold mor myȝt þan wiþ a blast of is mowþe gadyr togedyr al eorþe and
heuen and helle and al þat is þerin? Þer schul al stond at Crystis barre and
vndyrfong as hy habbyþ a seruyd, wel oþyr wo. Þus, þan, is dome derne, opin,

175 myȝtful. Take of derne 'd', of opin 'o', of myȝtful 'm', and þat wol make
dome. So þat dome of ys kund ys derne, opyn, and myȝtful. Nou Godde for
is mercy amiȝt, let vs scape þat dome aryȝt, and wynne þe blisse þat to vs diȝt.
Amen.

Headnote

Oxford, Bodleian Library, MS Hatton 96, is a paper manuscript, copied by several
scribes (McIntosh and Wakelin, 'John Mirk's *Festial* and Bodleian MS Hatton 96',
distinguished at least five major hands at work in it), and it contains for the most
part homiletic materials in English and Latin. The hands date to around the
middle of the fifteenth century, thus making Hatton the earliest of the vernacular
manuscripts studied here (the macaronic sermon in Dublin, Trinity College,

MS 75, may be nearly contemporary; see the headnote to Text E). The written dialect of the present sermon has been located by McIntosh and Wakelin in west Worcestershire, and this is probably the region of the language of the scribe's exemplar because this particular Hatton scribe (designated as scribe A in McIntosh and Wakelin's classification) seems to have been a *litteratim* copyist. It also seems possible that the manuscript was assembled by a priest for his personal use. Note in this respect the slip of paper inserted on fol. 49 which records on its verso a set of marriage banns in a contemporary hand; also, that the woman to be married was a servant of one Thomas Bewdley, whose surname might be thought to correspond to the eponymous town in Worcestershire. The Bewdley of the banns could never prove the manuscript's provenance, but given the West Midland complexion of some of its Middle English, Bewdley draws attention to the possibility that Worcestershire was indeed the county in which Hatton 96 was compiled.

Critical Notes and Glosses

2   oþer] A blotted letter, which could be *o*, has been expuncted at the start of this word by means of a single dot set above and below it.

3   perri] 'jewellery'.

5   Wisdome] Wisdomo MS.

5   sceldis] 'shields'.

6   goulis] 'gules'.

7   huche] 'each'.

11 couþe deuise þilke] 'knew how to explain the same'.

12 Biful ... scheldis] 'It happened that many came who wanted to enter but who did not know how to explain the shields'.

13 fyloȝofre] 'philosopher'.

16 þat noȝte ... hym] 'that nothing should escape him'.

17 dox, dasow] 'obscure, dim'.

18 Bewe] 'Fair' (a courteous form of address, deriving from the French word *beau*).

19 deþ] last letter unclear, possibly due to an alteration.

19–20 Þise Lorde God almyȝty] the sense is evidently disrupted by an ellipsis.

21 wyche] followed by *h* deleted.

22–23 for acordaunce ... rosys] 'on account of the likeness that is between man's nature and the nature of roses'.

23 defouling] 'crushing'.

26–27 now heer ... now wep] 'now ploughed, now sown, now ripe, now rotten, now whole, now sick, now laughing, now weeping'.

30 held] 'old age'.

31 vyrst hout ... lemys] 'first out and first suns its red gleams'.

33 quemfol] 'delightful'.

33 person] 'parson'.

36–37 is lems … most rode] 'its gleams are spread abroad and is at its greatest ruddiness'.

38 wiþ … a weniþ] 'with his long locks and other jollity he thinks'.

39–40 in is flouris] 'in his flowers' (i.e., 'is flourishing').

40–41 vadiþ, weltryþ, and welouþt] 'fades, withers and wastes away'.

42 falouyn and weltrin and swyndin] 'grows sere and withers and vanishes away'.

49 nim heod] 'take heed'.

53 huch step … fot] a possible elipsis here, 'each step that [cometh] of thy foot'?

55 onsykyrnes] 'uncertainty'.

57 byhot] 'promises'.

57 not] 'knows not'.

62 deol] 'mourning'.

63 sckylfolich] 'by reason'.

64 bynemiþ] 'deprives of'.

72 þoʒ a lyg] 'though he lies'; tapitis] 'tapestries'.

73 as swyþe as] 'as soon as'.

74 a party] 'somewhat'; herþe] 'earth'.

76 put] 'pit (of burial)'.

77 rof … on is mouþ] 'roof of his house lies on his mouth'; ber] 'bier'.

80 þilk … noʒt nay] 'that same man who owned everything [has] nothing at all'.

86–87 Þat schold … forʒut] 'They that ought to love [them] most, they have forgotten [them] soon enough'; As me saiþ on hold Englis] 'as it is said in old English'.

90–91 But wan … is way] 'But when Death comes, each goes its separate way'.

95 pine] 'affliction'; in reward of] 'in respect of'; ʒife a be] 'if he be'.

98 ondeþ] 'undoes'.

101–02 ne recchwhym neuir] 'no one cares at all'.

106 gastful and lolich] 'ghastly and loathsome'.

109 wyʒt] 'creature'.

109–10 þulk … pes] 'those that while she is alive will joust for her "of war" or "of peace"'.

111 onis] 'once'; manis … cou] 'man's nature is not repelled by a dead ox or cow'.

112 onneþ] 'hardly'

113 wlatsum] 'disgusting'.

116–18 of þe brain … inowe] 'for a toad breeds from the brain, and an adder breeds from the marrow of the *eschin* (shin-bone? ashes?)'.

120 king and] followed by an indistinct, deleted letter.

125 skylfollich] skyfollich MS.

129 chest] 'strife'.

130 sug] 'say'; in wom] 'in whom'.

133 ek hab þy cors] 'also have your curse'; Wodyr] 'whither'.

134 Þan] þᵗ MS.

141 gyst … oncouþe … herborouid] 'guest … stranger … gave lodging'.

142 Siþ] 'since'.

143–44 for Godis loue] fordisloue MS.

145 lybbyþ] 'live'; har] 'their'.

148 bygining] bygning MS.
149 go] we go MS ('we' having been repeated at the page break).
150 bout] 'without'; hab] not in MS.
156 Dern] 'secret'.
158–59 no man ... man] Matthew 24. 36. Something seems to be missing; the sense should be
     'no man but the Father knows it, nor does the Son know it in as much as he is a man'.
161 he] add. canc. b.
164 dampnacion] dampnacom' MS.
164 grisful] 'terrible'.
165 domisman and party] 'judge and litigant'.
168 sinful þus y-kaȝt ... biturþin] 'to where shall the sinful man caught in this way turn'.
169 Helie] 'cover'.
170–71 in eche halue] 'on every side'.
173 barre] 'bar (of Judgement)'.
174 vndyrfong] 'receive'.
177 amiȝt] 'almighty'; þat to vs diȝt] 'that [he] prepared for us'.

Apparatus fontium and Commentary

23–24 The use of the rose in eye balms is well attested in medieval recipes. Compare *The Liber
     de Diversis Medicinis*, ed. by Margaret Sinclair Ogden, EETS, o.s., 207 (London: Oxford
     University Press, 1938; repr. 1970), p. 11, lines 33–35.
26 The sense of 'lyȝe' as 'laughing' here antedates the first recorded example in the OED (1690).
28 Nunquam ... permanet: Job 14. 2.
31 The use of the verb *sonnyþ* in this sense antedates the first recorded example in the OED
     (1519).
43–48 This lyric and its lexis is discussed above; see also Fletcher, 'Death Lyrics' and below
     Chapter 9, pp. 293–94.
51 A litil ... oure lif: translating Wisdom 2. 1 ('Exiguum et cum taedio est tempus vitae nostrae').
52 mannis days ... toward þe: translating Job 14. 5 ('Breves dies hominis sunt; numerus mensium
     eius apud te est').
63 The motif that begins here of Death's three strokes, loosely comparable with the substance of
     the e Museo 180 text (Text B, lines 147–51), is more closely comparable with Lincoln 133
     (Text C, lines 99–103) and Trinity 75 (Text E, lines 37–40).
63–64 The reference here may be to some medieval laying-out practice.
65–70 This lyric and its lexis is discussed above (and see Fletcher, 'Death Lyrics').
77 rof ... on is mouþ: This is the common medieval conceit of 'grave as house'; see Christopher
     Daniell, *Death and Burial in Medieval England* (London: Routledge, 1997), pp. 68–69.
78 massis ... sauters: These are the traditional components of medieval exequies; compare Daniell,
     Death and Burial, p. 48, and *Mirk's Festial*, p. 296, lines 23–34.
87–88 Wan deþ ... forȝut: This rhymed proverb is not recorded in Whiting and Whiting,
     Proverbs, Sentences, and Proverbial Phrases, or in *NIMEV*.
100 Non est ... memoria: Ecclesiastes 1. 11.
107–08 I have not found anything close to this reference in St Augustine's works.

109–10 þulk ... pes: to joust 'of war' was to tilt with a sharp spear or lance, while to joust 'of peace' was to tilt with a blunted spear or lance.

126–27 Compare the citation here from 'St Jerome' with Lincoln 133 (Text C, lines 136–37).

128–29 Goþ, corsid gostis ... last: Matthew 25. 41.

139–41 For Ich wes hongry ... ʒe ne herborouid me noʒt: Matthew 25. 42–43.

159–60 But ... tyde: Matthew 25. 13.

161–64 I have not located this reference in St Bernard's works.

164–67 This matter attributed to 'Gregory' derives in fact from Anselm of Canterbury, *Meditatio*, 1 (St Anselm of Canterbury, *Sancti Anselmi Opera omnia*, ed. by F. S. Schmitt, 6 vols (Edinburgh: Nelson, 1946–61), III, 78–79).

168–69 The ideas in this line derive from similar ones found in Revelation 6. 16, 'Et dicunt montibus, et petris: Cadite super nos, et abscondite nos a facie sedentis super thronum, et ab ira Agni' (compare also Hosea 10. 8 and Luke 23. 30).

Text E

Dublin, Trinity College, MS 75, fols 2ᵛ–3ʳ

Sermo. Doctor Curteyse. Dominica in Passione. 'Christus assistens pontifex proprium sanguinem introiuit in Sancta.'

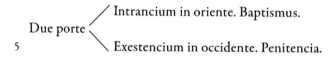

Due porte
Intrancium in oriente. Baptismus.

5   Exestencium in occidente. Penitencia.

Que habent vnum drawʒht brigge. Aperta iacet in die huius vite, et clauditur in nocte mortis, quando tenebre oriuntur in sensibus et aues cantare cessant, et ffures vagare desiderant, et laborare incipiunt executores, familia, heredes, et cetera. Inter has portas omnes sacramentales.

10 Narracio poetica.

Quidam philosophus quesiuit requiem. Fecit diuersis passagiis iter ad diuersas regiones. Demum in deserta patria requieuit super baculum, et iuxta orbitam, id est, bypaht, vidit turrem celestem depictum et ornatum curiosissime, splendentibus clipeis circumornatum. Cuius muralis edificii
15 nomen ab hostiario requirens, respondeatur, 'Hec diuinalis sapiencia'. 'Quod edificium', dixit hostiarius, 'non intrabis, nisi scuta apposita apertissime enucliare te disponas.' Philosophus amore diuinalis sapiencie motus, videbat supra portam tria scuta. Primum fuit of golde with iij roses of gowles. Hanc rosam considerans philosophus, et per primas litteras trium diccionum in

20 rosis scriptas que ffuerunt, L. I. F., adiunxit et faciunt 'Lif'. Prima rosa fuit·
borgening, budded and closed. In ista prima rosa fuit scripta 'Litel'. Secunda
rosa fuit fresscheli spred and opened. In ista fuit scripta 'Yvell'. Tercia rosa
fuit weltred, steyned and faded. In ista fuit scripta 'Fikell'. Sic intellexit
hanc rosam fore consideracionem tocius status humane condicionis. Per
25 primam ʒowht considerando formam illius rose et scripturam eius. Per
secundam manhode and sad wommanhode moraliter considerando illam
rosam cum scriptura. Per terciam age and febilnesse considerando, et cetera.
Et notandum est quod sicut rosa licet sit pulcherima crescit super a scharp
þorn, |fol. 3ʳ| sic humanitas nostra cressit super a scharp pricked stalk, scilicet
30 in natiuitate clamando, 'repletur multis miseriis'. Et sunt tres thornes illius
stalk humanitatis nostre, scilicet sekenes, besines, remors of synne. Secundum
scutum ffuit off sable cum tribus gladijs argenti. Scribebatur in primo gladio
'Departinge'; in secundo gladio 'Endynge'; in tercio gladio 'Tornynge'.
Considerauit philosophus hec tria principia istorum trium verborum et
35 percepit 'Deht'. ʿApplica narracionem de domina cum tribus filiis et v
ffiliabusʾ ffiliabus obsessa in castro per tortores mortis. Ffugit ad cameram
cordis vbi deponentes secreta vite thesaura. Isti tres gladij percutiunt in
morte tres asperimos ictus, quia smitiht awey all a manys wittes, all a manis
goodes, all a manis ffrendis, þre cruel and scharpe strokis, quia 'post mortis
40 morsum, vertit dileccio dorsum'. Tercium scutum quod ffuit de celestina
azura with iij trompis off golde. Scribebatur in primo 'Demavndyng'; in
secundo 'Opening'; in tercio 'Manassyng'. Adiunxit philosophus tria principia
istorum verborum et resultat 'Dome', id est, extremi iudicij. Pro primo,
'Surgite, mortui, venite ad', et cetera. Pro secundo, 'Opening'. Manifestabunt
45 consideranda, quia noluisti per penitenciam in via aperire cameram peccati,
et facit ʿsineʾ dilatione econtrario modo quibus dicitur, 'Venite benedicti
Patris mei', et cetera. Pro tercio, 'Manassing'. 'Esuriui, et non dedisti mihi',
et cetera. 'Ite maledicti', et cetera.

Numery primo, nota Iosephum antiquitus et Liram.

50 Ad instanciam populi, Moyses dedit eis a Deo vj c xiiij precepta. Rabi
Moyses, libro primo Iudaice legis, dicit quod de predictis preceptis, iij c lxvj
ffuerunt precepta negatiua, quia tot dies in anno in quolibet illorum precipit
non offerendo Deo, et de predictis preceptis ij c xlviij fuerunt affirmatiua,
quia tot ossa et iuncture sunt in humano corpore, sic totum hominem et
55 quamlibet eius partem voluit seruire Deo et fore seruientem Dei. Applica
illud ad Pascha. Post transitum mare, id est, penitenciam quadragesimalem.

Ffilii Israel videntes Deum, id est, cristicole. Per affeccionem sicco pede, nota sine slyme, id est, affeccione carnalis peccati. Aqua moyste, id est, desiderio terrestri. Petiuit a Moyse, id est, curato, obligari Deo in signum transitus
60 maris. Per nouam legem, id est, sacramenta data a Deo. Et applica vt supra omnem diem et totum hominem. Postea scribitur per Moysen quomodo Deus considerauit fragilitatem humane memorie, igitur tollebat illam multitudinem preceptorum et solum dedit x precepta Decalogi. Deinde in perfeccione legis, Matthei 5, sermo Domini in monte, dixit Saluator,
65 'Dictum est antiquis', et cetera, et dedit solum duo precepta: 'dilige Dominum ex toto corde,' et cetera, 'et proximum tuum sicut te', et cetera. 'In his duabus pendet', et cetera. Vltimo per suum secretarium Paulum dedit totum vnum dictum, 'Plenitudo legis est dileccio'. Et nota quando Moyses dabat populo vj c xiiij precepta, vt supra patet, accepit Moyses, id est, curatus, sanguinem
70 auium et vitulorum, id est, sacramentum Ihesu Christi, et ascendebat in locum, id est, altare eminentem, et vngebat seipsum. Et postea sanguinem, id est, Christi, qui fuit vitulus christianorum in die Passche, super capita populorum respersit et vocauit sanguinem federis, id est, reconsiliacionis; quasi diceret, 'hodie ffeceritis pro beneficiis suis nouam proffessionem obseruare
75 legem desideratam per vos et acceptam', scilicet istorum preceptorum. Qui sanguis in facie iudicii extremi vos accusabit nisi eam obseruaueritis.

Splendet in his scutis tibi gens doctrina salutis.
Vita qua viuis lex mortis, iudicij vis.
Vita nota rosis est mala, plena dolosis.
80 Mors habet hec certe tria: termino, diuido, verto.
Monstro tubis qualis venio iudex generalis.
Surgo latenter, pando patenter, flecto potenter.

Istos versus posuit philosophus super portam vt aperiretur sensus scutorum accedentibus.

Headnote

Dublin, Trinity College, MS 75, is an imposing parchment manuscript whose various scribal stints, and the identity of one scribe in it with a copyist whose hand features elsewhere in another group of contemporary manuscripts, are particularly important to hold in focus. This is so not only because the affiliation that Trinity 75 contracts with this manuscript group sheds light on the cultural context in which the sermon of 'Doctor Curteyse' is situated, but also because it bears upon larger questions concerning the propagation of vernacular and Latin Wycliffite writings between c. 1400 and the middle of the fifteenth century. For the fact is that, wherever Trinity 75 was copied, its earliest portions, the work of scribe A in the scribal analysis below, were executed at some centre of Lollard book production, if not indeed one of England's chief centres of Lollard book production (? London). Scribe A, whose hand is the one reappearing in the affiliated manuscript group, was a copyist of key Lollard texts and was active c. 1400. The hand of the scribal monogram 'Peruei', added at the foot of folio 217^r, col. b, most nearly resembles that of scribe A, but there is too little script in the monogram to make the identification stick. (The possibility that the monogram was that of John Purvey, an eminent Lollard, is for some unexplained reason rejected by Anne Hudson, 'John Purvey: A Reconsideration of the Evidence for his Life and Writings', in *Lollards and their Books* (London: Hambledon, 1985), pp. 85–110 (p. 104 n. 92) (first publ. in *Viator*, 12 (1981), 355–80).) Scribe A's work in Trinity 75 was subsequently corrected and supplemented around the middle of the fifteenth century by scribe B (and in any event after c. 1440–41; see further below on this). Scribe B, also a copyist of Lollard materials, was probably responsible for marrying the two originally separate parts which constitute Trinity 75; I believe the rubricator at work in the second part of the manuscript to be one and the same with scribe B identified in my scribal analysis (see also John Scattergood and Guido Latré, 'Trinity College Dublin MS 75: A Lollard Bible and Some Protestant Owners', in *Texts and their Contexts: Papers from the Early Book Society*, ed. by John Scattergood and Julia Boffey (Dublin: Four Courts, 1997), pp. 233–40, especially p. 229). These facts give pause for thought: what business had a sermon as thoroughly orthodox as that of 'Doctor Curteyse' in a manuscript such as this, one whose contents are predominantly Wycliffite — even the seemingly innocent letter of the rector of Chiddingfold, fols 255^r, col. a–257^r, col. a, makes (unacknowledged) use of John Wyclif's *Opus evangelicum* — and whose Wycliffite tenor is respected and further amplified by scribe B? The sermon of 'Doctor Curteyse', by contrast, elects a preaching style that Lollards and Lollard sympathizers characteristically abhorred. Furthermore, there is good palaeographical reason to believe that none other than the coordinating scribe B copied and included the sermon. Possible explanations for why some scriptorium evidently committed to disseminating Lollard material may also have disseminated at least some material that was impeccably orthodox are suggested in *PPPLME*, pp. 119–42, but the account there (p. 131) of the scribal stints of the Trinity manuscript is misleading and requires revision according to the scribal analysis below.

The most comprehensive published account of the scribal stints of Trinity 75 is in *LALME*, I, 76–77. To conform the scribal analysis below as closely as possible to this, I have followed *LALME*'s scribal designations. As a result, my analysis begins, not serially from A, as otherwise would be appropriate, but with scribe B. Corrections made by scribe B to the work of scribe A (for example, B has added a line of text, 'who of ȝou schal haue a frende', omitted by A when copying Luke 11. 5, in the right margin of fol. 71ʳ, col. b) have not been recorded in the analysis.

1ʳ–2ᵛ	Latin harmony of certain gospel episodes	Scribe B (s. xv med.)
2ᵛ–3ʳ	Macaronic sermon of 'Doctor Curteyse'	Scribe B
4ʳ–11ʳ	Latin table of epistle and gospel lections	Scribe A (s. xiv/xv)
11ᵛ–13ᵛ	English Prologues to Mark, Luke, John and the Apocalypse	Scribe B
14ʳ–217ᵛ	English Wycliffite New Testament, generally, though not exclusively, Early Version	A, with stints by B on fols 106ᵛ (15 lines in col. a) 107ʳ (bottom, 9 lines) 133ᵛ (21 lines in col. b) 134ʳ (29 lines in col. a) 157ʳ (15 lines in col. b) 168ᵛ (8 lines in col. b) 179ʳ (bottom, 5 lines) 182ᵛ (bottom, 4 lines) 185ʳ (bottom, 6 lines) 187ʳ (bottom, 6 lines) 189ᵛ (bottom, 4 lines) 190ᵛ (8 lines in col. a) 193ᵛ (7 lines in col. b) 196ʳ (bottom, 4 lines) 196*ʳ (bottom, 3 lines) 196*ᵛ (bottom, 13 lines); with stints by scribe C (s. xv¹) on fols 66ʳ⁻ᵛ 214ʳ–15ᵛ; with stints by scribe D (s. xv med.) on fols 148ᵛ–53ᵛ

| 218ʳ–81ʳ | Wycliffite Prologue to the Old Testament, items on the Prologue to the Psalter, excerpt concerning the four senses of Scripture from the General Prologue to the Wycliffite Bible, a prayer in English, the twelve articles of the Faith in English, an exposition of Mark 16. 12–20 in English, a Latin letter of John Witton, rector of Chiddingfold, c. 1441, to Cardinal Henry Beaufort, and the Old Testament lections read during the Church year in English. | Scribe E (s. xv med.), corrected by B on fols 222ʳ, col. b (right margin) 225ʳ, col. b (right margin) 231ʳ, col. a (left margin) 235ʳ, col. b (right margin) 237ᵛ, col. a (left margin) 238ʳ, col. a (left margin) 248ᵛ, col. a (left margin) 249ʳ, col. a (left margin) 252ᵛ, col. a (left margin) |

Critical Notes and Glosses

2 Sancta] *om.* MS.

4 opposite in the left margin: Anthema. Probably written in error for Antethema.

11 iter] *om.* MS (added here for the sake of the sense).

17 diuinalis] dimanalis MS.

18 opposite in the left margin: Primum scutum.

23 weltred] 'withered'.

26 moraliter] inoriter MS.

31–32 Secundum scutum] these words are written in the left-hand margin.

37 percutiunt] percutunt MS.

40 Tercium scutum] these words are written in the left-hand margin.

40 celestina] celestin MS.

53 opposite in left margin: nota.

66 duabus] duobus MS.

68 opposite in the left margin: A 'pasch'.

69 xiiij] *om.* MS.

73 respersit] *om.* MS (added here for the sake of the sense, and based on the Vulgate reading at Exodus 24. 8).

77 opposite in left margin: Versus pro tribus scutis.

Apparatus fontium and Commentary

1 Doctor Curteyse: 'Doctor Curteyse' may conceivably be a sobriquet (compare such well known examples as the 'Doctor Evangelicus', the 'Doctor Seraphicus', or the 'Doctor Irrefragibilis') as much as a proper name preceded by title (and moreover, no actual 'Doctor Curteyse' is on record at the Universities of Oxford and Cambridge who would be eligible). Whatever the case, I have not succeeded in determining who he may have been.

1–2 Christus assistens ... in Sancta: The lemma condenses Hebrews 9. 11–12, the opening of the epistle for Passion Sunday.

30 repletur multis miseriis: Job 14. 1.

35 Applica: note here the direct instruction to the user/preacher of the sermon, and its implications; such direct instructions appear also at lines 49 and 55.

35–37 Where the 'Doctor Curteyse' derived this *narracio* of a woman besieged in a castle with her sons and daughters from I have not been able to determine.

39–40 post mortis morsum ... dorsum: apparently proverbial, though I have traced no exact Latin source; but compare Middle English proverbs on the theme that the dead have no friends listed in Whiting and Whiting, *Proverbs, Sentences, and Proverbial Phrases*, p. 120, D71.

44 Surgite, mortui, venite ad: this citation is non-biblical; I have not located its source.

46–47 Venite benedicti Patris mei: Matthew 25. 34.

47 Esuriui ... mihi: Matthew 25. 35.

48 Ite maledicti: Matthew 25. 41 (the Vulgate reads, 'Discedite a me maledicti ...').

49 Numery primo, nota Iosephum antiquitus et Liram: The function of this note drawing attention to Joseph in the first chapter of Numbers (a reference to the tribe of Joseph appears in verse 32) is puzzling. The note has the air of being another informal, obiter dictum addressed to the person using the sermon. Probably *Liram* refers to some gloss of Nicholas de Lyra on this portion of Scripture.

65 Dictum est antiquis: Matthew 5. 21.

65–66 Dilige Dominum ... sicut te: Matthew 22. 37–39.

66–67 In his duabus pendet: Matthew 22. 40.

68 Plenitudo legis est dileccio: Romans 13. 10.

82 Surgo latenter, pando patenter, flecto potenter: this seems like a *distinctio* tagged on from some untraced source.

PREACHING IN LATE MEDIEVAL IRELAND:
THE ENGLISH AND THE LATIN TRADITIONS

Introduction

A book professing itself concerned with late medieval preaching in Britain and Ireland must necessarily range over a wider territory than has been implicitly covered in the discussions conducted so far. Hitherto, the provenance of every sermon manuscript commented upon has been English. In the present chapter, therefore, a preliminary exploration will be made of a much neglected field of study, preaching in late medieval Ireland, so that some justice may be done to the geographical range that the title of the book aspires to. In order to establish an appropriate comparative connection with what has gone before, however, the present chapter will focus principally on the preaching traditions within late medieval Ireland that are most germane to the preaching that previous chapters have examined. Thus, while preaching in the Irish language will be glanced at here, it is not this chapter's primary concern; indeed, it is a field better reserved for a separate specialized study of its own. Instead, the English and Latin preaching traditions of late medieval Ireland will constitute the primary subject of attention.

Some Qualifications

Before embarking on this subject, the chapter will do well first to strike a note of caution about its own chosen title, for reasons that have precisely to do with its occlusion of the preaching tradition in the Irish language that has just been announced. In one important sense, the title of the chapter entails a doubtful distinction. To cordon off an 'English' and a 'Latin' tradition of preaching in Ireland is to ignore the fact that at least some preachers, especially ones whose mobility brought them to those areas of the island where Irish was the dominant, in many places the exclusive, language, would not have recognized such a distinction as either particularly significant or meaningful. Such men would have needed to be linguistically versatile in order to fulfil their charge. The orders of friars come principally to mind in this respect, for while the secular clergy, and those of the regulars who preached, operated mainly at a local level, it was the essence of the mendicant movement to undertake preaching tours that ranged over wide territory, and hence, in late medieval Ireland, through different linguistic environments. Broadly speaking, English was to be heard in the walled towns and cities, and especially within the Pale, that area of the east coast with Dublin at its centre and where the English administration had its headquarters. Out in the countryside beyond the Pale, Irish was the predominant, if not the exclusive, language. Egregious in their response to the evangelical precept to preach the gospel to all nations (Matthew 28. 19), the friars, as has already been noted in Chapter 3, became associated with itinerancy, so much so that their detractors would seize upon it as a sign of their lapse into mere vagrancy and interloping. The examples from England of an association made in the minds of the critics of the friars between mendicant itinerancy and vagrancy are plentiful, but in the present context, an Irish example seems à propos. In about 1319, Alexander de Bicknor, Archbishop of Dublin, preached a sermon in Christ Church Cathedral, Dublin, against sloth. In it, he cited as cases in point the large numbers of vagrants and vagabonds filling the Dublin streets, nor were the mendicants spared his criticism, but included in the tally.[1]

The career of a mid-thirteenth-century Irish Franciscan, Tomás Ó Cuinn, told from the sympathetic perspective of a contemporary associate and member of his order, indirectly illustrates this mendicant wanderlust. At one stage Ó Cuinn had been guardian of the Franciscan house in Drogheda, County Louth, that most English of towns in late medieval Ireland, and yet he was evidently originally an indigenous, Gaelic-speaking Irishman. His situation in Drogheda suggests that he had acquired a competence in English. The confrère who related his activity was the English compiler of the late thirteenth-century *Liber exemplorum*, a work to which we shall return. He wrote approvingly of a sermon that Friar Tomás had preached against local superstition — it may well have been against popular

---

[1] Aubrey Gwynn, 'The Medieval University of St. Patrick's, Dublin', *Studies*, 27 (1938), 437–54 (p. 441).

belief in the fairies, though these were conceived by the compiler as having been devils — in the diocese of Clonfert, in the province of Connacht in the west of Ireland and on the other side of the country. Ó Cuinn had evidently and characteristically for his order gone on tour. The (lay) congregation at his Clonfert sermon must have comprised Irish speakers, and thus it must have been in Irish that he preached.[2] But he probably reported what he said to the English friar compiler of the *Liber exemplorum* either in English, since the latter, a native either of Warwickshire or of Worcestershire, would no doubt have been less familiar with Irish than Friar Tomás was, or perhaps even in Latin.[3]

Although the distinction proposed at the outset of the chapter, an English and a Latin preaching tradition, as opposed to an Irish one, may therefore be far from watertight, for the purposes of the present discussion it nevertheless remains convenient, and connects the preaching resources extant from late medieval Ireland to those hitherto discussed in preceding chapters with which the Irish ones have most in common.[4] Yet, more may be said for the distinction than mere taxonomic convenience, for in another sense, it is historically justified. As is well known to students of late medieval Irish history, the Church in Ireland was plagued by the factionalism of the two 'nations', between the Church of the native Irish, on the one hand, and that of the colonial settlers, on the other.[5] Demarcation lines drawn up between a Church *inter Anglicos* and *inter Hibernicos*, as it was termed, would necessarily complicate, if not compromise, the Church's mission as a single, coordinated enterprise. Even certain of the friars, famous boundary-crossers between different ethnicities, as Friar Tomás's career eloquently testifies, eventually succumbed to a partitionist thinking that a combination of historical

[2] See John A. Watt, *The Church in Medieval Ireland*, 2nd edn (Dublin: University College Dublin Press, 1998), pp. 77–78. Ó Cuinn became Bishop of Clonmacnoise in 1252; his Connacht preaching had occurred before that date.

[3] *Liber exemplorum ad usum praedicantium*, ed. by A. G. Little, British Society of Franciscan Studies, 1 (Aberdeen: Typis academicis, 1908), p. vii, proposed that the English compiler originated in Warwickshire, but the place names of Arley and Astley occur also in close proximity in Worcestershire.

[4] For a preliminary survey of the later medieval preaching tradition in the Irish language, see Murdoch, 'Preaching in Medieval Ireland'; the diaspora of the friars, notably the Franciscans, throughout the Irish-speaking territories is discussed by Colmán N. Ó Clabaigh, 'Preaching in Late-Medieval Ireland: The Franciscan Contribution', in *Irish Preaching*, ed. by Fletcher and Gillespie, pp. 81–93.

[5] See John A. Watt, *The Church and the Two Nations in Medieval Ireland*, Cambridge Studies in Medieval Life and Thought, ser. 3, 3 (Cambridge: Cambridge University Press, 1970).

circumstances conspired to bring about.[6] If we take as illustration a manuscript well known in literary circles, the Franciscan miscellany of verse and prose now preserved as London, British Library, MS Harley 913, we could arguably regard it as epitomizing this polarizing drift. Its palaeography suggests that it was assembled, probably by one scribe, in the 1330s, by which time the sorting even of the friars in Ireland into the two 'nations' was well under way. And what we discover on opening it is its presentation in the three chief languages of late medieval England (that is, English, French, and Latin). Its English is undoubtedly Hiberno-English, a dialect variety whose distinctiveness depends in part on its occasional lexical borrowings from Irish, but in Harley 913 there is no Irish per se to be found. On the face of it, therefore, the manuscript seems to be very much the product of such polarized cultural circumstances, and indeed, the balance of the evidence suggests that its provenance, entirely consistent with such circumstances, was the anglicized walled town of Waterford.[7] We will return to this manuscript too in the course of the chapter, since like the *Liber exemplorum*, Harley 913 also serviced to some extent the culture of preaching.

So our isolation of an English and a Latin from an Irish preaching tradition may have some historical justification provided, that is, that the distinction be not insisted upon too rigorously nor allowed to harden into a rigid orthodoxy. For even in the era of the Church *inter Anglicos* and *inter Hibernicos*, the situation on the ground was not entirely diametrically opposed, nor were the different ethnicities hermetically sealed off from one another quite as tightly as the administrative categories *inter Anglicos* and *inter Hibernicos* might suggest. Whatever the early fourteenth-century Harley 913 might seem to imply about a segregation is countered by another Franciscan product of the century to follow, copied *c.* 1455 and possibly in a conventual house in the west of Ireland in County Clare,[8] which witnesses to a rapprochement of the English, Latin, and Irish traditions in a remarkably telling way. Apart from the fact that the manuscript, Dublin, Trinity

[6] The support of some Franciscans for the Bruce invasion of 1315, for example, proved divisive within the order (Watt, *The Church in Medieval Ireland*, p. 80).

[7] Michael Benskin, 'The Style and Authorship of the Kildare Poems — (I) Pers of Bermingham', in *In Other Words: Transcultural Studies in Philology, Translation and Lexicography Presented to Hans Heinrich Meier on the Occasion of his Sixty-fifth Birthday*, ed. by J. Lachlan Mackenzie and Richard Todd (Dordrecht: Foris, 1989), pp. 57–83 (p. 59).

[8] Robin Flower, 'Ireland and Medieval Europe', *PBA*, 13 (1927), 271–303 (p. 282), although its origin in either Nenagh or Limerick has also been suggested by Ó Clabaigh, 'Preaching in Late-Medieval Ireland', p. 90.

College, MS 667, contains English, Irish, and Latin texts presented in comfortable proximity to each other, the very hybridity of the mise-en-page of the texts in the Irish language testifies, in the face of any notions of segregation, to ethnic cross-fertilization and exchange (see Figure 2). The style of the *litterae notabiliores*, rubricated and complemented by trailing pen flourishes (see for example the four letter *A*'s in the left-hand column), is wholly consistent with contemporary English, as opposed to insular Irish, manuscript layout. Conversely, the script of the text is otherwise unmistakeably Irish in character. MS 667 is another to which we shall return.

Gathering the Evidence

Having justified and qualified our focus, then, we next need to establish a corpus of manuscripts for study. Medieval preaching, no less in Ireland than everywhere else, is notoriously ephemeral. Like any oral performance predating the era of recording technology, it comprised evanescent words carried away on the air in the moment of their utterance. Such traces as survive do so, necessarily, only in written form, and for a host of reasons written form may not fully reflect what was actually preached.[9] Sermons in manuscript may, for example, have been originally conceived as model sermons, designed not for preaching as they stood but as quarries for subsequent preachers to mine in their search for their own preachable matter. Again, manuscript sermons may be literary, more sophisticated workings of what was actually said after the event itself, as may be the case with the sermons preached between 1348 and 1356 and recorded in the sermon diary of Richard FitzRalph, Archbishop of Armagh;[10] and so forth. Thus for a variety of cultural considerations, sermons on the page may stand at a remove from their counter-parts in oral delivery. Perhaps the best evidence for what early preachers actually said is to be found in the *reportatio* (that is, an account taken down of the sermon as preached), but from medieval Ireland there survive, as far as I am aware, no such *reportationes*; indeed, they are rare enough in medieval Britain generally.[11] We only approach, and that obliquely, something having *reportatio* status in the account that Friar Tomás Ó Cuinn gave of his own preaching as related to the English compiler of the *Liber exemplorum*. But the account is fleeting. If we take

---

[9] See the discussion in the introduction to Chapter 2, above.

[10] See Gwynn, 'The Sermon-Diary'.

[11] See Chapter 2, p. 12 and n. 2.

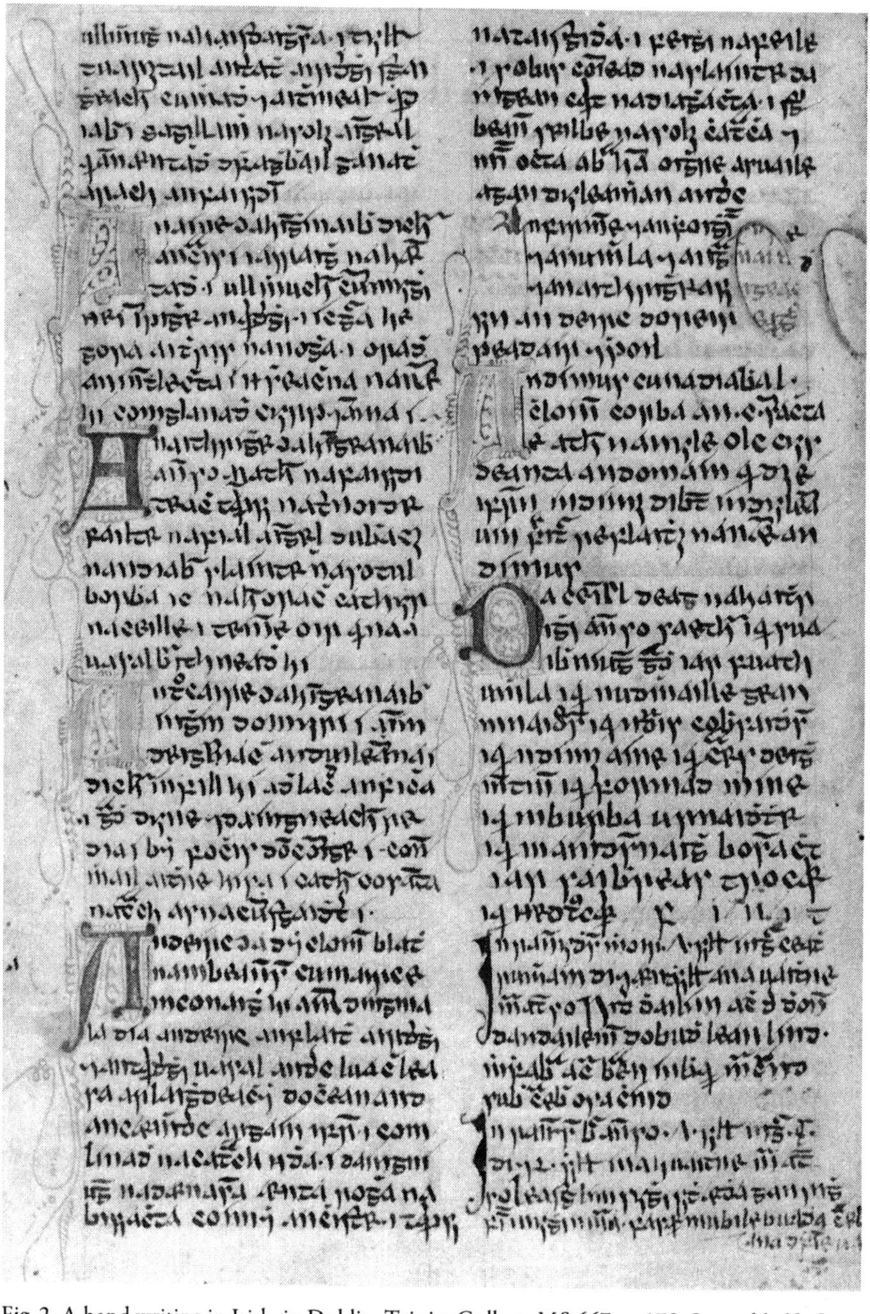

Fig. 2. A hand writing in Irish, in Dublin, Trinity College, MS 667, p. 178. Second half of the fifteenth century. Reproduced with permission of the Board of Trinity College, Dublin.

a little liberty with this category, it could be widened to include a discourse that features in the earliest morality play known from these islands, *The Pride of Life*, a play possibly written in medieval Dublin at the beginning of the fifteenth century.[12] In this play, whose former manuscript context suggests that it may have been produced under the aegis of the Canons Regular of St Augustine — men in the forefront of late medieval preaching and some of whose efforts were presented earlier in Chapter 5 — there occurs a scene in which a bishop preaches to an arrogant anti-hero, the King of Life, about life's transitoriness and the futility of earthly pride. What the play's audiences and the King of Life were evidently being treated to was a facsimile, albeit in the context of a play, of an actual sermon. That the Bishop, like the other characters in the play, spoke in verse does not necessarily detract from the possible resemblance between the play sermon and a real one; there existed such things as verse sermons, and indeed, MS Harley 913 contains one which, both in terms of its metre and some of its content, resembles the sermon of the Bishop in the play very closely.[13] But again, the play sermon is a lone witness, and thus its inclusion would extend the *reportatio* category only marginally.

Ireland is therefore no exception to the rule, and we are heavily reliant for our understanding of the English and Latin traditions of its late medieval preaching on texts of the sort liable to represent whatever may have been preached in reality filtered according to taste and preoccupation. The evidence consists in manuscripts containing sermons (principally or exclusively), in clerical miscellanies and anthologies in which sermons are included, or in materials intended for the use of preachers when they came to compose sermons of their own (from such materials it may be possible to conjecture the sort of preaching to which they may have given rise). The evidence also consists in library catalogues (which, at the very least, illustrate what sermons or sermon-related materials were in circulation, even if the catalogued originals may have subsequently vanished),[14] or in references to the activities of preachers and to preaching that occasionally appear in historical documents of other sorts. For the purposes of this chapter, I propose

---

[12] For the play, see *Non-Cycle Plays and Fragments*, ed. by Norman Davis, EETS, s.s., 1 (London: Oxford University Press, 1970), pp. 90–105. Its auspices are discussed in Alan J. Fletcher, *Drama, Performance and Polity in Pre-Cromwellian Ireland* (Toronto: University of Toronto Press, 2000), pp. 82–83 and 121–23.

[13] As Davis points out, *Non-Cycle Plays*, p. xcviii.

[14] The library catalogue of the Franciscans of Youghal is a famous example; see Ó Clabaigh, 'Preaching in Late-Medieval Ireland', pp. 85–88.

to concentrate on the first, second, and third classes of evidence (since the second and third sometimes overlap, however, they should not be regarded as absolutely exclusive): that is, manuscripts principally or exclusively containing sermons; sermons in clerical miscellanies and anthologies; and finally, sermon-related materials. The first and second classes are easier to identify than the third because, irrespective of what their exact nature may have been if they were indeed preached, the sermon status of a written text, more often than not, is relatively self-evident, while the homiletic applicability of a text of the third class may be much less so: St Paul's sanguine maxim that everything that is written is written for our learning promises a cornucopia from which preachers in future ages might choose, but at the same time holds out a dismal prospect for academic pigeon-holing. Nevertheless, at the risk of appearing arbitrary, I will confine discussion of works of the third class to ones that have overt and ostensible relation to preaching, compilations like the *Liber exemplorum* cited earlier.

Manuscripts Imported and Indigenous

John Watt, in his studies of the medieval Church in Ireland, was in essence right to regret a 'virtual disappearance of sermon literature' (and the examples of it that he cites suggest that he was thinking chiefly of sermons from the English and the Latin traditions before ones from the Irish tradition). Nevertheless, a little more survives for investigation than his bleak statement might suggest, especially if material be included that may have been imported from England for use in Ireland.[15] It is striking that both of the earliest sermon manuscripts representing the English and the Latin traditions in Ireland that have survived from the late medieval period are associated with the mendicant orders, although one, Oxford, New College, MS 88, arrived in Ireland, it is to be presumed, only from some date in or after 1397, the year in which its owner, Thomas Cranley (1337–1417), became Archbishop of Dublin.[16] Although nothing of his own work is known to survive, Cranley was by all accounts a celebrated preacher.[17] Thus New College 88 was

---

[15] Watt, *The Church in Medieval Ireland*, p. 210. Oxford, New College, MS 88 was imported, and Dublin, National Library of Ireland, MS 9596 may have been, though this is not entirely clear.

[16] Emden, *Biographical Register*, I, 510–11.

[17] The fulsome praise lavished on Cranley by the fifteenth-century Dublin chronicler Henry Marlborough does not omit to mention Cranley's stature as a preacher: he was a 'vir largus et elemosinarius, magnus clericus, doctor sacre theologie, egregius predicator [...] sibi diceretur

precisely the kind of manuscript that he would have found useful, containing as it mostly does sermons *de tempore* and *de sanctis*. A note on fol. 1ᵛ declares that he purchased it in Oxford.[18] It is a stocky little compilation (493 leaves, these measuring 152 × 107 mm),[19] and its portable format is wholly typical of a genre of manuscript books produced by mendicant preachers for use in their travels and illustrated earlier in Chapter 2. Indeed, the other manuscript of this earliest group, Dublin, Trinity College, MS 347, is of comparable dimensions, measuring 159 × 110 mm. Internal indications also put the original mendicant auspices of New College 88 beyond any doubt, although whether it was a product of mendicants in Oxford, where Cranley acquired it, is less clear.[20] In addition to items of mendicant (and particularly Franciscan?) interest,[21] on fol. 491ᵛ the following inscription can be seen under ultraviolet light: 'Iste Liber [...] conceditur fratre Roberto [...] ad terminum vite sue. qui hunc titulum deleuerit anathema sit. fiat/fiat amen (This book [...] is granted by Friar Robert [...] to the end of his life. May whoever shall have deleted this inscription be anathema. Fiat, fiat. Amen). It seems that Friar Robert's book never returned to his order from the unknown grantee, but eventually passed by some route into Cranley's hands. In it he would have found not only the wide selection of ready-made Latin sermons mentioned earlier, but also extensive sermon materials, some of which included occasional verses in Middle English.[22] Selected examples of these verses are worth citing, since they crystalize favourite sermon motifs and give some impression of what the

speciosus forma pre filijs hominum' (cf. Psalms 44. 3; 'a generous man and an alms-giver, a great cleric, a doctor of sacred theology, an outstanding preacher [...] of whom it might be said that he was in form fairer than the sons of men'; Troyes, Bibliothèque municipale, MS 1316, fol. 52ᵛ).

[18] Fol. 1ᵛ: 'Liber Magistri Thome Cranle quem emit Oxon' (The book of Master Thomas Cranley which he purchased in Oxford).

[19] London, British Library, MS Harley 913, discussed below, is roughly comparable. Its leaves measure approximately 140 × 95 mm.

[20] Margaret Laing, to whom I am grateful for advice, would tentatively locate the dialect of the Middle English appearing in New College, MS 88 in the region of south-east Herefordshire or south-west Worcestershire.

[21] A tract *De modo confitendi*, fols 211ʳ–214ᶠ, begins: 'Frater qui confessiones auditurus est' (The friar about to hear confessions). And a note running across the foot of fols 89ᵛ–90ʳ reads: 'Contra illos qui dicunt quod mundus melior ante aduentum fratrum' (Against those who say that the world was better before the coming of the friars).

[22] There is also a little French, as for example in the sermon on St Thomas Becket (fols 31ʳ–32ʳ), and a prayer to Jesus (fol. 477ʳ).

thematic centres of preaching were around which many medieval sermons *ad populum* in Ireland tended to converge.

The first piece of verse in New College 88 was written *c.* 1300 in the hand of a contemporary annotator who supplied marginalia throughout the entire manuscript:

> Wanne Ich þenche þinges þre,
> Ne mai [Ich] neure bliþe be.
> Þat on is, Ich sal awe.
> Þat oþer is, Ich ne wot wilk day.
> Þat þridde is mi meste kare:
> I ne woth nevre wuder I sal fare.[23]

(When I think on three things I may never be happy. The one is, that I must pass away. The other is, I don't know which day. The third is my greatest care: I have no idea where I shall fare to.)

This lyric introduces the mind-focusing prospect of death, and induces fear of an uncertain hereafter (purgatory and hell were traditionally presented as being more populous than heaven, moreover), in order to make those who heard it pliably receptive to the Church's prophylaxis for the two postmortem states that were to be feared. The lyric's strategy is common enough to lyrics written anywhere in medieval Britain and Ireland, but considered in a specifically Irish context, it begs comparison with the *memento mori* emphasis of the sermon of the Bishop in *The Pride of Life* play,[24] or with sentiments expressed in the Song of Michael of Kildare (a Harley 913 lyric whose author names himself as a Franciscan friar), or with sentiments in another Harley 913 text, this time an actual verse sermon,[25] or again with the moralized digits in Dublin, Trinity College, MS 667 (see Figure 3), a late fifteenth-century manuscript discussed at the end of this chapter. The lyric seems to be a reflex of this particular contemporary preoccupation, one whose appearance as late as MS 667 shows how resilient it would prove to be within the preaching of the mendicant orders.

---

[23] New College, MS 88, fol. 32ʳ. The lyric seems to have been popular; for discussion, see Woolf, *The English Religious Lyric*, p. 86.

[24] *Non-Cycle Plays*, pp. 100–02, lines 327–406, and pp. 103–04, lines 435–48.

[25] Respectively, *Anglo-Irish Poems of the Middle Ages*, ed. by Angela M. Lucas (Dublin: Columba, 1995), p. 74, lines 17–18, and pp. 82–84, lines 153–68. This latter text also identifies the typical stuff of mendicant preaching as being heaven, hell, joy, and torment (ibid., p. 80, lines 109–10): 'freris prech of heuen and helle, | Of ioi and pine to mani man'.

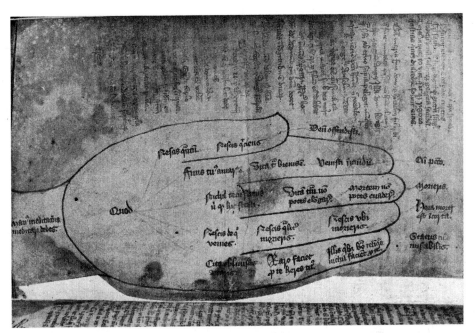

Fig. 3. The moralized 'Manus meditacionis', in Dublin, Trinity College, MS 667, p. 252. Second half of the fifteenth century. Reproduced with permission of the Board of Trinity College, Dublin.

Another New College 88 lyric that commandeers and Englishes a favourite sermon theme, this time copied by one of the manuscript's three principal scribes and embedded into a set of notes on the Passion, runs as follows:

> Man and wyman, loket to me
> U muchel pine Ich þolede for þe.
> Loke upone mi rig, u sore Ich was i-biten.
> Loke to mi side, wat blode Ich haue i-leten.
> Mine uet an mine honden nailed beth to þe rode.
> Of þe þornes prikung min hiued urnth a blode.
> Fram side to side, fro hiued to þe fot,
> Turn mi bodi abuten, oueral þu findest blod.
> Man, þin hurte, þin hurte þu turne to me,
> For þe vif wndes þe Ich tholede for þe.[26]

[26] New College, MS 88, fol. 181ʳ.

(Man and woman, look upon me, how much torment I endured for you. Look at my back, how grievously I was beaten. Look at my side, how much blood I have shed. My feet and my hands are nailed to the cross. My head streams with blood from the pricking of the thorns. From side to side, from head to foot, turn my body about, you find blood everywhere. Man, turn your heart, your heart, to me, for the five wounds that I suffered for you.)

Here, the verses offer a version (whose opening lines have evidently also been influenced by one of the *improperia* from the Good Friday liturgy, *O vos omnes qui transitis per viam*) of a preceding Latin text beginning *Respice in faciem Christi tui* (Psalm 83. 10; this Psalm verse was itself frequently chosen as a *thema* for sermons).[27] The lyric, patently in touch with the widespread, late medieval tradition of affective piety, evokes a speaking Christ intent on requisitioning, ultimately for their spiritual benefit, the audience's attention and pity. To that extent, the lyric's manipulation of salvific emotion compares with that of 'Wanne Ich þenche þinges þre'. And once again, though here in an unequivocally Irish context, Harley 913's poem Fall and Passion, which versifies a selection of key Bible narratives from the fall of Lucifer until the Resurrection, nevertheless elects to dwell on the Passion preponderantly.[28]

A third lyric in New College 88 appears alongside other snippets of Middle English within a set of memoranda concerning those who dangerously defer penance. In order to illustrate how most of the theological notes in this manuscript await the finishing touches of their actual users for their final arrangement and presentation — the notes of New College 88 are sermon materials in the most fundamental sense — their immediate Latin context has also been provided here:

Exemplum: difficile est auem senem docere ad loquendum, scilicet 'Richard'. Similiter, equum senem ad ambulandum. Exemplum: de malo garcione qui necgligenter surgit, uocante eum domino suo, 'Robin, Robin, up aris!' Iacet autem et dormit donec tercio uel quarto uocetur. Augustinus, *Libro confessionum*: 'Non erat quid responderem tibi ueritate conuictus dicenti mihi, "Surge qui dormis, et exurge a mortuis, et illuminabit tibi Christus"

[27] Woolf, *The English Religious Lyric*, p. 43 n. 1, notes that the lyric's opening is not an exact verbal parallel to *O vos omnes*. True, but the opening is possibly responsive to sermon protocols, where the expression 'good men and women', certainly by the fourteenth century, was a favoured form of opening audience address. For a repertoire of sermons on the theme *Respice in faciem Christi tui* by named preachers active in the later thirteenth century, see Schneyer, *Repertorium*, I, 312; II, 662, 673; III, 287, 289, 291; IV, 45. Interestingly, the authors of these were all friars.

[28] *Anglo-Irish Poems*, pp. 102–14 (especially pp. 108–12, lines 113–79). Friars' sermons were typically wont to capitalize on Passiontide emotions too, even if Passiontide was not explicitly named as a favourite mendicant preaching topic in the poem of MS Harley 913 entitled Sarmun.

(Ephesios 5) nisi uerba lenta et sompnolenta, "Modo, ecce modo, sine paululum." Sed "modo" et "modo" non habebat modum, et "sine paululum" in longum ibat.' Similiter est de differentibus penitencie:

'Louerd, þu clepedest me
An Ich nagt ne ansuarede þe
Bute wordes scloe and sclepie.
"Þole yet, þole a litel."
Bute "yiet" and "yiet" was endelis,
And "þole a litel" a long wexis.'[29]

(*Exemplum*: it is hard to teach an old bird to speak, that is, [to say] 'Richard'. Likewise, [it is hard to teach] an old horse to amble. *Exemplum*: concerning the bad boy-servant who gets up negligently as his master calls him, 'Robin, Robin, get up!' But he lies and sleeps until the third or fourth time he is called. Augustine, in [his] *Book of Confessions*: 'There was nothing that I, convinced by [your] truth, might reply to you as you said to me, "Get up, sleeper, and arise from the dead, and Christ will give you light" (Ephesians 5. 14), other than slow and sleepy words. "Soon, see now, soon, endure a short while." But "soon" and "soon" had no measure, and "endure a short while" was long lasting.' It is similar with those who defer penance: 'Lord, you called me and I answered you nothing except slow and sleepy words. "Endure yet, endure a little." But "yet" and "yet" was endless, and "endure a little" grows into "a long".')

If Cranley ever preached material such as this before his Irish audiences, he would first have had to trim it into sermon shape. By the late Middle Ages, preaching and the practice of confession and penance were often twinned enterprises and thus, understandably, the centrality of the sacrament of confession was frequently preached about, or affective sermons might be contrived to induce in their hearers the preliminary disposition, namely, contrition, from which effective confession could grow (these things have already been well exemplified in sermons presented in Chapters 4, 5, and 6, above).[30] If art had power to move, it could be enlisted to the preacher's purpose, and this is the purpose that probably called the New College 88 lyric into being. Compare, again, the Song of Michael of Kildare in Harley 913, which urges confession and due penance upon its hearers.[31]

---

[29] New College, MS 88, fol. 181ᵛ; the reference to St Augustine is to Book VIII, section 5, subsection 12 of his *Confessions*: *Sancti Augustini Confessionum Libri XIII*, ed. by L. Verheijen, CCSL, 27 (Turnhout: Brepols, 1981), p. 120, lines 42–47.

[30] For further discussion of the late medieval consortium of preaching and confession, see Alan J. Fletcher, 'The Essential (Ephemeral) William Langland: Textual Revision as Ethical Process', *YLS*, 15 (2001), 61–84. And compare notably the thinking of Thomas Cyrcetur in this respect, whose preaching was considered earlier in Chapter 6.

[31] *Anglo-Irish Poems*, p. 72, lines 117–24.

Equally pragmatic, if less emotionally evocative, is this final illustration which, in versifying one of the essentials of catechesis that from the Lambeth Council of 1281 preachers were widely enjoined to communicate, the Decalogue, dresses it in mnemonic rhyme.[32] Thus set forth, it would have been more liable to lodge profitably in the heads of the audience:

> On God þu sal aue in wrchepe,
> Ne takyn natte is name in idelchepe.
> Hold wel þe haliday.
> Fader a[nd] moder þu wrchep ai.
> Ne sclo þe nevre no man.
> Lecherie ne do þu non.
> Loke þat natt þu ne stele,
> Ne no fals withnesse þu ne bere.
> Affter oþer mannes wif natt te ne longe,
> Ne natt of his haue wid wronge.[33]

(You shall worship one God. Do not take his name in vain. Keep the holy day well. Always honour father and mother. Never slay any man. Do no lechery. See that you do not steal, nor bear any false witness. Do not hanker wrongfully after another man's wife, nor after anything that he has.)

And again, finally, we may compare a poem devoted to the Decalogue in Harley 913 and which, with four other poems in this manuscript, has the formal stylistic features of sermon register. These would have suited it for preaching.[34]

We turn now to another manuscript of approximately similar date and also produced in a mendicant context, though this time actually in Ireland. Dublin, Trinity College, MS 347, is so remarkably similar to New College 88 in format

[32] For the relevant section of the Lambeth Constitutions of 1281 (the decree beginning *Ignorancia sacerdotum*), see *Councils and Synods*, II, 900–05. Archbishop John Pecham, who issued the Constitutions, was himself a Franciscan. Only one explicit reference to the Irish adoption of *Ignorancia sacerdotum* is currently known, and appears in the registers of the late medieval diocese of Armagh.

[33] In the manuscript, the line 'Lecherie ne do þu non' is written finally, and marked to replace the line originally written, 'Bute bi þi wif ne li þu bi no wiman'; the latter line has accordingly been omitted here. The annotating hand adds this rhymed Decalogue at the foot of fol. 490[v]. I am indebted to Margaret Laing for checking and correcting my transcriptions from New College, MS 88.

[34] *Anglo-Irish Poems*, pp. 116–21. There are five 'sermon poems' in this manuscript (using Lucas's titles, they are: Sarmun, Fifteen Signs before Judgement, Fall and Passion, Ten Commandments, and Seven Sins).

and in the general complexion of its content that both manuscripts between them might be thought to witness to a high degree of consistency in the late thirteenth-century mendicant approach to pastoral care throughout Britain and Ireland. A note of ownership in an early fifteenth-century hand on folio 1ʳ declares: 'notandum quod iste liber est fratris Iohannis knoces accomodatus domino Iohanni hothum rectori de clogheran sine pecunia et quicumque istum titulum deleuerit anathema sit' (It is to be noted that this is the book of Friar John Knock, loaned to Master John Hothum, rector of Cloghran, without money. And may whoever deletes this inscription be anathema). It seems that MS 347 had stayed in mendicant hands from the time of its copying (the various scribes at work in it were all roughly contemporary, *c*. 1300) until it passed to John Hothum, rector of Cloghran (probably the place with that name situated a few miles north of Dublin).[35] In this respect again like New College 88, therefore, MS 347 was permitted to migrate from mendicant to secular clerical use — John Hothum was most probably the secular canon of the same name serving at St Patrick's Cathedral who was active in the early part of the fourteenth century[36] — and this suggests some mendicant collaboration with and support for the seculars in their exercise of the *cura animarum*, irrespective of bouts of hostility that sometimes marred relations between them and that in Ireland especially clustered around the campaign of Richard FitzRalph. If any clerical infighting registers in MS 347, it is not against the seculars but against the monastic regulars that it occurs.[37] The manuscript was possibly assembled at the Franciscan house at Multyfarnham, County Westmeath.[38]

It principally contains Latin sermons, *de tempore* and *de sanctis*, and sermon materials, and its occasional vernacular verses, like those of New College 88, are used to vivify and enliven fundamental Christian catechesis. The prime example

[35] Cloghran was part of the rich prebend of Swords which returned funds directly to the economy of St Patrick's Cathedral, Dublin.

[36] He is on record as a canon there between 1306 and 1313. He appears in the *Dignitas Decani* of the cathedral as a co-signatory to the initiative of the canons in 1306 to be vigilant on behalf of the cathedral's temporalities; see *The 'Dignitas Decani' of St. Patrick's Cathedral Dublin*, ed. by Newport B. White, with an introduction by A. Gwynn (Dublin: Stationery Office, 1957), p. 82. The inscription of ownership is found at the foot of fol. 1ʳ.

[37] Note its verses on bad monks (fol. 9ʳ), for example; compare also the anti-monastic Latin and English satires present in MS Harley 913.

[38] Its contents are fully catalogued in Marvin L. Colker, *Trinity College Library Dublin: Descriptive Catalogue of the Mediaeval and Renaissance Latin Manuscripts*, 2 vols (Aldershot: Scolar, 1991), I, 710–40.

of their use occurs within a passage against dancers, in which six aspects of dancing are each envisaged as profaning one of the Church's sacraments. The verses, in English and French, are interpolations into a passage which derives ultimately from the influential *Summa de vitiis* of the thirteenth-century French Dominican, William Peraldus.[39] (The passage is itself an interpolation into a larger work, the *Summa* or *Distinctiones* of Gilbert the Minorite.)[40] The passage is worth quoting, since it shows how an Irish preacher, obliged, in accordance with Church injunction, to discant annually on the sacraments, was being offered the resources to do so imaginatively. The passage's simultaneous attack on dancing has the additional advantage of serving as a device whereby the individual sacraments might be remembered:

Qve choreas ducunt faciunt quodammodo contra omnia sacramenta ecclesie. Prima contra baptismam, quia frangunt pactum quod inierunt cum Deo in baptismo cum patrini earum dixerunt pro eis, 'Abrenuncio diabolo et pompis eius.' Pompam siue processionem diaboli intrant cum choreas intrant. Vnde patrini earum possunt timere, ne de promissione illa rei apud Deum inueniantur, si non admonuerint eas diligenter ne choreas intrent. Contra sacramentum ordinis. Sunt enim qui simie clericorum et tale seruicium diabolo offerunt, quale clerico Deo, et per cantus earum impediuntur [lege impeditur] cantus ecclesiasticus et contempnitur, quia qui deberent interesse uesperis, intersunt choreis. Contra matrimonium, quia maritis multum detrahitur, quibus dicitur:

> 'Pur mun barun, fi!
> Vn plus bel me at choisi'.

Et Anglice dicitur:

> 'Of my husband giu I noht.
> Another hauet my luue y-bohit
> For tuo gloues wyht ynoht.
> If Hic him luue,
> Y naue no woht.'

Multi et incitantur ad faciendum contra matrimonii fidem. Aperte uero contra legem matrimonii predicatur cum cantatur quia pro prauo uiro uxor dimittere non debet quin amicum faciat. Vnde:

---

[39] As Wenzel, *Preachers, Poets, and the Early English Lyric*, p. 216, has observed.

[40] Its incipit is: 'Accidiosus siue piger est fertilis ad multiplicandum uicia'. For other manuscripts, see Morton W. Bloomfield and others, *Incipits of Latin Works on the Virtues and Vices, 1100–1500 A.D.*, Medieval Academy of America, 88 (Cambridge, MA: Medieval Academy of America, 1979), p. 30, item 0178.

'Lete þe cukewald syte at hom
And chese þe another lefmon.
Lete þe chorl site at hom and pile,
And þu salt don wat þu wile.
God hit wot, hit nys no skile.'

Cum secundum legem Dei et leprosum dimittere non debeat, quin loco et tempus [lege tempore] debitum ei reddat si ipse uoluerit. Contra confirmacionem, in quo [lege qua] in fronte signum crucis susceperunt, tanquam empte Passione Christi. In choreis uero signo Christi abiecto, signum diaboli pro eo in capite posuerunt; signum, scilicet uenalitatis, quasi Christus non emerit eas. Christus posuerat uexillum suum in eminenti parte, scilicet in fronte, tanquam in eminen |fol. 200ʳ| ciori parte castri, et ipse uexillum diaboli pro eo posuerunt, non absque magna contumelia Christi. Sicut faciunt qui furantur equos signatos, delent enim signum et ponunt signum suum. Contra sacramentum penitencie, per quam Deo reconsiliate erant in quadragesima, dum pacem illam frangunt, et in excercitum diaboli uadunt. Contra sacramentum altaris, quia ad mensam Dei panem celestem susceperunt et postea nichilominus Dei terram igne infernali incendunt. Similes inde qui cum comedisset ad mensam Domini, accepit choortem a pontificibus et phariseis, uenit contra Ihesum.[41]

(Those women who lead dances in a certain way act contrary to the Church's sacraments. First, against baptism, because they break the agreement with God that they entered in baptism when their godparents said on their behalf, 'I renounce the devil and his pomps.' They enter into the pomp or procession of the devil when they enter into dances. Wherefore their godparents may fear lest they be found guilty before God because of that promise, if they have not admonished them diligently not to enter into dances. Against the sacrament of Orders. For there are those who ape clerics and offer such service to the devil as a cleric does to God, and through their songs the song of the Church is impeded and despised, because those who ought to attend vespers attend dances. Against marriage, because husbands are much disparaged, of whom it is said, 'Fie upon my husband! I have been chosen by one more handsome.' And in English it is said, 'I care nothing for my husband. Another has bought my love for two very white gloves. If I love him, I have no sorrow.' Many are also driven to behave contrary to the faith of marriage. Indeed, it is openly preached against the law of matrimony when it is sung, because a wife ought not dismiss [her husband] on account of a faithless man but rather make him her friend. Whence [the verses], 'Let the cuckold sit at home and choose yourself another lover. Let the churl sit at home and pluck [his hair] and you shall do what you will. God knows, it's entirely appropriate.' Since according to God's law she might not abandon even a leper, but that at the right place and time let her repay [her husband] his debt if he wishes it. Against confirmation, in which they received the sign of the cross on their forehead, as if purchased by Christ's Passion. But in dances, having thrown aside Christ's sign, they have set the devil's sign in its place on their head, a sign, that is, of venality, as if Christ may not have bought them. Christ had set his banner in a prominent place, that is, the forehead, as if in the higher part of a camp, and they have set up in its stead the devil's banner, not

---

[41] I have ignored the scribe's mechanical copying errors and self-corrections.

without great insult to Christ. Those who steal horses behave similarly, for they remove the sign [of ownership] and impose a sign of their own. Against the sacrament of penance, by which they were reconciled with God in Lent, until they shatter that peace and enter the devil's army. Against the sacrament of the altar, because they have received heavenly bread at God's table and nevertheless afterwards they set God's land ablaze with infernal fire. Thereupon they are like the man who, when he had eaten at the table of the Lord, received a troop of soldiers from the priests and Pharisees and came against Jesus.)

The last of the late thirteenth-century preaching compilations needing notice has already been mentioned, so it can be dealt with summarily. It is the collection of sermon exempla known, appropriately enough, as the *Liber exemplorum*, preserved in Durham, University Library, MS Cosin B.IV.19. Though the manuscript itself was copied about the middle of the fourteenth century, the work was composed, as A. G. Little has shown, between 1270 and 1279, and probably in the latter part of this period, between 1275 and 1279. The peppering of sermons with short, lively narratives or exempla was a condiment that many friars applied liberally, doubtless because members of the laity, whose taste for tales and vivid illustrations had long been acknowledged by preaching theorists and practitioners alike, were especially targeted by friars. They also sought the laity out in those regions which the seculars often did not reach, fastened as the latter generally were to their local livings.[42] The appearance of mendicant exempla collections compiled as preaching resources therefore comes as no surprise, and the *Liber exemplorum*, among the more substantial specimens of this genre to have survived, is of Irish origin. Its anonymous compiler, an English friar, distributed the exempla he gathered — some from common pan-European sources, others by word of mouth from friars active like himself in Ireland — between two broad categories, the 'higher' and the 'lower matters'. He classified as 'higher' those exempla on topics like the life of Christ, the sacrament of the altar, and the Virgin Mary.[43] As 'lower' he classified, for example, exempla about the Seven Deadly Sins (perennial preaching matter since, like the sacraments itemized in the passage on the evils of dancing quoted above, these too were part of the established preaching programme).[44] Also classi-

---

[42] Even if the clergy did not reside in their livings, provision was normally made for resident vicars and deputies to serve in their stead.

[43] A very large number concern the Blessed Virgin Mary (twenty-six); compare, too, the way in which the Marian exempla cluster in Dublin, Trinity College, MS 667. Other exempla topics classified under the 'higher' section concern, for example, the cross (the well known story of the nun and the lettuce features here), the angels, and St James.

[44] Sloth (four examples); Avarice (five examples); Gluttony (six examples); Envy (two examples); Wrath (two examples); Lechery (seventeen examples); Pride is not present, because the collection, arranged alphabetically, is atelous, with the result that Superbia is missing.

fied here are exempla on assorted, more mundane topics, including specific social ones like the vices of lawyers, merchants, evil clerics, and executors.[45] Since it can be safely assumed that the substance of some of the material in this exempla collection was indeed preached, portions of the *Liber exemplorum* open a window onto things actually heard by medieval Irish audiences.[46]

Into the Fourteenth Century

Just as certain topics of the *Liber exemplorum* were similarly favoured in the other early mendicant sermon manuscripts that have been considered thus far, so too they would echo later in the first of the fourteenth-century compilations to which we may now turn, another Franciscan product, London, British Library, MS Harley 913.[47] Such thematic consistency suggests that between *c.* 1270 and *c.* 1330, mendicant preaching in Ireland wove variations on a repertoire of characteristic themes. On the basis of the evidence considered in this chapter, this repertoire could fairly be summarized as having comprised affective preaching about cardinal New Testament (and a few apocryphal) narratives and persons (for example, about Passiontide and about the Blessed Virgin Mary), and elementary catechetical preaching and moral exhortation. (Indeed, this consistent picture would not be disturbed by any apparent departures in the content of fifteenth-century sermons either, as will shortly be seen.) If we take, for example, two topics from the *Liber exemplorum*'s 'lower matters', the Seven Deadly Sins and the Fifteen Signs before Doomsday, we find them again centrally positioned in two of the 'sermon poems' of Harley 913.[48] Harley 913 has five 'sermon poems' in all. A third 'sermon poem', on the Decalogue, refurbishes another catechetical chestnut

---

[45] Also included are exempla about carnal thoughts, baptism, marriage, confession, alms, excommunication, those who injure the Church, those who work on feast days, those who tithe badly, inordinate games, backbiting, humility, indulgences, vainglory, the joy of heaven, oaths, Judgement (including the Fifteen Signs before Doomsday), the memory of death, etc. The original topical emphasis of this section on 'lower things' is distorted because the manuscript is atelous, but judging by what survives, the prominent themes are social complaint, Christian living, and catechesis. For further comment on the different methods used to organize exempla collections, see Claude Bremond, Jacques Le Goff, and Jean-Claude Schmitt, *L'Exemplum*, Typologie des sources du moyen âge occidental, 40 (Turnhout: Brepols, 1982).

[46] Friar Tomás Ó Cuinn's sermon, for example.

[47] An edition of the entire manuscript is projected by Michael Benskin and Alan J. Fletcher.

[48] *Anglo-Irish Poems*, pp. 90–101 and 140–49.

(recall the vernacular verse Decalogue prominent in MS New College 88), while a fourth and a fifth, respectively the Fall and Passion 'sermon poem' and the 'sermon poem' simply entitled Sarmun by its recent editor, rehearse, respectively, summaries of key biblical narratives from the fall of Lucifer to Christ's Resurrection and Ascension, accenting the Passion, and contempt for the vanity of this fleeting world. Harley 913 additionally keeps company with the earlier Franciscan MSS New College 88 and Trinity College 347 in terms of its small, portable format (Cosin B.IV.19, the *Liber exemplorum* manuscript, is substantially bigger, but this work was made to be consulted, not to provide a friar with a vade mecum).

It seems impossible to determine whether significance, or mere coincidence, should be attached to the fact that this early clutch of manuscripts are mendicant (indeed, Franciscan) products. Unquestionably, the mendicants comprised an important preaching corps in medieval Ireland; were manuscript quantity alone a reliable indicator, the mendicants would emerge as the most important, the prime movers on the preaching scene. Whatever the historical truth of this, it is interesting to note that it was partly in reaction to mendicant activity that the first major name to emerge among secular preachers in fourteenth-century Ireland defined his mission. The career of Richard FitzRalph (1299/1300–1360) has been amply charted elsewhere, but here some notice of his Irish preaching is warranted.[49] He came to Ireland twice, as Archbishop of Armagh, first between April 1348 and the early summer of 1349, and next from about the summer of 1351 until the early summer of 1356.[50] In this time his sermon diary records him having preached some twenty-eight sermons, all but two of which were in English. All were committed to parchment, however, in Latin.[51] The two sermons preached in Latin were, unsurprisingly, to clerical congregations, and delivered at synods held in Drogheda, on 7 February 1352 and 5 February 1355 respectively.

FitzRalph's first recorded sermon in Ireland, delivered the previous year also in London, was preached on 24 April 1348 in Dundalk on the six petititions of the *Pater noster*. The *Pater noster*, like the Decalogue and sacraments, was one of

---

[49] In addition to Gwynn's study (cited in n. 6, above), see Katherine Walsh, *A Fourteenth-Century Scholar and Primate: Richard FitzRalph in Oxford, Avignon and Armagh* (Oxford: Clarendon Press, 1981). A précis of his preaching style and career is given in *LSCLME*, pp. 31–35.

[50] He was probably absent with the King for most of summer and autumn of 1353.

[51] None of the sermon diary manuscripts is holograph, however (for a catalogue of these, see Gwynn, 'The Sermon-Diary').

the staples of elementary catechesis, and eminently suitable fare for a sermon *ad populum*. He managed to work into his preaching other catechetical favourites, too. The Seven Deadly Sins, for example, feature in a sermon of his delivered at Louth on 27 April 1348.[52] As occasion required, he was also prepared when preaching to make topical references, though these seem to have touched on the moral conduct of particular social groups rather than on broad political issues. Thus his memorandum of a sermon delivered in Drogheda on 2 December 1352, for example, notes that 'ibi fiebat dilatacio sermonis ad mercatorum fraudes et falsitates' (at that point the sermon was expanded to touch on the frauds and deceits of merchants),[53] and in another sermon delivered at Skreen on 21 June 1355 he noted that there existed in the deanery there 'vsurarij, falsidici et receptores furtorum et furum tanquam collectores' (usurers, liars, and harborers and collectors, as it were, of thieves and robbers).[54] Since all of his sermons delivered in Ireland in English were nevertheless recorded in Latin, and since most, furthermore, were preserved as précis or digests, we cannot know precisely what FitzRalph said, with the exception, perhaps, of the two Latin synodal sermons, and of the *obiter dicta*, like those at Drogheda and Skreen, that he notes having uttered. FitzRalph's sermons were cast in the 'modern' form of preaching, and he employed exempla, especially favouring them in sermons preached *ad populum*, as might be expected.

During his first visit FitzRalph is known to have preached in Dundalk, Louth, Ardee, Drogheda, and Mansfieldstown, all in County Louth. His second visit saw him again in these places, excepting Louth and Mansfieldstown, but now also including to the south of Dundalk his manor at Dromiskin and to the north-east of Drogheda his manor at Termonfekin. On this second visit he ventured a little further afield, preaching also in County Meath at Trim, Athboy, Kells, Skreen, and Greenock, and in one notable case, even travelling to the northern-most part of his diocese to preach on 8 September 1351 in Coleraine. But most of his time was spent in the relatively more domesticated reaches of the Dublin Pale.

[52] Oxford, Bodleian Library, MS Bodley 144, fols 42ᵛ–43ʳ.

[53] MS Bodley 144, fol. 63ʳ. Criticism of merchants was a sermon commonplace, to be sure, but in Drogheda, which had an established mercantile community, FitzRalph's comments, even if they were not actually intended as imminently topical, would doubtless have seemed so.

[54] MS Bodley 144, fol. 72ʳ.

Into the Fifteenth Century

FitzRalph's activity, however, seems to be something of an exception to prove the rule, for precious little preaching ascribable to seculars is in evidence before the fifteenth century. Even then, some well-known secular preachers, like Archbishop Thomas Cranley of Dublin, have left no sermons that are known of to posterity. In Cranley's case, the only preachable material surviving from his personal library was mendicant, and whether he actually preached it in Dublin or not is likely to remain forever obscure. A further exception should be made in the case of one mid-fifteenth-century preacher who achieved considerable notoriety. Philip Norreys, secular canon of St Patrick's Cathedral, Dublin, caused a stir both in Ireland and England by the provocative nature of some of his sermons. Following in de Bicknor's and FitzRalph's footsteps in respect of his view of the friars, Norreys also preached and taught against their four orders. So intemperate does he appear to have been that he succeeded in drawing papal censure down upon himself. A petition to Henry VI lodged against him by an unknown party outlines the circumstances. The King was petitioned 'to consider howe that the articles the which Maister Philip Norys preched and taught in Englond and Ireland ayenst the .iiij. ordres of freres were dampned in the Court of Rome, as it was shewed vnder lede in Englond to-fore you and your Counseil. And aftir that in Irelond the Archebisshop of Develyn, bi vertue of the bulles of Pope Eugeny, accused him in Develyn', whence Norreys came to England, where he was arrested and brought to answer before the Archbishop of Canterbury. Norreys then appealed to the Court of Rome, 'and thider went dyuers freres and had his appele denied for nought, and also had the sentence of the seid Archebisshop of Develyn confermed, and had him accursed for a sismatyk and an heretyk, and all his fauters and helpers'.[55] Although the sermons of this turbulent secular priest are not known to survive, it seems clear that polemical preaching was capable of causing as much of an uproar in Ireland as it was in England, and Norreys's involuntary

---

[55] London, National Archives, E28/82/1. The petitioner went on to ask for letters under Privy Seal to the Lieutenant of Ireland or his deputy, to the Archbishop of Dublin or the Bishop of Kildare, the Chancellor of Ireland or his deputy, the Prior of Kilmainham, the Mayor of Dublin, and all officers and liegemen in Ireland, to do due execution on Norreys wheresoever he might be found in Ireland, according to the Pope's bulls, until Norreys were to obey and fulfil the content of the said bulls. A sign manual at the top right of the petition, 'Rh', is the King's signature of authorization. It is minuted as 'Yeuen at Westminster þe ij day | September'. In a post-medieval hand on the dorse is written '30 Hen. VI' (i.e., the petition is dated 2 September 1451). I am grateful to Michael Benskin for providing me with his transcription of the petition, which I have here further edited for the modern reader's convenience.

pilgrimage to Rome to fight his corner seems very much a replay of FitzRalph's in the previous century.

The fifteenth-century sermon manuscripts that have survived contain preaching that was far more measured than Norreys's seems to have been, though occasionally some of it has topical application. Of the four manuscripts to which we must finally turn (Dublin, Trinity College, MSS 201, 204, and 667, and Dublin, National Library of Ireland, MS 9596), three were certainly produced in Ireland (MSS 201, 204, and 667), while the fourth (MS 9596) possibly was. Of these four, one may have served secular clergy (MS 201), another probably did (MS 9596), another may have been produced by mendicants (MS 204) and the last certainly was (MS 667).[56] The earliest of them, MS 201, is the only late medieval sermon manuscript surviving from Ireland whose contents are almost entirely in English. It contains an (incomplete) copy of the massively popular *Festial* of John Mirk, Augustinian canon of Lilleshall Abbey, Shropshire.[57] The name of one 'Dominus Thomas Norreys' copied at the top of fol. 22[r] seems to be in the hand of the principal scribe of the manuscript. Norreys's hand dates to the first half of the fifteenth century (possibly the second quarter) and, given that the written dialect of Middle English that he reproduced is Hiberno-English, it is likely that he was trained to write in Ireland.[58] In fact, a Thomas Norreys, chaplain, who is conceivably the same man, appears first on record in Dublin on 3 May 1447, when along with two other chaplains he was granted a messuage in the centre of the city in High Street.[59] Given the similarity of surname, and medieval Dublin being a relatively small place, it may be that he was a clerical relative of the infamous Philip whose career as an incendiary preacher was outlined earlier. Thomas also appears in one of the deeds of Christ Church Cathedral, Dublin, for 10 December 1455. Here, along with two other chaplains, he was granted two messuages and three gardens in Dublin by one William Hogge.[60] His last recorded appearance is

---

[56] In certain cases their content is older, antedating the fifteenth century.

[57] See also Chapter 2 above, p. 21 and n. 32, for further comments on this sermon collection.

[58] Angus McIntosh and M. L. Samuels, 'Prolegomena to a Study of Medieval Anglo-Irish', *MÆ*, 37 (1968), 1–11; unless, of course, Norreys was copying *literatim*.

[59] H. F. Berry, 'History of the Religious Gild of S. Anne, in S. Audoen's Church, Dublin, 1430–1740, Taken from its Records in the Haliday Collection, R.I.A.', *PRIA*, 25 (1904–05), 21–106 (p. 68, item 75). He also appears in property deeds connected with St Anne's Guild dated 20 February 1451, 12 May 1468, and finally June 1470 (see respectively Berry, ibid., p. 69, item 77, p. 70, item 84, and pp. 87–88, item 135).

[60] *Christ Church Deeds*, ed. by M. J. McEnery and R. Refaussé (Dublin: Four Courts, 2001), no. 961.

in June 1470. He is referred to as chaplain again but now also as a warden, with one Henry Yonge, of the Guild of St Anne.[61] It is not known whether Norreys, like the author of the sermon collection he copied, John Mirk, may have been an Augustinian canon too, though with three houses in medieval Dublin, the canons were well represented and would have contributed significantly to the city's clerical complement. Furthermore, it was in connection with one of those houses, Christ Church, that the Norreys of the deed of 1455 appeared. In any event, Norreys's possession of the *Festial* is evidence of the importation into Ireland, and presumably use there, of one of late medieval England's most influential vernacular sermon collections.

The writing of the *Festial*, a work stoutly orthodox and stocked full of ex-empla, some of which, indeed, are tastelessly sensational, may partly have been prompted in reaction to other contemporary preaching propagated by those op-ponents of orthodoxy, the Lollards: these had set their faces against the sort of fables and tales in preaching that Mirk, like many of the friars, relished. Yet the avoidance of racy narratives was not simply a means whereby Lollard radicals implicitly declared their opposition to the conservatives within the Church; even amongst the conservatives, including the friars, can be found sermons of chaster pitch, as Chapter 6, above, has already noted in connection with the preaching of Thomas Cyrcetur of Salisbury. The second fifteenth-century manuscript from Ireland containing the sermons of a single author, this time ones in Latin, is Dublin, Trinity College, MS 204, and it conceivably had mendicant auspices.[62] The two major sermon cycles in it, the *Sermones dominicales* and the *Sermones de sanctis et festis* of Nicholas de Aquevilla, were the work of a Franciscan who flourished early in the fourteenth century, and MS 204 represents an Irish appropriation of this other, highly popular but far less flamboyant, sermon collection. The style of Nicholas de Aquevilla's sermons, in utter contrast to John Mirk's, is restrained, and they tirelessly employ a tight, schematic 'modern' mode of preaching. The manuscript's exact provenance within Ireland is unknown, nor is anything known of the identity of one Nicholas Katwell, who declares his ownership in a fifteenth-century hand on fol. 278ᵛ.[63]

---

[61] Berry, 'History of the Religious Gild of S. Anne', pp. 87–88, item 135.

[62] Fully described by Colker, *Trinity College Library Dublin: Catalogue*, I, 391–92.

[63] Not Kantwell, *pace* Colker, *Trinity College Library Dublin: Catalogue*, I, 392, although, to be sure, an -*n*- may have been omitted; the name Cantwell had strong associations with the Kilkenny region. Some names of Gaelic Irish owners, listed in Colker, ibid., are also to be

Whether or not MS 204 originated within the Dublin Pale, the third fifteenth-century sermon manuscript of present concern, if indeed it originated in Ireland, seems likely to have done. At least by the sixteenth century, it was circulating in the town of Drogheda, County Louth. Dublin, National Library of Ireland, MS 9596 has no perceptible affiliation with any particular order within the Church, though that said, mendicant auspices seem perhaps the least likely. The late medieval core of this manuscript was copied by two scribes in hands dating to the second half of the fifteenth century. By the sixteenth, it had come into the lay possession of a Drogheda burgess family, the Burnells, and parchment leaves originally left blank between many of its items were subsequently filled by Burnell family members (notably by Robert Burnell, Mayor of Drogheda in 1570) with pious or practical memoranda.[64] However, our concern here is with the manuscript's late medieval core. Its first substantial item is a set of notes on the Decalogue,[65] each commandment being accompanied by commentary and illustrated with exempla of the type that many orthodox preachers, as has been seen, would have approved. For example, the second commandment, not to take God's name in vain, includes telegraphic notes such as the following which seem to assume in their readers a previous acquaintance with the narratives alluded to:

> Quidem lusor ad taxillos, cum semel perdidisset, multum iratus cepit iurare et blasphemare Deum. Et in signum perdicionis, iecit sagittam contra celum, quasi volens Deum sagittare. Mox que sagitta ad pedes eius ad detestacionem peccati redijt cruentata. Nota et de illo qui perdiderat primogenitum, vxorem et oculum dextrum, et tandem diuina vlcione percussus interijt. Nota et de periurio et iuramento super reliquias in libro de *Alphabeto narracionum*.[66]

found. Nicholas de Aquevilla was a Franciscan and his sermons were also copied widely beyond the mendicant orders. MS 204 additionally contains the *Super Deuteronomium* of Thomas Docking, OFM. (Two snatches of Middle English, the words *dysclosyd* and *deseysyd*, appear on fol. 145ᵛ.)

[64] Perhaps the most important of these post-medieval insertions, from the historian's point of view, is a unique, but hitherto unnoticed, account of the land-gavel of Drogheda, copied between fols 41ᵛ–52ᵛ in the first half of the sixteenth century. This invaluable source for Drogheda history, which merits publication, was not noticed in Susan O'Connor, 'Tudor Drogheda', *Journal of the Old Drogheda Society*, 10 (1996), 86–110, or in John Bradley, *The Topography and Layout of Medieval Drogheda* (Drogheda: Old Drogheda Society, 1997).

[65] Dublin, National Library of Ireland, MS 9596, fols 2ʳ–19ʳ.

[66] MS 9596, fol. 5ᵛ. See also Tubach, *Index exemplorum*, no. 324. The *Alphabetum narracionum* (the *Alphabet of Tales*) was an alphabetically arranged collection of exempla.

(A certain dice player, when he had lost on one occasion, was greatly enraged and started swearing and blaspheming God, and shot an arrow against heaven as a sign of his perdition, as if wishing to pierce God. To his detestation, this arrow soon returned bloodstained to his feet. Also, note about the man who had lost his first-born son, his wife and his right eye, and at length he died, struck by divine vengeance. Also, note in the book of the *Alphabet of Tales* about the perjurer and his oath upon the relics.)

Next, a discussion of lechery is followed by a series of alphabetically arranged topics with accompanying notes.[67] The sermons proper start on folio 124ᵛ with an opening for a Palm Sunday sermon, followed by full sermons for, respectively, the fourth Sunday in Lent (fols 125ʳ, col. a–127ᵛ, col. b), the first Sunday in Lent (fols 127ᵛ, col. b–131ʳ, col. a), the fourth Sunday in Advent (fols 131ʳ, col. a–134ʳ, col. a),[68] and Passion Sunday (fols 134ʳ, col. a–136ᵛ, col. b). Since Advent, Lent, and Passiontide were prime preaching seasons, the content of the manuscript at this point, like the content of various other manuscripts surveyed in the previous chapters, may reflect preaching's traditional seasonal investment. Then follow two openings of sermons, respectively for the first and second Sundays in Advent (fol. 136ᵛ, col. b), and lists of sermon *themata* (*de tempore themata* on fol. 137ʳ⁻ᵛ and on fols 137ᵛ–38ᵛ *de sanctis themata*, plus *themata* for visitation and synodal sermons, and sermons to congregations of religious living according to a Rule and to solitaries).[69] Next comes an opening for a sermon on the feast of relics (fol. 141ʳ),[70] and finally an atelous sermon of unknown occasion (fol. 144ᵛ).[71]

These sermons, cast like FitzRalph's and Nicholas de Aquevilla's in the 'modern' form, are probably all fifteenth-century compositions, and at least seven are likely to be by the same anonymous author.[72] He probably addressed

---

[67] Respectively, fols 20ʳ–25ʳ and fols 26ʳ–110ʳ. Various interpolations were later made on the folios originally left blank, the land-gavel of Drogheda being one such.

[68] This sermon concludes (fol. 134ʳ, col. a): 'quod Rychmund'. It is hard to know whether the name Rychmund was scribal or authorial.

[69] Note that the *themata* of the earlier sermons appear in these lists.

[70] References to the Normandy campaigns of Henry V here must date the sermon to some time in his reign or later (post-1422). The date of those other sermons in this manuscript that may be by the same author (see further below) is likely to be similar.

[71] However its *thema* (Hebrews 7. 26) derives from the epistle reading for the feast of several confessors in Sarum Use, so it may be for then. (The manuscript concludes with an alphabetical list of topics on fol. 145ʳ.)

[72] The incomplete sermon on fol. 141ʳ that refers to the Normandy campaigns of Henry V is one of those addressed to 'Reverendi domini' (Reverend masters).

clerical, or at least mixed, congregations, comprised as these were of 'Reuerendi domini et amici carissimi'.[73] Conceivably, therefore, the sermons, if delivered to congregations predominantly of clerics, would doubtless have been delivered, as recorded, in Latin, even though four also mark their thematic divisions with verses in Middle English.[74] Were they preached in Drogheda? Certainly, as remarked, the manuscript was kept there by the sixteenth century, and we have seen how in the fourteenth, FitzRalph had set a precedent for 'modern' Latin preaching in Drogheda where he addressed clerical congregations on at least two occasions. But the importation of MS 9596 from somewhere in England cannot be entirely ruled out.

Our final fifteenth-century manuscript takes us beyond the Dublin Pale and back once more to the friars with whom we began, and this time, its Irish origin is beyond dispute. Dublin, Trinity College, MS 667, cited earlier as witnessing to a close association, indeed symbiosis, of the material forms of two ethnic religious cultures on the island of Ireland, includes amongst its varied material two Latin sermons for the feast of Corpus Christi.[75] A modest investment, to be sure, but other sermons are in Irish, and the remaining contents would have commended the manuscript to friars whether *inter Anglicos* or *inter Hibernicos* as a preaching resource.[76] Its pertinence to preachers is clear from such items as a passage comparing the attributes and habits of a cockerel to those of a preacher, for example, or the notes on preaching's sister enterprise, confession.[77] Also of pulpit use were

---

[73] Compare the opening terms of address of one of FitzRalph's synodal sermons in Drogheda on 7 February 1352: 'Reuerendi domini, patres et fratres, et amici carissimi' (Reverend masters, fathers and brothers, and dearest friends); Oxford, Bodleian Library, MS Bodley 144, fol. 49ʳ.

[74] Those for the fourth Sunday in Lent, for the first Sunday in Lent, for the fourth Sunday in Advent, and for Passion Sunday. All are also addressed to 'Reuerendi' (Reverend ones).

[75] Dublin, Trinity College, MS 667, pp. 130–31 and 184–88 respectively. At least the second of these Corpus Christi sermons may be a fifteenth-century composition; its sensitivity to lay debate about the nature of the Eucharist leads one to suspect a composition after the 1380s when Eucharistic controversy was becoming topical among laity. (For further discussion of MS 667 within a Franciscan context, see Ó Clabaigh, 'Preaching in Late-Medieval Ireland', pp. 89–90.)

[76] Ó Clabaigh, 'Preaching in Late-Medieval Ireland', pp. 88–90, has a useful summary of this manuscript and its relations to a number of others that share similar Irish material. More work could profitably be done on this group of manuscripts, however.

[77] Dublin, Trinity College, MS 667, p. 82, col. a, and pp. 105, col. a–106, col. a respectively; in addition, a list of what sins are reserved for episcopal absolution appears on p. 81, cols a–b, and an Irish text on confession on p. 165, col. a.

its several Latin exempla, many on familiar and favourite sermon topics (on death
and the last things, for example, and on the Blessed Virgin Mary).[78] Trinity College, MS 667 also contains what may be considered the ultimate template for a
sermon, supremely portable in the best mendicant tradition: a moralized diagram
of the human hand appears on page 252 (see Figure 3). With the moral significance of its digits committed to memory, a preacher would never have lacked a
sermon of perennial (if gloomy) relevance: 'You don't know how greatly, nor how
often, you have offended God', proclaims the thumb; 'Your ending is bitter, your
life brief, and you have entered the world in sin', says the index finger; 'You will
take nothing hence other than your deeds, nor can you prolong your life nor evade
death', declares the middle finger; 'You don't know whence you come, nor how
nor when you will die', says the fourth finger; and the little finger concludes, 'You
will soon be forgotten by those dear to you, your heir will seldom make provision
for you [presumably, by commissioning postmortem spiritual suffrages for your
soul], nor will those do any differently to whom you leave your wealth.'[79] Thus
without needing either book or sermon notes, the preacher's very hand might
serve as an aide-mémoire.

The fact that the two actual sermons chosen for preservation in MS 667 are
both for Corpus Christi is itself of interest. The second, being the more substantial, may conveniently serve for illustration. It is organized according to the
'modern' form, and like some of the 'modern' sermons noted previously in MS
9596, it too introduces a threefold rhymed division of its matter in Middle
English into its Latin.[80] But unlike the MS 9596 sermons, the likelihood is that
this Corpus Christi sermon was originally preached in the vernacular. It is edgily
aware that some among the laity were asking many questions about the sacrament
of the altar, where more properly they ought simply to believe what the Church
told them and hold themselves content.[81] Advice of this sort to the laity is familiar

---

[78] Respectively, Dublin, Trinity College, MS 667, pp. 32, col. b–36 col. a; pp. 199, col. b–214,
col. b, and pp. 222, col. a–231, col. b.

[79] Though termed a 'manus meditacionis' (a hand of meditation), the diagram stocks the
mind with preachable matter.

[80] The division is summarized at the foot of p. 184: 'Condiciones corporis Christi: hyt ys
dredefull in takyng; hyt ys nedefull in reseuyng; hyt ys medefull to belyuyng' (The conditions of
Christ's body: it is dreadful in the taking; it is necessary in the receiving; it is beneficial to
believing).

[81] Interestingly, this sermon seems to have been copied by the Irish scribe Donaldus O
Maelechlaynd.

in orthodox sermons in England at about this date; Hugh Legat's preaching reviewed earlier in Chapter 4 is a case in point.[82] Moreover, such admonitions would remain unheeded if left ring-fenced in priestly Latin, a language normally beyond the laity's reach. Recommendations that the laity be acquiescent also strongly suggest that the sermon was composed some time in the wake of the Eucharistic controversies of the 1380s that Lollardy had precipitated. Evidently, some friars in fifteenth-century Ireland felt moved to champion orthodox teaching on the Eucharist, as their English confrères had been doing, and choosing as their forum for doing so a singularly appropriate feast day.[83]

Conclusion

It is difficult to be confident that any summary of what this relatively small collection of manuscripts suggests about the history of English and Latin preaching traditions in late medieval Ireland may not suffer from partiality: John Watt was essentially right, after all, when he regretted Ireland's scarcity of medieval sermon literature. This being so, the picture is necessarily incomplete. Yet, a few points have emerged that are worth drawing together, especially since they are consistent with what other classes of evidence described at the beginning of this chapter suggest. The aggregated manuscript evidence suggests that in late medieval Ireland, the Church's preaching mission was being staunchly undertaken by the friars. Indeed, mendicant efforts seem to eclipse those of the seculars, though it must be admitted that since the activity of seculars tended in the nature of things

---

[82] To cite but two instances, a sermon on the *thema*, *Panis dat vitam* (John 6. 33) in Worcester, Cathedral Library, MS F.10, fols 30ᵛ–32ʳ, and repeated on fols 85ᵛ, col. b–87ʳ, col. a, preserved in Latin but doubtless delivered in English, warns the laity against being inappropriately curious and inquisitive about the Eucharist, as similarly does an Easter Day sermon on *thema*, *Qui manducat hunc panem vivet in eternum* (John 6. 59) in Hereford, Cathedral Library, MS O.iii.5, fols 21ᵛ, col. a–24ʳ, col. b (see fol. 22ʳ, col. b).

[83] It is interesting also to note that an Irish sermon on the Eucharist, possibly intended for delivery on Corpus Christi, found in Rennes, Bibliothèque municipale, MS 598, fols 29ʳ, col. a–30ᵛ, col. a, a manuscript with which Dublin, Trinity College, MS 667 shares some overlap of content, is aware of the circulation of heretical teaching about the nature of the Eucharist. None of this teaching, as far as the sermon describes it, is obviously commensurate with characteristic Lollard positions, however. The Rennes manuscript was copied probably not long after 1475; see Ó Clabaigh, 'Preaching in Late-Medieval Ireland', pp. 88–90. Its sermon on the Eucharist was edited by James A. Geary, 'An Irish Homily on the Holy Eucharist: Text and Translation', *Catholic University Bulletin*, 18 (1912), 460–75.

to be more locally circumscribed, it would have been somewhat less conspicuous. And as if by way of corollary, we find cases where the preaching of the seculars was directly facilitated by resources originally mendicant. The mendicant preaching machine was also being serviced in Ireland as early as the second half of the thirteenth century with preaching aids like the *Liber exemplorum*. It may, therefore, be more than a mere cliché of antimendicant propaganda that Alexander de Bicknor and Richard FitzRalph uttered when they lamented the ubiquitousness of the friars: in Ireland, it seems, they would indeed have been surrounded by them. Nor did any division of the late medieval Irish Church *inter Anglicos* and *inter Hibernicos* hamper their collaborative activity on the preaching front, at least not in the fifteenth century. And as for the matter that they most typically preached, it combined key scriptural (sometimes apocryphal) narratives with practical moral exhortation. This matter might be artistically and imaginatively vivified — here exempla played an important part — to render it at once palatable and memorable. Little that was preached, judging by what the manuscripts disclose, was historically unique and specific: when the inhabitants of Drogheda and Skreen were admonished by FitzRalph, for example, it seems to have been more for such venalities as the flesh is ever heir to, as well as for besetting class sins, than for circumstances peculiar to Drogheda and Skreen. This does not, of course, necessarily imply that preaching, if in general indifferent to contemporary politics, always confined itself exclusively to timeless matters of morality.[84] Perhaps those timeless matters could as occasion required be tailored to specific social situations. Occasionally there is evidence of preaching's targeted social application: for example, the prior of the Dominican house of St Saviour, in the suburb of Oxmantown, Dublin, seems to have delivered an annual sermon on the subject of civic rights and responsibilities to the newly elected mayor and his company in the context of what appears to have become a regular event in the civic calendar.[85] However, the prevailing impression left by the aggregated evidence for the English

---

[84] The friars in Ireland were commissioned to preach the crusades on various occasions: for example, in 1250, Henry III requested that they do so (*Calendar of Documents, relating to Ireland, preserved in Her Majesty's Record Office, London*, ed. by H. S. Sweetman, 5 vols (London: Longman, 1875–86), I, 457). Amongst the seculars, FitzRalph preached topically when he targeted the claims of the friars.

[85] The event came complete with a procession of the new mayor and his officers from the city centre, over the bridge on the river Liffey and to the northside suburb of Oxmantown in which the priory was located. See Benedict O'Sullivan, 'The Dominicans in Medieval Dublin', in *Medieval Dublin: The Living City*, ed. by Howard B. Clarke (Dublin: Irish Academic Press, 1990), pp. 83–99 (p. 89) (first publ. in *Dublin Historical Record*, 9 (1946–48), 41–58).

and Latin preaching traditions in late medieval Ireland is of a relative consistency in the matter preached that is remarkable. Its longevity over nearly three centuries, moreover, is impressive. Such was its tenacity that its characteristic concerns echoed into sixteenth-century Ireland and beyond.[86]

Although the manuscript resources that can be marshalled to throw light on the English and Latin preaching traditions in late medieval Ireland are thus far sparser than the resources for those parallel traditions in Britain, they nevertheless speak of a history of preaching in many ways closely comparable to, yet in others divergent from, that history as it was evolving in Britain. Attention to the traces of Ireland's parallel but alternative history can only add depth and richer complexion to our understanding of the history of preaching in these islands generally. Hitherto, that understanding has largely, if understandably, been pursued within a British context. It is time now to redress the balance a little.

---

[86] For a study of preaching in Ireland in the early modern period and its continuation of medieval matter and form, see Bernadette Cunningham, '"Zeal for God and for Souls": Counter-Reformation Preaching in Early Seventeenth-Century Ireland', in *Irish Preaching*, ed. by Fletcher and Gillespie, pp. 108–26.

LITERATURE AND PULPIT:
THE LYRIC IN THE SERMON

Introduction

A declared aim of this book has been towards exploring examples of one of
medieval preaching's commonest contexts, namely, preaching conducted
coram populo, in the presence of the general laity, and as this was practised across all the major departments of the late medieval Church. While other,
more specialized areas of preaching call for study in their own right (for example,
preaching at the universities, parliamentary preaching, or preaching to the clergy
at times of synod, general chapter, or visitation), areas which may complement
by contrast and comparison our understanding of preaching as the laity experienced it, they have nevertheless been glanced at only obliquely in these pages. The
present emphasis has been instead upon those quarters of preaching that most
preoccupied the preachers, if for no other reason than that those quarters
accommodated the bulk of the population of late medieval Britain and Ireland.

Preaching delivered to the laity was also the type that most absorbed the
attention of Gerald R. Owst, that twentieth-century scholar who more than any
other brought medieval preaching and sermons in England to wide literary critical
notice. The first of his two seminal books, *Preaching in Medieval England*, published in 1926, while certainly conscious of preaching's more elite contexts, chose
for the greater part to dwell on the kinds of sermon and sermon material that
more ordinary folk are likely to have encountered. This popular accent is even
more pronounced in Owst's second major work, *Literature and Pulpit in Medieval England*, first published in 1933 and then in 1961 reissued in a revised
edition, in which he excavated, although as most would now agree with an excess

of zeal, characteristic preaching themes and content in a selection of popular vernacular literary and dramatic texts.

The present chapter is named in honour of Owst's pioneering project, although it will not further that project in Owst's preferred terms. Even students whose concerns lie narrowly with medieval preaching may be interested in observing how that preaching, especially popular preaching, was liable to incorporate other textual genres in order to achieve itself, or even to extend its influence into genres that originally had no close affiliation with preaching at all. Instances of the absorption into the sermon of other genres, or of the infiltration into other genres of sermon-related themes and forms, help measure through a two-way commerce the extent of the cultural reach that medieval preaching had. Thus this chapter not only offers an implicit retrospective on Owst but an investigation of some of the ways in which his project has been, and can continue to be, pursued a couple of generations after his inauguration of it. The chapter will chart the relation between the culture of the preachers and the medieval English lyric. In keeping with a book that has chosen preaching's popular dimension for its subject, this particular literary genre may similarly and in large part be deemed 'popular', its popularity nevertheless tolerant of incorporating robust moral considerations without being compromised by them. Indeed, some of the lyrics to be reviewed in this chapter are capable of marrying popular and moral agendas in remarkably sophisticated ways. Yet, these ways are not inevitably obvious, and benefit from fuller explanation. The question of the lyric in the sermon and the nature of the liaison between vernacular lyric poetry and preaching generally, has been extensively researched in recent years, although still more remains to be said about it.[1] In the course of providing a general survey of this field, this anthology's concluding substantive chapter will also discuss some lyrics that have hitherto been neglected or only recently come to light.

'Only connect'

This leitmotif that E. M. Forster threaded throughout *A Room with a View* provides one of the handiest watchwords that anyone engaging with any kind of medieval text could wish for. Again it comes into its own when broaching the present subject, for it is now time to turn to consider the *ad populum* sermon

---

[1] See especially the various contributions by Siegfried Wenzel cited in the bibliography of *LSCLME*.

both as a host for, and also as a generator of, vernacular lyric poetry. The sermon context of that poetry connected it so organically to a wider set of preacherly aims and obligations that its existence solely as some self-referential, literary event was forbidden: in its sermon context, poetry as mere word game, as literary *jeu de mots* paying no more than incidental heed to the real world in which its readers lived, moved, and had their being, would never thrive. Instead, the sermon context recruited and anchored poetry precisely in order to re-dimension strategically the existential outlook of the congregation experiencing it. Therefore poetry's potential playful volatility could only be approached with caution, and allowed room only under the preacher's watchful eye. The chapter thus concerns poetry's partnership with preaching and the collaboration with preaching's agenda that was visited upon it.

The task ahead will be to survey how lyrics in sermons functioned, and to consider the sorts of lyric that preaching collected, or indeed, that in many cases it first called into being in order to further its ends. By adjusting the way we look at this particular lyric species, choosing to see its examples not in isolation and out of their sermon context but as integral participants in preaching's wider enterprise, a healthier understanding of it may be possible, and with that an appreciation of the weight of cultural work that these sermon lyrics were allowed to shoulder. It follows that any excision of such lyrics from the sermons in which they feature obscures their essential role as collaborators in preaching's wider objective. For preaching was a dedicated intervention whose social consequences are hard to overestimate, and in it, many of the lyrics examined in this chapter took root. Preaching presented ordinary men and women with the salvific maps by which they could trace the narrow way to heaven and avoid the primrose path to the everlasting bonfire. It was one of the Church's key means for helping them navigate their living and dying, and for interpreting all of life's experiences in between into one intelligible design.[2] Thus the preacher shouldered much responsibility, in principle, for purveying personal and social meaning. As he discharged that responsibility, he necessarily explained a sanctioned order and enjoined it

---

[2] The modalities of medieval religious formation were, of course, multiple, and customized according to the stage of life from cradle to grave. In the schoolroom, for example, the entry of the child into the symbolic order, the realm of letters, was presided over by religion (abecedaria were normally accompanied by the *Pater noster* and other prayers), and on the deathbed, the last sight a dying person might expect to see was a crucifix held before his or her eyes. In between, the sermon, especially in conjunction with confession, offered repeated opportunities for religious formation.

upon his congregations. For many preachers (although, as we will see, not for all), a popular lyric utterance could help inscribe and activate that order in the mind.

The category of poetry, while not an entirely a self-evident one, is nevertheless widely agreed to reveal itself in a certain linguistic intensity, contrived by various means, that distinguishes its discourse, marking it off from more routine forms of communication. Through its taut use of language poetry stands out and becomes arresting, and this in ways often experienced as pleasurable. Poetry may also deliver the delightful shock of the familiar made strangely new. When it comes to medieval vernacular poetry, however, this freshening of the familiar was more usually effected in local than in wholesale ways. That is, the freshening that poetry might afford was carefully calibrated: more usually it entailed a re-cognition of the familiar than a defamiliarization of the familiar that was so radical that its former truth-claims risked losing their hold.[3] So this poetry, while it might take eye- and brain-catching risks with the presentation of its familiar subject matter, nevertheless finally offered a consoling repetition: familiar subject matter was redelivered fundamentally intact. And in the same moment that poetry emerged colourfully from the grey routine of the everyday, at once arresting and pleasuring its receivers, the familiar subject matter into which it was infused also acquired memory value, lodging in their heads.

Stating these things about early poetry's mnemonic power is to state little more than the writers on rhetoric and the arts of poetry who were read in the Middle Ages had already appreciated, but for present purposes, what might be borne in mind is the extent to which many medieval preachers shared that rhetorical awareness.[4] Making the matter they preached pleasurably memorable was an art that had powerful spiritual endorsement; no frivolous decoration, it was a cultivation warranted in serving a sacred end. Whether or not medieval preachers directly consulted the textbooks for guidance in rhetorical ways for commanding attention, accomplished preachers would have understood, as much from on-the-job instinct and experience as from any written authority, how important it was to make an occasion out of their pulpit performance. Hence it is easy to imagine that the pleasurable conquest and colonization of the congregation's imagination, even were it not the declared primary purpose of preaching, might nevertheless

---

[3] Although sometimes the authority is re-delivered at the cost of a certain audacity, even risk; compare, for example, the lyric *I syng of a mayden* considered briefly below, where the approach of Christ to his mother Mary in the moment of her conception is daringly, if gently, eroticized.

[4] For an informative study, see Mary J. Carruthers, *The Book of Memory: A Study of Memory in Medieval Culture* (Cambridge: Cambridge University Press, 1990).

be an important incidental goal for the preacher to aim at.[5] The stakes that a preacher played for were high — winning souls and confirming them in their faith — yet circumstances were often against him.

Given that the lyrics considered in this chapter were so context-sensitive, it seems worthwhile, before moving on to examine them, to devote a few pages to evoking in outline the medieval preaching scene, recalling some of the inhospitable circumstances ever likely to thwart even the best attempt of the preacher to get his message across. Some circumstances were intractable, but there were others that he might try to take control of, and against which he might usefully mobilize the power of lyric poetry in his battle for attention.

Wandering Minds

The medieval preacher, then, generally had an uphill task. To begin with, while he urged familiar matter of eternal consequence, he did so through a necessarily ephemeral medium, spoken words, that as soon as uttered vanished on the air. If interest in familiar matter was to be rekindled, and if he was to turn his congregation's recollection of it into salvific pleasure, the preacher must be memorable both in the moment of utterance and also in a way that outlasted the medium in which he worked. The spiritual benefit of his words might only prove durable if they had an afterlife in his congregation's minds. Yet congregations then, no less than ones now, might find their minds wandering away from their pursuer. And understandably. If the preacher were honourable in intent, no mere showman wielding rhetoric for unscrupulous ends,[6] then no matter how favourable an impression he might make, he still in the end came stalking his congregation's souls like a spiritual huntsman. Or, to recall the evangelical simile, he was a fisherman casting to catch their souls in his nets. Before he had any hope of reeling those souls in, he must recognize that they inhabited bodies that had to be reckoned with first. And bodies might be recalcitrant for a whole host of reasons. For example, they might be cold and uncomfortable. One need only recollect the advice given to parish priests by one assiduous late fourteenth-century preacher

---

[5] The doctrine of *docere et delectare*, that teaching should combine with delighting, was ancient. Each was not to be the other's nemesis, but both organically fused. By this doctrine, therefore, the most effective preaching would have mixed both.

[6] The outstanding literary paradigm of the abuse of the *officium predicatoris* is found in Chaucer's Pardoner; see *PPPLME*, pp. 249–65.

mentioned in passing elsewhere in this book, the Augustinian canon John Mirk, about what to do if the wine froze solid in their chalice while they were celebrating Mass, to capture the seasonal chill of many a medieval church.[7] Climate would not always have been on the side of a congregation's attention span. People might also be distracted from listening for all sorts of other reasons: by the children they had brought with them to church, for example. One fifteenth-century English sermon offers a little vignette of exemplary maternal patience in a dialogue that it reports as having taken place between a mother and her son in church. Like all young children, the little boy is inquisitive:

> And upon a certen tyme þei were in there chyrche, and faste this childe behelde ever the rode, and seyde to his moder þus, 'Madame, is that a man or a childe that is so nayled up on yonder tree? What menythe it þat he is so arayed?' Sche answerd and seyd, 'Sonne, this is the similitude of Cristis Passion that he sufferde for us to bryng us to the ioyes of heven.' 'And moder, whi stondithe that woman so by hym?' 'A sonne, that is the moder of Ihesu, his owne modur.' 'And saw sche [all] tho peynes that he sufferd for us?' '3ee certen, sonne', seyd sche. Then seyde þe childe to his moder, 'It wolde greve 3ow ri3t sore at 3owre hert, and case were þat 3e saw me so farde witheall.' Then seyd sche, '3ee sonne, the moste hevynes it were to me that my3te be devised by eny possibil reson.' 'In certen, moder, then it semythe to my reson that sche was full of hevynes when sche saw hyr sonne Ihesu suffer so grete tribulacion.'[8]

> (And once upon a time they were in their church, and this child kept gazing steadfastly at the rood, and said thus to his mother, 'Madam, is that a man or a child nailed so on the tree over there? What is the reason he is arrayed in that way?' She answered and said, 'Son, this is the likeness of Christ's Passion that he suffered to bring us to the joys of heaven.' 'And mother, why is that woman standing by him in that way?' 'Ah, son, that is Jesus's mother, his own mother.' 'And did she see all those pains that he suffered for us?' 'Yes indeed, son', she said. Then the child said to his mother, 'It would grieve your heart very sorely if you saw me treated in the same way.' Then she said, 'Yes, son, it would be the greatest sorrow that could be devised for me in any possible manner'. 'To be sure then, mother, it seems to me that she was full of sorrow when she saw her son suffer such great affliction.')

The promise that the child's lively mind shows does not disappoint, for he ends up following a distinguished clerical career in Oxford. Nevertheless, his repeated sleeve-tugging cannot have improved his mother's concentration. Only transfer

---

[7] Mirk's *Manuale sacerdotis* advises: 'Si sanguis Christi in calice frigore congelatur, per aspiracionem dissolvatur et gluciatur' (If Christ's blood freezes in the chalice because of the cold, let it be thawed by breathing and swallowed) (Oxford, Bodleian Library, MS Bodley 549, fol. 157ʳ). Mirk's prescription is itself based on earlier canonical precept.

[8] Oxford, Bodleian Library, MS e Museo 180, fol. 85ʳ⁻ᵛ, edited with minor emendation.

his childlike persistence to the occasion of a sermon being delivered in the same church and, short of quickly finding a way of keeping him quiet, his mother would have had little chance of taking everything in.

Churches, too, were full of distractions of other far less edifying kinds, not least those introduced by people who had gone along precisely for the purpose of eyeing each other up and gossiping.[9] The same was true outdoors. Many sermons were preached outside in the open air, in outdoor pulpits, whether temporary or permanent, or at preaching crosses, or in cemeteries and churchyards. Here, in addition to distractions of the sort already glanced at, others might invade. The weather could be the chief enemy, for example. Unless the preacher had the saintly resources of a St Edmund of Abingdon who, when preaching outdoors could reprimand any menacing storm clouds and cause them to scud obediently away, rain might stop play.[10]

No matter how resolute they were, preachers less favoured with divine aid would have been powerless to hold their congregations in a downpour. But there was one intangible enemy over which they might seek to develop a greater degree of direct control, one more insidious than the threat of inclement weather. Of all the frailties that the flesh is heir to, the one most bedevilling the preacher's efforts would have been plain boredom, and it was particularly lethal when mixed with a dash of resistance, of disinclination to listen to what the flesh found uncongenial to hear. Since the path of salvation is trod at a certain fleshly cost, the flesh is usually reluctant to pay it. Preachers themselves knew the danger that the unpalatable parts of their message 'commeþ in at þe on ere and goyþ oute at þe oþur'.[11] Furthermore, neither boredom nor disinclination were respecters of class boundaries. Sometimes the loftiest in society, whom fond hope might fancy would be seen setting an example to the rest, simply marched out if they felt that the sermon was dragging on too long. Alternatively, the congregation might even heckle. Early in the thirteenth century, Stephen Langton, Archbishop of Canterbury, is related to have suffered this affront, and he, enjoying no less a nickname than Stephen *de lingua tonante* (Stephen 'of the Thundering Tongue'), was by

[9] Geoffrey Chaucer's Wife of Bath makes a good example of this type; she frankly declares her habit of going to sermons in order to see and be seen (*Riverside Chaucer*, p. 112, lines 555–59).

[10] Matthew Paris relates St Edmund's rain-averting abilities in the Life of him that he wrote; see Clifford H. Lawrence, *St. Edmund of Abingdon: A Study in Hagiography and History* (Oxford: Clarendon Press, 1960), p. 236.

[11] *Middle English Sermons: Edited from British Museum MS. Royal 18 B.xxiii*, p. 166, lines 22–23.

all accounts no mean preacher.[12] On one occasion, the grandee unconcerned about letting his impatience show was King John himself. If King John vented his exasperation, there was little hope that those beneath him would behave any better.[13] A few centuries later, nothing had changed. According to an early Tudor account of a sermon and the response it provoked, a friar who upbraided a wife in his congregation for chattering while he preached got an impertinent comeuppance when the wife retorted, 'I beshrowe his harte that babeleth more of us two.' Nor was the congregation embarrassed by this: 'At the which seyng the people dyd laughe, because they felte but lytell frute in hys sermonde.'[14] So, sensible preachers knew that they had to get on with it and not to wear out the patience of their congregations by making needless demands on them.

Of course, uncongenial subject matter notwithstanding, the force of a preacher's personality and his sheer moral authority, in addition to whatever rhetorical skills he might muster, could go a long way towards holding his audience's attention. The corollary of this is implicit in the frequently reiterated insistence of late medieval clerical authors that if a preacher's life did not conform to his words, his words would be held in contempt and his preaching scorned. Thus, one sermon writer was moved to apply to the discredited preacher two homely similes: he was like an ass that bears loaves to market, but never tastes a single one of them; or like a scarecrow set in a field to terrify birds from the corn — at first, this trick works, but when the birds finally realize that they have nothing to fear from a lifeless manikin, they simply foul it with their droppings.[15] Such forlorn images of benighted ass and soiled scarecrow picturesquely captured what was self-evident, that if the preacher's life agreed with his message, he was more likely to be attended to than if it did not.

But apart from burnishing personal moral authority and its concomitant power to command respect (or less demandingly, from simply practising the widely acknowledged virtue of brevity), the astute preacher had other tricks up his sleeve for keeping his audience gripped. These were not always as drastic as those

---

[12] See Phyllis Barzillay Roberts, *Stephanus de Lingua-Tonante: Studies in the Sermons of Stephen Langton*, Studies and Texts, 16 (Toronto: Pontifical Institute of Mediaeval Studies, 1968), p. 51.

[13] *Magna Vita Sancti Hugonis*, ed. by Decima L. Douie and D. H. Farmer, 2 vols (Oxford: Clarendon Press, 1985), II, 143.

[14] From *Shakespeare Jest-Books: II. Mery Tales and Quicke Answeres from the Rare Edition of 1567*, ed. by William Carew Hazlitt (London: Willis and Sotheran, 1881), p. 85.

[15] Oxford, Bodleian Library, MS Barlow 24, fol. 178ᵛ.

that the sixth-century preacher Caesarius of Arles might employ, who is reputed
to have had the church doors locked before starting to preach.[16] This 'bolt the
doors, I'm about to begin' approach seems, however, to have been an exceptional
method for securing a captive audience. A more subtle tactic was that mentioned
earlier, the targeting of the sermon at the imaginations of the congregation.
Wooing those might finally prove the preacher's best resort, since any less-
compromising methods he chose to employ would be tacit admissions of defeat.
If the sermon aspired to being memorable, it might also aspire to being appropriately entertaining, to the extent that entertainment might be compatible with
spreading God's Word without detracting from it. Many preachers, for example,
thought the occasional joke permissible. The tradition of *risus paschalis* (literally,
'Easter laughter') is a case in point, and seems to have been regarded as fair game
amongst some for whom it licensed seasonal flickers of fun; the tradition may be
seen working its leaven into the Easter Day sermon edited above in Chapter 5, for
example. Preachers did not have to hold in their sides for the larger part of the
year, however; several examples are recorded of the medieval preacher having
his little joke, and not just at Eastertide. The fourteenth-century Dominican
friar, John Bromyard, for example, whose massive preaching resource, the *Summa
predicantium*, still awaits a modern edition, told the tale of a *truffator* (trifler,
trickster) who made himself ill by excessive drinking. When the doctor warned
him that 'the cup is killing you', he quipped, 'Had I'd known that, I'd have drunk
from the saucer'.[17] And another contemporary and equally esteemed Dominican,
Robert Holcot, whose contributions to preaching, as Chapter 7 has illustrated,
had a long shelf life, told the tale of an artist who painted superbly, but whose
children were startlingly ugly. When the discrepancy was pointed out to him, he
replied, 'Ah yes, you see, when I'm producing my paintings I work during daylight
hours when I can see what I'm doing.'[18] Neither Bromyard nor Holcot seems to
have restricted outings like these to one festival day in the year, although it seems
reasonable to suppose that jokes during the Church's penitential seasons would
have been rather less likely out of respect for seasonal decorum.

[16] Owst, *Preaching in Medieval England*, p. 181.

[17] Translated from an entry under 'Mundus', M.XIII, §19, in John Bromyard's *Summa
predicantium* (see London, British Library, MS Royal 7.E.iv, fol. 361). See also Tubach, *Index
exemplorum*, no. 5322.

[18] Translated from an entry in *lectio* 194A in Robert Holcot's *In Sapientiam* (see Oxford,
Balliol College, MS 27). The joke circulated widely; see Tubach, *Index exemplorum*, no. 3574.

Sterner, Bible-based preachers and reformists would set their faces against such levity as this, condemning it as an adulteration, and lumping it together with the frivolous, vain tales that they claimed certain preachers confected their sermons with merely to curry favour with their audiences and to pander to a degenerate taste. And in this condemnation verse might be included.[19] The position statement issued in the Prologue to the *Mirrour*, a late fourteenth-century Middle English translation of a French sermon cycle that Robert de Gretham authored early in the thirteenth century, articulates an important thread of late fourteenth-century English thinking in this regard. Perhaps most conspicuously and characteristically this temper of thinking is displayed in the writings of the followers of John Wyclif.[20] In censuring people who wanted to hear romances and heroic tales read to them, the *Mirrour* translator also attacked the composers of these secular 'songes and gestes', accusing them of lying when they said that all things that are written are to be believed:

> Many men it ben that han in wille to heren rede romaunce and gestes. That is more than idilchip, & that Y wil wele that alle men it witen; for hii ben controved thurgh mannes wit that setten here hertes to folies and trufles. As the leiyer doth, he maketh his speche queynteliche that hit may ben delicious to mennes heryng for that it schuld be the better listen[d]. [...] And therfor Ich have sette myn herte for to drawen out a litel tretice of divinite, that men that han wil for to here swiche trufles, that hii mow tur[n]en her hertes therfro. [...] And for men seyn that al thynges that ben writen it ben for to leven, & hii gabben; for hii that maken thes songes and thes gestes, hii maken hem after weneinge, & men seit on old Englisch that weneinge nis no wisdome. Loke nou to Tristrem, other of Gii of Warwike, other of ani other, & thou ne schalt finde non that ther nis mani lesinges & gret.[21]

---

[19] The austere, anti-poetic disposition is perhaps most stridently vocal in the criticisms of Wyclif and his fellow travellers, but this criticism, although theirs characteristically, seems nevertheless to have focused a more generally found distrust of poetic artifice.

[20] See Thomas G. Duncan, 'The Middle English Translator of Robert de Gretham's Anglo-Norman *Miroir*', in *The Medieval Translator*, ed. by Roger Ellis, René Tixier, and B. Weitemeier, The Medieval Translator, 6 (Turnhout: Brepols, 1998), pp. 221–31.

[21] *The Middle English Mirror: Sermons from Advent to Sexagesima, Edited from Glasgow University Library, Hunter 250*, ed. by Thomas G. Duncan and Margaret Connolly (Heidelberg: Universitätsverlag Winter, 2003), p. 3. It is interesting to note that de Gretham's Middle English translator, censuring those who say that everything that is written is to be believed, claims that they *gabben* (prate), and in so doing, he uses one of the disparaging words favoured in radical Lollard discourse (Anne Hudson, 'A Lollard Sect Vocabulary?', in Hudson, *Lollards and their Books*, pp. 165–80 (p. 178 n. 27) (first publ. in *So meny people longages and tonges: Philological Essays in Scots and Mediaeval English presented to Angus McIntosh*, ed. by Michael Benskin and M. L. Samuels (Edinburgh: Middle English Dialect Project, 1981), pp. 15–30).

(There are many men that want to hear romances and tales read out. That is something greater than idleness, and I really want all men to know it; for they are contrived by men's wit, and they incline men's hearts to folies and trifles. As the liar does, he devises his speech artfully to delight men's hearing, so that it should be the better attended to. [...] And therefore I have resolved to develop a short treatise of divinity, so that men who desire to hear such trifles may turn their hearts from them. [...] And because men say that everything that is written is to be believed; and they prate; for those who make these songs and these tales, they make them according to idle fancy, and it is said in old English that fancy is not wisdom. Consider now Tristram, or Guy of Warwick, or any other, and you will not find one of them but that there are many great lies there.)

Not surprisingly, the sermons of the Middle English *Mirrour* do not come larded with lyrics. Along with those arch-evangelicals and promoters of the vernacular, the Wycliffites, the *Mirrour* translator repeatedly affirmed his reliance on Holy Writ, as, indeed, had Robert de Gretham himself over a century earlier.[22] No matter what its ostensible purpose, lyric utterance for such people as these was too closely associated with reprobate secular taste to warrant any toehold in sacred discourse.

Yet, wiser churchmen knew that just as jokes and tales, provided they were judiciously used and diverted towards a pious end, might earn their place in preaching, so might poetry. Through poetry, a preacher might catch the attention of many a layman and laywoman who otherwise might find those main staples of the sermon menu — pastoralia and catechesis — indigestible if served ungarnished. For not only might the syllabus of salvation be rebarbative for reasons explained earlier; as far as it concerned the laity, it was also relatively concise, and by that same token, liable to bore them, so wearily familiar had it become, and thus prone to the sort of audience resistance described earlier. Even if 'Friar John x. commandments', as he got called behind his back, ended up having the last laugh, his case, itself introduced in the context of a joke, shows the perennial truth of the maxim that familiarity breeds contempt. The story goes that Friar John had only one sermon, on the Ten Commandments, and got pilloried for trotting it out on all occasions. His accusers said that everyone knew what he was going to say before he even opened his mouth. But, said he, if it were really true that they knew what he was going to say, they could surely rise to the challenge of telling him what the Ten Commandments were. Put on the spot, one of his

[22] It may be of interest to note that one of the *Mirrour* manuscripts, Oxford, Bodleian Library, MS Holkham misc. 40, resembles in its choice of script, production quality, and general format the characteristics of several manuscripts made *c.* 1400 containing vernacular Wycliffite material.

accusers triumphantly recited 'pride, covetousness, sloth, envy, wrath, gluttony and lechery'.[23] Verses to season his Decalogue might have helped the discountenanced critic remember it better, and so escape his embarrassment; indeed, sermons intercalated with a Decalogue versified can be found, as has already been illustrated, for example, in the previous chapter on sermon manuscripts that circulated in late medieval Ireland.[24] Consequently, many sermons were content to include verse, objectors notwithstanding.[25]

Verses in Sermons

Before turning squarely to lyrics and verses in sermons, however, we must first enter a distinction. Sermon verse is broadly classifiable into one of two main categories. I will distinguish these as the 'structural' and the 'non-structural'. By structural, I intend verse which, though sometimes mistaken by modern literary critics as lyric poetry,[26] originally had no existence independent of the structure of the sermon in which it participated (as, conversely, a lyric poem might have); normally, the function of verse of this structural sort was to focus nodal moments in the development of sermons constructed according to rules characteristic of what some contemporary theorists referred to as the 'modern' mode of preaching. To recall the explanation of this mode given in Chapter 3 above, 'modern' sermons opened with a *thema* normally selected from Scripture, and then, usually after a short introductory preamble or *prothema*, they proceeded to repeat this *thema* and announce a division of it into a number of 'principals' or 'members' (often totalling three, less often four, but occasionally even more). The systematic development and amplification of these 'principals' or 'members' generated the remaining bulk of the sermon. Thus, for example, the extract given below from an unpublished sermon copied early in the fourteenth century has an opening *thema* announced in Latin, *Audi, filia, et vide* (Psalm 41. 11), followed by a short introduction. At the end of the introduction, this *thema* is repeated and then translated into a Middle English couplet, 'My doȝter, my derlyngge, | Herkne my lore, y-se my thechynge'. At this point of repetition the *thema* is made to

---

[23] *Mery Tales and Quicke Answeres*, p. 83.

[24] See Chapter 8, p. 254, above.

[25] It seems almost axiomatic that sermons containing verses are not likely to be Lollard.

[26] For a classic exposé of this, see Siegfried Wenzel, 'Poets, Preachers, and the Plight of Literary Critics', *Speculum*, 60 (1985), 343–63.

generate four 'principals' or 'members', rhymed in English, which are amplified serially until the sermon has run its course. Additionally, just before the repetition of the theme, it might be noted that another English couplet is used to translate the gospel verse quoted from John 9. 11:

'Audi, filia, et vide', in Psalmo. Refert Solinus in colectaneis, capitulo de mirabilibus Sardinie, quod in regione illa sunt fontes mirabiliter salutares [...] sunt tres ille in divinis persone; si possem ab eorum quolibet unam guttam inpetrare, a Patre a drope of hys miȝty, a Filio a drope of hys wytte, a Spiritu Sancto a drope of his milce, possem dicere secure cum ceco nato, 'Lavi oculos meos et vide[o]', Iohannis nono capitulo:

> 'Loverd Ihesus, herye þe of al þy myȝtty.
> Ich have myn ighe i-wasse and habbe myn syȝte.'

Ad istud ergo lumen clare intuendum dat nobis propheta sanum consilium in verbis thematis preassumpti, dicens, 'Audi, filia, et vide.' Anglice sic:

> 'My doȝter, my derlyngge,
> Herkne my lore, y-se my thechynge.'

[...] Audi et vide: principium a quo processisti; privilegium quale suscepisti; preiudicium quantum commisisti; precipicium in quod incedisti. Si consideremus sicud prius þe busynesse of Cristes godnesse, videlicet, wyþ what mastrie he hat man y-wrouȝt; wyþ what curtaysie he ys to man y-brouȝt; wyþ what marchandie he hat y-bouȝt; and what seynorie he hat to man y-þouȝt, non mirum si querat eum dirigere, wyssy and rede mannes sole, tamquam filiam specialissimam, dicens, 'Audi, filia, et vide.'

> 'My doȝter, my derlyng,
> Herkne my lore, y-se my techyng.'

Et hec materia sermonis. Primo dicere potest Deus humano generi, 'Audi et vide how mankende furst bygan; in what manschep stow ys man; what wykednesse man hat y-do; what ioye and blisse man ys y-broȝt [to].'

> 'My doȝter, my derlyng,
> Herkne my lore, y-se my thechyng.'[27]

('Hear, daughter, and see', in the Psalm. Solinus in his collectanea, in his chapter on the wonders of Sardinia, reports that there are wonderfully health-giving springs in that region [...] there are three persons in divinity; if I might obtain from each of them a drop, from the Father, a drop of his might, from the Son, a drop of his wit, from the Holy Spirit, a drop of his mercy, I might say with the man born blind, 'I have washed my eyes and see', in the ninth chapter of John: 'Lord Jesu, I praise thee for all thy might | I've washed my eyes and have my sight.' Therefore, the prophet gives us sound advice for seeing that light clearly in the words of the *thema* taken up earlier, saying, 'Hear,

---

[27] Oxford, Bodleian Library, MS Bodley 26, fols 192ʳ–193ᵛ, edited with minor emendation.

daughter, and see.' In English thus: 'My daughter, my darling, | Hearken to my lore, heed my teaching.' [...] Hear and see: the beginning from which you have issued; what kind of privilege you have received; how great the damage you have committed; the precipice into which you have fallen. If we were to consider as before the activity of Christ's goodness, namely, with what power he has wrought man; with what courtesy he is brought to man; with what merchandise he has redeemed; and what lordship he has intended for man; it would not be surprising were he to seek to guide him, to guide and advise man's soul, like a most cherished daughter, saying, 'Hear, daughter, and see.' 'My daughter, my darling, | Hearken to my lore, heed my teaching.' And this is the matter of the sermon. First, God can say to the human race, 'Hear and see how mankind first began; in what manship set is man; what wickedness man has done; what joy and bliss man is brought to.' 'My daughter, my darling, | Hearken to my lore, heed my teaching.')

The Latin/English intermixture of this extract is broadly representative of a macaronic style found in a substantial number of late medieval sermons whose nature was discussed earlier in Chapter 3. Vernacular verses are sewn into the Latin prose, as are also occasional English words or phrases (note, for example, the Latin/English alternation in the sentence 'non mirum si querat eum dirigere, wyssy and rede mannes sole, tamquam filiam specialissimam').[28] Flexible though the categories arrived at may be for classifying the Middle English lyric, it is doubtful whether structural verses like these warrant inclusion in any of them.[29]

Conversely, the sermon verses that I have classified as non-structural, like the Decalogue verses referred to earlier, have every reason to be included in the Middle English lyric corpus.[30] Verses of this category, many of which already had independent existence outside the sermons in which they were allowed to make guest appearances, were by that same token unlike the verses mechanically cranked out by the machinery of 'modern' sermon form. The use of non-structural verse in sermons was thus far less predictable, and its functions more flexible and diverse.

In principle, any verse known to the preacher might be recruited for his purposes. This offered him a potential repertoire sufficiently broad to include verses that were bluntly secular. Such lyrics had an attention-catching value and, if corralled within a Christian moral frame, the potentially subversive secular con-

---

[28] The question of the language in which such sermons were delivered is disputed; see Chapter 3, above.

[29] Robbins, 'The Earliest Carols', p. 243, mistakenly believed that there was an unnoticed, if fragmentary, carol embedded in the *Audi, filia, et vide* sermon.

[30] Even when these lyrics are not especially 'lyrical' in the modern sense, but robustly practical, like Decalogue verses.

notations that they imported from their original field of use could be tamed and piously harnessed. A famous example is the thirteenth-century 'Atte Wrastlinge' sermon, where the preacher, almost certainly a friar, made sermon capital out of a risqué verse detached from what was originally a dance song or *carole*: 'Atte wrastlinge my lemman I ches | And atte ston-kasting I him forles' (I chose my lover at wrestling, and I lost him at stone casting); or again on another occasion when the preacher, possibly this time a Cistercian monk, drafted into his sermon lines from an almost equally bracing lullaby, odd though the appearance of such material in a lullaby today might seem: 'Wake wel, Annot, þi mayden boure, | And get þe fra Walterot, for he es lichure' (Keep your maiden bower well, Annot, and get yourself away from little Walter because he's a lecher).[31] A typical place within the sermon for lyric material of this friskier sort was at or near its beginning, providing the kind of opening gambit still used by preachers today for capturing attention before moving on to more solid fare. Whenever the secular material sailed close to the wind, as in the cases just cited, the need to police its application was naturally more pressing. However, even secular poems far less suggestive than these might find themselves being rigorously disciplined before being admitted. Take, for example, the following case of a lyric embedded in a sermon exemplum. If we were to excise it from its exemplum context, allowing it to return to what in all likelihood was its pristine form before the preacher incorporated it, it would read as follows:

> Þe dew of Averil
> Havetʒ y-maked þe grene lef to sprynge.
> My sorow is gon.
> My ioye is comen.
> Ich herde a foul synge.

(The dew of April has made the green leaf grow. My sorrow is gone, my joy is come. I heard a bird sing.)

---

[31] The 'Atte Wrastlinge' sermon is published in M. Förster, 'Kleinere Mittelenglischen Texte', *Anglia*, 42 (1918), 145–224; for 'Wake wel, Annot', see *PPPLME*, p. 32, lines 20–21. There were also examples of preaching woven around secular songs in French; a famous case, a copy of which also appears in the manuscript that yields the poem *Wan the turuf* discussed below, is found in Cambridge, Trinity College, MS 323, fol. 34ᵛ. This Latin sermon, attributed in some of its manuscripts, perhaps mistakenly, to Stephen Langton (see Roberts, *Stephanus de Lingua-Tonante*, p. 24 and n. 46, p. 63 n. 160, and p. 194), discants morally on the song *Bele Alys matyn se leva* (Pretty Alice rose up one morning).

Here, in the lightest and most economical of touches, its speaker sketches nature's revival in springtime (first two lines), declares his/her sorrow to be replaced by joy (second two lines), and ends by merging this now joyful, narrating 'I' with the revived world through remarking on having heard a bird sing. By leaving the speaker faceless and genderless, the experience related in the lyric becomes all the more readily assimilable by anyone receiving it. Working towards a similar end is the lyric's delicate reticence about how, exactly, it should be that people make the connections that they do between signs of natural and personal revival. There is no question but that people do this; springtime revival is commonly 'felt under the skin' by any of us. Yet, how does this happen, precisely? The indeterminacy here, which the lyric mimics, leaves the mind free to feel, rather than to understand intellectually, the associational connections in precisely the way people often do when they know in their bodies the unspoken seasonal miracle; having invited the reader's active participation in any connection-making, the lyric draws the reader into its experience by making him/her responsible for imaginatively completing it.

That may be one way of describing how the lyric works when it existed in its freestanding state, and there is further formal justification for reading it like that when, as the eye scans the manuscript page on which the poem is written, the Middle English vernacular of the lyric seems to surface strikingly from its surrounding sea of Latin, appearing in the process almost to detach itself visually and linguistically and to insist on respect being accorded to a separate sort of integrity and expressive potentiality that reside in its sheer vernacularity. In its Latin context, the vernacular seems honoured as a place where certain things perhaps not possible in Latin become possible. But in the sermon, the morally unburdened *reverdie* of the vernacular lyric is also given a ballast of Latin glosses that aim to steady its vernacular significances more strictly around the sermon's exemplum. As mediated there, the lyric now reads somewhat differently:

> Þe dew of Averil, id est gracia et bonitas Spiritus Sancti; Haveʒ y-maked þe grene lef to sprynge, id est Beatam Virginem; My sorow is gon, id est pena pro meritis; My ioye is comen, scilicet per Dei Filium vita beata; Ich herde a foul synge, id est angelum, scilicet Ave Maria.[32]

> (The dew of April, that is, the grace and goodness of the Holy Spirit; has made the green leaf grow, that is, the Blessed Virgin; my sorrow is gone, that is, punishment in proportion to merits; my joy is come, namely, blessed life through God's Son; I heard a bird sing, that is, the angel, namely, 'Ave Maria'.)

---

[32] Worcester, Cathedral Library, MS F.126, fol. 248ʳ. See Wenzel, *Preachers, Poets, and the Early English Lyric*, pp. 58 and 223–24.

It is as if the preacher were trying to connect into simultaneity two realms of experience, neither of which was wholly commensurable. The 'secular' experience he located in the vernacular, and the 'religious' in the disciplining Latin. While both areas of experience seem to move towards a certain mutual rapprochement that the Latin initiates as it reaches out to take hold of the vernacular and restrain it, neither experience seems wholly integrated with the other; but then, whole integration would efface distinctive lineaments of one or the other experience. And so instead, both experiences manage to exist in a tension, amounting to a textual polyphony comparable, if we may apply a medieval musical analogy, to that heard in certain motets of the contemporary musical styles known as the *ars antiqua* and the *ars nova*: in these motets, the tenor line in which the melody is held is grounded in a Latin religious text, while above it in the upper voices float secular vernacular verses whose sentiments often seem incongruous with that of the voice beneath them even as musically they are supported by it.

Nevertheless, invaluable to preachers though purely secular lyrics occasionally were, by far the largest number of sermon lyrics of the non-structural sort were, not surprisingly, religious, even when these were robust enough internally to accommodate various secular strains and resonances that set their religious appeal on a more complex basis. Lyrics of such sophisticated internal tonality may epitomize locally within the sermon certain stylistic objectives of the sermon at large, its aim to supply a warmth of approachably human *experiencia* to often chilly propositions of *auctoritas*. In many cases, non-structural religious lyrics, already suitable for potential sermon use by virtue of their subject matter, waited in the wings ready against the day of their pulpit appearance. While these sermon lyrics in waiting have not come down to us in actual sermon texts, the reason for this may simply be want of evidence. As it is, they are recorded in the antechamber to preaching, in a group of manuscripts widely produced in the later Middle Ages that, while they may contain no actual sermons, were evidently intended to assist preachers and had pulpit needs in mind. These manuscripts ranged from the informal notebooks of *materia predicabilis* that individual preachers made to formal encyclopedias of similar material at the other end of the scale, vast quarries of *predicabilia* like the *Summa predicantium* of John of Bromyard cited earlier, one of medieval England's most ambitious examples of the genre.

This sense of the 'sermon lyric in waiting', the lyric in the antechamber of preaching, as it has been termed here, attends one of the most haunting of the Middle English Passion lyrics to have survived. It is also one of the earliest. We may turn to it now as an eloquent witness to the sort of complex simplicity which the religious lyric could distil. It seems likely that its author was none other than the famous St Edmund of Abingdon, whose rain-banishing skills were mentioned earlier. He was, by all accounts, a dedicated preacher, and indeed, the contemporary artist and chronicler, Matthew Paris, took the trouble to record one of St Edmund's sermons, preached to the monks of Pontigny on the subject of Christ's seven utterances from the Cross, in the Life of St Edmund that he composed.[33] In fact, St Edmund's very topic on that occasion, the seven utterances, follows closely upon the English lyric of present concern in the treatise in which the lyric appears. This is the *Merure de Seinte Eglise*, a work written by St Edmund in French, *c.* 1239–40, and dedicated to the Pontigny monks.[34] The *Merure* is a devotional, consultative work, not a sermon, but, as his own practice plainly proves, his material on the Passion was versatile, capable of appearing in either treatise or sermon form. So, while the lyric quoted below does not appear in a sermon proper, it can justly be regarded as belonging to the 'sermon lyric in waiting' class. Chapter 24 of the *Merure* invites meditation on, among other things, the sorrow of the Virgin at seeing her crucified son. Momentarily the chapter modulates from French into English, focusing this sorrow in a single and, relative to the French, single-minded, quatrain:

> Ci doit tu penser de la duce Marie
> De quel angusse ele estoit replenie
> Quant estut a son destre
> E receust le disciple pur le mestre;
> Cum ele avoit grant dolur
> Quant le serf receust pur le Seignur —
> Le fiz au peschur
> Pur le fiz al emperor —
> Iohan, le fiz Zebedeu,
> Pur Ihesu, le fiz Deu.
> E pur ceo poeit el dire de soi
> Ceo ke dist Neomi:
> 'Ne me apelez des or ne avant;
> Kar de amerte e dolur grant
> M'ad replenie le tot pussant.'
> Meimes cele tenuire
> Dit ele en le chancon de amur,
> 'Ne vus amerveillez mie

---

[33] Lawrence, *St. Edmund of Abingdon*, pp. 286–89.

[34] Pontigny is where he died, not long after having left England, in 1240.

> Que io su brunecte e haslee
> Car le solail me ad descoluree.'
>
> E pur ceo dit un Engleis en teu manere de pite:
>
> Now goth sonne under wode,
> Me reweth, Marie, thi faire rode.
> Now goth sonne under tre,
> Me reweth, Marie, thi sone and thee.[35]

(At this point you must think upon sweet Mary, upon what anguish she was filled with when she was at his right side and received the disciple in the stead of the Master; how great a grief she had when she received the servant in the stead of the Lord, a sinner's son in the stead of the Emperor's son — John, Zebedee's son — in the stead of Jesus, God's son. And because of this, she can say of herself what Naomi says, 'Do not call me [Naomi] in the past or from henceforth, for the Almighty has filled me with bitterness and grief.' She says a similar matter in the Song of Love, 'Be not amazed that I am brown and discoloured for the sun has burnt me.' And about this an Englishman says in the following pitying manner: 'Nou goth sonne [...]', etc.)

Although both Middle English lyric and French text establish a Marian focus, the single-mindedness of the lyric compared with the French accesses a different realm of feeling entirely. Gone are the somewhat learned biblical references and allusions of the French which tend to scatter attention centrifugally towards the wide hinterlands of Passion exegesis. They make way for an almost exclusively centripetal attention to Mary at the end of the dying day: the sun/son sinks beneath the wood/cross; the speaker pities Mary's fair face; the sun/son sinks beneath the tree/cross; the speaker pities Mary and her son. This coalescence of what could be a timeless sunset with a time-bound historical event, the crucifixion, blends both in a moment at once in and out of time and in which, having established the mood of a dying day, the speaker merges that mood with absolute naturalness into a compassionate pondering of Mary's face. Then, by a small increment, the speaker further merges that compassionate pondering into a similar pondering of Mary and her son. Why should the speaker find her face, and her situation with her son, so moving? With a radical understatement, not unlike that already seen in the secular lyric *The dew of Averil*, the reader is again provoked to supply the connections that frame an answer. S/he is left to infer the precise

---

[35] St Edmund of Abingdon, *Le Merure de Seinte Eglise by Saint Edmund of Pontigny*, ed. by Harry Walcott Robbins (Lewisburg, PA: H. W. Robbins, 1925), p. 63; the lyric, however, is given as it appears in *Medieval English Lyrics, 1200–1400*, ed. by Thomas G. Duncan (London: Penguin, 1995), p. 118.

nature of the scene that the lyric's emotional reasoning is starting to suggest: the speaker grieves, we infer, because Mary's face, and her (unspoken) situation with her son, express something that cannot fail to elicit grief. This inferential process set in motion by the poem's profound reticence prompts the reader's mind to imagine what it will in terms of Mary's grief-touched face and of the fleshing out of the situation in which she finds herself. Thus the reader assumes responsibility for inventing much of the poem's meaning, personally bringing it to life out of the poem's economical promptings of her or his prior cultural awareness and knowledge of the content of the crucifixion narrative. The reader, in completing that experience out of her or his own resources, comes to possess that experience uniquely by collaborating in its construction. The reader therefore is led to own the experience gestured at in the lyric in the closest way possible: the reader in some measure is encouraged to stand in the powerful position of author. As with *The dew of Averil*, the art of this lyric too locates in the way it encourages the reader to colonize and take personal responsibility for a set of related experiences to which it only briefly alludes.

Lyrics on the Passion comprise an extremely important subject group among the verses that appear in sermons. Apart from the generally affective pitch of their content, they draw extensively on reservoirs of emotion that only the intimacies associated with a mother tongue can most readily access, channelling this emotion into the events of sacred history. Yet, the linguistic province of sacred history was chiefly Latin, and thus the mother tongue had the advantage of bringing sacred history's temporal distance emotionally up close: it was seen in the lyric just discussed, *Nou goth sonne under wode*, for example, how the event was narrated in a timeless, eternal present in which its historical distance tended as a result to be elided. According to the standard affective piety of the age, the feeling of emotional identity with the characters of sacred history was thought to have salvific value, and necessarily, feelings of identity with the past could only be achieved in the surrogacy of the present.

Another group of sermon lyrics, found somewhat less frequently than Passion lyrics but which still form a conspicuous group, are lyrics on old age and dying, and again like Passion lyrics, they typically rehearse emotional repertoires that were thought to work towards salvific ends. This time, it was most frequently feelings of sad resignation to mortality, or even mortal fear, that were evoked, and these feelings might be compounded with what some theologians called *timor servilis*, alarm at the prospect of dire eternal consequences for a life lived badly.[36]

---

[36] On the theology of *timor servilis*, see Woolf, *The English Religious Lyric*, p. 72.

Here it may be helpful to consider a number of examples, chosen to illustrate something of the variety that exists within this group.

The first will be relatively unfamiliar, because it has never appeared in any modern anthology of Middle English lyrics. It features within an item in prose published *in extenso* in Chapter 7, above (Text D), and to which the reader is referred so that the way the lyric operates in its general prose context can be appreciated. It is printed again here with its introductory discourse on how the life cycle of the rose may be thought to figure the life cycle of man:

And skylfollich mannis lif is tokind to þe rose, for þre statis þat is in mannis lif: the furst is chyldhede; the secund is manhed; þe þryd is held. By þe rose, wan he comiþ vyrst hout and sonnyþ furst is red lemys in May, his bytoknyd a chyld on is norice lappe of on ȝer old oþir two þat is fayre and lykful, for ȝong þing is comunlich quemfol. Þan he schall be a person, a byssoppe, a gret lord. But wel were is modir ȝiff he mowe boe a god sepherd, for to þe sepherdys broȝt furst þe angel tyþingys of Goddis burþe, aftyr a fewe of Goddis derlingys, Mary and a fewe oþir. Þe secund stat of the ros is lems buþ sprad abrod and is in most rode, and bytokniþ a man in is best stat with ful rode and ful streynþe. And wiþ is long lokkus and othir ioliftese a weniþ he schal never be feblyr ne foulir þan he is þan. And þarfor me sayþ, he is in is flouris. Bote it wol far of hym |fol. 194| as it fariþ of þe rose. Furst he vadiþ, weltryþ, and welouþt, and wrynkeliþ, fallyþ to þe eorþe an rotiþ. So schal man in held falouyn and weltrin and swyndin away. Wan:

> Wan þat is wyte waxit falou,
> And þat is cripse waxit calau,
> Wen þi neb ryveliþ as a roket,
> And þin hein porfilin as scarlet,
> And þi nose droppiþ as a boket,
> Than þou beon y-clipid kombir-flet.[37]

(And by reason a man's life is expressed by the rose, because of three conditions in which man's life consists: the first is childhood; the second is manhood; and the third is old age. By the rose, when it first comes out and first suns its red petals in May, there is signified a child a year or two old who is fair and delightful on his nurse's lap, for a young thing is often pleasant. Then he shall be a parson, a bishop, a great lord. But his mother is well satisfied if he may be a good shepherd, because it was to the shepherds that the angel first brought tidings of God's birth, and next to a few of God's dear ones, to Mary and a few others. The second condition of the rose is when its petals are spread wide and when it is in its greatest redness, and this signifies man in his best condition, with full complexion and strength. And with his long locks of hair and other revelries he thinks he will never be any febler or worse off than he then is. And therefore it is said, he is in his prime. But for him it will come to pass as it comes to pass for the rose. First he fades, [then] falters,

---

[37] Oxford, Bodleian Library, MS Hatton 96, fols 193ᵛ–194ʳ.

turns sere, shrivels, falls to the earth, and rots. So shall man grow sere in old age, and falter, and dwindle away. Whence [the verse]:

> When what is white grows yellow,
> And when curly hair becomes bald,
> When your face wrinkles like a rochet,
> And your eyes are rimmed with scarlet,
> And your nose drips like a bucket,
> Then you'll be called 'space-waster'.)

The rose is a familiar image in medieval literary texts, as are also narratives in which the rose takes centre stage and which allegorize events in a man's life. The most famous literary example of rose narrative is of course the thirteenth-century *Roman de la Rose*, where the rose at the heart of the garden stands for the desired woman towards whom the lover steadily makes his way in the course of his wooing, encountering en route various encouragements or obstacles. Thus the rose was well known from the secular literary canon for the associations it contracted with the earthly love interests of mankind. In the sermon, however, the association takes a different turn in a religious and moral direction. The three stages in the rose's life cycle unfold as the three ages of man, beginning in infancy, when the child shows promise of being a valued member of whichever of medieval society's three estates awaits him (traditionally, either the clergy, the aristocracy, or the labouring classes). The next stage is maturity, when man's powers are at their height. But finally and unstoppably come decrepitude and death. It is at this dark terminus, when the passage is describing the bleakest point of the cycle, that the lyric enters to distil the prose's concluding mood and crystalize its sentiment in a vivid series of images of old age. The lyric thus memorably focuses what the prose has built up towards, and leaves the reader's or hearer's imagination hesitating at the point where the next inevitable step on the downward path into the pit is about to be taken; indeed, where it may just as well be taken, for the old man, bereft of dignity, has been reduced to mere clutter. The last line dismisses him as a *kombir-flet*, a 'space-waster', an encumbering irrelevance. The lyric, then, seems a natural outgrowth and summation of the theme of the prose. Whether it was originally a freestanding poem drafted into the service of its context, or whether composed expressly for its use here, is not clear. What is clear is the way that it works smoothly in a prose-and-poetry ensemble, and its function is the better understood for seeing it in that context.

The second example from the death lyric repertoire will not be familiar to readers at all, since it is published here for the first time. The same fourteenth-century manuscript that gave us *The dew of Averil* also contains in another of its

Latin sermons this brief, *ubi sunt* reflection on the great and the good who have passed away in death like a shadow and are seen no more:

> Rogo vos dicatis michi ubi sunt principes gencium, et cetera.
> 'Where beþ þys lordes þat holden sted in stall,
> Hawkes and houndes in boure and eke in hall,
> Þat gold and selver leyden op and wenden never a down fall?'
> Et statim respondet propheta,
> 'Þe soules beþ in hell, þe bodyis stynkeþ all,
> And oþer beþ up in her sted of wham schoul so byfall.'[38]

> (I ask you if you can tell me where are the princes of the peoples, et cetera.
> 'Where are these lords who have horses in stables,
> Hawks and hounds in bower and also in hall,
> Who stored up gold and silver, and never expected a downfall?'
> And the prophet at once may reply,
> 'The souls are in hell, the bodies all stink,
> And others are up in their stead to whom it shall befall similarly.')

Readers already familiar with Middle English lyrics will immediately recognize affinities of phrase and sentiment between this lyric and a longer one, whose earliest manuscript, like that of this lyric, also hailed from the West Midlands. The longer poem, *Where ben they before us were*,[39] outstrips *Where beþ þys lordes þat holden sted in stall* in its ambitious scope, but by that same token, it sacrifices the formal compression that the latter lyric achieves not only in terms of its comparative brevity, but also of its relentless monorhyme. Whereas the pit's-brink symptoms of old age listed in *Wan þat is wyte waxit falou* are universal, death in *Where beþ þys lordes þat holden sted in stall*, as also in the longer poem *Where ben they before us were*, is presented as knocking specifically at the door of society's rich and powerful. Many lyrics in the death repertoire targeted this upper-class audience, and the next to be considered here singles out from the favourite target audience a particular representative.

Sometimes the melancholic, reflective tone of voice assumed by speakers of death lyrics — compare that of the first voice heard in *Where beþ þys lordes þat holden sted in stall* — is substituted by a voice more stern and unsparing — compare that

---

[38] Worcester, Cathedral Library, MS F.126, fol. 29ᵛ, col. a (in a sermon on the *thema*, *Respicite, et levate capita vestra*; Luke 21. 28).

[39] *Medieval English Lyrics, 1200–1400*, pp. 62–63.

lyric's second voice, which is clearly distinguished as being a second voice by the intercalated Latin sentence that attributes it to a *propheta*. It is this sterner sort of prophetic voice that may also be heard in another powerful little lyric similarly busy with the death of beauty and status, *Whan the turuf is thy tour*. This lyric is preserved uniquely in a manuscript of the second half of the thirteenth century, evidently copied for the use of preachers in view of its content, and whose relatively small format and multiplicity of scribes strongly suggests its production amongst the friars.[40] *Whan the turuf is thy tour* colludes with a traditional medieval preaching theme in choosing to warn the powerful not to be overconfident in their position, since no one, not even the nobility, may finally escape unscathed from death. The lyric displays a superb literary compression, again comparable to some of the lyrics already discussed, and also resembles them in its kindred ability to nudge readers into fleshing out for themselves details of a scenario only fleetingly hinted at. It appears in a section of the manuscript in which verses in Latin are rendered by English equivalents:

> Cum sit gleba tibi turris
>
> Tuus puteus conclavis,
>
> Pellis et guttur album
>
> Erit cibus vermium.
>
> Quid habent tunc de proprio
>
> Hii monarchie lucro?

---

[40] See Chapter 2, above, p. 15 and n. 13, for a discussion of the characteristic codicology of mendicant preaching books. Seth Lerer, 'The Genre of the Grave and the Origins of the Middle English Lyric', *MLQ*, 58 (1997), 127–61, dates Cambridge, Trinity College, MS 323 too early ('the first half of the thirteenth century'; p. 148), and perhaps also implies for it a monastic readership (p. 153), whereas the manuscript's use is more likely to have been not monastic but mendicant. Wenzel, *Preachers, Poets, and the Early English Lyric*, p. 8, implicitly agrees with *Religiöse Dichtung im englischen Hochmittelalter: Untersuchungen und Edition der Handschrift B.14.39 des Trinity College in Cambridge*, ed. by Karl Reichl (Munich: Fink, 1973), pp. 49–58 (though Reichl is not cited by name) in considering the manuscript a preacher's notebook. Reichl's suggestion, ibid., that the manuscript was a mendicant product has been challenged, though not in my view convincingly, by John Frankis, 'The Social Context of Vernacular Writing in Thirteenth Century England', in *Thirteenth Century England I*, ed. by P. R. Coss and S. D. Lloyd (Woodbridge: Boydell and Brewer, 1986), pp. 175–84 (pp. 181–82). Frankis omits to consider such codicological possibilities as were discussed above in Chapter 2 that the relatively small and portable format of the manuscript, combined with its multiplicity of scribes (some twelve or more different hands have been identified in it), all of whom are engaged in copying material more or less obviously useful to preachers, suggest circumstances typical of mendicant book production.

Unde anglice sic dicitur:

Whan the turuf is thy tour,
And thy pit is thy bour,
Thy fel and thy white throte
Shullen wormes to note.
What helpeth thee thenne
Al the worilde wenne?[41]

(When the glebe is your tower and a pit your chamber, skin and white throat will be
worms' food. What will these possess of their own wealth of the kingdom then?
Wherefore it is said in English thus:

When the turf is your tower,
And the pit is your bower,
Your skin and white throat
Shall be the concern of worms.
What do all the world's delights
Help you then?)

The English achieves a concentration that the Latin does not: note, for example,
its accusatory, second-person singular thrust maintained throughout; the Latin,
by contrast, disperses its attack in a generality, concluding with a much remoter,
third-person plural reference. The implied addressee of the English lyric must also
be female — something rather less clear in the Latin — and an aristocratic one
into the bargain.[42] The tower and the bower, where she seems to reside, are
dedicated architectural spaces within a castle, for the castle is where such things
as towers and bowers coincide, the latter word in medieval English usage also
characteristically signifying the bedchamber of a lady. Our imagined aristocratic
female is challenged by the stern prophetic voice of the lyric speaker to consider
what good her present worldly joy will do her when death comes. But that voice
does not actually name death as such; instead, life's end is figured indirectly,
via a dramatic change of residence and an alternative group of grisly admirers
that crawl around the (fair) skin and the white throat. These two physical en-
dowments, characteristically enjoyed by the ideal medieval mistress and often
celebrated in secular love poetry, will come in the fullness of time to the exclusive
attention of worms. In this horrid exchange, future worms stand in for present

[41] *Medieval English Lyrics, 1200–1400*, p. 59.

[42] Woolf, *The English Religious Lyric*, p. 82, mistook the addressee as male.

suitors as the stern, prophetic voice wrenches the joys of the present time out of joint. The voice makes the secular 'now' a hostage to the sacred 'then': the ephemeral 'now' has its towers, bowers, (fair) skin, and white throats; in the eternal 'then', these will yield to turf, pit and worms, the harbingers of the postmortem realm of God's dispensation. The lyric's imagery turns not only on this moral-temporal axis of forwarding-looking prophecy, but also on a moral-spatial one. The lyric's remorseless, one-way direction, twice repeated, is that of *flattening*: death is inferred metonymically from within this lyric in images of falling and levelling, as (elevated) tower falls into the (flatness of) turf and (eminent) bower suffers an even deeper subterranean collapse into a pit. This blunt alliteratively conjoined alteration of state, from which this poem derives much of its impact, resembles in its brutality the equally brutal sentiment of a widely circulating sermon exemplum with which the sentiment of this poem begs for comparison. In the exemplum, a one-time lover, now turned religious, keeps the rotting body of his erstwhile mistress in his cell as a reminder that the charms he so admired in days gone by have been shown by the march of time merely to have been the acceptable face of carrion.

Not only driven by their perennial theme, then, the vernacular lyrics on death served preachers from every wing of the orthodox medieval Church: *Wan þat is wyte waxit falou* is to be found in a sermon anthology probably used by seculars; *Where beþ þys lordes þat holden sted in stall* in a Benedictine sermon anthology; and *Whan the turuf is thy tour* in an anthology probably compiled by mendicants. Two hitherto unpublished death lyrics might be added from the fifteenth-century sermon anthology likely to have been compiled under the aegis of the Canons Regular of St Augustine, examples of whose preaching were studied in Chapter 5, above. They both appear in a Lenten sermon on the *thema, Penitentiam agite* (Matthew 3. 2; readers are referred to the edition of that sermon in Chapter 5, above, where may be found the fuller Latin context in which the lyrics are embedded):

> Mirabiles enim sunt mortis condiciones, videlicet, iste:
> Deth of frendis maketh fon;
> Deth þer was love maketh none;
> Deth of riȝth maketh wrong;
> And rufull is þe dede songe.[43]

---

[43] Hereford, Cathedral Library, MS O.iii.5, fol. 49ᵛ. Mechanical scribal copying errors are not noticed.

(Death's conditions are wonderful, and namely the following:

Death makes foes of friends;

Death nullifies love;

Death turns right into wrong;

And doleful is the death song.)

The second quatrain follows on after this a little further down the page:

Nam quondam fuerunt duo quorum vnus dilexit alium sicut se ipsum. Tamen post mortem vnius alius superuiuens superueniens dixit,

> When þu myght no lengur spek,
>
> And þi body is in erth rek,
>
> No force is woder þu wende,
>
> Bot gret hym wele at þe londis ende.

Quia post mortem homines diligere desinunt, nam hec est condicio mortis, þat deth þer was love, et cetera.[44]

(For there were once two men, one of whom loved the other as himself; however, after the death of one of them, the other surviving one came along and said,

> When you might no longer speak,
>
> And your body is reeky in earth,
>
> It matters not where you got to.
>
> But greet him well at the land's end.

Because after death, men cease loving, for this is death's condition, that death nullifies love, etc.)

The first quatrain presents death's interruption of an individual's status quo in terms of a set of *mirabiles condiciones*, the first three of which focus either some kind of reversal or negation: death turns friends into foes; death obliterates love; death turns right into wrong; and death's song is doleful to hear. The first three of these 'wonderful conditions' leave it up to the audience to imagine concrete personal examples, should they so choose, of the situation so aphoristically condensed and alluded to within each line. The fourth *mirabilis condicio* bluntly states that the 'dede songe' is 'rufull' to hear, and again teases the audience into amplifying the meaning of this: perhaps the line refers to the music of the liturgy of the dead, or perhaps it describes with a twist of grim irony as a 'dede songe' the sound of the death rattle that dying persons make as they breathe their last.

---

[44] Hereford, Cathedral Library, MS O.iii.5, fol. 49ᵛ. Mechanical scribal copying errors are not noticed.

Although the four lines cluster here in a group, they are also detached from each other and stitched singly elsewhere into the texture of the sermon, where each becomes an individual topic for discussion and development. Their suturing into the sermon's structure in this way also helps the lines to lodge in the heads of the audience by an incremental process of piecemeal reiteration. Thus the lyric *Deth of frendis maketh fon* functions both structurally, in helping the sermon to develop, and also stands freely, as in its occurrence cited above when its four lines emerge as a unit for recitation en bloc. The second quatrain, by contrast, is not used structurally but features once and solely as a free-standing unit, even though its appearance is rooted within a sketchily indicated narrative context, an exemplum-like situation of two men, one of whom loved the other as himself, until death intervened and separated them. The lyric is then introduced and attributed to the survivor in the exemplum-like narrative. He seems to address the first three lines of the lyric to the audience directly, in a kind of moralization derived from his experience with his dead friend that is then applied to each of them. The fourth line seems to turn its back on each addressee in the audience by abandoning the second-person pronoun and shifting to the third-person pronoun, thereby putting 'þu' firmly out of the way by the substitution of 'hym': 'Bot gret hym wele at þe londis ende'.[45]

All the death lyrics surveyed so far are relatively short, their shortness being another characteristic means whereby the impact of their terminal theme can be maximized. But very occasionally the vernacular death lyric in the sermon expatiates. Our last and longest example from the death repertoire, *Man mai longe him lives wene* (picturesquely called *Death's Wither-Clench* by some editors), also introduces the final dimension of the lyric in the sermon that I wish to consider, the possibility of the lyric in the sermon as a *musical* event, whether literally, as the preacher sang lines in the course of his preaching, or at least minimally, by his allusion to the lyric's sung reception. While the earliest text of *Man mai longe him lives wene*, where it is accompanied with a musical setting, does not actually appear in a sermon, its wider manuscript context is nevertheless 'a closely written mass of sermons and pieces useful to a preacher',[46] and it is known to have been popular with preachers from certain of its other later appearances and reminiscences:[47]

---

[45] The exact meaning of this last line remains mysterious; perhaps a reference is intended to some practice of affording a final greeting to a dead body as it is borne towards its grave?

[46] Neil Ripley Ker, *Medieval Manuscripts in British Libraries*, III: *Lampeter-Oxford* (Oxford: Clarendon Press, 1983), p. 317.

[47] The music of the lyric is published in E. J. Dobson and F. L. Harrison, *Medieval English Songs* (London: Faber, 1979), p. 242. Although Wenzel, *Preachers, Poets and the Early English*

Man mai longe him lives wene,
Ac ofte him lyeth the wrench;
Fair weder ofte him went to rene,
An ferliche maketh is blench.
Therfore, man, thou thee bi-thench,
Al shal falewi thy grene.
Weilaway, nis king ne quene
That ne shal drinke of Dethes drench.
Man, er thou falle of thy bench,
Thy sinne aquench.

Ne mai strong, ne starck, ne kene
Ayein Dethes wither-clench;
Young and old and bright and shene,
Al he riveth an his strength.
Fox and ferlich is the wrench,
Ne may no man thertoyene,
Weylaway, threting ne bene,
Mede, list, ne leches drench.
Man, let sinne and lustes stench,
Wel do, wel thench!

Do bi Salomones rede,
Man, and so thou shalt wel do;
Do als he thee taught, and hede
What thin ending thee bringth to,
Ne shaltow never misdo —
Sore thou might thee adrede!
Weylaway, swich wenth wel lede
Long lyf, and blisse underfo,
There Deth luteth in his sho
To him fordo.

Man, why niltow thee bi-knowe,
Man, why niltow thee bi-se;
Of foule filth thou art i-sowe,
Wormes mete thou shalt be.

Lyric, p. 204, says of the lyric's earliest manuscript, Maidstone Museum, A.13, that it cannot 'be definitely shown to have been compiled for use in preaching', Ker's view of its function is surely correct (see the previous note).

Her nastou blisse dayes three,
Al thy lif thu drist in wowe;
Welaway, Deth thee shal throwe
Doun ther thou wenst hye ste;
In wo shal thi wele te,
In wop thy gle.

World and wele the biswiketh
Iwis, they ben thine ifo;
If thy world mid wele thee sliketh
That is for to do thee wo.
Therfore let lust overgo,
Man, and eft it wel the liketh.
Weylaway, hou sore him wiketh
That in one stunde other two
Werkth him pine evermo.
Ne do, Man, swo![48]

(Man may expect a long life for himself but the quirks of fate deceive him. Often fair weather turns rainy and suddenly plays its trick. Therefore, man, take heed, all your greenness shall fade. Alas, there is neither king nor queen who shall not drink Death's draught. Man, overcome your sin before you fall off your bench. Neither the strong, the mighty, nor the bold may prevail against Death's hostile grip. Young and old, and bright and beautiful — he tears all to pieces in his strength. His twist is crafty and sudden. No man may prevail against it, alas, neither may threats, entreaty, bribes, cunning, nor the doctor's potion. Man, abandon sin and lust's stench. Do well, consider well! Man, act according to Solomon's advice, and you shall do well. Do as he taught you, and take heed of what your ending brings you to, and you shall never do amiss. Sorely you may fear for yourself! Alas, such a man fully expects to lead a long life and to enjoy happiness, while Death lurks in his shoe to destroy him. Man, why will you not acknowledge your nature? Man, why will you not consider yourself? You are begotten of foul filth, and you shall be worms' meat. Here you do not have three days' worth of joy. All your life you endure in sorrow. Alas, Death shall throw you down when you expect to rise high; your prosperity will pass into misery, and your merriment into weeping. The world and prosperity deceive you. Certainly, they are your foes. If your world flatters you with prosperity it is to cause you harm. Therefore, man, let lust pass, and afterwards it will please you well. Alas, how sorely it serves him who in an hour or two earns everlasting torment for himself. Man, do not do so!)

The lyric weaves variations on certain staple motifs of the death tradition in its attempt to bring people to realize their transitoriness and to egg them on to the

---

[48] *Medieval English Lyrics, 1200–1400*, pp. 54–55.

moral resolutions that that realization encouraged, based on the biblical principle of 'Memorare novissima tua, et in eternum non peccabis' (Be mindful of the last things, and you will not sin eternally; Ecclesiasticus 7. 40). The first stanza evokes the sort of reversals in the natural world that are regularly vehicles for medieval death meditation — fair weather turns rainy, greenness grows sere and fallow — and with these may be compared the blossoming and fading rose of the sermon material cited earlier. The first stanza also trades on the familiar idea that no social estate is immune, not even king or queen. But it also introduces a motif not encountered in the specimens cited so far, one which, especially after the Black Death crisis of the mid-fourteenth century, would come to loom ever larger: Death personified. The lyric develops this vision of Death abroad in the world and stalking a quarry in a steady accumulation of detail through all the remaining stanzas (save the last, by which time the poet is ready to devote his conclusion to exhorting mankind to make an appropriate moral response). The encounter of Life with Death is presented in the lyric as an unequal struggle, a fated contest. Its presentation thus perhaps echoes a medieval conceptualization of the encounter of Life with Death as a duel; for example, the Easter sequence *Victimae paschali laudes* projects such an encounter, the ironic difference being that in the Easter sequence, Life triumphs, since it is Christ who is doing the duelling.[49] In mankind's case, however, the victor will always be Death.

It may be fanciful to go as far as imagining some preacher singing the whole of this lyric in the course of his sermon. Yet, since each individual stanza has a self-contained moral, it may have been worth his while to lift stanzas singly for such a purpose. Maybe he lifted and sang snatches briefer still. Many Middle English lyrics were, of course, more heard as song than read on the page as literary events, and the prospect of a preacher's sung delivery of at least some non-structural sermon lyrics which are known to have been set to music does not stretch credibility.[50] Given the battle for the congregation's attention that every preacher waged as soon as he stepped into the pulpit, music might have offered another welcome means of holding that attention; we know that the friars, so frequently alluded to in this chapter and whose raison d'être was preaching, were widely known for their musical abilities. St Francis had styled his followers *ioculatores Dei*

---

[49] The line in *Victimae paschali laudes* runs: 'Mors et vita duello conflixere mirando; dux vitae mortuus regnat vivus' (Death and life have struggled together in a great battle; the Lord of life who died, now in life reigns) (in free translation).

[50] Even though there is comparatively little direct evidence of clerics performing music in a preaching context.

(God's jesters), by which we should understand not only a taste for wit of the sort illustrated earlier, but also for music, the medieval jester being not just a comedian but an all-round entertainer whose skills might include musical performance. In the century after St Francis, Geoffrey Chaucer would show such a musical ethos alive and well in the person of his Friar Huberd: 'And in his harpyng, whan that he hadde songe, | His eyen twynkled in his heed aryght | As doon the sterres in the frosty nyght.'[51] And in the century after Chaucer, an assiduous Franciscan preacher, Nicholas Philip, who himself incorporated both structural and non-structural verse in his sermon booklets (introduced above in Chapter 2) included within his sermon collection bars of musical notation, revealing himself in the process to be a true heir of a long musical tradition within his order.[52] One of the most celebrated Middle English lyrics to have survived, *I syng of mayden*, a poem in praise of the Blessed Virgin Mary and her acquiescence in the Incarnation, is recorded in a single manuscript copy.[53] Yet, were it not for the industry of a late fourteenth- or perhaps early fifteenth-century sermon writer, a man of whom we know nothing save his surname — Selk — we would lack clear external proof that *I syng of mayden* was originally a song, and that it was commonly heard in England.[54] These are things that a single surviving manuscript copy, *prima facie*, might not encourage us to believe. Selk included a reference to *I syng of mayden* in a sermon that he compiled, in Latin, for the feast of the Assumption. Among all the exalted comparisons in Latin that he lavished on Mary, Selk made time to recall a vernacular one. Mary 'absque dolore peperit, cum omnes alie in dolore pereant. Unde communiter de eo [*read* ea] canitur, "Mayde, wyff and moder whas never but ye. | Well may suche a lady Goddys modyr be"' (Mary gave birth without pain, when all others may die in pain. Whence it is commonly sung about her, 'Maid, wife, and mother was never but she. Well may such a lady be God's mother').[55] Maybe at this point Selk, or whoever else may have preached from his sermon anthology, actually sang a snatch of *I syng of mayden*. We will never know

---

[51] *Riverside Chaucer*, p. 27, lines 266–68.

[52] *PPPLME*, pp. 41–57; see p. 56.

[53] *Medieval English Lyrics, 1200–1400*, p. 111.

[54] For a summary description and inventory of its contents, see *LSCLME*, pp. 203–06 and 545–50 respectively.

[55] Oxford, Bodleian Library, MS Barlow 24, fol. 188ᵛ; on the date of the collection, see Alan J. Fletcher, '"I Sing of a Maiden": A Fifteenth-Century Sermon Reminiscence', *N&Q*, n.s., 25 (1978), 107–08. The sermon, found on fols 188ʳ–189ᵛ, is on the *thema*, *Tu supergressa es universas* (Proverbs 31. 29).

for sure. But what we can certainly know is that some preachers were fully aware of the musical dimension that certain of their non-structural sermon verses accessed. At the very least, we can observe their willingness to allude to that dimension as they sought to hold the attention of their congregations.

Conclusion

In the sermon, then, and especially in the popular sermon, Middle English lyrics found a natural, if clerically patrolled and supervised, habitat, and we risk restricting our understanding of how some lyrics worked if we persist in isolating them from preaching's wider enterprise; their artistry, some of whose sophistication was glimpsed earlier in this chapter, helped preaching take root in hearts and minds. From structural verses to non-structural ones, the range of sermon lyrics (those on the Passion, on death, and on the Virgin, being only three of the more prominent subject areas) expressed a corresponding range of poeticized experience. The perceived benefits of the reception of this experience in the lives of those who heard or read the lyrics were equally diverse in turn: the lyric might provide aesthetic pleasure that helped memorialize sermon content, or it might move to moral resolve and a better conduct of life according to Christian principles. But fundamentally, the lyric in the sermon helped the preacher to help members of his congregation to construct the right sort of hopes and fears for themselves as they made their way charily, but also not without a due measure of rejoicing, through the moral landscape of middle earth.

'Good Men and Women'

To settle popular audiences in a position from which they could recognize with unobstructed view how the landscape of their lives was in fact a morally charged landscape, one in which the routes that they took would finally lead to different eternal consequences, could be said to be the ultimate aim of each of the various popular sermons anthologized here. Even the very mode of audience address characteristic of that late medieval popular preacher par excellence, the Augustinian canon John Mirk, whose favoured form of words was chosen as the heading for this book's epilogue, may be thought to encapsulate in small this essential enterprise of pastoral orientation: the 'good men and women' congregated before the preacher were 'good' once brought within the sheepfold that his preaching would go on to circumscribe and define. The good sheep of that sheepfold would know their shepherd's voice, and in recognizing it, they would acknowledge and own for themselves what he stood for as he herded his flock obediently together within the sheepfold's walls. Such, at least, was the shepherd-preacher's aspiration, and this book has illustrated something of the diversity of means whereby that aspiration, *Deo adiuvante*, might be achieved.

Signposts, then, were set up by popular preachers in the landscape of their audiences' lives which might stand as prominent points of reference and moral orientation that preachers could usefully allude to. Sometimes the landscape in which the signposts were erected was already a thoroughly literal and familiar one. Thus to return for a moment to the example of John Mirk, we hear him in his sermon for the dedication of a church telling the story of three ox-rustlers of Lilleshall in Shropshire, one of whom, having died unconfessed of his ox-rustling, had continued to haunt the locale, 'and soo feeryd þe parysch þat aftyr þe sonne going downe þer dyrst no man go out of his yn', until the ministrations of the local parish priest, Thomas Wodward, succeeded in laying his ghost.[1] Mirk's home base was in Lilleshall Abbey, and so he is found here in this particular sermon sowing a landscape whose geography was already well known to him personally, and doubtless also to many of his immediate audience, with the seeds of a supernatural narrative; its harvest might fruitfully be turned to the sermon's purpose at this point. This seems to have been the raising in that familiar landscape of a pastorally appropriate crop: the audience's everyday reality was narrated by Mirk as vulnerable to being overrun by supernatural agencies that only representatives of the Church had the ability to confront and reckon with; lay deference to clerical prerogatives was implicitly being advocated here.

While the sermons of the present anthology, being free of immediate local allusion, do not operate in an exactly comparable way, in some cases their *social* and *political* topographies may nevertheless have been already comparably familiar and ripe for a similar sort of clerical conquest and plantation. Thus items like the luxurious finery, modish hairstyles, banquets, and love tokens evoked in the Advent sermon edited in Chapter 3, all redolent of the courtly world and of high society's values, if they were not merely delicious dream commodities with which the preacher teased the minds of an audience that in real life was unaccustomed to such things, may alternatively and conceivably have been commodities with which the audience already had some actual social acquaintance. If so, those things promptly lent themselves to the preacher's further manipulation, and as the sermon clearly shows, this entailed a soul-saving exchange of the common secular coin of high society for more spiritual goods.[2] Similarly, the contemporary political immanence and anxiety that respire throughout Hugh Legat's Lenten sermon edited in Chapter 4 seem to have induced him to try to use preaching as a means to mould the outlook of his popular audience into conformity with his own. A world where unity between clergy and laity was known from experience to be under threat seems to have been for Legat an important *exemplum horrendum*; harmony between society's estates was needed, and might perhaps be assisted by his rhetorical attempts from the pulpit to conjure up a picture of the ill effects of discord and then to draw the parties away from its brink by bonding them closely

---

[1] *Mirk's Festial*, ed. by Erbe, p. 281, lines 18–19. The best manuscript of the *Festial*, preserved in London, British Library, Cotton Claudius A.ii, adds that Thomas Wodward was afterwards 'parson of Rokeley' (probably Ruckley, about six miles south-south-east of Shrewsbury in Shropshire).

[2] Compare, too, the description and social pitch of the Castle of Prudence exemplum edited in Text D in Chapter 7, above.

together in a set of reciprocally defining roles and mutually enhancing aims. Thus Legat, too, seems to have acknowledged and addressed a political reality already known to his audience, and had sought to work upon it in his preaching so that the old traditional clerical and lay alignment, one that incidentally also underwrote his own social position, might prevail once again as it had in happier days.

Careful inspection of late medieval popular preaching in Britain and Ireland may therefore reveal it to be aware of the local circumstances of its audience in ways not always the most immediately apparent. While moral, social, and political orientation was one of their central concerns, popular sermons had a variety of additional purposes, capacities, and limitations, each varying according to the nature of the sermon's occasion, the composition of the audience, and the talents of the preacher; the detail of some of these variables was glanced at in Chapter 9. But the business of evoking and then rewriting according to clerical precept the laity's perception of a number of aspects of their experience was one in which each of the popular sermons gathered in this anthology was in its own way engaged. In order to transact that business the sermons cultivated distinctive sorts of strategy of the kind just mentioned, and that might generally be characterized as the harmonizing of the secular with the spiritual; the desired outcome was that the former might subtly be amalgamated with, if not indeed sometimes be actually displaced by, the latter.

When different kinds of topical resource, be they those furnished by familiar literal, social, or political topographies, were not being refurbished with a view to their salutary reinstallation in the audience's imaginations, unfamiliar resources might be drawn on to lead those imaginations on morally supervised flights of fancy. Preachers doubtless hoped that even departures from the familiar, too, might affect the audience's disposition in a similar way: the propulsion of their imaginations into terrains that were, by contrast, unfamiliar, sometimes indeed strangely exotic, might yield a comparable net result. John Mirk again was also fully capable in this regard and took this particular tack with his audience many times; in fact, he took it far more frequently than starting from places that his audience already knew. In the present anthology, the lake in Judea whose water is thrice bitter and thrice sweet in the course of a day (see the Easter sermon edited in Chapter 5) provides but one such example from a preacher probably himself belonging to some branch of that same Augustinian regular tradition to which Mirk belonged; another in the same sermon is provided in the Egyptian fountain that extinguishes lighted firebrands but paradoxically ignites extinguished ones. Packing the mind with marvels like these sent it on a holiday from its routine contact with mundane reality. Once abroad in the realm of the imagination, it opened itself more easily to infusion with the preacher's confected moral matter. Not all popular preachers drew on the tricks of the fantastical repertoire, the evocation of geographically or temporally remote countries where people could be relied on to exert that characteristic fascination of doing things differently. Thus the Good Friday sermon edited in Chapter 6 allowed itself to be geographically and temporally removed from its audience only to the extent that its bulk was taken up with a synthetic account derived strictly from the gospels of the story of Christ's Passion. Yet even while technically remote from the audience's experience in its reference to distant times and places, biblical matter of such common currency as this had been made by the Church's repeated evangelical efforts so thoroughly domestic and familiar a part of the laity's stock religious awareness that there was really nothing unusual about it at all. Indeed, the preacher of that same Good Friday sermon, Thomas Cyrcetur, showed a consistency of approach, for elsewhere in his work he chose to avoid the fabulous. Seemingly, this particular common resource of popular preaching whereby the imaginations of an audience might be hijacked for pious purposes was not for him.

Instead, Cyrcetur preferred to work upon the emotions of his audience whenever the occasion lent itself to that. He encouraged the desired clerical/lay symbiosis by speaking as if his personally declared affective state chimed completely with the affective state of those listening to him. Thus here again, though expressed in a different set of terms, we encounter the popular preacher's instinct for seizing the opportunity to construct moments of clerical and lay unison. In this particular case, the shared condition was devotional synchronicity. Emotions might be pastorally tended in preaching so that everyone feeling them might thereby be corralled into a common affective community promoted and sanctioned by the Church. Of course, the affective fervour of the preacher himself had necessarily in some measure to be a rhetorical contrivance, for self-evidently, if he were too moved to speak he may not in turn have been most easily able to move his audience; Cyrcetur spoke of both weeping and preaching almost as if simultaneous events, but the prospect of their actually having been entirely so is hard to conceive. There must necessarily have been some insulation of detachment between him and the affective heat that he claimed had chafed his words. Effective popular preaching, sensitive to its audience's circumstances, receptivity, and state of mind, might therefore aim to harness a wide range of emotional responses, and not merely the tearful ones (something that the Easter Sunday sermon edited in Chapter 5 makes quite clear), although to be sure, sorrowful moods that stimulated penitence, as earlier chapters have noted, scored highly as a preaching target.

How effective the popular sermons anthologized in this book actually were in stirring up and capturing the emotions of their audiences is something we will never know.[3] The late medieval popular preacher's success in this respect is only infrequently reported in contemporary accounts from Britain and Ireland of actual cases of audience response. These are precious witnesses whenever they occur, although, as is often the nature of the historical record, extreme examples of various kinds are what tend to prevail in reports, since commonly what is ordinary will pass unremarked. By the time of the end of the period covered in this book, a cultural legacy of affective piety had accumulated over several generations; its techniques for inducing emotional states considered conducive to the health of the soul were well developed, and sermons had available an extensive repertoire of them on which they could draw as it suited their purposes. Add to that the fact that sometimes members of a sermon's audience were already susceptible to emotionalism for one reason or another, whether because of external social conditioning in the customary affective responses, or because of some internal psychological predisposition, and the resultant mixture could easily be imagined to have produced a spectacular outcome. Perhaps the most famous case on record from our period is that of Margery Kempe of Lynn in Norfolk. Little effort is required to speculate on what the affective topics in a sermon preached on the *thema* 'Ihesu is ded' may have been that managed to set her off,[4] but whatever the surprise, embarrassment, suspicion, or annoyance that her devotional outbursts were capable of provoking, there seem always to have been some who were less quick to dismiss her and who saw her emotionalism, rather, as a God-given grace. Thus, for example, when on another occasion in Lynn a sermon was to be delivered on the Assumption, Margery already had her advocate, one Thomas Constance, a Dominican friar, who approached the preacher in advance of the sermon to alert him to Margery's likely reaction and to request that he bear with it indulgently. Constance is reported as having commended Margery's cryings in a conversation that he had had with her, parts of which read as if they were lifted from the pages of some textbook collection of sermon exempla: 'Margery, I haue red of an holy woman whom God had ʒouyn gret grace of wepyng and crying

---

[3] Strictly speaking, of course, we do not know that any of them was in reality preached because no external evidence survives which would confirm that. Yet, even if that takes scepticism a step too far, if actually preached, their manner of delivery and their preachers' relative skills in putting them across could necessarily never be known.

[4] *The Book of Margery Kempe*, I: *Text*, ed. by Sanford Brown Meech and Hope Emily Allen EETS, o.s., 212 (London: Oxford University Press, 1940; repr. 1961), p. 167.

as he hath don onto ʒow' (Constance then proceeds to relate the woman's story).[5] When the priest in Constance's little narrative could not tolerate the said woman's weeping and crying and had sought her removal from the church, she prayed that God would incite similar devotion in him. God obliged, stirring the priest to such devotional transports at Mass that he could not contain their effects. Perhaps, then, when we hear of contexts like this, Thomas Cyrcetur's talk of an occasion when preaching and weeping could coincide may seem less out of the ordinary. Even without the accreditation provided by appeals to this story of the noisily devotional but divinely endorsed laywoman, the tradition of boisterous devotion went back a long way. It was known even at the foundations of Constance's own order: no less than St Dominic himself had been famous for his loud weeping and praying; his conversations with God might rise to such a pitch that they became audible everywhere.[6] Margery's behaviour, therefore, had some impeccable precedents, and whatever her detractors said about the demerits of her conduct, there would be others, conversely, who knew those precedents and who would thus be likely to approve of it. When it came to preaching as the context for emotional outpourings of this kind, the course likely to win the most all-round approval was doubtless one of moderation, as the mendicant author of the Advent sermon edited in Chapter 3 seems to have appreciated. He condoned balance: while the 'warm tear in the eye' had its proper place, any sobbing that accompanied it should nevertheless not be 'on high'.[7] Perhaps he showed us here that already in the late thirteenth century there existed those who, like Margery in the early fifteenth, were inclined to let their devotional exuberance get the better of them.

The late medieval popular sermon, then, needed to engage its audience if it were not to remain an arid exercise and wither on the vine. Consequently, preachers might find themselves treading a fine line between disaffecting their audiences and affecting them too much. The content and structure of the sermon had to be well prepared, of course, but only in delivery would it stand or fall in the moment that its preacher's rhetorical mettle was put finally to the proof. We find in the sermons edited in this anthology some of the traces of those preachers' competence, and they are traces only, for reasons that have already been discussed. The

---

[5] *The Book of Margery Kempe*, pp. 165–66.

[6] Cited in Simon Tugwell, *The Way of the Preacher* (London: Darton, Longman, and Todd, 1979), p. 47.

[7] See above, p. 41, line 41. Also, it may be that he was recommending such moderation more generally, in *any* devotional context, and not only during preaching.

introduction to this book announced at the outset that what was offered in it was an anthology that necessarily and of its nature would be more representative than it could ever hope to be considered comprehensive. Along with their accompanying studies, the book's chapters have taken a number of snapshots of the genre of popular preaching over a period of some two hundred years. It goes without saying that much more room remains in the album for other snapshots to be included, and to be sure, not until as many of those as can be taken have been taken will we be in the best possible position to appraise the nature of the general picture that this particular genre of preaching presents. Until that day arrives, the current collection has aimed to take an interim step along the desired path and to offer others an incentive to pursue ever further for themselves the twists and turns that it may take.

I. Primary Manuscript Sources

Aberdeen

University Library, MS 154

Cambridge

Jesus College, MS 13
Peterhouse, MS 210
Trinity College, MS 43
Trinity College, MS 323
Trinity College, MS 1285
University Library, MS Gg.6.16
University Library, MS Ii.3.22

Dublin

National Library of Ireland, MS 9596
Trinity College, MS 75
Trinity College, MS 114
Trinity College, MS 201
Trinity College, MS 204
Trinity College, MS 347
Trinity College, MS 667

Durham

University Library, MS Cosin B.IV.19
University Library, MS Cosin V.III.5
University Library, MS Cosin V.IV.3

Gloucester

Cathedral Library, MS 22

Hereford

Cathedral Library, MS O.iii.5

Hertford

Record Office, ASA/AR1 (Stoneham Register, 1415–70)

Lincoln

Cathedral Library, MS 50
Cathedral Library, MS 51
Cathedral Library, MS 133

London

British Library, MS Additional 41321
British Library, MS Additional 49619
British Library, MS Arundel 384
British Library, MS Cotton Claudius A.ii
British Library, MS Cotton Faustina A.v
British Library, MS Cotton Vespasian D.xiv
British Library, MS Harley 913
British Library, MS Harley 2383
British Library, MS Harley 2624
British Library, MS Harley 4894
British Library, MS Royal 7.E.iv
British Library, MS Royal 18.B.xxiii
Lambeth Palace Library, MS 487
National Archives, E28/82/1

Longleat House

Longleat House, MS 4

Maidstone

Maidstone Museum, MS A.13

Oxford

Balliol College, MS 27
Bodleian Library, MS Ashmole 750

Bodleian Library, MS Ashmole 759
Bodleian Library, MS Barlow 24
Bodleian Library, MS Bodley 26
Bodleian Library, MS Bodley 95
Bodleian Library, MS Bodley 144
Bodleian Library, MS Bodley 216
Bodleian Library, MS Bodley 279
Bodleian Library, MS Bodley 320
Bodleian Library, MS Bodley 474
Bodleian Library, MS Bodley 549
Bodleian Library, MS Bodley 649
Bodleian Library, MS Bodley 687
Bodleian Library, MS Bodley 709
Bodleian Library, MS Bodley 806
Bodleian Library, MS Bodley 832
Bodleian Library, MS Bodley 859
Bodleian Library, MS Digby 86
Bodleian Library, MS e Museo 180
Bodleian Library, MS Hatton 96
Bodleian Library, MS Holkham misc. 40
Bodleian Library, MS Junius 1
Bodleian Library, MS Lat. th. d. 1
Bodleian Library, MS Laud misc. 528
Bodleian Library, MS Laud misc. 706
Bodleian Library, MS Rawlinson C.751
Bodleian Library, MS Rawlinson G.99
New College, MS 88
Oriel College, MS 10
Trinity College, MS 30
University College, MS 28
University College, MS 109

Rennes

Bibliothèque municipale, MS 598

Salisbury

Cathedral Library, MS 13
Cathedral Library, MS 36
Cathedral Library, MS 39
Cathedral Library, MS 40
Cathedral Library, MS 55
Cathedral Library, MS 81

Cathedral Library, MS 84
Cathedral Library, MS 87
Cathedral Library, MS 97
Cathedral Library, MS 113
Cathedral Library, MS 126
Cathedral Library, MS 166
Cathedral Library, MS 167
Cathedral Library, MS 170
Cathedral Library, MS 174

Shrewsbury

Shrewsbury School, MS 13

Troyes

Bibliothèque municipale, MS 1316

Worcester

Cathedral Library, MS F.10
Cathedral Library, MS F.126
Cathedral Library, MS Q.53

II. Primary Printed Sources

Aelred (of Rievaulx), *Opera omnia II: Sermones I–XLVI (Collectio Clarævallensis prima et secvnda)*, ed. by Gaetano Raciti, CCCM, 2A (Turnhout: Brepols, 1989)
——, *Opera omnia III: Sermones XLVII–LXXXIV (Collectio Dunelmensis sermo a Mattheo Rievallensi Servatus sermones Lincolnienses)*, ed. by Gaetano Raciti, CCCM, 2B (Turnhout: Brepols, 2001)
Anselm (of Canterbury), *Sancti Anselmi Opera omnia*, ed. by F. S. Schmitt, 6 vols (Edinburgh: Nelson, 1946–61)
——, *St Anselm's Proslogion*, ed. and trans. by Maxwell John Charlesworth (Oxford: Clarendon Press, 1965)
Aristotle, *Ethica Nichomachea: Translatio Roberti Grosseteste Lincolniensis sive 'Liber Ethicarum'*, *B. Recensio recognita*, ed. by René Antoine Gauthier, Aristoteles Latinus, XXVI, 1–3, Fasciculus Quartus (Leiden: Publications universitaires, 1973)
Augustine (of Hippo), *Sancti Augustini Confessionum Libri XIII*, ed. by L. Verheijen, CCSL, 27 (Turnhout: Brepols, 1981)
Beadle, Richard, ed., *York Plays* (London: Arnold, 1982)
Bede, *Bede's Ecclesiastical History of the English People*, ed. by Bertram Colgrave and Roger A. B. Mynors (Oxford: Clarendon Press, 1969)

Bestul, Thomas H., ed., *Walter Hilton: The Scale of Perfection* (Kalamazoo: Medieval Institute Publications, 2000)

Biblia sacra cum glossa ordinaria, 6 vols (Antwerp: [n. pub.], 1617)

Biblia sacra iuxta Latinam Vulgatam versionem (Rome: Typis polyglottis Vaticanis, 1926–)

Bland, Cynthia Renée, *The Teaching of Grammar in Late Medieval England: An Edition, with Commentary, of Oxford, Lincoln College MS Lat. 130*, Medieval Texts and Studies, 6 (East Lansing, MI: Colleagues; Woodbridge: Boydell and Brewer, 1991)

Bradshaw, Henry, and Christopher Wordsworth, eds, *Statutes of Lincoln Cathedral*, 2 pts in 3 vols (Cambridge: Cambridge University Press, 1892–97)

Brinton, Thomas, *The Sermons of Thomas Brinton, Bishop of Rochester, 1373–1389*, ed. by Mary Aquinas Devlin, Camden Society Third Series, 85–86 (London: Royal Historical Society, 1954)

Brown, Carleton, ed., *Religious Lyrics of the XIVth Century*, 2nd edn, rev. by G. V. Smithers (Oxford: Clarendon Press, 1957)

Cartlidge, Neil, ed., *The Owl and the Nightingale* (Exeter: Exeter University Press, 2001)

Charland, T. M., *Artes praedicandi: Contribution à l'histoire de la rhétorique au moyen âge*, Publications de l'Institut d'études médiévales d'Ottawa, 7 (Paris: Wetteren, 1936)

Chaucer, Geoffrey, *The Riverside Chaucer*, gen. ed. Larry D. Benson, 3rd edn (Boston: Houghton Mifflin, 1987)

Cigman, Gloria, ed., *Lollard Sermons*, EETS, o.s., 294 (Oxford: Oxford University Press, 1989)

Davis, Norman, ed., *Non-Cycle Plays and Fragments*, EETS, s.s., 1 (London: Oxford University Press, 1970)

——, *The Paston Letters: A Selection in Modern Spelling* (Oxford: Oxford University Press, 1963)

Davis, Norman, Richard Beadle, and Colin Richmond, eds, *Paston Letters and Papers of the Fifteenth Century*, EETS, s.s., 20–22 (Oxford: Oxford University Press, 2004–05)

Dobson, E. J., and F. L. Harrison, eds, *Medieval English Songs* (London: Faber, 1979)

Douie, Decima L., and D. H. Farmer, eds, *Magna Vita Sancti Hugonis*, 2 vols (Oxford: Clarendon Press, 1985)

Duncan, Thomas G., 'A Transcription and Linguistic Study of the Introduction and First Twelve Sermons of the Hunterian MS Version of the "Mirror"' (unpublished B.Litt. thesis, University of Oxford, 1965)

Duncan, Thomas G., and Margaret Connolly, eds, *The Middle English Mirror: Sermons from Advent to Sexagesima, Edited from Glasgow University Library, Hunter 250* (Heidelberg: Universitätsverlag Winter, 2003)

Duncan, Thomas G., ed., *Medieval English Lyrics, 1200–1400* (London: Penguin, 1995)

Eccles, Mark, ed., *The Macro Plays*, EETS, o.s., 262 (London: Oxford University Press, 1969)

Forshall, J., and F. Madden, eds, *The New Testament in English* (Oxford: Clarendon Press, 1879)

Förster, M., 'Kleinere Mittelenglischen Texte', *Anglia*, 42 (1918), 145–224

Fowler, J. T., ed., *Rites of Durham*, Surtees Society, 107 (Durham: Andrews, 1903; repr. 1964)

Frere, W. H., and L. E. G. Brown, eds, *The Hereford Breviary*, Henry Bradshaw Society, 26 and 40, 2 vols (London: Harrison, 1904–10)

Friedberg, Emil, and Emil Ludwig Richter, eds, *Corpus iuris canonici*, 2nd edn, 2 vols (Leipzig: Tauchnitz, 1879–81; repr. Graz: Academische Druck- u.Verlagsanstalt, 1959)

320   *Bibliography*

Geary, James A., 'An Irish Homily on the Holy Eucharist: Text and Translation', *Catholic University Bulletin*, 18 (1912), 460–75

Gradon, Pamela, and Anne Hudson, eds, *English Wycliffite Sermons*, 5 vols (Oxford: Clarendon Press, 1983–96)

Greene, Richard Leighton, ed., *The Early English Carols*, 2nd edn (Oxford: Clarendon Press, 1977)

Grisdale, Dora M., ed., *Three Middle English Sermons from the Worcester Chapter Manuscript F. 10*, Leeds Texts and Monographs, 5 (Leeds: Wilson, 1939)

Hamesse, Jacqueline, ed., *Les Auctoritates Aristotelis* (Louvain: Université catholique de Louvain, Publications de CETEDOC, 1974)

Hazlitt, William Carew, ed., *Shakespeare Jest-Books: II. Mery Tales and Quicke Answeres from the Rare Edition of 1567* (London: Willis and Sotheran, 1881)

Hingeston-Randolph, F. C., ed., *The Register of John de Grandisson, Bishop of Exeter AD 1327–1369)*, 3 vols (London: Bell, 1894–99)

Horner, Patrick J., 'Benedictines and Preaching in Fifteenth-Century England: The Evidence of Two Bodleian Library Manuscripts', *Revue Bénédictine*, 99 (1989), 313–32

——, 'An Edition of Five Medieval Sermons from MS Laud misc. 706' (unpublished doctoral dissertation, State University of New York, Albany, 1975)

——, 'A Funeral Sermon for Abbot Walter Froucester of Gloucester (1412)', *American Benedictine Review*, 28 (1977), 147–66

Horner, Patrick J., ed. and trans., *A Macaronic Sermon Collection from Late Medieval England*, Studies and Texts, 153 (Toronto: Pontifical Institute of Mediaeval Studies, 2006)

Hudson, Anne, ed., *The Works of a Lollard Preacher*, EETS, o.s., 317 (Oxford: Oxford University Press, 2001)

——, *Two Wycliffite Texts: The Sermon of William Taylor 1406, The Testimony of William Thorpe 1407*, EETS, o.s., 301 (Oxford: Oxford University Press, 1993)

Langland, William, *Piers Plowman: A Parallel-Text Edition of the A, B, C, and Z Versions*, ed. by A. V. C. Schmidt, I: *Text* (London: Longman, 1995); II: *Introduction, Textual Notes, Commentary, Bibliography, and Indexical Glossary* (Kalamazoo: Medieval Institute Publications, 2009)

Lindsay, W. M., ed., *Isidori Hispalensis Episcopi Etymologiarum sive originum libri XX*, 2 vols (Oxford: Clarendon Press, 1911; repr. 1966)

Little, A. G., ed., *Liber exemplorum ad usum praedicantium*, British Society of Franciscan Studies, 1 (Aberdeen: Typis academicis, 1908)

Lombard, Peter, *Magistri Petri Lombardi Sententiae in IV libris distinctae*, Collegium S. Bonaventurae, Spicilegium Bonaventurianum, 3rd edn, 2 vols in 3 parts, 4–5 (Grottaferrata: Editiones Collegii S. Bonaventurae ad Claras Aquas, 1971–81)

Loserth, Iohann, ed. *Iohannis Wyclif Sermones*, Wyclif Society, 11–14, 4 vols (London: Trübner, 1887–90; repr. New York: Johnson Reprint, 1966)

Lucas, Angela M., ed., *Anglo-Irish Poems of the Middle Ages* (Dublin: Columba, 1995)

Lumiansky, R. M., and David Mills, eds, *The Chester Mystery Cycle*, EETS, s.s., 3 (London: Oxford University Press, 1974)

McElwain, Mary Belle, ed., *The Stratagems and the Aqueducts of Rome*, with trans. by Charles E. Bennett, LCL, 174 (London: Heinemann; and New York: Putnam's, 1925)

McEnery, M. J., and R. Refaussé, eds, *Christ Church Deeds* (Dublin: Four Courts, 2001)

Maitland, Frederic William, ed., *Year Books of Edward II*, I: *1 and 2 Edward II, A.D. 1307–1309*, Publications of the Selden Society, 17 (London: Quaritch, 1907; repr. London: Professional Books, 1974)

Meech, Sanford Brown, 'An Early Treatise in English Concerning Latin Grammar', in *Essays and Studies in English and Comparative Literature*, University of Michigan Publications, Language and Literature, 13 (Ann Arbor: University of Michigan Press, 1935), pp. 81–125

Meech, Sanford Brown, and Hope Emily Allen, eds, *The Book of Margery Kempe*, I: *Text*, EETS, o.s., 212 (London: Oxford University Press, 1940; repr. 1961)

Mirk's Festial: A Collection of Homilies, ed. by Theodor Erbe, EETS, e.s., 96 (London: Paul, Trench, Trübner, 1905; repr. Millwood, NY: Kraus, 1973)

Morris, Richard, ed., *Old English Homilies and Homiletic Treatises*, EETS, o.s., 29 (London: Trübner, 1868)

——, *An Old English Miscellany*, EETS, o.s., 49 (London: Trübner, 1872; repr. New York: Greenwood, 1969)

Neilson, Nellie, ed., *Year Books of Edward IV: 10 Edward IV and 49 Henry VI, A.D. 1470*, Publications of the Selden Society, 47 (London: Quaritch, 1931; repr. London: Spottiswoode, Ballantyne, 1965)

Nelson, William, ed., *A Fifteenth Century School Book from a Manuscript in the British Museum (MS. Arundel 249)* (Oxford: Clarendon Press, 1956)

Nevanlinna, Saara, ed., *Northern Homily Cycle: The Expanded Version in MSS Harley 4196 and Cotton Tiberius E vii*, Mémoires de la Société Néophilologique de Helsinki, 3 vols (Helsinki: Société Néophilologique, 1972–84)

O'Mara, Veronica, *A Study and Edition of Selected Middle English Sermons: Richard Alkerton's Easter Week Sermon Preached at St Mary Spital in 1406, a Sermon on Sunday Observance, and a Nunnery Sermon for the Feast of the Assumption*, Leeds Texts and Monographs, n.s., 13 (Leeds: University of Leeds, 1994)

Oesterley, Hermann, ed., *Gesta Romanorum* (Berlin: Weidmann, 1872; repr. Hildesheim: Olms, 1963)

Ogden, Margaret Sinclair, ed., *The Liber de diversis medicinis*, EETS, o.s., 207 (London: Oxford University Press, 1938; repr. 1970)

Pantin, William A., ed., *Documents Illustrating the Activities of the General and Provincial Chapters of the English Black Monks, 1215–1540*, Camden Third Series, 45, 47, and 54, 3 vols (London: Royal Historical Society, 1931–37)

Powicke, Frederick M., and C. R. Cheney, eds, *Councils and Synods with Other Documents Relating to the English Church*, 2 vols (Oxford: Clarendon Press, 1964)

Procter, Francis, and Christopher Wordsworth, eds, *Breviarium ad usum insignis ecclesiae Sarum*, 3 vols (Cambridge: Cambridge University Press, 1879–86)

Reichl, Karl, ed., *Religiöse Dichtung im englischen Hochmittelalter: Untersuchungen und Edition der Handschrift B.14.39 des Trinity College in Cambridge* (Munich: Fink, 1973)

Reimer, Stephen R., ed., *The Works of William Herebert, OFM*, Studies and Texts, 81 (Toronto: Pontifical Institute of Mediaeval Studies, 1987)

Riley, Henry T., ed., *Annales monasterii S. Albani a Johanne Amundesham, Monacho, ut videtur, conscripti, A.D. 1421–1440; Quibus praefigitur Chronicon rerum gestarum in Monasterio S. Albani, A.D. 1422–1431, a quodam auctore ignoto compilatum*, RS, 28, 2 vols (London: Longman, 1870–71)

——, *Gesta abbatum monasterii Sancti Albani, a Thoma Walsingham [...] compilata*, RS, 28, 3 vols (London: Longman, Green, Reader, and Dyer, 1867–69)

Robbins, Harry Walcott, ed., *Le Merure de Seinte Eglise by Saint Edmund of Pontigny* (Lewisburg, PA: H. W. Robbins, 1925)

Ross, Woodburn O., ed., *Middle English Sermons: Edited from British Museum MS. Royal 18 B.xxiii*, EETS, o.s., 209 (London: Oxford University Press, 1940; repr. 1960)

Sabatier, P., ed., *Bibliorum sacrorum latinae versiones antiquae*, 3 vols (Paris: Didot, 1751)

Seneca ad Lucilium epistulae morales, ed. by Richard M. Gummere, 3 vols, LCL, 75–77 (London: Heinemann; Cambridge, MA: Harvard University Press, 1917–25)

Shakespeare, William, *Love's Labour's Lost*, ed. by Richard David, 5th edn (London: Methuen, 1956)

Shirley, W. W., ed., *Fasciculi Zizaniorum Magistri Johannis Wyclif cum Tritico*, RS, 5 (London: Longman, 1858)

Stevens, Martin, and A. C. Cawley, eds, *The Towneley Plays*, EETS, s.s., 13–14, 2 vols (Oxford: Oxford University Press, 1994)

Sweetman, H. S., ed., *Calendar of Documents, Relating to Ireland, Preserved in Her Majesty's Record Office, London*, 5 vols (London: Longman, 1875–86)

Tolkien, J. R. R., and Eric Valentine Gordon, eds, *Sir Gawain and the Green Knight*, 2nd edn, rev. by Norman Davis (Oxford: Clarendon Press, 1967; repr. 1985)

Valerii Maximi factorvm et dictorvm memorabilivm libri novem, ed. by Karl Kempf (Leipzig: Teubner, 1888)

Van Banning, Joop, ed., *Opus imperfectvm in Mattheum: Praefatio*, CCSL, 87B (Turnhout: Brepols, 1987)

Von Nolcken, Christina, ed., *The Middle English Translation of the 'Rosarium Theologie'*, Middle English Texts, 10 (Heidelberg: Universitätsverlag Winter, 1979)

Voragine, Jacobus de, *Iacopo da Varazze, Legenda Aurea*, ed. by Giovanni Paolo Maggioni, 2nd edn, Millennio Medievale 6, Testi 3, 2 vols (Florence: SISMEL, Edizioni del Galluzzo, 1998)

White, Newport B., ed., with an introduction by A. Gwynn, *The 'Dignitas Decani' of St. Patrick's Cathedral Dublin* (Dublin: Stationery Office, 1957)

White, R. M., ed., *Ormulum*, rev. by R. Holt, 2 vols (Oxford: Clarendon Press, 1878)

Wilkins, David, ed., *Concilia Magnae Britanniae et Hiberniae*, 4 vols (London: Gosling and others, 1737; repr. Brussels: Culture et civilisation, 1964)

Wyclif, John. See *Iohannis Wyclif Sermones*, ed. by Iohann Loserth

Year Book (London: Wyllyam Myddylton, [n.d.])

III. Secondary Sources

d'Avray, David L., *The Preaching of the Friars: Sermons Diffused from Paris before 1300* (Oxford: Clarendon Press, 1985)

Ball, R. M., 'Thomas Cyrcetur, a Fifteenth-Century Theologian and Preacher', *JEH*, 37 (1986), 205–39

Bataillon, Louis-Jacques, *La Prédication au XIIIe siècle en France et Italie: Études et documents*, Variorum Collected Studies Series, 402 (Aldershot: Ashgate, 1993)

Benskin, Michael, 'The Letters <þ> and <y> in Later Middle English and Some Related Matters', *Journal of the Society of Archivists*, 7 (1982), 13–30

——, 'The Style and Authorship of the Kildare Poems — (I) Pers of Bermingham', in *In Other Words: Transcultural Studies in Philology, Translation and Lexicography Presented to Hans Heinrich Meier on the Occasion of his Sixty-fifth Birthday*, ed. by J. Lachlan Mackenzie and Richard Todd (Dordrecht: Foris, 1989), pp. 57–83

Benskin, Michael, and M. L. Samuels, eds, *So meny people longages and tonges: Philological Essays in Scots and Mediaeval English presented to Angus McIntosh* (Edinburgh: Middle English Dialect Project, 1981), pp. 15–30

Berry, H. F., 'History of the Religious Gild of S. Anne, in S. Audoen's Church, Dublin, 1430–1740, Taken from its Records in the Haliday Collection, R.I.A.', *PRIA*, 25 (1904–05), 21–106

Binkley, Peter, 'John Bromyard and the Hereford Dominicans', in *Centres of Learning: Learning and Location in Pre-Modern Europe and the Near East*, ed. by Jan Willem Drijvers and Alasdair A. MacDonald (Leiden: Brill, 1995), pp. 255–64

Bloomfield, Morton W., and others, *Incipits of Latin Works on the Virtues and Vices, 1100–1500 A.D.*, Medieval Academy of America, 88 (Cambridge, MA: Medieval Academy of America, 1979)

Bradley, John, *The Topography and Layout of Medieval Drogheda* (Drogheda: Old Drogheda Society, 1997)

Bremond, Claude, Jacques Le Goff, and Jean-Claude Schmitt, *L'Exemplum*, Typologie des sources du moyen âge occidental, 40 (Turnhout: Brepols, 1982)

Caerwyn Williams, J. E., 'Medieval Welsh Religious Prose', in *Proceedings of the Second International Congress of Celtic Studies held in Cardiff, 6–13 July, 1963* (Cardiff: University of Wales Press, 1966), pp. 65–97

Carruthers, Mary J., *The Book of Memory: A Study of Memory in Medieval Culture* (Cambridge: Cambridge University Press, 1990)

Clark, James G., *A Monastic Renaissance at St Albans: Thomas Walsingham and his Circle c. 1350–1440* (Oxford: Clarendon Press, 2006)

Colker, Marvin L., *Trinity College Library Dublin: Descriptive Catalogue of the Mediaeval and Renaissance Latin Manuscripts*, 2 vols (Aldershot: Scolar, 1991)

Cunningham, Bernadette, '"Zeal for God and for Souls": Counter-Reformation Preaching in Early Seventeenth-Century Ireland', in *Irish Preaching*, ed. by Fletcher and Gillespie, pp. 108–26

Dahmus, John W., '*Dormi Secure*: The Lazy Preacher's Model of Holiness for his Flock', in *Models of Holiness in Medieval Sermons*, ed. by Kienzle and others, pp. 301–16

Daniell, Christopher, *Death and Burial in Medieval England* (London: Routledge, 1997)

Dickinson, John Compton, *The Origins of the Austin Canons and their Introduction into England* (London: S.P.C.K., 1950)

Diller, Hans Jurgen, 'Code-Switching in Medieval English Drama', *CompD*, 31 (1997–98), 506–37

Doyle, A. I., 'English Books in and out of Court from Edward III to Henry VII', in *English Court Culture in the Later Middle Ages*, ed. by John Scattergood and J. W. Sherbourne (London: Duckworth, 1983), pp. 163–81

Duncan, Thomas G., 'The Middle English *Mirror* and its Manuscripts', in *Middle English Studies Presented to Norman Davis in Honour of his 70th Birthday*, ed. by Douglas Gray and Eric Gerald Stanley (Oxford: Clarendon Press, 1983), pp. 115–26

——, 'The Middle English Translator of Robert de Gretham's Anglo-Norman *Miroir*', in *The Medieval Translator*, ed. by Roger Ellis, René Tixier, and B. Weitemeier, The Medieval Translator, 6 (Turnhout: Brepols, 1998), pp. 221–31

Duncan, Thomas G., ed., *A Companion to the Middle English Lyric* (Cambridge: Brewer, 2005)

Edwards, Kathleen, *The English Secular Cathedrals in the Middle Ages: A Constitutional Study with Special Reference to the Fourteenth Century*, 2nd edn (Manchester: Manchester University Press, 1967)

Eldredge, L. M., ed., *The Index of Middle English Prose Handlist IX: A Handlist of Manuscripts Containing Middle English Prose in the Ashmole Collection, Bodleian Library, Oxford* (Cambridge: Brewer, 1992)

Ellegård, A., *The Auxiliary Do: The Establishment and Regulation of its Use in English*, Gothenburg Studies in English, 2 (Stockholm: Almquist and Wiksell, 1953)

Emden, A. B., *A Biographical Register of the University of Oxford to A.D. 1500*, 3 vols (Oxford: Clarendon Press, 1957–59)

Erb, Peter C., 'Vernacular Material for Preaching in MS Cambridge University Library Ii. III. 8', *MS*, 33 (1971), 63–84

Fletcher, Alan J., '"Benedictus qui venit in nomine Domini": A Thirteenth-Century Sermon for Advent and the Macaronic Style in England', *MS*, 56 (1994), 217–45

——, 'The Criteria for Scribal Attribution: Dublin, Trinity College, MS 244, Some Early Copies of the Works of Geoffrey Chaucer, and the Canon of Adam Pynkhurst Manuscripts', *RES*, 58 (2007), 1–36

——, 'A Death Lyric from the *Summa Predicantium*', *N&Q*, n.s., 24 (1977), 11–12

——, 'Death Lyrics from Two Fifteenth-Century Sermon Manuscripts', *N&Q*, n.s., 23 (1976), 341–42

——, *Drama, Performance and Polity in Pre-Cromwellian Ireland* (Toronto: University of Toronto Press, 2000)

——, 'The Essential (Ephemeral) William Langland: Textual Revision as Ethical Process', *YLS*, 15 (2001), 61–84

——, 'The Genesis of *The Owl and the Nightingale*: A New Hypothesis', *ChauR*, 34 (1999), 1–17

——, '"I Sing of a Maiden": A Fifteenth-Century Sermon Reminiscence', *N&Q*, n.s., 25 (1978), 107–08

——, 'John Mirk and the Lollards', *MÆ*, 55 (1987), 59–66

——, 'The Liturgy and Music of the Medieval Cathedral', in *St Patrick's Cathedral, Dublin: A History*, ed. by John Crawford and Raymond Gillespie (Dublin: Four Courts, 2009), pp. 120–48

——, 'The Lyric in the Sermon', in *A Companion to the Middle English Lyric*, ed. by Thomas G. Duncan (Cambridge: Brewer, 2005), pp. 189–209

——, 'The Meaning of "Gostly to owr purpos" in *Mankind*', *N&Q*, n.s., 31 (1984), 301–02

——, '*Pearl* and the Limits of History', in *Studies in Late Medieval and Early Renaissance Texts in Honour of John Scattergood*, ed. by Anne Marie D'Arcy and Alan J. Fletcher (Dublin: Four Courts, 2005), pp. 148–70

——, 'Preaching in Late-Medieval Ireland: The English and the Latin Tradition', in *Irish Preaching*, ed. by Fletcher and Gillespie, pp. 56–81

——, 'Unnoticed Sermons from John Mirk's *Festial*', *Speculum*, 55 (1980), 514–22

——, 'Variations on a Theme Attributed to Robert Holcot: Lessons for Late-Medieval English Preaching from the Castle of Prudence', *MS*, 66 (2004), 27–98

Fletcher, Alan J., and Raymond Gillespie, eds, *Irish Preaching 700–1700* (Dublin: Four Courts Press, 2001)

Fletcher, Alan J., and Anne Hudson, 'Compilations for Preaching and Lollard Literature', in *The Cambridge History of the Book in Britain*, II, *1100–1400*, ed. by Morgan and Thomson, pp. 317–39

Fletcher, Alan J., and Susan Powell, 'The Origins of a Fifteenth-Century Sermon Collection: MSS Harley 2247 and Royal 18.B.XXV', *LeedsSE*, n.s., 10 (1978), 74–96

Flower, Robin, 'Ireland and Medieval Europe', *PBA*, 13 (1927), 271–303

Ford, Judy Ann, *John Mirk's 'Festial': Orthodoxy, Lollardy and the Common People in Fourteenth-Century England* (Cambridge: Brewer, 2006)

Forde, Simon, 'New Sermon Evidence for the Spread of Wycliffism', in *De ore Domini: Preacher and Word in the Middle Ages*, ed. by Thomas L. Amos, Eugene A. Green, and Beverly Maine Kienzle, Studies in Medieval Culture, 27 (Kalamazoo: Medieval Institute Publications, 1989), pp. 169–83

Frankis, John, 'The Social Context of Vernacular Writing in Thirteenth-Century England', in *Thirteenth-Century England: I*, ed. by P. R. Coss and S. D. Lloyd (Woodbridge: Boydell and Brewer, 1986), pp. 175–84

Greatrex, Joan, 'Benedictine Monk Scholars as Teachers and Preachers in the Later Middle Ages: Evidence from Worcester Cathedral Priory', in *Monastic Studies*, II: *The Continuity of Tradition*, ed. by J. Loades (Bangor: Headstart History, 1991), pp. 213–25

——, 'Benedictine Sermons: Preparation and Practice in the English Monastic Cathedral Cloister', in *Medieval Monastic Preaching*, ed. by Muessig, pp. 257–78

Gwynn, Aubrey, 'The Medieval University of St. Patrick's, Dublin', *Studies*, 27 (1938), 437–54

——, 'The Sermon-Diary of Richard FitzRalph, Archbishop of Armagh', *PRIA*, 44 (1937–38), 1–57

Haines, Roy Martin, 'Church, Society and Politics in the Early Fifteenth Century as Viewed from an English Pulpit', in *Church, Society and Politics*, ed. by Derek Baker, Studies in Church History, 12 (Oxford: Blackwell, 1975), pp. 143–57

——, *Ecclesia Anglicana: Studies in the English Church of the Later Middle Ages* (Toronto: University of Toronto Press, 1989)

——, '"Our Master Mariner, Our Sovereign Lord": A Contemporary Preacher's View of King Henry V', *MS*, 38 (1976), 85–96

——, 'Reginald Pecock: A Tolerant Man in an Age of Intolerance', in *Persecution and Toleration*, ed. by William J. Sheils, Studies in Church History, 21 (Oxford: Blackwell, 1984), pp. 125–37

——, '"Wilde Wittes and Wilfulness": John Swetstock's Attack on those "Poyswunmongeres," the Lollards', in *Popular Belief and Practice*, ed. by G. J. Cuming and Derek Baker, Studies in Church History, 8 (Cambridge: Cambridge University Press, 1972), pp. 143–53

Hanna, Ralph, *London Literature, 1300–1380* (Cambridge: Cambridge University Press, 2005)

Heffernan, Thomas J., 'The Authorship of the "Northern Homily Cycle": The Liturgical Affiliations of the Sunday Gospel Pericopes as a Test', *Traditio*, 41 (1985), 289–309

——, 'Sermon Literature', in *Middle English Prose: A Critical Guide to Major Authors and Genres*, ed. by A. S. G. Edwards (New Brunswick, NJ: Rutgers University Press, 1984), pp. 177–207

Heffernan, Thomas J., and Patrick J. Horner, 'Sermons and Homilies', in *A Manual of the Writings in Middle English 1050–1500*, ed. by Peter G. Beidler (New Haven: Connecticut Academy of Arts and Sciences, 2005), XI, 3969–4167

Herbert, J. A., and H. A. Ward, eds, *Catalogue of Romances in the British Museum*, 3 vols (London: Trustees of the British Museum, 1883–1910; repr. 1961–62)

Hudson, Anne, 'John Purvey: A Reconsideration of the Evidence for his Life and Writings', in Hudson, *Lollards and their Books*, pp. 85–110

——, 'A Lollard Compilation and the Dissemination of Wycliffite Thought', in Hudson, *Lollards and their Books*, pp. 13–30

——, 'A Lollard Sect Vocabulary?', in Hudson, *Lollards and their Books*, pp. 165–80

——, *Lollards and their Books* (London and Ronceverte: Hambledon, 1985)

Hudson, Anne, and Helen L. Spencer, 'Old Author, New Work: The Sermons of MS Longleat 4', *MÆ*, 53 (1984), 220–38

Humphreys, Kenneth Williams, *The Book Provisions of the Medieval Friars 1215–1400*, Studies in the History of Libraries and Librarianship, 1 (Amsterdam: Erasmus, 1964)

Hunt, Tony, *Teaching and Learning Latin in Thirteenth-Century England,* 3 vols (Cambridge: Brewer, 1991)

James, Montague Rhodes, *A Catalogue of the Medieval Manuscripts in the University Library of Aberdeen* (Cambridge: Cambridge University Press, 1932)

——, *A Descriptive Catalogue of the Manuscripts in the Library of Lambeth Palace: The Mediaeval Manuscripts* (Cambridge: Cambridge University Press, 1932)

Jurkowski, Maureen, 'Lollard Book Producers in London in 1414', in *Text and Controversy from Wyclif to Bale: Essays in Honour of Anne Hudson*, ed. by Helen Barr and Ann M. Hutchison, Medieval Church Studies, 4 (Turnhout: Brepols, 2005), pp. 201–26

Kelly, J. N. D., *The Athanasian Creed* (London: A. and C. Black, 1964)

Ker, Neil Ripley, *Catalogue of Manuscripts Containing Anglo-Saxon* (Oxford: Clarendon Press, 1957)

——, *Medieval Manuscripts in British Libraries*, I: *London* (Oxford: Clarendon Press, 1969)

——, *Medieval Manuscripts in British Libraries*, III: *Lampeter-Oxford* (Oxford: Clarendon Press, 1983)

Kienzle, Beverly Mayne, ed., *The Sermon*, Typologie des sources du moyen âge occidental, 81–83 (Turnhout: Brepols, 2000)

Kienzle, Beverly Mayne, and others, eds, *Models of Holiness in Medieval Sermons*, Textes et études du moyen âge, 5 (Louvain-la-Neuve: Fédération internationale des Instituts d'études médiévales, 1996)

Knowles, David, 'The Censured Opinions of Uthred of Boldon', *PBA*, 37 (1951), 305–42

Knowles, David, and R. Neville Hadcock, *Medieval Religious Houses: England and Wales*, 2nd edn (London: Longman, 1971)

Latham, Ronald Edward, *Revised Medieval Latin Word-List from British and Irish Sources* (Oxford: Oxford University Press, 1965; repr. 1983)

Lawrence, Clifford H., ed., *St. Edmund of Abingdon: A Study in Hagiography and History* (Oxford: Clarendon Press, 1960)

Lerer, Seth, 'The Genre of the Grave and the Origins of the Middle English Lyric', *MLQ*, 58 (1997), 127–61

Leyser, P., *Historia poetarum et poematum medii ævi* (Halle: Sumptu novi bibliopolii, 1721)

Machan, Tim William, *English in the Middle Ages* (Oxford: Oxford University Press, 2003)

Madan, Falconer, and H. H. E. Craster, *A Summary Catalogue of Western Manuscripts in the Bodleian Library at Oxford*, 7 vols (Oxford: Clarendon Press, 1895–1953)

Matthew, H. C. G., and Brian Harrison, eds, *Oxford Dictionary of National Biography*, 60 vols (Oxford: Clarendon Press, 2004)

McIntosh, Angus and M. L. Samuels, 'Prolegomena to a Study of Medieval Anglo-Irish', *MÆ*, 37 (1968), 1–11

McIntosh, Angus, and Martyn F. Wakelin, 'John Mirk's *Festial* and Bodleian MS Hatton 96', *NM*, 84 (1983), 443–50

Mifsud, G., 'John Sheppey, Bishop of Rochester, as Preacher and Collector of Sermons' (unpublished B.Litt. thesis, University of Oxford, 1953)

Migliorini, Bruno, *The Italian Language*, abridged, recast and rev. by T. Gwynfor Griffith (London: Faber, 1984)

Morgan, Nigel, 'The Introduction of the Sarum Calendar into the Dioceses of England in the Thirteenth Century', in *Thirteenth Century England: Proceedings of the Durham Conference 1999*, ed. by Michael Prestwich, Richard Britnell, and Robin Frame (Woodbridge: Boydell and Brewer, 2001), pp. 179–206

Morgan, Nigel, and Rodney M. Thomson, eds, *The Cambridge History of the Book in Britain*, II: *1100–1400* (Cambridge: Cambridge University Press, 2008)

Morrison, Stephen, 'Lollardy in the Fifteenth Century: The Evidence from Some Orthodox Texts', *Cahiers Élisabéthains*, 52 (1997), 1–24

Muessig, Carolyn, ed., *Medieval Monastic Preaching*, Brill's Studies in Intellectual History, 90 (Leiden: Brill, 1998)

Murdoch, Brian, *Cornish Literature* (Cambridge: Brewer, 1993)

——, 'Preaching in Medieval Ireland: The Irish Tradition', in *Irish Preaching*, ed. by Fletcher and Gillespie, pp. 40–55

Murphy, James J., *Rhetoric in the Middle Ages: A History of Rhetorical Theory from Saint Augustine to the Renaissance* (Berkeley and Los Angeles: University of California Press, 1974)

——, 'The Teaching of Latin as a Second Language in the 12th Century,' *Historiographia Linguistica*, 7 (1980), 159–75

Mustanoja, Tauno F., *A Middle English Syntax*, Mémoires de la Société néophilologique de Helsinki, 23 (Helsinki: Société néophilologique, 1960)

Myers-Scotton, Carol, *Contact Linguistics: Bilingual Encounters and Grammatical Outcomes* (Oxford: Oxford University Press, 2002)

Mynors, Roger A. B., and Rodney M. Thomson, *Catalogue of the Manuscripts of Hereford Cathedral Library* (Cambridge: Brewer, 1993)

Nighman, Chris L., 'Commonplaces on Preaching among Commonplaces for Preaching? The Topic *Predicacio* in Thomas of Ireland's *Manipulus florum*', *Medieval Sermon Studies*, 49 (2005), 37–57

——, 'The Electronic *Manipulus florum* Project (www.manipulusflorum.com)', *Medieval Sermon Studies*, 46 (2002), 97–99

Norris, Herbert, *Costume and Fashion*, II: *Senlac to Bosworth* (London: Dent; New York: Dutton, 1924)

Ó Clabaigh, Colmán N., 'Preaching in Late-Medieval Ireland: The Franciscan Contribution', in *Irish Preaching*, ed. by Fletcher and Gillespie, pp. 81–93

O'Connor, Susan, 'Tudor Drogheda', *Journal of the Old Drogheda Society*, 10 (1996), 86–110

O'Mara, Veronica, and Suzanne Paul, eds, *A Repertorium of Middle English Prose Sermons*, Sermo, 1, 4 vols (Turnhout: Brepols, 2007)

O'Sullivan, Benedict, 'The Dominicans in Medieval Dublin', in *Medieval Dublin: The Living City*, ed. by Howard B. Clarke (Dublin: Irish Academic Press, 1990), pp. 83–99 (first publ. in *Dublin Historical Record*, 9 (1946–48), 41–58)

Ogilvie-Thomson, Sarah J., ed., *The Index of Middle English Prose Handlist VIII: A Handlist of Manuscripts Containing Middle English Prose in Oxford College Libraries* (Cambridge: Brewer, 1991)

Ong, Walter, *Interfaces of the Word: Studies in the Evolution of Consciousness and Culture* (Ithaca: Cornell University Press, 1977)

Owst, Gerald R., *Literature and Pulpit in Medieval England: A Neglected Chapter in the History of English Letters and the English People*, 2nd edn (Oxford: Blackwell, 1961; repr. 1966)

——, *Preaching in Medieval England: An Introduction to Sermon Manuscripts of the Period c. 1350–1450* (Cambridge: Cambridge University Press, 1926; repr. New York: Russell and Russell, 1965)

Palmer, Nigel F., 'Das "Exempelwerk der englischen Bettelmönche": Ein Gegenstück zu den "Gesta Romanorum"', in *Exempel und Exempelsammlungen*, ed. by W. Haug and B. Wachinger, Fortuna Vitrea, 2 (Tübingen: Niemeyer, 1991), pp. 137–72

Parkes, Malcolm B., *English Cursive Book Hands 1250–1500* (Oxford: Clarendon Press, 1969; repr. with minor revisions, London: Scolar, 1979)

——, 'Tachygraphy in the Middle Ages: Writing Techniques Employed for "Reportationes" of Lectures and Sermons', *Medioevo e Rinascimento*, 3 (1989), 159–69

Pfander, Homer G., 'The Medieval Friars and Some Alphabetical Reference Books for Sermons', *MÆ*, 3 (1934), 19–29

——, *The Popular Sermon of the Medieval Friar in England* (New York: New York University, 1937)

Poplack, Shana, 'Sometimes I'll Start a Sentence in Spanish y termino in espanol: Toward a Typology of Code-Switching', *Linguistics*, 18 (1980), 581–618

Robbins, Rossell Hope, 'The Earliest Carols and the Franciscans', *MLN*, 53 (1938), 239–45

Roberts, Phyllis Barzillay, *Stephanus de Lingua-Tonante: Studies in the Sermons of Stephen Langton*, Studies and Texts, 16 (Toronto: Pontifical Institute of Mediaeval Studies, 1968)

Robinson, Pamela R., 'The "Booklet": A Self-Contained Unit in Composite Manuscripts', *Codicologica*, 3 (1980), 46–69

Rouse, Richard H., and Mary A. Rouse, 'Biblical Distinctions in the Thirteenth Century', *Archives d'histoire doctrinale et littéraire du moyen âge*, 49 (1974), 27–37

——, *Preachers, Florilegia and Sermons: Studies on the 'Manipulus Florum' of Thomas of Ireland*, Studies and Texts, 47 (Toronto: Pontifical Institute of Mediaeval Studies, 1979)

Ruddock, G. E., 'Siôn Cent', in *A Guide to Welsh Literature, 1282–c. 1550*, ed. by A. O. H. Jarman and Gwilym Rees Hughes, rev. by Dafydd Johnston (Swansea: Davies, 1976), pp. 150–69

Sankoff, David, and Shana Poplack, 'A Formal Grammar for Code-Switching', *Papers in Linguistics: International Journal of Human Communication*, 14 (1981), 3–45

Scattergood, John, and Julia Boffey, eds, *Texts and their Contexts: Papers from the Early Book Society* (Dublin: Four Courts, 1997)

Scattergood, John, and Guido Latré, 'Trinity College Dublin MS 75: A Lollard Bible and Some Protestant Owners', in *Texts and their Contexts*, ed. by Scattergood and Boffey, pp. 233–40

Schendl, Herbert, 'Linguistic Aspects of Code-Switching in Medieval English Texts', in *Multilingualism*, ed. by Trotter, pp. 77–92

Schneyer, Johannes Baptist, 'Eine Sermonesliste des Nicolaus de Byard, O.F.M.', *AFH*, 60 (1967), 3–41

——, *Repertorium der Lateinischen Sermones des Mittelalters, für die Zeit von 1150–1350*, Beiträge zur Geschichte der Philosophie und Theologie des Mittelalters, 43, 11 vols (Munster: Aschendorff, 1969–90)

Sharpe, Richard, *A Handlist of the Latin Writers of Great Britain and Ireland before 1540*, Publications of the Journal of Medieval Latin, 1 (Turnhout: Brepols, 1997)

Smalley, Beryl, *English Friars and Antiquity in the Early Fourteenth Century* (Oxford: Blackwell, 1960)

Spencer, Helen L., 'The Fortunes of a Lollard Sermon-Cycle in the Later Fifteenth Century', *MS*, 48 (1986), 352–96

——, 'Middle English Sermons', in *The Sermon*, ed. by Beverly Maine Kienzle, Typologie des sources du moyen âge occidental, fasc. 81–83 (Turnhout: Brepols, 2000), pp. 597–660

Strang, Barbara M. H., *A History of English* (London: Methuen, 1970)

Thomson, David, *A Descriptive Catalogue of Middle English Grammatical Texts* (New York: Garland, 1979)

Thomson, Rodney M., *Catalogue of the Manuscripts of Lincoln Cathedral Chapter Library* (Cambridge: Brewer, 1989)

——, *Manuscripts from St Albans Abbey, 1066–1235*, 2 vols (Woodbridge: Boydell and Brewer, 1982)

Thomson, Rodney M., with Gullick, M., *A Descriptive Catalogue of the Medieval Manuscripts in Worcester Cathedral Library* (Cambridge: Brewer, 2001)

Thomson, Samuel Harrison, *The Writings of Robert Grosseteste Bishop of Lincoln, 1235–1253* (Cambridge: Cambridge University Press, 1940; repr. New York, 1971)

Thorndike, Lynn, *A History of Magic and Experimental Science during the First Thirteen Centuries of our Era*, History of Science Society Publications, n.s., 4, 8 vols (New York: Columbia University Press, 1923–58)

Treharne, Elaine, 'The Form and Function of the Twelfth-Century Old English *Dicts of Cato*', *JEGP*, 102 (2003), 465–85

Trotter, David A., ed., *Multilingualism in Later Medieval Britain* (Cambridge: Brewer, 2000)

Tubach, Frederic C., *Index exemplorum*, FF Comunications 86, no. 204 (Helsinki: Suomalainen Tiedeakatemia, 1969)

Tugwell, Simon, *The Way of the Preacher* (London: Darton, Longman, and Todd, 1979)

Voigts, Linda Ehrsam, 'What's the Word? Bilingualism in Late-Medieval England', *Speculum*, 71 (1996), 813–26

Von Nolcken, Christina, 'An Unremarked Group of Wycliffite Sermons in Latin', *MP*, 83 (1986), 233–49

Wakelin, Martyn F., 'The Manuscripts of John Mirk's *Festial*', *LeedsSE*, n.s., 1 (1967), 93–118

Walsh, Katherine, *A Fourteenth-Century Scholar and Primate: Richard FitzRalph in Oxford, Avignon and Armagh* (Oxford: Clarendon Press, 1981)

Walther, Hans, *Initia carminum ac versuum medii ævi posterioris latinorum*, Carmina medii ævi posterioris latina, 1, 2 pts (Göttingen: Vandenhoeck and Ruprecht, 1969)

Wardhaugh, Ronald, *An Introduction to Sociolinguistics* (New York: McGraw-Hill, 1986)

Watson, Andrew G., *Catalogue of Dated and Datable Manuscripts c. 700–1600 in The Department of Manuscripts, The British Library*, 2 vols (London: The British Library, 1979)

Watson, Nicholas, 'Censorship and Cultural Change in Late-Medieval England: Vernacular Theology, the Oxford Translation Debate, and Arundel's Constitutions of 1409', *Speculum*, 70 (1995), 822–64

Watt, John A., *The Church and the Two Nations in Medieval Ireland*, Cambridge Studies in Medieval Life and Thought, ser. 3, 3 (Cambridge: Cambridge University Press, 1970)

——, *The Church in Medieval Ireland*, 2nd edn (Dublin: University College Dublin Press, 1998)

Webber, Teresa, and Andrew G. Watson, eds, *The Libraries of the Augustinian Canons*, Corpus of British Medieval Library Catalogues, 6 (London: The British Library, 1998)

Weinreich, Uriel, *Languages in Contact: Findings and Problems*, Publications of the Linguistic Circle of New York, 1 (New York: Linguistic Circle of New York, 1953; repr. The Hague: Mouton, 1963)

Wenzel, Siegfried, *Macaronic Sermons: Bilingualism and Preaching in Late-Medieval England*, Recentiores: Later Latin Texts and Contexts (Ann Arbor: University of Michigan Press, 1994)

——, *Monastic Preaching in the Age of Chaucer*, Morton W. Bloomfield Lectures on Medieval English Literature, 3 (Kalamazoo: University of Western Michigan, 1993)

——, 'Poets, Preachers, and the Plight of Literary Critics', *Speculum*, 60 (1985), 343–63

——, *Preachers, Poets, and the Early English Lyric* (Princeton: Princeton University Press, 1986)

——, *Verses in Sermons, 'Fasciculus Morum' and its Middle English Poems*, Medieval Academy of America, 87 (Cambridge, MA: Medieval Academy of America Press, 1978)

Whiting, Bartlett Jere, and Helen Wescott Whiting, *Proverbs, Sentences, and Proverbial Phrases from English Writings mainly before 1500* (Cambridge, MA: Belknap, for Harvard University Press, 1968)

Wilmart, André, 'L'Hymne de la charité pour le Jeudi-Saint', in *Auteurs spirituels et textes dévots du moyen âge latin* (Paris: Études augustiniennes, 1932), pp. 26–36

——, 'Un répertoire d'exégèse composé en Angleterre vers le début du XIIIe siècle', *Mémorial Lagrange* (Paris: Gabalda, 1940), pp. 307–46

Woolf, Rosemary, *The English Religious Lyric in the Middle Ages* (Oxford: Clarendon Press, 1968)

Wright, Laura, 'Bills, Accounts, Inventories: Everyday Trilingual Activities in the Business World of Later Medieval England', in *Multilingualism*, ed. by Trotter, pp. 149–56

INDEX OF PERSONS AND PLACES

SERMO: STUDIES ON PATRISTIC, MEDIEVAL, AND REFORMATION SERMONS AND PREACHING

All volumes in this series are evaluated by an Editorial Board, strictly on academic grounds, based on reports prepared by referees who have been commissioned by virtue of their specialism in the appropriate field. The Board ensures that the screening is done independently and without conflicts of interest. The definitive texts supplied by authors are also subject to review by the Board before being approved for publication. Further, the volumes are copyedited to conform to the publisher's stylebook and to the best international academic standards in the field.

Titles in Series

Ruth Horie, *Perceptions of Ecclesia: Church and Soul in Medieval Dedication Sermons* (2006)

Veronica O'Mara and Suzanne Paul, *A Repertorium of Middle English Prose Sermons* (2007)

Constructing the Medieval Sermon, ed. by Roger Andersson (2007)

In Preparation

Kimberly A. Rivers, *Preaching the Memory of Virtue and Vice: Memory, Images, and Preaching in the Late Middle Ages*

Holly Johnson, *The Grammar of Good Friday: Macaronic Sermons of Late Medieval England*